Joyce's Anatomy of Culture

Cheryl Herr

JOYCE'S ANATOMY OF CULTURE

University of Illinois Press

Urbana and Chicago

Publication of this work was supported in part by a grant
from the Andrew W. Mellon Foundation.

This book is printed on acid-free paper.

Library of Congress Cataloging-in-Publication Data

Herr, Cheryl, 1949–
Joyce's anatomy of culture.

Bibliography: p.
Includes index.
1. Joyce, James, 1882–1941—Political and social
views.   2. Joyce, James, 1882–1941—Knowledge—Ireland.
3. Ireland in literature.   4. Ireland—Popular culture.
I. Title.
PR6019.09Z582   1986   823'.912   85-20790
ISBN 0-252-01234-8 (alk. paper)

For John

Contents

Preface

In recent years, literary theorists have called for attention to the historical pressures that shape the composition of even the most aggressively reflexive work. This study directly addresses the impress of social history on the fiction of James Joyce from *Dubliners* through *Finnegans Wake*. I view these works as cultural acts that expose the shaping operations and ideological practices characteristic of urban Ireland at the turn of the century. Attentive to the need to link fundamentally the work and its social environment, *Joyce's Anatomy of Culture* charts two intersecting courses. On the one hand, I use previously ungathered information to specify the functions and subtexts of Irish mass culture. On the other hand, I analyze Joyce's formal uses of the popular media—the newspaper, the pantomime, the music-hall "turn," and the sermon—which he selected to further his dissection of social forces in early modern Ireland. I concentrate on such forms as themselves bearing meanings which were perhaps second nature to Joyce's contemporaries but which must be reconstructed for many of today's readers. The significance of communications from the press, the stage, and the pulpit involved not only the messages of specific newspaper articles, theatrical performances, and sermons but also the ideological practices and positions characteristic of the institutions responsible for those communications as well as the forces typically brought to bear on those institutions. We have long recognized the interpretive value of Joyce's literary, historical, philosophical, and other allusions; this study defines the allusive force inherent in the forms of popular discourse on which he models large sections of his writing.

In contrast to this approach, much recent criticism of Joyce's works has concentrated on the role of narrative voice and the function of style. Of course, the very idea of "voice," like that of a narrator who chooses and changes styles, leads inevitably to increasingly vexed questions of intentionality and challenges much traditional thinking about the nature of narrative. While I would hesitate to dispense altogether with the concept of a narrator, I have attempted to swing the discursive pendulum in the direction of those social phenomena that Joyce insists upon as constituting the voices through which his characters find themselves speaking—the press, the stage, and the church being among the most formally prominent of those forces in Joyce's texts and in his culture. Ultimately, I argue that institutional stylizations remain such in Joyce; they are never given the status of persons even when they mimic the tones through which human voices acknowledge the profound influence of social institutions on individuality.

Exchanging, then, the focus on individuals for Joyce's recurrent concern with institutions, I have found his works to involve messages and tensions that are strikingly congruent with those of Irish popular culture. In particular, when the fictions enact subversions of the reigning institutional ideologies of Joyce's day, those same subversions are discoverable within the larger culture. To be sure, I do not argue that Joyce's narratives simply mirror their context but rather that they were produced within and worked transformations on the cultural conditions which generated various popular texts in Ireland. My effort is to document the symptoms of both domination and resistance in modern Irish history and in Joyce's narratives, which systematically isolate the major contradictions and stress points characteristic of Irish society during his lifetime. This exposure, although not itself politically doctrinaire, nonetheless implies Joyce's essentially political attention to the alternative positions resident within the ascendant and often censoring culture. Further, this exposure highlights the economic basis of cultural contradictions and institutional interaction in Joyce's Dublin, both of which are key topics of this book. Given Joyce's pervasive treatment of commodification and class difference, it is surprising and significant that to date Joycean economics has been studied only minimally.

This volume traces Joyce's anatomy of institutional competition and collusion, of economic pressures and social practices, of suppression and subversion, all of which shaped his culture's concepts of gender and selfhood, courtship and marriage, family life, the social order, national identity, and Anglo-Irish relations, as well as the moral and spiritual values that characterized the Joyce age in Ireland.

Acknowledgments

The scholar who does not live in Ireland is necessarily disadvantaged in doing research on Irish culture. For helping me to overcome that disadvantage, I am grateful to the Center for Programs in the Humanities at Virginia Tech and to the American Philosophical Society for funding trips to Dublin during the summers of 1981 and 1982. I am also indebted to the National Endowment for the Humanities for granting me a year-long fellowship and for paying for a third trip to Dublin in 1983. For permission to reprint parts of my essays previously published, I thank the University of Delaware Press ("Irish Censorship and 'The Pleasure of the Text': The 'Aeolus' Episode of Joyce's *Ulysses*," *Irish Renaissance Annual*, ed. Dennis Jackson, 3 [1982], 141–79), the editors of *Language and Style* (volume 15), and the editors of the *Journal of Modern Literature* (volume 11).

Occasionally, I have had the experience of discussing my project with people who disagreed with my approach to Joyce and to Irish popular culture. Such confrontations served to whet my appetite for the project, something especially helpful during the cold summer days of 1981, and I am glad that they occurred. On the other hand, I have more often met with enthusiastic assistance. To the staffs at the National Library of Ireland, Trinity College (Dublin), the Central Catholic Library (Dublin), the Irish Theatre Archive, Virginia Polytechnic Institute and State University, and the Beinecke Rare Book and Manuscript Library at Yale University, I owe much, as I do to both Raymond Mander and Colin Mabberley of the Raymond Mander and Joe Mitchenson Theatre Collection (London). My thanks also to Walton Litz and to Sean White, Dean of the School of Irish Studies, for help and encouragement. Dr. Cyril Cusack graciously shared with me his early experiences in the Irish theater; Noel Purcell and Elaine Marmion Purcell generously contributed much useful information about the Irish pantomime; Lorcan Bourke spent an afternoon taping recollections and opinions about the music hall and pantomime and answering my many questions about the technical side of theatrical productions in Ireland; and Peter McBride talked with me about the Irish music hall before and during World War I. For conversations with Matthew Murtagh, Joe Cairns (manager of the Gaiety Theatre), and A. G. Cruise (then manager of the Olympia Theatre), I am also grateful. Chief among these patrons of the book has been Séamus de Búrca, who has given many hours to educating me in the theatrical traditions of which he is a dedicated historian. Finally, my special thanks to Brendan O Hehir and Fritz Senn for their incisive suggestions about the book and to Robert Siegle, who read the manuscript at several stages. His complex vision of the work in which American English departments should be engaged remains a tonic, not to say a goad. Finally, I am indebted to the Society of Authors as the literary representative of the Estate of James Joyce, to Faber and Faber Limited, to Random House, Inc., and to Viking Penguin Inc. for permission to quote from Joyce's writings; I am also very grateful to Ann Lowry Weir and Michael Kaufman of the University of Illinois Press for their careful editing of this volume.

Blacksburg, Va.
Swarthmore, Pa.

Notes on the Text

References to Joyce's works are noted in my text parenthetically, as cited below, and are to these editions:

Dubliners: *Text, Criticism, and Notes*, ed. Robert Scholes and A. Walton Litz (New York: Viking Press, 1969)—(D).

Stephen Hero, ed. John J. Slocum and Herbert Cahoon (New York: New Directions, 1963)—(SH).

A Portrait of the Artist as a Young Man: *Text, Criticism, Notes*, ed. Chester G. Anderson (New York: Viking Press, 1968)—(P).

Ulysses (New York: Random House, 1961)—(U). Quotations from *Ulysses* have been silently emended to agree with *Ulysses*: *A Critical and Synoptic Edition*, prepared by Hans Walter Gabler with Wolfhard Steppe and Claus Melchior (New York: Garland Publishing, 1984).

Finnegans Wake (New York: Viking Press, 1939; 1967)—(FW).

Because little research has been done on the history of Irish censorship, Irish music hall, Irish pantomime, and Irish sermons between 1880 and 1930, the book ends with a bibliography which includes sources for the study of Irish popular culture.

Texts of the Culture

> To re-integrate himself with worldly actuality, the critic of texts ought to be investigating the system of discourse by which the 'world' is divided, administered, plundered, by which humanity is thrust into pigeonholes. . . .
>
> Edward Said, *Diacritics* (1976)

> Yet to concentrate solely on the literal sense or even the psychological content of any document to the sore neglect of the enveloping facts themselves circumstantiating it is just as hurtful to sound sense (and let it be added to the truest taste) as were some fellow in the act of perhaps getting an intro from another fellow turning out to be a friend in need of his, say, to a lady of the latter's acquaintance, engaged in performing the elaborative antecistral ceremony of upstheres, straightaway to run off and vision her plump and plain in her natural altogether. . . . Who in his heart doubts either that the facts of feminine clotheiring are there all the time or that the feminine fiction, stranger than the facts, is there also at the same time, only a little to the rere? Or that one may be separated from the other? Or that both may then be contemplated simultaneously? Or that each may be taken up and considered in turn apart from the other? (FW 109.12–20, 30–36)

Joyce's Allusions

No doubt a startling number of Joyce's most dedicated readers began their love affairs with Leopold Bloom or Anna Livia Plurabelle either by recognizing in the fictions a previously unidentified allusion or by trying to track down the source of a phrase that had the special feel of the culturally referential. From sending a note on one's discoveries to the *James Joyce Quarterly* or *A Wake Newslitter* to stepping into Davy Byrne's pub in Dublin is a somewhat expensive but often traveled route, and there are no signs that the transatlantic traffic is lessening. Whether Joyce alludes to a song or a place, to "In Old Madrid" or the Royal Canal, we tend both to search for the identity of the reference and to justify its presence in the marvelously complex works that continue to give resident Dubliners opportunities to regale the world's Joyceans with sometimes doubtful facts and that continue to purchase for Joyce more and more space on the library shelf.

This is not to say that the attraction of allusion is limited to Joyce's fictions. Certainly there are important matters to be identified in the works of most major writers, but like few others, Joyce teases us beyond the bounds of what seems necessary to sustain an aesthetic or ethical point. Perhaps for this reason, the usual explanations of his frenetic referentiality are unconvincing. One argument—unfortunately much too widely accepted by readers at all levels of sophistication—holds that Joyce's sensibility caused his allusiveness. Highstrung, well-read, mnemonically retentive, and more than a bit given to obsessive behavior, Joyce indulged in compositional techniques that directly reflected his anxieties about creativity and his neurotic need to impose order. Dissatisfied with the world around him, Joyce created his own cosmos—and so successfully that, at least in his own eyes, his self-styled "encyclopedic" texts substantially replaced experience.[1] Joyce, because he came more and more to live within his creations, neurotically wove into them as many details and facts as possible. Burdened with a vision for the coincidental and with a belief in something like fate, Joyce painfully composed fictions which are great partly because of their comprehensiveness and partly in spite of it.[2]

To this position, I would respond that even if anxiety in fact motivated Joyce when he wrote, his allusions do more than merely reflect one man's obsessions. Such charges overlook what Joyce was acutely sensitive to—the force of culture on the writer, the extent to which what we conceive to be a continuous individual consciousness is composed of materials derived from sources outside the mind. Because author and culture are both shaped by the ideas and events that allusions memorialize, it is oversimple and self-defeating strictly to separate authorial psychic needs from the larger ever-allusive cultural operations that bind writer, work, and reader.

A second explanation for the Joycean reference—one a good bit sounder but still not fully satisfying—is that Joyce turned to the allusion as the most efficient means of establishing both subtle thematic reinforcement of ideas and a complexity resonant with historical depth and breadth. Within the confines of the life of one young Irishman presented in *A Portrait of the Artist as a Young Man*, or the day in turn-of-the-century Dublin displayed in *Ulysses*, or the night in one Chapelizod household dealt with in *Finnegans Wake*, allusions establish the cultural context of the Western mind across the ages. The very process of alluding seems to attest to the universal and atemporal value of such knowledge. Hence, the Stephen Dedalus of "Proteus" is not limited to his own thoughts as he shapes his antagonistic relationship with his father; rather, he can call on Aristotle, Boehme, Aquinas, and even the likes of the heretic Sabellius to build a framework for that troubled relationship that helps him to outgrow being the son and perhaps to find the father within himself.

This approach to Joyce's allusions has yielded extraordinary scholarship on many fronts. M. J. C. Hodgart, Mabel P. Worthington, Zack Bowen, Adaline Glasheen, William York Tindall, J. S. Atherton, Roland McHugh, Don Gifford, Robert J. Seidman, Louis O. Mink, Weldon Thornton, Clive Hart, Fritz Senn, Richard Ellmann, Bernard Benstock and Shari Benstock are among the many readers who have shared with the Joycean community their extensive identifications and annotations. Their investigations have performed the invaluable function of linking Joyce's works to specific examples of the culture on which he draws. Yet, given the immense body of information currently available about Joyce's sources, we still need to understand the relationship among allusion, narrative form, and cultural operations. It is with the effort to connect these three terms that my project began. Moving from a focus on the immediate allusion to consider the process of alluding, I have studied the cultural forms of which Joyce's phrasal references are fragments.

Allusion and Institutional Discourse

The "Aeolus" episode includes references to journalists, ads, columns, and newspapers, but the episode does more than just deal quite specifically and in some historical depth with Irish journalism. The presence of headlines and captions throughout the text casts it into the *form* of newspaper copy.[3] This episode, in fact, is the focal point in Joyce's works for organizing information about journalism because the newspaper is put forth as a key cultural institution and primary shaper of consciousness in modern Dublin. In this book, I discuss the significance of the newspaper as a form; that is, rather than investigate Joyce's use of the press on the micro-level of the allusion, I have devoted chapter 2 of this book to Joyce's presentation of the newspaper as a mode of communication that defines its own cultural space and defends that space against the encroachment of other, censoring discourses like those (to name the other institutions on which my study concentrates) of the stage or the church. Such cultural establishments dictated the conditions of possibility for Joyce's characters, for his society, and for his art. One thesis of this volume is that the daily newspaper, the popular play, and the sermon are thus signs for the institutions whose ideological practices they embody and articulate. The process of allusion in Joyce points to the cultural dynamics by which these major institutions competed for discursive power over the demotic mind.

It might be objected at this point that to call the journalistic establishment an "institution" is to project onto the press a coherence it has never had. For the purposes of this study, however, I have used the term "institution" to mean any collective creator of discourse that tends to repeat its messages and to shape social behavior through that repetition.[4] As Joyce's fiction portrays these cultural forces, their communication occurs through characteristic formats. The institution is not a presence as such but is dissolved into ideologically charged conventions and assertions. When Joyce uses the format of a newspaper, a play, a playbill, a song, or a sermon, he foregrounds the repetitive nature of institutional messages, for these passages in his fictions direct attention to the strictly conventional packaging of experience by institutions. A text like *Ulysses* navigates between specific allusion and larger form, to the end that the narrative shows how little (if anything) of what the reader perceives as stream of consciousness, idea, and action can be seen as separate from the social dialectic of individual and institution. By and large, the Joycean character lives out only the possibilities of social conventions and lives within a thoroughly allusive—and thus constantly repetitive (many of the allusions seem to make the same point)—cultural space.

Such repetition most obviously characterizes popular culture. All three of the institutions studied here are popular forces, and especially so in this regard. No single sermon was as important to Joyce—not even the Pinamonti work on which he modeled the sermon in *Portrait*—as was the often monotonic discursive presence of the church in Irish life—hence my emphasis on allusion as form rather than as source-marker. Daily and weekly, the Irish were exposed to religious lectures and sermons at mass, all of which shared not only a standard set of topics but also a well-worn weltanschauung. Constantly repeating itself, the church was like the press. Certainly, an individual issue of the *Freeman's Journal* was not as important to Joyce's portrayals of journalism as were the patterned interchanges among a variety of politically charged papers. Similarly, Joyce's allusions in "Circe" and in *Finnegans Wake* to the popular stage rely on our being familiar with the range of performance styles and dramatic modes typical of his era—with music-hall acts, with melodramatic conventions, with pantomime and its characteristic themes and devices. All three institutions conformed to well-defined conditions of expressive possibility.

The repetitions of formal discourse are targets for parodic imitation in Joyce's work. The simulation of cultural form and operation in his narratives makes his mimeses speak their social burden even while the fictions re-perform those communications in critical burlesque. Moreover, the productions of press, stage, and church often masked ideas counter to those to which most Irish women and men of Joyce's day would have given lip service. It is both convention and countermessage that Joyce's allusive network makes evident when we examine it as an anatomy of cultural forms rather than as a catalogue of thematic accents. Hence, through Joyce's works, we can eavesdrop on the culture's dialogue with itself.

Institutions and Ideology, Fiction and History

Certainly a survey of journalistic, theatrical, and homiletic forms in Joyce's day does not cover all of the decisive interest groups in Ireland during that time or all of the cultural forces that touched Joyce's fiction, but his treatment of press, theater, and church suggests that the interrelationships among societal forms map out the site of culture as we know it. Joyce's fictions, therefore, present the life of a community not as natural but as constructed. Again and again he strands on Viconian astro-turf the reader seeking the grounds of certitude. In Joyce, the artificial terrain of Western culture includes no knowledge that has not been humanly made and, as often as not, institutionalized.

Much of Joyce's effort is thus to erode the concept of nature and to indicate the fabricated quality of all social experience. When in *Finnegans Wake* Joyce indicates the interpenetration of religion and economics, when in "Aeolus" he deals with the relationship of church and press, when in "Circe" he explores the artifices of gender definition and the popular theater's play with those stereotypes, we see the texts unraveling ideological practice and exposing it as such. Separate neither from each other nor from their cultural environment, the institutions receiving Joyce's formal attention are his prime means of anatomizing his culture and thereby of demonstrating that ideological (rather than absolute) values are transmitted on the stage, in the press, and from the pulpit. This is not, however, to see Joyce's fiction as propaganda. Alive to specific abuses of power, the texts certainly imply political correctives, and yet Joyce wrote less what has recently been called the "literature of commitment" than a literature of exposure. His anatomies of cultural constructions and operations enable rather than determine the reader's political or socioeconomic stances.

Hence, although many critics have argued that Joyce's art is nondidactic and apolitical, this position calls for questioning. Products of their social situation, works like *Ulysses* and *Finnegans Wake* both respond to ideological practices and are part of the culture. His fiction inevitably adumbrates the practices of literary and other institutional discourses. In fact, it is possible to study contiguously and *as continuous* the popular media and Joyce's works because the two classes of phenomena emanate from the same historical ground and speak to the same structures and practices. That is, the three forms of cultural expression that control my inquiry were complexly conditioned by historical forces. They were visible and often controversial forms of expression and entertainment, rich in conventional material and yet necessarily in touch with the diverse events of their day. These forms played out both the major social tensions of the era and the society's ways of coping with them.[5]

To defend this position is not to privilege history as the only source of meaning in a literary text but to see Irish culture as a narrative composed of various myths and versions of reality, each one the product of institutional needs and conventions. This narrative runs parallel to those Joyce wrote; exploring some of the multiple relationships of these parallel texts is the task of this book. I am interested both in *how* culture operates and *that* a work like *Ulysses* betrays the operations of the institutions composing Irish social life in his day. In fact, *Ulysses* is a model of cultural processes, the themes and limitations of cultural expression affecting not only such popular material as newspapers and stage productions but also an avant-garde work under the "conscious" control of an individual writer.

To understand fully this dimension of Joyce, modernists must ultimately specify the conditions of cultural expression—what could be said by one institution but censured by another, which institutional conventions became straitjacketing constraints.

But readers of Joyce are only beginning to understand the importance of placing his fictions within their sociological setting. Most critics, in considering his relation to matters of institution, class, and politics, have remained within the bounds of traditional literary history. They have directed their efforts to pinning down what Joyce believed and how his beliefs influenced the meanings of his fiction. Recently, two books and a brief review in the *James Joyce Quarterly* have addressed these issues and, taken together, have suggested more interesting lines of investigation. The first study is Richard Ellmann's *The Consciousness of Joyce* (1977).[6] Ellmann argues that, partly because of Joyce's "indirectness," readers have underestimated the presence of political material in his works. But as Ellmann indicates, Joyce demonstrated interest in socialism and anarchism, in Arthur Griffith, Mikhail Bakunin, Peter Kropotkin, and Pierre-Joseph Proudhon. Further, he sees Joyce's politics as bound up with his aesthetics, especially through the pun, which joins sense and "countersense." As far as characterization is concerned, Ellmann maintains that Bloom and Stephen "anatomize and deride Church and State alike"; that is, Stephen wants his countrymen "to walk untrammelled by petrified dogmas," and Bloom wants them to live according to a humanitarian "mutuality of concern." Hence, Joyce's characters critique the sterilities of both idealism and materialism.

Developing this provocative approach to Joyce in much greater detail, Dominic Manganiello's *Joyce's Politics* (1980) testifies to the profoundly political nature of Joyce's writings. Through often original research on the relationship of Joyce's expressed opinions about politics, the political moments in his fictions, and the historical movements and figures (including Guglielmo Ferrero, Arturo Labriola, Benjamin Tucker, Bakunin, Kropotkin, Proudhon, Tolstoy, Arthur Griffith, and Eamon de Valera) in which he was interested, Manganiello documents beyond a doubt the fact that we cannot take seriously Joyce's protests of his own apolitical nature.

A valuable consideration of this book and an important statement in its own right about Joyce's politics is Sidney Feshbach's review of Manganiello in the *James Joyce Quarterly* for Winter 1982.[7] Feshbach links the work of Ellmann and Manganiello in terms of their biographical approach to literary scholarship ("Joyce knew x person and read y book; he used these in the construction of character or event z"). Praising the value of their investigations, Feshbach also notes the "simplistic" nature of conclusions based on this kind of scholarship. Quoting John Lauber, he suggests that the time has come for our movement beyond the definition of Joyce's beliefs to articulate the ideology of his works. Feshbach suggests that *Ulysses*, rather than expressing primarily socialism or anarchism, is the "Epic of Liberalism," and doing so he moves us toward the ideological reading that he desires. Like Franco Moretti, who in 1976 argued that the very structure of *Ulysses* expresses the "crisis of . . . liberal capitalism,"[8] Feshbach makes the leap from biographical detail and authorial opinion to assessment of the entire work.

I address Joyce's works at the level of institutional discourse, where the form of communication conveys specific ideological practices and where Joyce's beliefs are not as important to our understanding as are his formal experiments. Certainly, Joyce's textual dissection of culture critiques the institutional functions that shaped his works. *Ulysses* and *Finnegans Wake*, because of their peculiar comprehensiveness, provide information about the production of ideology in the Joyce era's newspapers, theatrical productions, and sermons. In particular, the areas of cultural contention into which Joyce's fictions insert themselves include personal autonomy, gender definition and sexual mores, family life, and the social order. Hence, I have come to see the culture and the fictions under consideration—*Dubliners*, *Portrait*, *Ulysses*, and *Finnegans Wake*—as parallel texts, that is, as reflexively related versions of an unrecoverable historical experience, which nonetheless expose the process by which social reality takes conceptual form.

Texts of the Culture

Given their comprehensive connections with history, both *Ulysses* and *Finnegans Wake* may be considered what Cesare Segre, following Juri M. Lotman, has called "texts of the culture." Lotman states: "A necessary property of a text of the culture is its universality. Its picture of the world is correlative to the whole world and, in principle, embraces *everything*. Asking what there is outside such a framework is, from the point of view of a given culture, as absurd as if the question were to be posed of the entire universe."[9] But Segre,

Lotman, and Boris A. Uspensky caution that no text can be taken as unfiltered evidence about the period in which it was written. As the latter two observe: "The conversion of a chain of facts into a text is invariably accompanied by selection; that is, by fixing certain events which are translatable into elements of the text and forgetting others, marked as nonessential. . . . The text is not reality, but the material for its reconstruction."[10] In other words, a "text of the culture" is necessarily ideological.

Joyce's efforts, of course, were consistently toward the encyclopedic, and his own discriminations taken into account, the self-conscious pose of his great fictions involves the premise that they are not *only* fictions but also compilations of details emergent from the cultural mythoi dominant in their author's lifetime. However selective Joyce was, the urge for totality speaks itself even in his practices of composition and revision. But, as I have suggested, this urge is not politically neutral. *Ulysses*, for example, reflects the always-ideological attempt to subsume all relations into its own design and to shape all information according to its own structuring principles while encompassing and projecting as significant only selected data about the culture and its operations. Continuously accretive, Joyce's fictions stylize all information to fit the text's needs and ends. To be sure, Joyce's attention to Flaubert's *Bouvard et Pecuchet* provides evidence that he understood such encyclopedism to be absurd. Not straightforwardly compendious but rather parodic of the whole project of human knowing, Joyce's fictions critically simulate the cultural process of accretion.[11] As it seems fair to describe the ideological stance informing that process as bourgeois, Joyce's fictions both operate within the philosophical structures that marked his early rearing and critique their own ideological surface by revealing the inevitable failure of cultural acquisitiveness (what critics to date have often dealt with as authorial neurosis). Hence, the "texts of the culture" which Lotman isolates for their efforts at comprehensiveness reflect ideological complacency. They announce their cultural sufficiency (we have all of the truth that is necessary, useful, or possible to have, and we can *present* it all here). Perhaps in partial contrast, Joyce's fictions also reveal the fissures in his society's structure and the contradictions between its prevailing attitudes and historical realities.

Joyce's major works, then, circle back on the cultural processes that shaped their composition as well as on the social realities inscribed by those operations. These processes, like Joyce's narratives, may be described partly in semiotic terms. For example, it is accurate to say that it is because of Dublin that Joyce was able to write *Ulysses* and *Finnegans Wake*, that he wrote as much out of the texture and patterns of city life as out of literary styles and conventions. Growing to adulthood within a highly insulated urban space, Joyce was exposed constantly to the accidental significances cutting across its conventionalities. The historical and geographical Eccles Street, for instance, is aggressively not an ecclesiastical site; its name suggests much more to those readers of Joyce who see *Ulysses* as a celebration of the human spirit than to the casual resident of Dublin who was less attuned than Joyce to etymology and semantics. The gap between semiotic accident and history (sacred significance and profane fact, the institutional and the everyday) defines a binary opposition on which many of Joyce's fictive ironies rest. His reliance on Dublin to provide the structuring relations (ordinary experience, spiritual significance) and the "chance" collocations of meaning in which he delighted led him to the semiotic crossings and retracings that structure thought as well as coincidence and that adumbrate the network of tensions, oppositions, and contradictions readily observable in any city.

Similarly, it has long been thought that the parallels between Bloom and Stephen indicate affinity or consubstantiality between spiritual father and spiritual son. However, the word *consubstantiality* suggests (in a literary work that is, after all, limited in its life to the mind of the reader in interaction with the signs he perceives) only that the sets of signs that point to Bloom intersect with the sets of signs that we connect with Stephen. This semiotic webbing is sometimes very obvious, sometimes barely noticeable, but it occurs repeatedly, perhaps an infinite number of times if we consider both the signs Joyce included in his text and the connotations that those words suggest to one reader or another, or—a daunting thought— to all who have read *Ulysses* since its publication. If we were able to construct a multidimensional chart of those connotations, we would, no doubt, notice significant overlapping from one reader's cultural connections to another's. We would also find radical differentiations in readings, as the massive body of Joyce criticism testifies. The tinker-toy model that might result from such a charting would "mean" something; it would suggest that the same kinds of sign-nexi or ideological practices link not only Joyce's readers but also Stephen and Bloom in the minds of those readers. In a city as small as Dublin and in which specific institutions and traditions shape much of the political, economic, religious, intellectual, and social life of the inhabitants, parallel experience among residents is more predictable than not.

That Joyce enhanced our awareness of this sharing of social experience indicates his concern in fiction with cultural conventionality—how it masks itself, how much of that which individuals consider to be personal choice is in fact controlled by larger forces and systems of signification. Such paralleling does not and cannot indicate the consubstantiality of persons except insofar as that sharing of being is understood on a semiotic level, as a fiction which is part of the larger Western myth-making on which Joyce draws. Culture sets the conditions for parallels; Bloom and Stephen live them out; readers have tended to code these characters as "consubstantial" because of the numerous semiotic strands connecting them and because the culture's repertoire of ideas includes that of consubstantiality, via transmission from the powerful institution of the church.[12] Hence, what has often led to discussion of individuality and selfhood may lead instead to consideration of the institutions and discursive forms constituting cultural experience.

As parallel texts, then, early modern Irish culture and Joyce's works exemplify similar mechanisms of operation and conform to similar conditions of possibility—especially insofar as they conceptualize matters such as being, freedom, personal authenticity, and fidelity. The measure of Joyce's awareness that these notions are inherently ideological is the fact that his texts do not affirm them; the works merely generate discourse about them and gesture toward the institutional purveyors of these concepts. Hence Joyce wrote portions of his fiction which aggressively insisted on the context to which they alluded, as in the sermon, theater, and press portions of his works that are the subject of this book. Those forms brought with them code systems asserting ideological content that, ironically and insistently, Joyce's texts undermine by establishing the artificial, semiotic, and self-serving qualities of cultural systems of meaning. Although each code system formally announces its dominance, its disregard of other forms, contexts, codes, and institutions clearly establishes the incomplete vision of any isolated institution in Joyce's world. Joyce critiques the effects of even seemingly innocent institutions like the press, which appear to announce quite openly their political affiliations, and he does so to indicate the vast substructure of economic and political coercion that informs the policies of seemingly disparate organizations. In Joyce's works, culture is the space in which ideologies perform, each institutional message struggling to eliminate ambiguity while masking its motivations for imposing its interests on a too-receptive public.

To a large extent, Joyce criticism has focused on those philosophic issues that the culture uses to mask the "concrete social relationships and given material conditions of life."[13] Discussing the way beyond ideology, Umberto Eco points to two paths, revolution or exposure, the latter occurring "through a survey of the contradictory format of the semantic universe, getting back toward its sources as far as is possible by moving along the branches of the content systems and across the various code shiftings and concretions of different sign-functions [to demonstrate] . . . how much broader than most ideologies have recognized is the format of the semantic universe." This tracing of sources neatly describes Joyce's use of allusions and obvious teasing of the reader by them, as if each reference were an imperative—go and find the origin. But what then are we to make of Joyce's motivation in so doing? Eco comments: "A critical semiotic survey of ideological discourses does not eliminate the speaker's pragmatic and material motivations and therefore does not change the world (or the material bases of life). It can only contribute to making them more explicit." Part of the aim of this book is to make such contradictions explicit, whether they occur in Joyce's texts or in the parallel texts of Irish culture, as Joyce does when he uses the newspaper, the play, and the sermon as signifying forms. One outcome of such an aim is to conceive of political engagement not only as specific commitment but also as the anatomical exposure that Joyce practices.

Theory of Culture

Although Joyce's works do not explicitly advance a theory of culture, both contemporary semioticians and Marxist theorists suggest perspectives on cultural theory useful in considering the parallel texts of Joyce and of Irish history. As models of cultural operation, Joyce's composing process and his fictions both display at least three basic functions, which are aligned with a semiotic theory of culture: accretion, binary structuring, and repression.[14] An encyclopedic interweaving of facts, the processing of raw data into ideology, and the selective masking of economic and other social realities have shaped the version of Irish experience registered in Joyce's fictions, both before and after composition. *Ulysses* is a "text of the culture" not only because of its apparent desire to synopsize the society portrayed but also because it represents the mechanisms of culture at a second remove and to a higher power than in unmediated experience.

In addition, semioticians join other analysts in noting the tendency of societies to be composed of both contemporary forms and forms of social interaction characteristic of earlier historical eras. Cesare Segre, in "Culture and Modeling Systems," singles out one aspect of this historical depth and functional multiplicity when he notes that "every culture contains sedimented texts from its remote past, texts which were constructed to conform to different concepts of the world."[15] Similarly, Michel Foucault asserts the existence in the modern episteme of former epistemic modes, and Fredric Jameson reminds us that all modes of production operative before the advent of high capitalism are present within high capitalism. Joyce, also conscious of this fact, used Vico's cycles to structure *Finnegans Wake*. In doing so, Joyce allowed for the presence of early cycles within later ones, part of the point no doubt being that in a cyclic theory such as Vico's, early and late become impossibly relative terms, but also that culture is cumulative and can tolerate all sorts of contradictions while continuing to "burst in systems" (FW 429.12).

No doubt this layering partly accounts for the way that new information is ordered, but Segre, interpreting Lotman, maintains that it is ideologies that "polarize the elements within the system [of culture]": ". . . ideologies . . . block out a first rough plan for structuring the culture's semiotic values."[16] This theory is significant in terms of the fact that, as Foucault points out and Joyce's texts amply demonstrate, cultural institutions tend to set up themselves and their discourses in opposition to the rules and ideas of other institutions. But this opposition is not purely binary. In considering the discourse of one Irish institution, say the church, around the turn of the century, one might focus readily on its attempts to censor the press and on the press's attempts to retaliate, but these ideological skirmishes in newspaper and pulpit are only symptoms of a larger political flow of power within the Irish capital, one in which the church's role is to aid sometimes the Irish resistance, sometimes the

British, sometimes no political party at all. In this context, many actions of the church become political or economic; the discursive opposition of religion to press, world, flesh, and devil is redefined in the complex relations among societal forces. In Irish culture one might first recognize a code by its difference from other systems, but this relationship may be traced, as Eco suggests, to the code's intertwining with various other systems.

This interaction of cultural components is so complete that no inside or outside of an institution may be defined; ideologies which appear to be "pure" are actually contaminated, through their use of the same dominant language, by adjacent institutional ideologies. Thus discourse does make poachers of us all, principally because signs are not univocal but are capable of operating in varied institutional code systems and of reentering their own system trailing connotations which make the resident ideology ambiguous. Certainly, the complexity of Irish cultural relations, even among the three institutions on which Joyce chose to focus attention, indicates the historical contradictions which characterize most social formations. As often as not, one institution may incorporate or agree with the rhetoric of another—even an opposing one—and one institution may be informed by more than one ideological position.[17] At times, Joyce's texts may seem to obscure that fact and to simplify the historical terrain, but the pressure of specific allusions on formal parody counters that tendency, and the way that such alluding draws the historical into Joyce's texts ensures that even the most straightforward comment recognizes these complexities. The distortion of reality which one institution imposes on a semantic field[18] operates endlessly in a culture composed of many competing institutions. Joyce's own texts address this ambiguity, "reality"-distortion, and semantic richness in the intense linguistic and formal "experimentation" of *Ulysses* and *Finnegans Wake*.

The perspective offered by contemporary semioticians, especially those of the Tartu-Moscow group, suggests that culture in general and therefore Irish culture in particular is marked by these defining characteristics:

1. The operations of culture take place at the level of signification, and all meaning depends on the frames of reference for those signs which the culture generates.
2. Culture is a mechanism which produces itself in texts—works of literature, newspapers, sermons, and the like.

3. Culture displays both unity and diversity on a number of levels and in a number of ways. It tends to assimilate new data into accepted or at least functioning ideological codes as well as sedimented ones, but it also accommodates countercodes and subversive ideas.

4. Culture forges the identities of individuals according to a system of constraints, standardization, and stereotyping. In the endless productivity of culture, there is mostly repetition of well-defined but often masked ideologically charged images and goals. Thus productivity becomes a kind of censorship.

The structuring principles of binarism, of conventionalizing, and of censorship form repeated themes in my treatment of the press, the stage, and the church in chapters 1 through 7.

By the light of this definition of culture, it is clear that (even though for convenience I continue to use the term "popular culture") to distinguish between low and high culture is less than accurate and especially inappropriate in studying Joyce, who did not discriminate in his works between the value of an allusion to the popular and a reference to a work of higher social status. It is a commonplace that many ordinary Irish people had some degree of classical learning and that all classes attended and appreciated the run of plays and light operas (*Maritana*, *The Bohemian Girl*) that were common entertainment in Dublin. Molly Bloom is no music-hall artiste, but her songs (such as "The Young May Moon" and "Love's Old Sweet Song") had a broad range of appeal nonetheless and were part of many musical evenings of the time. In addition, Joyce's insistent use of popular forms and performers suggests his desire to create the avant-garde out of the demotic. This inter-scripting draws attention to the issue of class values in his works.

Class and Culture: Contradiction, Absence, and Domination

Marxist critics today often speak of a literary work as a "strategic intervention" into the "contested terrain" of a society's ideological practices or, following Fredric Jameson, as "symbolic acts" of the "political unconscious." These terms identify topics that few Joyceans have addressed, even though Joyce's fictions critique cultural formations by adopting the stylizations of institutional communications and exposing the practices hidden by those stylizations. His transformations of received discourses mark the entrance of his fictions as cultural productions in their own right into the censored and embattled landscape of Irish history. Because the dialectic relationship of history and narrative explored in this volume exposes the pressures of ideology on the social sites under consideration in Joyce's works, I shall direct attention here to some of the contradictions marking Joyce's society and work and to the varieties of domination characteristic of modern Ireland.[19]

Responding to these dominating forces, Joyce's fictions become complex subversions in two ways. First, addressing ascendancy at all levels, they critique the fundamental social relations of the middle class in Ireland (institution/individual, upper class/lower class, British/Irish, male/female, Protestant/Roman Catholic, priest/layperson) by defining these relations as ideological and their source as institutional. As Joyce was acutely aware, only certain views of life in Dublin were legitimated by the publishing industry of his day; similarly, only certain social roles and relations received the imprimatur of the press, stage, and pulpit. What passes muster with such institutions often goes uninterrogated by the popular consciousness, which becomes composed of fossilized experience in the form of clichés and conventions.

In Joyce's fictions, these frozen traces of institutional activity are shown to be such, experienced by the reader in works which are in every way continuous with though not identical to history. As Ian Craib suggests, "The work is the trace of an experience that is framed by . . . social and ideological structures. . . . It is something more than its raw materials because it is a way of living those materials." He continues, "The conceptual space between different forms of explanation is, I would suggest, the reflection of a real, if often miniscule, area of human freedom."[20] For Joyce, however, that freedom is circumscribed by the intricate scriptings of culture, which contrapose one convention against the others. In place of freedom, we have something more usable—a structuring culture which enables speech by providing a framework within which meaning is composed and in which discourse may be strategically pitted against prevailing practice. That the cultural would mark out the experiences and relations possible in a given time and place follows from the very function of the ideological. As Terry Eagleton observes, ideology "is the product of the concrete social relations into which men enter at a particular time and place; it is the way those class-relations are experienced, legitimized and perpetuated." Not "a simple reflection of a ruling class's ideas," ideology "consists of a definite, historically relative structure of perception which underpins the power of a particular social class."[21] And viewing the "dominant ideological formation" of a society as a result of its general mode of production, he finds such a formation "constituted by a relatively coherent set of 'discourses' of values, representations and beliefs which, realized in certain material apparatuses and related to the structures of material production, so reflect the experiential relations of individual subjects to their social conditions as to guarantee those misperceptions of the 'real' which contribute to the reproduction of the dominant social relations."[22]

The institutional discourses with which I am concerned are not merely forms of communication but also the public arenas in which dominant conventions are legitimated. These institutional discourses defined the categories by the use of which Irish society was subjugated (British/Irish, upper class/lower class, male/female, and the like). They also propagated as natural the operations by which the culture created such distinctions. Circumscribing the way that middle-class Dubliners thought, both by labeling them "bourgeois" and by strictly defining other class groups, these operations link the culture, its texts, and its critics even today. In Joyce's fiction, all power is discursive, just as much domination begins with labeling. When in *Ulysses* and *Finnegans Wake* Joyce questions and undermines the absolutism of institutions like the church, when he demystifies their hegemonic presence by stressing the artificial status of the institution, he manifests that critique in the very discursive format which perpetuates the power of enfranchised social groups. Doing so, he clears a textual space in this "text of the culture" for other class practices and concerns, including the interests of the economically dominated.

There is a second way in which Joyce's narratives may be seen as subversive. The fictions principally call attention to those cultural sites where ideological or semiotic conflict occurs—where one set of institutional values clashes with another or where ideological practice is crumbling under the pressure of lived experience. For example, in my study of the Irish press, I focus on its censorship battles with church and state, while in my section on the theater, I address the conflict between traditional gender definition and dramatic transvestism, and in my chapters on the sermon, I examine the contradiction between the church's vision of the social order and the economic realities of the Irish experience. Relevant here is the dictum of Pierre Macherey that literary texts do more than simply reflect the ideological practices of their culture; the work of literature itself "is an authentic *production* rather than a reproduction."[23] Producing in fiction contradictions akin to those in his culture, Joyce transformed the messages and modes of press, theater, and church to undercut accepted relations and at least provisionally to voice alternative positions.[24]

Joyce's narrative subversions of dominating discourses are made possible partly by his extensive use of allusions. While they function as thematic reinforcers, they also bring into his works the fossilized forms of cultural activity, the bits and pieces of language that hardened into convention after emerging from the hotbed of cultural production. Each of the texts and discourses to which Joyce refers necessarily bears the traces of the historical state of affairs from which it was produced; each "real" detail that Joyce was at pains to check and double-check against the lived experience of the modern Dubliner speaks to the potent social relations, connections, sedimentations, and structurings of Irish culture. As important as Joyce's allusions, however, are the things to which he does not allude, that is, the silences and absences about which Macherey has spoken as the conditions of possibility for literary texts.[25] Conceiving of such absences in the most obvious sense, we can note that despite Joyce's claim to have captured the Dublin of his time on paper, his fictive city lacks many of its counterpart's historical components. Some of the deviations and lapses in Joyce's portraits of the city are addressed by J. C. C. Mays, who asserts that "Joyce presents a Dublin seen from betting-shop, bar and brothel. He ignores what the city looked like from Rathmines or Phibsborough just as he ignores Land Purchase in Connacht and Unionism in Ulster." But Mays's interesting essay about such differences is satisfied to argue for the creativity of Joyce's vision of Dublin, for the "strange radiance" which the book conveys in its "pervasive and longlived ability to change the way we see."[26] It is perhaps more important to point out that in Joyce's works we see very little if anything of those whose names fill the "Fashionable Intelligence" columns of the *Irish Times* and precious little of the abject poor who filled Dublin's teeming and disease-ridden tenements. The social sites portrayed by Joyce are primarily urban, lower middle-class territories directly touched at the level of popular institutional communications; Joyce's protagonists read the newspaper, go to the theater and music hall, listen to sermons. Their experience of Dublin shares rather little with those thousands of impoverished people who lived in Dublin's slums.[27] Nonetheless, their experience is marked by domination of various kinds—not only at the level of class and family but also, as I discuss below, in the very definition of being Irish.

Similarly, these "texts of the culture" concentrate only on the urban experience and fail to present life in the country, far from the seat of political, religious, and economic power, far from the presence of the hegemonic Anglo-Irish ascendancy. Against this absent backdrop, Joyce composes the ideological relations which he labels "Dublin." But it would be wrong to criticize Joyce for his interests and for the limited range of his relatively brief adult experience of life in Ireland. The reader can discern in Joyce's essentially middle-class worlds an exploration of the ideological structure of bourgeois Dublin *positioned within* a hierarchical class system that is shadowed by the powers of British military force and the Roman Catholic church. It must be observed, then, that although Joyce does not present life in the slums or in the countryside, his writings evince the pressures of such things as the threat of poverty and the alienating artifices of urban existence. In particular, his fictions of middle-class life imply the relationships that define it as "middle."[28] While many readers have found Joyce insensitive to the problems of poverty in Dublin or lacking knowledge of suburban (or extra-urban) living or uninterested in the mores of upper-class life, it is nonetheless true that without the implied pressures of those social relations, Joyce's "texts of the culture" would lack their peculiar purchase on history.

The question of class in Joyce requires further comment, especially because it is occasionally stated that in Joyce's fictions there is no working class as such. At a recent meeting of the International Association for the Study of Anglo-Irish Literature (University College, Dublin, July 1982), for example, it was observed that the trouble with talking about the working class in *Ulysses* is that no one does any work in the novel, and the comment was greeted with general murmurs of approval. As a matter of fact, some labor does go on in *Ulysses:* "Grossbooted draymen" unload barrels of Guinness (U 116), H.E.L.Y.'s men carry their signs around town, prostitutes do their duties, newsboys hawk their papers, barmaids serve their customers, "Thirtytwo workmen" build the "new Bloomusalem" (U 484). All of these activities proceed in addition to the more exalted work of teaching (Stephen), cadging ads (Bloom), undertaking (Corny Kelleher), keeping the peace (constables), setting type (Nannetti), and the like. More important, we might observe that in Joyce's text absence *is* often the highest form of presence. That relatively little work is seen in progress in *Ulysses* suggests a society in which the status of the worker was highly ambiguous and in which poverty and unemployment were so widespread as to have disrupted the proportions typical of European class structure.

Again, at the Eighth International Joyce Symposium in Dublin in June of 1982, I chaired a panel on Joyce and the Music Hall, at which I argued that Dilly Dedalus becomes in "Circe" a focus for certain working-class problems (this paper has become part of chapter 5 of this study). One member of the audience objected that *Ulysses* has no working-class and that in any event the Dedaluses are firmly bourgeois despite their poverty at the time of the novel. There are two responses to this statement. First, the comment points chiefly to the inadequacy of our current terminology for class relations. Particularly in Ireland, where the unprecedented conditions of the Famine seriously depleted the size of the work force and where economic and political conditions militated against the establishment of a British-styled industrial class, the terms "working class," "bourgeoisie," and "upper class" fail accurately to describe the varieties and intersections of domination that occurred in Victorian and modern Irish society. The oppressions suffered by the Irish were at least as much political as economic, and it could be argued that in many instances of social interaction, class was defined as much by nationality as by financial condition. Her poverty, her ignorance, and her status as a colonized citizen make Dilly closer to the "working class" than to the prosperous bourgeoisie.

Second, if in his idleness Simon Dedalus cannot be called "working class," perhaps he should not be regarded in class terms alone. By birth and education bourgeois, he has fallen in the social ranks to the point at which his younger children are not receiving the private educations that opened doors in Irish society. Like his cohorts in the Ormond Hotel barroom, Simon has suffered, partly through temperament and partly through following the trajectory of Irish fortunes in general, an economic and social disfranchisement. His role in *Portrait* and especially in *Ulysses* is to signify that loss of power and a state of impoverishment which is political, economic, and social all at once. That a man of Stephen Dedalus' talents and education might be viewed as having many options open to him means only that he is more socially mobile than the rest of his less favored family.

That James Joyce, similarly educated and more talented than Stephen, was never able to function within Irish society as he might have wished, either economically or politically, indicates that the multiple dominations of Irish life played themselves out in Joyce's biography as they do in his fiction; both cases tutor us against over-simple labeling of significations, against dismissing poverty as irrelevant when a character is nominally middle class. Some of the absences in Joyce's fictions are adumbrated only as differential relations without which what is presented could not be signified as such; some of the absences are misnamed so, things like poverty being nonexistent in Joyce's texts only if we choose to regard certain silences as actual omissions. The silences of Joyce on some aspects of life in the lower classes speak eloquently of his culture's inability to deal with the seemingly insoluble problems of poverty and power.

Further, Joyce's fictions, though composed, it would seem, from a middle-class perspective, refuse to view classes as seamless wholes. As I observed above, Irish society was marked by class-crossing in cultural matters. While in England the halls celebrated their lower-class origins, in Ireland Dan Lowrey worked hard to establish his Star of Erin as a respectable place of entertainment even for bourgeois ladies. All but the poorest members of society seem to have been able to afford an occasional ticket to the Queen's for a melodrama. Joyce himself was a quite unwilling social spanner. Hugh Kenner observes that

> Joyce's subject began with the fact that he had been born in Rathgar, then Dublin's most prosperous suburb, eldest son of a substantial property owner, and was sent, before his sixth birthday, to Clongowes, the most fashionable boarding school in the keeping of the church's most prestigious teaching order; but by the time he was a college freshman the family for no clear reason was living in a slum, finishing breakfast consisted of draining a third cup of watery tea to the dregs, one crossed the city on foot to save penny tram-fares, and there was little to be done with one's BA save take it off to the continent to use

in bargaining for a job teaching English to foreigners. His theme, in short, was catastrophic decline, from affluence to patched trousers in perhaps ten years.[29]

As Raymond Williams reminds us, it is more accurate to speak of class "fractions" than of classes as wholes.[30] Thus James Connolly, though a working-class proponent of socialism, was martyred in the pursuit of a middle-class revolution.[31] And Stephen Dedalus betrays the markings of mixed socioeconomic influences in his upper-class pretensions and desires, middle-class values, a splinter-class intelligentsia viewpoint, and the unmistakable signs of poverty (rotten teeth, borrowed and ill-fitting clothes). Certainly, Stephen violates gentlemanly mores when he asks Haines, who has offered to collect his gnomic sayings, "Would I make any money by it?" (U 16). The class distinction, which surprises Haines, is as critical in defining the distance between the two men as is the political situation that the Englishman blames on history.

Cutting across the notion of class in Dublin are the forces of gender and of nationality. That is, Dilly is of interest to us in "Circe" partly because she signifies not just working-class disfranchisement but also the second-class status of most of the women in her city. She sits through breakfast with her sisters in the kitchen and watches her brother go off to college; she eats bread and drippings instead of wholesome food; she wears tattered clothing; she is a younger version of her abused and poverty-famished mother. It may be that she yearns to improve herself intellectually because of her sense that the men in her family are both better educated and more advantaged than she is; she seems to see speaking French as a means to the prerogatives of cultural power. In a city of words where most of the work is presented as discursive, she may be correct.

The social problems of women and men alike, however, were consolidated into a thoroughly oppressive system by the fact that Irish society was not constituted by a single class structure. The hierarchy of richer and poorer, of empowered and disfranchised, was cut across by British class fractions—by the imported power structure of Lord Lieutenant and Chief Secretary, of the "Castle" class and the Royal Irish Constabulary that did its bidding. Again, although these groups are not much in evidence in Joyce's fictions, their presence is unmistakably felt. When, for instance, the Lord Lieutenant and his wife travel through Dublin on the way to the Mirus Bazaar, they attract the attention and virtual homage of many of those crossing their path. Poor as he is, Simon Dedalus aligns himself with the power structure by obsequiously removing his hat; the Ormond barmaids are aflutter with excitement over seeing the carriages; and the cavalcade is saluted or otherwise affirmed by Tom Kernan, the Rev. Hugh C. Love, Gerty MacDowell, Tom Rochford, Buck Mulligan, Dennis Breen, Patrick Dignam, some "male walkers," and "two small schoolboys" (U 255).

Since the truly empowered class in Ireland was British, it is not surprising that Irish entrepreneurs like Michael Gunn, the manager of the Gaiety Theatre, and Grant Richards, a publisher who enraged Joyce, were far from being political radicals. Publishers, theater managers, music-hall owners, and church leaders stood to lose money or power if their ends were not met in public debates over religion, politics, and economics; those who shared in either the political or economic side of British power had to align themselves with its ideological premises. Hence, in general, the Irish middle-class is presented in Joyce's fictions as having acceded to the economic motivations it shared with the British. Assenting to the imperialist ideological practice of its class, the Irish bourgeoisie in many ways complied with the oppression of Ireland; at least, Joyce's works imply such collusion.[32] Dubliners are especially implicated when they give not a political but a class response to the Lord Lieutenant's entourage and demonstrate how thoroughly Irish popular culture was scripted by British mores and ideologies. Without necessarily taking the British to their bosoms, the Irish took their ideas into their culture and consciousness. As I argue in chapter 5, the presence in Joyce's fictions of music-hall songs indicates the impact of British working-class ideology on all of the Irish. Not only did the British dominate Ireland and create a Protestant upper class while attracting the Irish rich to this artificial Castle class, but at all levels the British-Irish connection created an alliance which would not be severed, regardless of Ireland's political status. In Ireland, the *concept* of class became imbued both with the imposed social structure of British imperialism and with native nationalism.[33]

The interpenetration of British class elements and the Irish social framework maps out a contradiction that is political and economic at the same time. Ultimately, far from being radically opposed, British and Irish groups defined themselves by transforming elements from each other. Doing so, these largest defining terms of Irish life suggest the way that culture itself is created of imposed, artificial oppositions which nonetheless interpenetrate and define themselves by using and transforming elements characteristic of "opposing" groups. Even more, this situation suggests the ambiguous place allotted to the Irish within the British empire: how could the citizen of Dublin be *both* British subject and Irish national? The British failure to respond adequately to the Irish famines of the mid- and late nineteenth century highlighted that conflict of interests. The exploitative nature of the British presence in Ireland aside, this situation illuminated the liminal element that Irishness constituted in nineteenth-century Ireland. Both part of the empire and ostracized from many of its benefits, Ireland existed on the margin of the British political and economic systems that scripted it. As D. P. Moran sadly reiterated in *The Leader*, being a modern Dubliner too often implied enacting British traits and attitudes learned from imported songs, popular theater, governmental procedures, and the like. Exiled from the urban culture of Dublin is a kind of Irishness which the likes of Stephen Dedalus and Gabriel Conroy fear, an Irishness which they construe to be natural, primitive, and somewhat alien, an Irishness which they are in no danger of finding within themselves. Their estrangement from Ireland is in large measure the fear of the bourgeoisie for the "rabblement" who inhabit the unimaginable space outside of bourgeois hegemony and the social institutions which support it.

Somewhat apart from yet also tied up with the political and economic system, the Roman Catholic church posed another contradiction; an external power source, the Italian church in many ways shaped the interaction of the Irish hierarchy and society. Neither inside nor outside, the church formed an undecidable element, essential to the modern conception of being Irish yet not native, freely prescribing political and social behavior, and yet largely out of step with the realities of social unrest.

As a colonized marginal site, Ireland before 1922 blended foreign scriptings with counterpressures, and Joyce's fictions both embody and exercise some of these forces against domination. Using Jameson's terms, I view Joyce's fictions as symbolic acts which enter the social system, each text carrying its own "social subtexts," each of the texts and forms on which it relies doing the same. Embedded in historical reality at multiple levels, these fictions directly and indirectly address not only the operations of culture but also the contradictions that threatened to tear apart Irish society as Joyce knew it. Surely, the fact that Joyce's works have frequently been censored signifies their efficacy in addressing the issues that cried out for resolution in Irish society. Yet in response to the ideological practices that effectively defined the space in which he could move as an artist, Joyce wrote fictions that are neither legitimating nor revolutionary. Rather, the narratives speak the endless stylizations of culture and transform them into exposures of the constructedness of all institutions and human goals. In effect, these fictions attest profoundly that, because of the semiotics of culture, no change in the political system, however beneficial, is likely to bring about anything resembling individual autonomy. Given the culture that Joyce shows us, what we normally mean by the term "freedom" is at best a theory and an illusion. If we take such positions as seriously as Joyce's texts do, we conclude that significant changes in the quality and character of individual lives can come about only in relation to changes in cultural institutions and social organization.

Although my study of Joyce concentrates on institutional communications, all of the fictions explore finally the pressure of such discourse on the individual. In a sense, culture is viewed in Joyce as a fabulist, whose institutions generate narratives with which various characters must fall into line. Through the domination of the press, the theater, the church, and the like, individuals are made, as Foucault might observe, into subjects, in both senses of the word.[34] Formed as persons with distinct characteristics, they are subjected to the prevailing institutional attitudes about gender, family relations, appropriate class behavior and expectations, race, and nationality. What *Portrait* describes, for instance, is the genealogy of Stephen Dedalus, his *subjecting* from birth to adulthood through the pressure of familial, educational, religious, and political institutions. *Dubliners*, *Ulysses*, and *Finnegans Wake* map out the trajectories of these pressures. Throughout Joyce's works we see individuals who blend within themselves various codes, ideologies, and censoring mechanisms. The triumph is that warring ideologies *are* internalized and continue forever their uneasy juxtaposition within the "text" of the individual persona. Even at the level of character, where we might often rest, fascinated with the contradictory qualities of Stephen or Molly or HCE, we are engaged with the encompassing arena of the ideological and institutional. And even if we begin our analysis with allusion, say, or with identity, Joyce's fictions push us relentlessly toward those considerations of form that describe the site of culture.

It is with the foregoing theoretical positions in mind that I turn in the chapters to come to the forms that Joyce used to anatomize his culture. My own dissection of that culture begins in chapter 1 with a history of censorship in Irish society between, roughly, 1880 and 1930. The omnipresence of censorship in Ireland made suppression and its varied conditions the subtext of all cultural productions of the era, whether journalistic, dramatic, homiletic, or Joycean. In fact, the lines of censorship in Irish society make difficult if not impossible the separation of press, stage, and church into discrete organizations with distinct motivations. Throughout this book, I work to specify the separate significance of the discursive forms used by Joyce, but chapter 1 asserts a caveat: each form signifies not only the ideology of one institution but also the relations among institutions which generated both censoring competition and subversive argument. Chapters 3, 5a, and 6 continue the documentation of historical conditions pertaining in Joyce's day to the production of Irish newspapers, pantomimes, music-hall "turns," and sermons. Chapters 2, 4, 5b, and 7 are reconsiderations and contextualizations, based on my historical research, of the sections of *Ulysses* and *Finnegans Wake* that bring into play the forms and subtexts of these institutional discourses. By devoting equal time to history and to Joyce, I document the complex relationships that I have, by way of introduction, asserted.

NOTES

1. A recent variation on this theme of world-creation is found in Hélène Cixous's *The Exile of James Joyce*, trans. Sally A. J. Purcell (New York: David Lewis, 1972).

2. Even a recent very fine book carries overtones of this attitude. Speaking of "the seemingly limitless number of details and styles" in Joyce, the author asserts, "One can view the encyclopedic nature of *Ulysses* as both a liberation from the constraints of the traditional novel form and a defensive strategy against the knowledge of the limitations of all writing." Hence, the writer claims that Joyce's "bravura performance is itself created out of anxiety. The compulsiveness of the inventories of possibilities reveals this

anxiety: it is a defense against the knowledge that all of life can never be contained within the book." Elsewhere, the writer speaks of Joyce's possible "fantasy of omnipotence."

3. I am aware that, owing to the terminological difficulties of Anglo-American criticism, it is impossible to discuss "form" without evoking a contrast with "content," that is, without seeming to lapse into a sterile and misleading distinction. This book often addresses situations in which the implications of a typographical format as such interplay with certain ideas which are evoked "within" that formal unit, but my use of the word "form" is provisional and always qualified by the above consideration.

4. See, for example, Paul Bouissac, "Semiotics and Spectacles: The Circus Institution and Representations," in *A Perfusion of Signs*, ed. Thomas A. Sebeok (Bloomington: Indiana University Press, 1977), who states, "Any spectacle implies an *Institution* which provides the means for recurrent displays of collective representations" (p. 143).

5. Cf. Fredric Jameson's work on the "ideology of form" (fictional genres) in *The Political Unconscious: Narrative as a Socially Symbolic Act* (Ithaca, N.Y.: Cornell University Press, 1981), esp. pp. 76, 98–99. An essay published too recently to be considered here but which takes a stance on Joyce's allusions complementary to my own is André Topia's "The Matrix and the Echo: Intertextuality in *Ulysses*," trans. Elizabeth Bell and the author, in *Poststructuralist Joyce: Essays from the French*, ed. Derek Attridge and Daniel Ferrer (Cambridge: Cambridge University Press, 1984), pp. 103–25.

6. Richard Ellmann, *The Consciousness of Joyce* (New York: Oxford University Press, 1977), pp. 77. Below I quote from 93, 84, 85.

7. Sidney Feshbach, review of Dominic Manganiello, *Joyce's Politics, James Joyce Quarterly* 19 (1982), 208–13.

8. Franco Moretti, "The Long Goodbye: *Ulysses* and the End of Liberal Capitalism," in *Signs Taken for Wonders: Essays in the Sociology of Literary Form*, trans. Susan Fischer, David Forgacs, and David Miller (London: Verso Editions and NLB, 1983), p. 186. This essay was originally published in *Studi Inglesi*, 1976–77. Although my work on *Joyce's Anatomy of Culture* was substantially completed by the time Moretti's book came to hand, I have found valuable the confirming parallels between his assessment of style and form in *Ulysses* and my own. Another book that bears mention here is Colin MacCabe's *James Joyce and the Revolution of the Word* (London: Macmillan, 1979). In the final two chapters of that study, MacCabe argues not only for the political content of Joyce's writings but also for the connection among identity, Irish nationalism, and sexuality. He states, "Rather than engaging in the direct espousal of political positions, Joyce's work poses new questions about the relation between reader and text" in such a way that the "practice of writing subverts traditional politi-

cal discourse" (p. 152). Further, MacCabe maintains: "Deprived of an audience that would allow his texts to function politically, Joyce's writing becomes a more and more desperate attempt to deconstruct those forms of identification which had allowed the triumph of the national revolution to mean the very opposite of a liberation of Ireland" (p.170). MacCabe's book is both provocative and exciting, but his focus on the process of writing and on psychoanalysis moves his work on form and politics outside the areas treated in my study.

9. Quoted in Cesare Segre, "Culture and Modeling Systems," trans. John Meddemmen, *Critical Inquiry* 4 (1978), 533. The passage from Lotman is quoted in Segre from an Italian translation of Lotman, "Il metalinguaggio delle descrizioni tipologiche della cultura," in Juri M. Lotman and Boris A. Uspensky, *Tipologia della cultura*, ed. Remo Faccani and Marzio Marzaduri (Milan, 1975), p. 150.

10. Juri M. Lotman and Boris A. Uspensky, "On the Semiotic Mechanism of Culture," trans. George Mihaychuk, *New Literary History* 9 (1978), 216. The authors discuss the culture's process of retaining some texts and excluding others. They argue also that culture is a "mechanism creating an aggregate of texts" (p. 218).

11. Ju. M. Lotman, B. A. Uspenskij, V. V. Ivanov, V. N. Toporov, A. M. Pjatigorskij, "Theses on the Semiotic Study of Cultures (As Applied to Slavic Texts)," in *Structure of Texts and Semiotics of Culture*, ed. Jan Van Der Eng and Mojmír Grygar (The Hague: Mouton, 1973), sec. 1.2.3. They propose that culture typically tries to include within it all phenomena with which it comes into contact.

12. This line of argument is supported by the highly persuasive theory of Umberto Eco in *A Theory of Semiotics* (Bloomington: Indiana University Press, 1976), that semiotics helps us to understand some of the "fundamental mechanisms" of culture (p. 22). Eco finds a text to be "a network of different messages depending on different codes, sometimes correlating different expressive substance with the same content" (p. 141).

13. Eco, p. 290. The mechanism of obscuring such conditions Eco defines as Marxist false consciousness. On ideology and contradiction, Eco remarks that a "non-ideological statement would be a meta-semiotic one that shows the contradictory nature of its semantic space" (pp. 292–93). The following two quotations are from Eco, pp. 298 and 296.

14. These functions are discussed in "On the Semiotic Mechanism of Culture." Overall, Lotman and Uspensky argue that culture is a "system of signs" (p. 211); it is "the generator of structuredness" (p. 213) as well as "the *nonhereditary memory of the community*, a memory expressing itself in a system of constraints and prescriptions" (p. 213). In addition, the cultural system incorporates several oppositions ("The old and the new, the unchangeable and the mobile . . . unity and multiplicity") and relies on het-

erogeneity for impetus (pp. 226–27). Hence, Lotman and Uspensky advance the position that culture is a mechanism which not merely generates within itself diverse forces and phenomena but both transforms those things into signs and organizes those signs into binary oppositions. Despite contradictions, the mechanism works to create a "myth" of unity which the members of the culture tend to accept (Lotman, et al., "Theses," sec. 9.0.2.).

15. Segre, p. 532. Cf. p. 531.

16. Ibid., p. 532.

17. Terry Eagleton argues usefully against viewing ideology as "monolithic." He states in "Marxism and Deconstruction," *Contemporary Literature* 22 (1981), that ideology must be "grasped as a heterogeneous, contradictory formation, a question of constant struggle at the level of signifying practices" (p. 487). In *Marxism and Literary Criticism* (Berkeley: University of California Press, 1976), he maintains that ideology is "always a complex phenomenon, which may incorporate conflicting, even contradictory, views of the world" (p. 7). I often follow Eagleton in speaking not merely of ideology but of ideology as practice.

18. Eco, p. 26.

19. The concept of "contradiction" has been extensively theorized in Marxism; a very useful overview of this material occurs in Jorge Larrain, *Marxism and Ideology* (London: Macmillan, 1983), pp. 129–68. Larrain argues, "A contradiction necessarily entails two extremes which cannot stand without each other and which negate each other. . . . not all conflicts in society are contradictions." My own use of the term here encompasses what Larrain would label simply "conflicts."

20. Ian Craib, "*Criticism and Ideology*: Theory and Experience," *Contemporary Literature* 22 (1981), 507.

21. Eagleton, *Marxism and Literary Criticism*, pp. 6–7.

22. Terry Eagleton, *Criticism and Ideology* (London: Verso Editions, 1978), p. 54. Eagleton discusses the exposure of ideology in *Finnegans Wake* on pp. 82–83.

23. Pierre Macherey, *A Theory of Literary Production*, trans. Geoffrey Wall (London: Routledge & Kegan Paul, 1978), p. 232. Cf. James H. Kavanagh, "Marxism's Althusser: Toward a Politics of Literary Theory," *Diacritics* 12 (1982), 25–45. Kavanagh agrees with Macherey that the text is "an *act*, operating its own transformative labor that 'resumes,' elaborates, and displays the ideological in a peculiar way, endowing it with a *visibility* that it did not have before the literary work" (p. 36).

24. In "The Politics of Impersonality: An East German Perspective," *James Joyce Broadsheet*, No. 8 (June 1982), Wolfgang Wicht speaks of "Joyce's dialectical method of portraying negating points of view and ideologies, in order to sharpen the reader's apprehension of alternatives" (p. 1). Wicht's

position recalls that of Louis Althusser. A convenient summary of Althusser's thought occurs in Tony Bennett's *Formalism and Marxism* (New York: Methuen, 1979); Bennett states that Althusser "has argued that the specific nature of literature consists in the transformations to which it subjects the categories of dominant ideology, distancing them from within, providing a 'vision' of them at work so that, within the literary work, the reader is to an extent divorced from the habitual mental associations which the forms of dominant ideology foster" (p. 42). Mikhail Bakhtin's exploration of "the carnivalesque" also investigates the counter-cultural possibilities of cultural space.

25. Macherey, pp. 85–89.

26. J. C. C. Mays, "Some Comments on the Dublin of 'Ulysses,'" in Ulysses *Cinquante Ans Après: Témoignages Franco-Anglais sur le Chef-d'Œuvre de James Joyce*, ed. Louis Bonnerot with J. Aubert & Cl. Jacquet (Paris: Didier, 1974), pp. 89, 96. See also Terence Brown's "The Dublin of *Dubliners*," in *James Joyce: An International Perspective*, ed. Suheil Badi Bushrui and Bernard Benstock (Gerrards Cross: Colin Smythe; Totowa, N.J.: Barnes and Noble, 1982), pp. 11–18. A comprehensive portrait of Dublin at the time is Joseph V. O'Brien's "*Dear, Dirty Dublin*": *A City in Distress, 1899–1916* (Berkeley: University of California Press, 1982).

27. O'Brien says that "according to reliable statistics . . . over one-quarter of the citizens in 1914 were in pressing need of the essentials of decent living" ("*Dear, Dirty Dublin*," p. 161).

28. Eugene Jolas remembers "reading to him [Joyce] a German translation from a speech by Radek in which the Russian attacked *Ulysses*, at the Congress of Kharkov, as being without a social conscience. 'Well,' said Joyce, 'all the characters in my books belong to the lower middle classes, and even the working class; and they are all quite poor.'" See "My Friend James Joyce," in *James Joyce: Two Decades of Criticism*, ed. Seon Givens (New York: Vanguard, 1948), p. 14.

29. Hugh Kenner, "Notes toward an anatomy of 'modernism,'" in *A Starchamber Quiry: A James Joyce Centennial Volume 1882–1982*, ed. E. L. Epstein (London: Methuen, 1982), pp. 16–17.

30. Raymond Williams, *The Sociology of Culture* (New York: Schocken Books, 1982), p. 74.

31. MacCabe, pp. 167–69.

32. Cf. Ellmann, *Consciousness of Joyce*, p. 80.

33. Cf. the account in Stephen Lucius Gwynn's *The Famous Cities of Ireland* (Dublin: Maunsel; New York: Macmillan, 1915): "The garrison was kept in Ireland to keep down the Irish, and that coloured the tone of Dublin society. The always growing civil service, mainly recruited from Ireland but mainly from the old ascendancy class, reflected the spirit of Dublin Castle, which at the beginning of the century was that of John

Beresford, yet became gradually mitigated and modified. The Viceroy and the Chief Secretary, with their combined and respective environments, summed up the social aspect of Dublin Castle—an administrative machinery for governing Ireland according to English opinion, tempered by the prepossessions and character of the official on the spot. This element, though less alien than the military, was neither wholly Irish nor English" (p. 258).

34. Michel Foucault, "Two Lectures," in *Power/Knowledge*: *Selected Interviews and Other Writings 1972–1977*, trans. Colin Gordon, Leo Marshall, John Mepham, Kate Soper, ed. Colin Gordon (New York: Pantheon Books, 1980): "We should try to grasp subjection in its material instance as a constitution of subjects" (p. 97). Moreover, the "individual is an effect of power, and at the same time, or precisely to the extent to which it is that effect, it is the element of its articulation" (p. 98).

CHAPTER 1

Culture as Censor

... there are certain statements which ought not to be, and one should like to hope to be able to add, ought not to be allowed to be made. (FW 33.19–21)

The censor upsets any hierarchy of values, muddles minds, and mixes things up so that it seems impossible to untangle them. The censor wins, because he imposes the game on everyone else. But is there anything besides the censor?

Tomas Venclova, *The New York Review of Books* (1983)

Joyce and Censorship

When in 1912 he left Ireland for the last time, Joyce fled from a Dublin which he identified with censorship. The year before, he had written to several newspapers about "the present conditions of authorship in England and Ireland" and the "legal, social and ceremonious" systems that had kept *Dubliners* unpublished.[1] Throughout his lifetime, a widespread intellectual vigilantism similarly forced Joyce to defend his writings against charges of obscenity, profanity, obscurity, libel, and tastelessness. The story of Joyce's bouts with publishers and printers is well known, mostly because the author himself communicated his troubles to the press, to friends, and to family. Richard Ellmann has detailed the controversies over the publication of *Dubliners*, *Portrait*, and *Ulysses*, and we have the record in Joyce's corrosive broadside "Gas from a Burner" of his sardonic rage against publishers like George Roberts[2] and printers like John Falconer. Although the myth persists that until 1929 Ireland was markedly free from censorship, what is most interesting about the objections to Joyce's works, the hasty burnings, and the litigations is their testimony to the simultaneous working of several distinct social forces in the country; clearly, more than one institution stirred itself to censure Ireland's greatest novelist. From the churches of Ireland and England emerged dictates against the explicit discussion of sexuality that Joyce found important; governmental and publishing establishments further took to heart economic considerations represented by the fear of libel suits.

In his fiction from *Dubliners* on, Joyce critiqued the groups that mobilized against his writings. For this reason, a study of Irish censorship is an excellent point of access to Joyce's anatomy of culture. In this chapter, I establish the general prevalence in Ireland of the impulse to suppress information. As the rest of this book demonstrates, for Joyce culture is largely constituted by the censoring efforts (that is, the conventionalizing, stereotyping, and hegemonic maneuvers) of institutions. From *Dubliners* through *Finnegans Wake*, Joyce's writings directly engage with points of cultural contradiction and institutional conflict, areas not usually exposed in the relentless manner of Joyce's comprehensive "texts of the culture." To date, however, little research has been done on Irish censorship in the late nineteenth and early twentieth centuries. In fact, the two major studies of this topic—Brian Inglis's *The Freedom of the Press in Ireland 1784–1841* (1954) and Michael Adams's *Censorship: the Irish Experience* (1968)—are not primarily interested in the Joyce era.

That the study of Joyce's fiction is the study of the cultural forces brought to bear on even his early work is made explicit in *Stephen Hero*. We are told that Stephen Dedalus reveals a sense—no doubt partly subjective—of being watched by the authorities and even by his own peers at University College. The students there "regarded art as a continental vice" and, in their confusion of pictorial art with the art that interests Stephen, favored only scriptural subjects. They felt that "really art was all 'rot': besides it was probably immoral; they knew (or, at least, they had heard) about studios." And Stephen has to resist this conservatism and work "all the more ardently since he imagined . . . [that his works] had been ⟨⟨put under ban⟩⟩" (SH 34). In fact, Stephen's essay is initially vetoed by Father Dillon after McCann submits it for approval. Stephen's troubles with censors also include his mother's desire to burn the books she believes have led him astray, and *Stephen Hero* presents ample evidence that many of the people with whom Stephen comes into contact read and think only those things for which their church provided an imprimatur. Similarly, in *Portrait*, Stephen's memory of the public uproar over *The Countess Cathleen* hovers in his mind as he gazes "for augury" (U 217) at the birds flying over the National Library—the memory constituting a portent of his own probable reception by the arbiters of Irish culture. And throughout *Ulysses* and *Finnegans Wake*, Joyce weaves moments of caution and of counterattack against the culture that makes the threat of censorship so pervasive that it becomes part of the motivation for art; to understand his own oppression, the artist describes the institutions responsible for it.

Yet a shift in strategy occurred between *Portrait* and *Ulysses*. Joyce's later major works of fiction approach society not through the experience of the individual who is stultified by it but through a mature anatomizing of the culture itself. *Ulysses* and *Finnegans Wake* provide evidence that in a large measure culture as Joyce conceptualized it *is* suppression of various kinds. More than a Freudian repression of libido,[3] this activity extended throughout the institutional network which created social attitudes, values, and relations. As I argue in chapter 2, it is in "Aeolus" especially that Joyce gives shape to a change from denunciatory irritation with ideologically middle-class characters and critics to a larger recognition that conventional constraints upon the imagination constituted modern reality. Such metaphorical but potent "censorship" extends to every aspect of textual production, from the author's scripting by familial, educational, and other codes to his efforts to engineer acceptance of his writing by publishers and the public. Joyce's works—despite their attack on systems of convention—were demonstrably shaped by those patterns and, having become part of the cultural fabric, in their turn have contributed to the perpetuation of selected ideas and customs. At least the works have often been read as reinforcing various social values—connubial love, pacifism, and the like. Yet the narrative rendering of these values contributes equally to the exposure of received ideas as such, and of all ideas as received.

Hence, Joyce's fiction was not only a response to this censoring and repressive society; it was also continuous with it, for, despite the outrage over his writings, the allusive nature of his work insured that the narratives largely contained material also found elsewhere in the culture. For example, "soft" pornographic books were easy enough to come by even in Dublin; in *Stephen Hero* Uncle John talks about the time when, as a boy, he was offered such books by a storekeeper, and Bloom, too, has his sources. But Joyce's sin was to mingle the codes reserved for pornographic writing with those governing other forms of literature and behavior. Bloom not only appreciates the eroticism of *Sweets of Sin* but also supports Arthur

Griffith's politics, which included a stance on sexual purity. The presence of such conflicting traits leads not just to our sense of Bloom as a complex character but also to the recognition that cultural areas usually kept separate are mingled within a text that both echoes and critiques its society. Joyce, then, did not articulate what no one else did; rather, he blended discourses usually regarded as mutually exclusive. Whereas it was easy for his contemporaries to dismiss simply obscene or simply seditious literature, Joyce's works question the logic of such labeling precisely through this erosion of the ideological boundaries set by the culture.

Similar unveilings take place when Joyce's fictions engage with popular anxieties over religion, nationalism, class, and gender. Far from resolving contradiction, the works keep social antagonisms alive. As chapter 2 illustrates, Joyce's presentation of ideological contests recasts binarism as complex multiple discriminations. Ernesto Laclau insists that society is not a closed system of difference and that there is no ultimately fixed relation or identity. Rather, following Derrida, he finds that meaning is constantly negotiated and constructed in discourse, which is a response to this "non-fixity."[4] By this logic, to study Irish censorship is to index the impossibility, which Joyce's writings foreground, of authoritative closure, of a static society composed of monolithic institutions and classes; the anatomy of censorship is the anatomy of culture. Of course, although one can discern within a text a fluidity of signifiers in relation to metaphysical categories, the corresponding economic and political categories that operated within a specific historical setting impose concrete restraints on our thinking. As much as we might like to, we cannot disperse past conditions of oppression into the play of signifiers. On the other hand, insofar as they investigate historical constraints, Joyce's narratives participate in the discursive competition that aired institutional differences. Joyce's texts situate themselves within social contradiction and institutional competition to reveal the mechanisms by which ideological practices perpetuate themselves and by which infinite possibility is masked as a series of moral choices.

Joyce introduced his texts into the specific historical conditions of composition, publication, control, and censorship that pertained in Ireland during his lifetime. In tracing that history, I find an array of incidents that articulate a system of prohibitions, a network of regulations, and a pattern of proprieties—all accepted at times as natural and even as reflecting an absolute system of right order. Further, I find that the tensions which appeared to separate institutions actually bound them to one another in their mutual underwriting of the social structure. In fact, charting the lines of censure casts into relief the symbiosis of one institution and another. Finally, I document the role of the censor in producing the culture's dominant discourses.

Censorship in Ireland: The Church

"A few years ago," lamented AE in 1928, "an advertisement which displayed a naked baby outraged our moral guardians so that the billposters in two counties had to go out with paintpot and brushes and put trousers on that infant."[5] The immediate reason for AE's complaint against such instances of what he called "moral infantilism" was the Censorship of Publications Bill then under consideration by the Dáil and passed in 1929. It is often noted by critics of Ireland that the institution of a puritanical censorship, following as it did upon the long-sought liberation of the country from British parliamentary control, constitutes an ironic trading of political domination for a kind of intellectual enchainment.[6] It is also recognized, however, that despite the relative freedom of Irish culture from official censorship, the attitudes for acceptance of such a program had never been dormant in nineteenth- and twentieth-century Ireland. During the century preceding the liberation, along with recurrent agitation for political change, attacks on free expression came from several sources. An informal curtailment of liberty combined with English control either impinged on or received attention from many of Ireland's journalists, politicians, and artists.

The major source of Irish censorship in terms of sheer longevity is the Roman Catholic church, yet just how the *Index Librorum Prohibitorum* applied to the "Pope's green island" (W. P. Ryan's phrase) became, by the end of the nineteenth century, a matter of some debate. In 1897, the Reverend W. McDonald published an article in the *Irish Ecclesiastical Record*, an orthodox journal mostly by and for the clergy, entitled "The Index in Ireland," in which he argued that the *Index* did indeed carry force throughout Christendom. Although admitting that most Catholics, even priests, ignored the *Index* in 1897, Father McDonald affirmed that not only was the Council of Trent "inspired by the Holy Ghost to provide . . . the Rules of the Index" but that these rules had "been duly promulgated for Ireland, as laws, by competent authority."[7]

One year later, the *Index* again received attention when the Reverend T. Hurley began to publish in the *Record* a ten-part series of articles on "The New Legislation on the Index." In February of 1897 Pope Leo XIII had published new rules for the *Index* that covered not only books but also newspapers, magazines, and any societies that have "a positive union" and are "directed in some way either against the church or State" (including Socialism, "Nihilism," "Internationalism," Fenianism, and Communism).[8] Father Hurley asserts, "The censorship of books is a jurisdiction conjoined with infallibility."[9] He defends the sustaining of the centuries-old *Index* (begun in 1557) partly by citing examples of secular governments in prohibiting harmful publications. "No one . . ." he argues (somewhat irrelevantly, one suspects, to the enemies of censorship), "can accuse the church of injustice in restricting our reading without accusing these governments; and to accuse governments of injustice in such a matter, would be to accuse them of being careful of their own preservation." Indeed, the new regulations on the *Index* made clear the church's self-interest; for instance, the *Index* strictly supported the rules set down by Pope Benedict XIV for the guidance of those officials making up the "Congregation of the Index," including adherence to criteria based on "the dogmas of the church, the common teaching of Catholics, the decrees of the general councils, the constitutions of the Roman Pontiffs, and the tradition of the fathers." Like any legislative body, the church provided its own frame of reference.

This traditional perspective is especially significant in the face of a critic like George H. Putman, whose study of Catholic and Protestant censorship maintained that the *Index* had made the Catholics of the world conform to "local Italian standards."[10] In response to Father Joseph Hilger (*Der Index der verbotenen Bücher*, 1904), who supported the *Index*, Putman claimed that the *Index* had "inconsistencies" and was sometimes the tool of one or another clerical order. This implicit undermining of the infallibility of the *Index* Putman joined with a characterization of the state censorships in various countries as having "had very little continued effect on literary development" and, at least as far as political censorship went, as having been the inconsistent tool of different parties and groups.

He concludes that Protestants often wanted to exercise the power of censorship through the state, but the many sects and opinions dispersed these efforts, and the limited powers of civil authorities likewise blunted their effectiveness. Putman's study points to the ongoing debate over censorship which Pope Leo's revision contributed to, and—more important—it argues that the inconsistencies and power-plays that Putman attributed to Rome also plagued institutional censorship in general.

Given the concern in the Leonine *Index* over obscene books, it is little wonder that various Catholic organs took up the censorship gauntlet in the early modern era and ultimately spearheaded Irish agitation for the 1929 Censorship of Publications Bill. It is also not surprising that Joyce felt his books under the ban of the church. In reality, the *Index* prohibited not only specific books but also classes of books.[11] On several counts, Joyce's fiction, read naively, fell into these proscribed categories. For example, the *Index* rules posited that "an author may assail any particular member of the hierarchy or any particular priest or religious, without incurring the censure of the present rule" but that denunciation of the priesthood "in the abstract" was still disallowed.[12] The Christmas dinner scene in *Portrait*, even apart from the blasphemies uttered by Mr. Casey, would thus qualify, from the standpoint of this rule, as questionable. Similarly, "all those books that impugn the Sacrament of Marriage as bad and immoral, that propose and endeavour to justify free sexual intercourse, or any other practice of a kindred nature, are strictly forbidden." One can understand why, even apart from mores of the times, Emma Clery strictly ignores Stephen after he proposes to her a night of love without benefit of wedlock or even commitment, and one can see that by this rule *Stephen Hero* could easily fall under ban (as it did in 1944 when it was forbidden by the Irish government).

Along these lines, Leo XIII had "proscribed obscene books" because they conduced "not only . . . to immorality, but also to heresy." That *Ulysses* includes not only Stephen's thoughts of the heretical Arius, Sabellius, and Valentine but also the blasphemies of Buck Mulligan and the mildly pornographic interests of Bloom and Molly attests to the remoteness of the *Index* rules from what *Ulysses* portrays as everyday experience. Further, Hurley states that "we are forbidden to publish, read, or retain books which teach or commend either fortune-telling, divination, magic, spiritism, or any other similar superstitious practice." Stephen, of course, browses through a book of "Charms and invocations" (U 243) in "Wandering Rocks." During the early twentieth century, the church's principles were even used in Ireland to promote religious agitation against detailed press reporting of divorces and murder cases.[13] Bloom's thoughts of divorce have always struck me as significant considering the difficulty of securing a divorce in Ireland in 1904; similarly, the references in *Ulysses* to the Childs murder case and to the trial of Mrs. Maybrick serve to pull such events into the fabric of ordinary consciousness, a situation which testifies to the church's defeat on this matter. It is thus no surprise that in 1925, in favor of a state censorship in Ireland, the Reverend R. S. Devane wrote: "It may be a stimulus to young and timorous legislators to know that various States have drawn up a 'Black List' of books and papers excluded from circulation within their territories. I have the Australian and Canadian lists beside me as I write. Why should not the Irish Free State make a beginning with such a list of its own, and, as a deterrent to the Dublin Cloacal School, open it with the notorious volume of a well-known degenerate Irishman?"[14] That Joyce's works were never formally banned by the church is thus beside the point; like Stephen, Joyce felt himself under ban, and in a real sense he was.

On the other hand, Catholicism was not just the source of self-legitimating prohibitions. Somewhat contradictorily, almost every aspect of popular culture that the church objected to found supporters among the clergy. For example, many priests spoke out against the music hall, in the Irish *Catholic Bulletin* and elsewhere, but the famous Jesuit preacher Father Bernard Vaughan blandly maintained that "In a foggy climate . . . [music halls] were a necessity."[15] Similarly, despite an active condemnation in the press and from the pulpit of many modern plays, the theater often found support from the clergy. Hence, although Séamus de Búrca recalls the statement of his father, the actor-manager-playwright P. J. Bourke, that his company was once closed down by a parish priest, Cyril Cusack speaks of instances in the 1920s in which the clergy influenced people "even from the pulpit" to attend the melodramas presented by the company of his stepfather, Brefni O'Rorke. Dr. Cusack maintains that the censorship of the Irish theater of that period was not official but clerical and not negative but "collaborative";[16] that is, the priest and the theater managers together sought the dramatic material most suited to popular requirements.

Again, the church opposed many aspects of Irish journalism but also used the press. The Irish writer Canon P. A. Sheehan called newspapers "utterly untrustworthy . . . scurrilous, false, and libellous" toward the Catholic church. Rightly, Sheehan points to the economic motivations of editors who, far from knowing Catholic doctrine, are paid to please the public.[17] So influential was the press that the church censured, censored, and feared it, but many priests also sought the power of the press. Thus, the Reverend Joseph Guinan came out in both the *Irish Monthly* (1910) and the *Catholic Bulletin* (Dublin, 1911) with a call for an "apostolate of the press." Far from showing only evil, the press could be "the heavenly post-man of good news" that would reach many more people than are touched by the preaching of sermons.[18] The Reverend Denis O'Shea agreed, stating in 1910 in the *Irish Ecclesiastical Record* that "the Sunday newspapers, in modern times, have taken the place of the pulpit and the preacher with the majority of people in Protestant countries. They appeal to a mighty congregation, therefore, and they are the best means at hand for explaining and defending Catholic truth."[19] Recommending active correspondence with editors, O'Shea provides evidence that the church did not univocally oppose the press but rather sought access to journalistic discourse.

Even advertising drew the church's attention. In the *Catholic Bulletin* the Reverend Patrick Forde asserted, "All the devices of the pushful trader and the more pushful quack must be used to bring our books before the public. . . . Daily we see that advertisement actually creates an appetite for the goods advertised. So it may be with Catholic literature."[20] This statement emphasizes the direct and pragmatic sense in which the church sought to operate according to capitalist principles like the manipulation of the consumer by the creation of demand. "We must realise," Forde continued, "that literature is marketable goods, and so must fight for its place in the market." Similarly, Guinan asserts that there should be inexpensive Catholic novelettes and even "a Catholic Tit-Bits."[21]

Along with appropriating these modern forces of the press and of advertisement, the church sought to organize its own forces to combat cross-channel literature of obscene and indecent tendencies. It promoted Vigilance Committees and used local sodalities and confraternities to patrol parishes, street by street, for shop windows and street vendors that did not conform to Catholic standards in the items they marketed.[22] These efforts were reported in and encouraged by Dublin's *Catholic Bulletin*, which began publication in 1911. Father Devane, writing in the *Irish Ecclesiastical Record* in 1925, discussed the work of one such Vigilance Committee in 1911 in Limerick, where two newsagents were "brought into line" in an admittedly illegal (but unspecified) manner,[23] and he cites the approval of Lord Aberdeen, then Lord Lieutenant of Ireland, of the overall success of the plan in getting the pledges of twenty-two newsagents that only unobjectionable material would be sold. Devane recommends similar organized agitation for action by the Irish Free State against "indecent literature."[24]

Another kind of religious censorship was, perhaps not surprisingly, directed at the church itself. As we discover in reading Gerard Manley Hopkins' sermons, at times a homily did not meet with the church's approval. For example, on Sunday evening, 25 January 1880, at St. Francis Xavier's church in Liverpool, Hopkins was to preach on "the Fall of God's First Kingdom." He claims, "I was not allowed to take this title and on the printed bills it was covered by a blank slip pasted over. The text too I changed to last week's, and had to leave out or reword all passages speaking of God's kingdom as falling." Again, his sermon for Monday evening, 25 October 1880, on the topic of "Divine Providence and the Guardian Angels," was censored. His notes for the sermon read: "God knows infinite things, all things, and heeds them all in particular. We cannot 'do two things at once', that is cannot give our full heed and attention to two things at once. God heeds all things at once. He takes more interest in a merchant's business than the merchant, in a vessel's steering than the pilot, in a lover's sweetheart than the lover, in a sick man's pain than the sufferer, in our salvation than ourselves." Hopkins maintained, "In consequence of this word *sweetheart* I was in a manner suspended and at all events was forbidden (it was some time after) to preach without having my sermon revised."[25]

Hence, through all major means of communication, the church attempted to exercise control, from childhood use of wholesome Catholic journals through the consumption of church-sponsored or approved books and newspapers. But Catholic authority was by no means unopposed. Frederick Ryan, for instance, in an article in *The Irish Review* (January 1912) called "The Latest Crusade," cites efforts of the church to combat the imported press, erotic novels, and the like, and asserts: "A much deeper and more sinister motive, however, actuates the real directors of the present crusade than the

mere exclusion of reports of divorce cases and criminal happen-
ings." Citing Cardinal Logue's efforts to suppress the *Irish Peasant*
when it "advocated some sort of popular control of primary education in Ireland," as well as the antipathy of the clergy to socialism
and "Rationalist literature," Ryan argues that the clergy cannot "discriminate between actual immorality or indecency and any rational
dissent from the views which they favour in religion and politics."
Allowing the law to handle cases of indecency is all the censorship
Ryan would have; the church would impose only an unnecessary
"political or theological tyranny."[26]

Further, Ryan implies that the church in Ireland was geared to
the maintenance and extension of its own power through the dominant capitalist system: he quotes a letter dated 10 December [1911]
from the Most Reverend Dr. Clancy, Bishop of Elphin, to the Sligo
Vigilance Committee, which argued that "Heresy, as we know, may
be an embodiment of principles, not only against revealed doctrine,
but also against the ethical principles which govern the relations between labour and capital." This theological support of the status
quo harmonized with the economic, political, and self-protective
motivations for church censorship evident both in the *Index* and
in local applications of it (a point to which I return in chapters 6
and 7). The positive shaping of behavior according to Catholic
mores joined with these projects to make the church a formidable
force in Irish culture; all avenues of public dialogue were affected by
it because of its alliances with and uses of the secular institutions it
frequently opposed.

Censorship in Ireland: The Theater

It would be easy to say that the installation of a state censorship in
1926 was totally the result of religious effort, but this was not the
case. Other institutions similarly implanted the censoring impulse
in the public mind. The theater, for instance, provides many instructive examples of censure and suppression. The impact in Ireland of
the British Lord Chamberlain, who from 1737 had been licensed to
prohibit plays before they were performed,[27] is especially interesting. Echoing Putman's concern over the inconsistencies of the *Index*, an author writing in 1908 who signed himself only "G. M. G."
cites examples of the capricious nature of the Lord Chamberlain's
activities and laments that official's freedom from citing reasons for
his decisions. However, the Lord Chamberlain's powers did not

extend to Ireland. As Michael Gunn testified when he appeared before a parliamentary committee in 1892, "None of the theatres in Ireland (not even the patent ones in Dublin) come under the jurisdiction of the Lord Chamberlain, but conditions of a stringent character are inserted in the patents as to no plays being produced which shall be contrary to good morals or manners, indecent, subversive of law and order, or inimical to religion or the government of the country."[28] Hence, when the British censor denied George Bernard Shaw a license for *The Shewing Up of Blanco Posnet*, he provided that great polemicist with an excellent excuse for publishing a rousing preface with the play. Far exceeding the length of the one-act drama, Shaw's statement (1910) railed against the absurdities of British theatrical licensing.[29] Because Dublin was legally exempt from that control, the play was eventually produced in the Abbey Theatre, and Joyce wrote a review of it. Although Joyce characteristically objected to Shaw's sermonizing in *Blanco Posnet*, he applauded the fact that the play was put on, and he noted that it had been well received by Dubliners. That reception demonstrated at least the pragmatic innocence of Shaw's play, for the Abbey Theatre had become notorious for its demonstrations against playwrights whom the audience saw as either slandering Ireland or outraging popular morality. In fact, it could be said that for a long while one of the most interesting things about Yeats's *The Countess Cathleen* or about Synge's *In the Shadow of the Glen* and *The Playboy of the Western World* was that the plays were received with verbal or physical violence when they were initially performed by the Irish Literary Theatre and the National Theatre Society. During the 1907 week-long production of *Playboy*, Lady Gregory and her players engaged in what she termed "a definite fight for freedom from mob censorship,"[30] and in *Our Irish Theatre*, she notes several productions in Ireland that submitted to actual or predicted audience disapproval as a criterion for rejecting or ceasing performance of a play.

Such instances of the intrusion of public opinion as a censoring power in the theater were reinforced by yet another source of censure, Dublin Castle. Lady Gregory's stand against the Castle's attempt to ban *Blanco Posnet* threatened to lose the Abbey its license, and yet the government's reason for desiring the play's banning was simply to avoid appearing to contradict the Lord Chamberlain. While informing Lady Gregory in writing that the production of Shaw's play probably violated the Abbey's patent, an official of the

Lord Lieutenant attempted personally to convince her to drop the play, citing the political awkwardness of the situation, the desire to avoid the Castle's involvement with the press (the *Irish Times* had published an article entitled "Have we a Censor?"), possible criticism by the Dublin aristocracy, Archbishop Walsh's conceivable concern over the play, and the desire to maintain a favorable "Public opinion."[31]

On a different stage, that of the Queen's Theatre, Irish melodrama often took on a decidedly nationalistic flavor. In obvious contrast to the melodramas performed in Ireland by English companies during this period—plays like *East Lynne*, *The Bells*, and *The White Slave*—in many Irish dramas the domestic arena is shot through with, if not overshadowed by, the demands of history. Like the music of the country, the melodramas sometimes took on the haunted tones of persistent persecution; they were, after all, written and performed under the political regime they challenged. That challenge occasionally became so forceful that the plays were not allowed to be performed, despite Ireland's freedom from the Lord Chamberlain. For example, the playwright and historian of the Queen's Theatre, Séamus de Búrca, tells of difficulties between his father, P. J. Bourke, and the Castle: "My father's play 'In Dark and Evil Days,' was suppressed by the British Military in 1916. The year before, 1915, my father had crossed the Liffey to the Abbey to present 'For the Land She Loved,' a play dealing with the love of General Monro (of the United Irish) and Betsy Grey. The Chief Secretary remonstrated with St. John Ervine, manager of the Abbey, and rapped his knuckles for permitting such a work of sedition to be performed in the Abbey."[32] Such suppression, surely spurred by the joint threats of World War I and the Easter Rising, involved not only the blocking of playbills from the hoardings but also the banning in 1917, after only one showing, of a film[33] called *Ireland a Nation*. That work, for which Bourke wrote the scenario and was the principal director, prominently depicts in silent film fashion the events of the Wexford Rising of 1798. And it is reported that in 1881 when Dion Boucicault visited Dublin, owing to "Castle interference," "he was not allowed to sing his own version of 'The Wearing of the Green' in *The Shaughraun* because of its rebel sentiments."[34]

But all parties are agreed that the most important vehicle of theatrical censorship was simply "public opinion," which was vexed and contradictory in Joyce's Ireland, despite—or rather because of—institutional efforts to control it. In general, the Irish public was assumed to be fairly unprogressive, and various periodicals of the era support that conclusion. Hence, the *Dublin University Magazine* for 1875, in a discussion of a Gaiety production of *The Merry Wives of Windsor*, "regretted that the wit and humour, the poetry and pathos, the plot and passion, of the old masters of our drama are often not only associated with, but mainly turn upon, what are now considered forbidden themes."[35] The play, it seems, had been cut to eliminate objectionable material, but some critics still found fault with "the matter and manner of speech"; even though the words had been changed, the "actions and intentions" of characters had not been sufficiently altered by the expurgators to turn Shakespeare's characters into conservative Victorian Dubliners.[36]

That Dublin was mainly populated by these conservatives is a common belief, but one further point might be made here. The managers of commercial theaters in Ireland strove to meet public taste at its broadest point, that is, not necessarily at its point of greatest rigidity nor of greatest toleration but at its point of greatest profit. Hence, if a play offended the conservative opinion often voiced by the press but also filled the house, the production was allowed to continue. This situation helps to explain the reception in Dublin, when Joyce was eleven years old, of Arthur Wing Pinero's *The Second Mrs. Tanqueray*. Certainly, for the managers of the Gaiety this play was memorable. They included the following report of it in their 25th Anniversary *Souvenir*: "In October, 1893, Mr. George Alexander and the St. James' Theatre Company opened an engagement which attracted a very great amount of public interest. It brought with it Mr. Pinero's clever, but in many respects unwholesome play, 'The Second Mrs. Tanqueray'—a play which, in a striking degree illustrated the license that had sprung up in the modern stage. The work, nevertheless, was a very remarkable dramatic achievement, and its performance was a revelation of good acting."[37] What is fascinating about the Gaiety's mentioning of the play is the distance they create by the use of the word "had" ("the license that had sprung up"), as though their role were simply to convey to the public whatever material the stage produced, and as though the event were far earlier than only the three years preceding the publication of the *Souvenir*. The managers place the responsibility for the work on a monolithic "modern stage." That a play be "remarkable" and well-acted appear to be the only criteria used by managers to determine the success of an engagement.

The press, however, was quick to condemn the play. In Trinity College is a Gaiety programme for 21 October 1893 to which the playgoer attached an unidentified press clipping that compares *Mrs. Tanqueray* with *La Dame aux Camelias*, which was banned by the Lord Chamberlain. The reviewer argues that *La Dame* "was not all bad," but in Pinero's drama, "one is presented with an almost sickening effort to meet the foreign masters of stage licentiousness on their own sweet ground and beat them with their own peculiar weapons." The reviewer's only explanation for the "squalid" theme of *The Second Mrs. Tanqueray* is "notoriety"; he admits, "The house last night was crowded to excess. . . ." And Joseph Holloway, that inveterate playgoer who recorded his theatrical impressions in a multivolumed diary, reports that "of course we were all shocked with the play, & wanted to know why Mr Pinaro [sic] was so naughty to go & write such, after all the nice things he has given us in the past & so on, and so on; but nevertheless we all went & enjoyed the offending [?] piece despite our 'oh, mys!' etc. How nice of us & so very consistent, wasn't it?" He confirms that "the house was packed from floor to ceiling with a thrilled audience."[38] But in 1900 the "Irish-Ireland" paper, *The Leader*, jeeringly recalled the occasion when the *Freeman's Journal* "went into superlatives" about the play, which the *Leader* writer had found "a morbidly disgusting performance."[39] If nothing else, the reception of *Mrs. Tanqueray* indicates that managers would and did book plays reputed to be scandalous, plays that drew forth at best the two-handed praise of "remarkable" and at worst were denounced on the grounds of being both disgusting and detrimental to Irish culture. While playwrights in England demanded an end to the Lord Chamberlain's arbitrary and sometimes inexplicable censorship, the managers of Irish commercial theaters spiritually joined their English brethren[40] in playing both sides of the fence as much as possible: censorship was good if it protected them from booking a play that would draw public ire; it was also good if it stirred up interest in a play that was viewed as only barely passable and that would consequently draw large crowds to the theater.

A good example of the use of a kind of suppression in the service of such purely economic interests is the late nineteenth-century controversy over the production of short plays and sketches in music halls. In December of 1892, Michael Gunn, manager of the Gaiety Theatre and of Leinster Hall, had a performance at Dan Lowrey's Star Theatre of Varieties halted. The authorities stopped Miss Cora Stuart from presenting "her well-known sketch, 'The Fair Equestrienne,'" because Gunn regarded the performance as a violation of his patent rights.[41] This limiting of what-could-be-performed-where shows Gunn's "censorship" to be a bald economic maneuver; as Stuart reported to the press, she had presented the same sketch at the Gaiety only a few years before. In addition to the economic motivation for suppression, politics occasionally entered the theatrical arena. During World War I, when national tensions ran high in Ireland, playgoers at the Theatre Royal in Dublin hissed "Rule Britannia."[42] Given that fining resulted from such behavior, *Éire-Ireland* reported one offense under the ironic banner, "THE FREEDOM OF THE THEATRE."

The Dublin public obviously accommodated a wide range of attitudes, with the hostile being ascendant in the "retrospective arrangement" in which we now see Irish theater of Joyce's day. Molly Bloom recalls "the one and only time we were in a box that Michael Gunn gave him to see Mrs Kendal and her husband at the Gaiety . . . I wont forget that wife of Scarli in a hurry supposed to be a fast play about adultery that idiot in the gallery hissing the woman adulteress he shouted I suppose he went and had a woman in the next lane running round all the back ways after to make up for it" (U 769). As Molly knows, even what is criticized on the stage describes someone's reality. Her irritation over the sanctimonious upholders of stage propriety brings to mind Stephen Dedalus as he recalls the cries of outrage against *The Countess Cathleen*. Yet, judging by the frequent comments in periodicals about "nudity" on the stage, the public was not averse to being controlled by the conventions of the upper and middle classes that sought to maintain hegemony not only over money but also over morals. Indeed, the correlation of religious mores with class-based critiques suggests that censorship habitually expresses the economic motivations that often determine both individual and institutional behavior. The facts are that managers were tied economically to the Crown as well as to the public, and that the public was ineradicably conditioned both by English mores and by the anguished contest over nationalism. Poli-

tics, economics, and class determinants such as "taste" and bourgeois morality together wove the fabric of the mass mind. Popular
opinion, therefore, cannot be seen as merely a range of attitudes; it
must also be recognized as the meeting site of ideological manipula-
tions and economic strategies.

Three points grow out of the evidence provided here and in modern Irish history as a whole. First, individuals are influenced by
many forces and play out their culture's contradictions, undermining the monolithic quality of any institution, however apparently uniform its discourse. Individual priests, dramatists and journalists have always been known to act and speak counter to the
institutions that provide them with a forum. Hence, despite the
church's general antipathy to the press, some Catholic priests advocated using newspapers as an expressive outlet. Sometimes priests
denounced the theater, and sometimes they recommended that their
parishioners attend plays. Some of the clergy preached duty to the
social order, and others advocated revolution. These institutional
contradictions often show up in a single person or in response to a
single event. As a representative of the publishing industry, George
Roberts says that a publisher should never be a censor, but he suppressed Joyce's *Dubliners*. Ireland was free from the Lord Chamberlain, but the Castle asked Lady Gregory not to produce *Blanco
Posnet*. The *Irish Times* for 16 June 1982 records the events sur-
rounding the centenary celebration in Dublin of Joyce's birth but
not the most interesting parts of what Richard Ellmann really said
on that occasion.

Second, institutional attitudes often highlight the socioeconomic
relationship of one public body with another. For example, the
church and state agree that scanty costumes on the stage are harmful
to society; what is important here is not their joint moral stance but
their common support of the social order that legitimates their
power.

The third conclusion: so pervasive was censorship and so fundamental to the texture of society in Joyce's day, that Irish culture during the era was a network of repression. These prohibitions caused
the society to manifest antagonisms and conflicts as well as institutional affiliations. Censorship became a means of articulating the
"nature" of Irish culture.

Censorship in Ireland: The Press

The best place to demonstrate the logic of the system is in an analysis of the Irish press between 1880 and 1930, precisely where Joyce located his commentary on the censorship of his day when he explores in "Aeolus" the relationship between public rhetoric and "private" consciousness (the subject of my next chapter). A survey of journalistic conditions of publication provides examples of three kinds of control: (1) cases in which one newspaper, slanting the news according to its own political and economic interests, sparred with another, (2) cases in which the church and press differed over political or other matters, and (3) cases in which the British shut down Irish newspapers or edited their output.

In some ways, the press in the era of Alfred Harmsworth and William Randolph Hearst was feared more than any other form of mass communication. The British reporter, Frederick J. Higginbottom, born in 1859 and in 1891 the London correspondent for the anti-Parnellite *National Press*, maintained: "The 'power of the Press' is no mere figure of speech; it is an actual force for the creation of public opinion and the domination of it. It exceeds the power of the Pulpit, and equals that of the Legislature itself. While the preacher addresses his few dozens or few hundreds once a week, the editor is speaking to millions daily; the Parliamentarian, in confiding his views and opinions to limited audiences of Lords or Commons, is dependent on reporters for the transmission of them to the country and the world."[43] During Joyce's era the press captured the imagination of many writers both inside and outside the journalistic establishment, their comments designed either to awe or to warn. On the less exultant side, for example, is R. J. Smith, in whose *Ireland's Renaissance* (1903) we find both a call for the Irish provincial press to "liberate itself from the undue influence of its big brothers in Dublin and Belfast" and the following cautionary words: "Newspaper history, theology, biography, and philosophy is one-sided and partisan. Newspapers are a hot-bed for the growth of bigots and fanatics. Irish voters, liberate yourselves from newspaper dictation, deception, and trickery! Emancipate yourselves! Read standard books on biography, history, travel, popular science, commerce, and the like."[44] Putting aside Smith's naive reliance on "standard" books as acceptable norms, we find that his fear of the partisan press and its power was more than justified by the numbers and kinds of news-

papers published in Ireland in his day as well as by the evidence that
remains of their intolerance of opposing or variant views. Apart
from examples of outright censorship, we have such comments
as the offhand discussion, in *The Insurrection in Dublin*, by James
Stephens about his response to an *Irish Times* article by Shaw, "Irish
Nonsense talked in Ireland." Irritated by the article, Stephens says,
"I wrote an open letter to him which I sent to the *New Age*, because
I doubted that the Dublin papers would print it if I sent it to
them. . . ."[45] So widespread was concern over the biases of the press
that it is with surprise that in 1909 the *Chicago Citizen* hailed the
Irish Independent as a newspaper "absolutely uncontrolled by any
political party"[46] (a debatable point given the strong enmity of the
proprietor, William M. Murphy, to labor organizer James Larkin).

Virginia E. Glandon, having surveyed early twentieth-century
Irish newspapers, calculates that from 1900 to 1922 "three major
political persuasions dominated the editorial pages of most Irish
journals: Nationalist, Unionist, and Labor. Exclusive of the pro-
and anti-Treaty newspapers that appeared after 1921, there were
172 journals of Nationalist persuasion; 73 of Unionist persuasion;
27 of Labor persuasion; and 60 journals of an independent persuasion."[47] The rhetorical crossfire among these journals was often
extreme and occasioned biased and censored reports on events involving the opposing camps. As always, D. P. Moran's *The Leader*
provides lively evidence to this effect, because the paper was itself
ostracized by the mainstream press[48] and constantly badgered papers like the *Freeman's Journal* and the *Irish Times* about their English affiliations. Those connections arose, according to *The Leader*,
from the economic motives of the newspaper establishment in Dublin. Complaining of both the *Irish Independent* and the *Freeman's
Journal* that "the truly national press is the real 'Dublin Castle'
of Ireland," one editorial maintained that "the journalistic trade
in Ireland has attracted many clear-sighted, brilliant and well-
intentioned men" who were "smothered" by editors who desired
only profits.[49] Presumably the same writer asserted that British papers routinely supplied for the Irish press syndicated columns of all
sorts—"the society column, the ladies' column, the joke column,
the metropolitan par. column and the serial story"—all of which
shaped Irish popular opinion and social aspirations.[50] Describing
one example of this influence, in which both Unionist and Nationalist papers printed notices in praise of the British Grenadiers's Band

which appeared in Dublin during Horse Show Week, another article laments, "At the present rate of going . . . [the Briton] will in a short time do everything for us, down to supplying our Nationalist newspapers with stereo blocks of seditious and patriotic cant at 2s. 6d. a column!"[51]

If any social organ disapproved of the money-hungry Dublin press more than the *Leader*, it was the Catholic church. A representative sample of that displeasure is an article published in 1913 in the *Catholic Bulletin*, "Social Unrest & Its Remedy." Like Moran, the author begins with the argument that the profit motive rules the press: "What pays must be published; but if truth is considered unprofitable, it must be suppressed, or twisted so as to make it palatable, and consequently make it pay." Hence, "An Orange outrage on the one side, is Hibernian hooliganism on the other. What according to the Liberal Press is a violation of the natural or national law, is in the Conservative papers quite right and proper." From this point of departure, the writer finds the press to be in many cases the *cause* of social unrest, including the strikes that from 1911 on rocked the British Isles.[52]

Other examples of hostility to the press and attempts to undermine its public power could easily be summoned. For example, when John O'Leary, the inspiration for much of Yeats's early interest in Irish politics, edited a newspaper called the *Irish People*, he ran into major trouble with the British government and with the church. Malcolm Brown sums up O'Leary's story: O'Leary tried to use this paper "to call Irishmen to arms," an attempt that "led to his arrest, trial, and conviction for treason felony," as well as to "five years in English prisons and another fifteen years in exile."[53] The O'Leary case was, of course, known to Joyce; in 1907 he published an essay about O'Leary in *Il Piccolo della Sera* called "Il Fenianismo. L'Ultimo Feniano." Joyce explains the resistance of the Irish revolutionaries to both "the English political parties" and Irish "parliamentarians," a resistance expressed by the "intransigent press" in which O'Leary played a part.[54]

Joyce presents O'Leary more as a political leader betrayed by a lone Judas than as a journalist silenced by the state, but in fact O'Leary fits both roles. The militancy of those associated with the *Irish People* antagonized and frightened the English; when in 1865 they were able to procure indicting evidence against O'Leary and the Irish Republican Brotherhood (IRB), they took the opportunity to destroy the office of the newspaper.[55] As Marcus Bourke states, "Every scrap of paper—stationery, account books, proofs, correspondence, manuscripts, even obviously personal letters—was seized; the very floorboards were ripped up lest anything might be overlooked. A police float was summoned from the Castle and the entire type-setting machinery was loaded on to it, removed to the Castle yard and there unceremoniously dumped in an irreparable condition." Finally, "all over the country copies of the last issue of the *Irish People* were seized and confiscated by the police. . . ." That O'Leary's paper had called for Irish independence did not, however surprisingly, cause the publication to be outlawed until an arrest was made possible by the government's obtaining of hard evidence about IRB sedition, but the paper inevitably was killed when the arrest occurred. Certainly O'Leary's ultimate defense, that whatever he was to England he was no traitor to Ireland, did not save any of his work from being considered treasonous. Notably, the church had anticipated such an end and had warned its members not to read the paper. Archbishop Cullen of Dublin even publicly "thanked the authorities for the suppression of the *Irish People*."

A much milder but equally instructive case of suppression of the press involves the Irish journalist W. P. Ryan. Ryan strongly supported a renewal of Irish culture, both by the stimulation of interest in Gaelic matters and by the initiation of debate over contemporary problems in education, agriculture, politics, legislation, and religion. F. S. L. Lyons writes, "For a time in the early years of the new century he ran a widely read paper, the *Irish Peasant*, until it fell foul of the church and was obliged to close down, an episode described by Ryan himself in a novel, *The Plough and the Cross*."[56] Ryan's account of this episode,[57] which is also presented in the introduction to his book of "review" and "reverie" entitled *The Pope's Green Island*, shows how complicated and frustrating such falling foul could be, even to the most enthusiastic Irish editor. Ryan's report of his 1905 to 1910 editorship reveals persistent old-guard clerical antagonism to the intellectual debate that Ryan tried to foster in his publication. The *Irish Peasant* was edited by Ryan for only a year before the owner of the newspaper gave up its publication in acquiescence to the displeasure of Cardinal Logue, a censure that followed much clerical pressure on the owner's family. Although Ryan asserts that his paper found support from "a more hopeful new order of Irish ecclesiastics," Logue, in a letter to the owner, accused the *Irish Peas-*

ant of being "'anti-Catholic'" and stated his intention "to denounce it publicly and prohibit the reading of it in the archdiocese" under his control. It is worth noting, though, that after some public discussion of the case, Cardinal Logue "left the 'anti-Catholic' note," and Ryan moved the paper from Navan to Dublin. When Ryan's paper—later called the *Irish Nation*—finally folded, its demise was over financial, social, and political issues rather than religious ones, despite the fact that the paper had continued fighting with "the more rigid and formalistic clerics."

Hence, while the church did not necessarily ban objectionable publications out of hand, ecclesiastical power tended toward maintenance of conservative views and public ignorance. Ryan comments that during 1906, "There was . . . the feeling on the part of the older priests that, as a friendly young priest informed me, it [the *Irish Peasant*] was 'telling the people too much.'" Judging by the tenor of the time, a reader can accept this unsubstantiated report as at least credible. The Irish press was under attack both from a hostile foreign government and from an often equally hostile native church, both of which sought to prevent the press from diminishing their own cultural dominance.

In addition, from the death of Parnell to the beginning of the Free State, many small journals, most but not all of them short-lived, cycled through Irish culture in various kinds of support of "the Separatist, Sinn Fein and Irish Ireland Movements" as well as the socialist labor movement. (The National Library of Ireland has some 112 "Radical Newspapers" on microfilm, a collection mostly covering from 1900 through the 1930s.) Labeled the "Mosquito Press"[58] in token perhaps not only of their annoyance but also of their persistence, these journals are characterized mainly by their resistance to always imminent suppression. Typically, when a paper was suppressed, it immediately reappeared under a changed name or with a slightly masked policy. P. S. O'Hegarty, who knew many of the editors he mentions, cites several radical papers in his article on the "Mosquito press": *The Northern Patriot, The Shan Van Vocht, The United Irishman, Sinn Féin, Nationality, The Leader, New Ireland, The Nationalist, The Republic, Peasant and Nation, Irish Freedom, Éire, Scissors and Paste, Fianna Fáil, The Spark, Honesty, An Barr Buadh, Na Bac Leis, The Irishman, Irish Opinion, The Irish Nation, New Ireland, An Saoghal Gaedhealach, The Republic, Eire Og, The Gael,* and *The Leitrim Guardian.* W. P. Ryan and Arthur Griffith

PLATES 1 and 2. The publishing history of William O'Brien's *United Ireland* exemplifies the mechanics of much censorship in early modern Ireland. In *The Press in Ireland: A Survey and a Guide* (1937; reprinted New York: Lemma, 1971) Father Stephen J. Brown reports that in its early years the paper "was produced in at least ten cities successively—London, Liverpool, Glasgow, Manchester, Paris, etc." as the authorities responded repressively to its Home Rule Stance (p. 38). By the end of 1890, however, the newspaper had assumed an anti-Parnell stance. On the 15 December of that year, in response to Parnellite pressure, this halfpenny paper was printed under the banner "SUPPRESSED"; although *United Ireland* began publication in 1881, the issue styled itself "Vol. 1.–No. 1." The National Library of Ireland's microfilm of this journal is missing the issue for December 16th, but the following day's paper shows that Parnell's supporters had been unable to stop the news from hitting the streets. Volume 1, number 3 of the "SUPPRESSED," invoking a familiar Celtic emblem in its support, insisted on being "INSUPRESSIBLE." (Photographs courtesy of the National Library of Ireland.)

proved to be among the most persevering editors, each of them having his current publication suppressed by the British government only to start right up again with a newly named paper. As Dorothy Macardle confirms,[59] Griffith's *Sinn Féin*, born on the death of *The United Irishman*, was replaced by *Nationality* and then by *Éire* and *Scissors and Paste*. Another tenacious editor was William O'Brien, whose *United Ireland* was suppressed by supporters of Parnell in December of 1890, only to reappear during the same month as the *Insuppressible*. Notably, Bloom recalls both *Scissors and Paste* (U 117) and "the auspicious occasion when they broke up the type in the *Insuppressible* or was it *United Ireland*" (U 649–50, 654—see Plates 1 and 2). The *Insuppressible* also finds its way into the *Wake* as the "*Instopressible*" (FW 568.16).[60]

Much of this suppression on the part of the British took place during World War I, when the Defence of the Realm Act (D.O.R.A.—1914) created the opportunity for press censorship in Ireland; until the end of April in 1919, Lord Decies was the Press Censor for Ireland, Bryan Cooper taking over only for the final four months that the office operated in Dublin. Under D.O.R.A., the British censors could proscribe the printing of any information not consistent with maintenance of security on military matters. However, they clearly could not resist the chance to educate the Irish while defending the realm. As early as November of 1914, the London *Daily Mail* was quoted in *Éire* as being opposed to government censorship, which it was claimed was being extended from protection of military information in the press to "a censorship over opinion."[61] Yet *Éire* also reported in November that "The London 'Globe' . . . called for the suppression of the Nationalist Press in Ireland."[62] This difference in attitude characterizes the Censor's role in Ireland. On the one hand, the Censor informed Irish newspaper editors that submission of material to his office was voluntary; on the other, the Censor regularly issued dictates to the press about materials that could not be published without violating D.O.R.A., and many Irish papers were suppressed as seditious almost from the outset of the wartime regulations. Clearly, the international conflict, which postponed the already legislated separation of Ireland and England, created an excellent opportunity for the British government to attempt to shape opinion in Ireland on a host of issues that did not relate directly to military maneuvers and supplies. Home Rule was won, but the war had to be over before the British govern-

ment would give up Dublin Castle and control of the Irish. Given
the imminence of independence, the search and destroy tactics carried out on various newspapers were especially ironic.

Nationalist papers were suppressed partly because they tended to
exhort Irish men to resist recruitment in the English army and navy;
these calls were considered seditious.[63] But as the Griffith-edited
Éire suggested, the degree to which the suppression of information
went and the nature of that action were equaled in caprice only by
what was left untouched by the Censor's blue pencil. For instance,
on 1 December 1914 *Éire* reported under the banner "PASSED BY
THE CENSOR": [64] "The 'Evening Herald' announces that a French
cat has violently attacked and overcome a German infantryman,
who is now in hospital, 'his face one mass of bloody pulp.'" Silliness
and distortion appeared to hallmark the Censor's office, at least in
the public mind. Again, *Éire* reported that the London *Times* had
charged the British government with distorting news from Ger-
many and sending it to the press as truth; the headline was "THE
INVENT AND SUPPRESS BUREAU."[65]

Distortion and censorship had serious implications for Irish politics and civil rights. Not just news of foreign military proceedings
was altered; even if some newspapers were allowed to operate, the
news from home was also often controlled. Thus, when Hanna
Sheehy Skeffington, the widow of the martyred patriot and feminist, visited Britain, Lord Decies "requested" that the Irish press
"not . . . publish any letters or extracts from letters from Mrs. Sheehy
Skeffington which may be sent them without previous submission
to this Office" (Plate 3).[66] Other circulars from the Censor now in
the National Library of Ireland banned the publication of statements in political elections, speeches about rebellion against the
British or about antimilitary ideas, seditious statements even when
part of the transcript of judicial proceedings, anti-British leaflets circulated at meetings, notices about Sinn Féin Volunteers' parades,
and selected information about the British treatment of jailed Irish
prisoners.

Intended to block the news, such circulars sometimes served only
to circulate it further. For example, Lord Decies's 7 March 1918 notice to Irish editors, marked "Confidential. Not for Publication or
Communication" and warning against inflammatory printing of information about the hunger striking of prisoners in Irish jails, was
reprinted as a throwaway headed "How Ireland is Gagged. Men

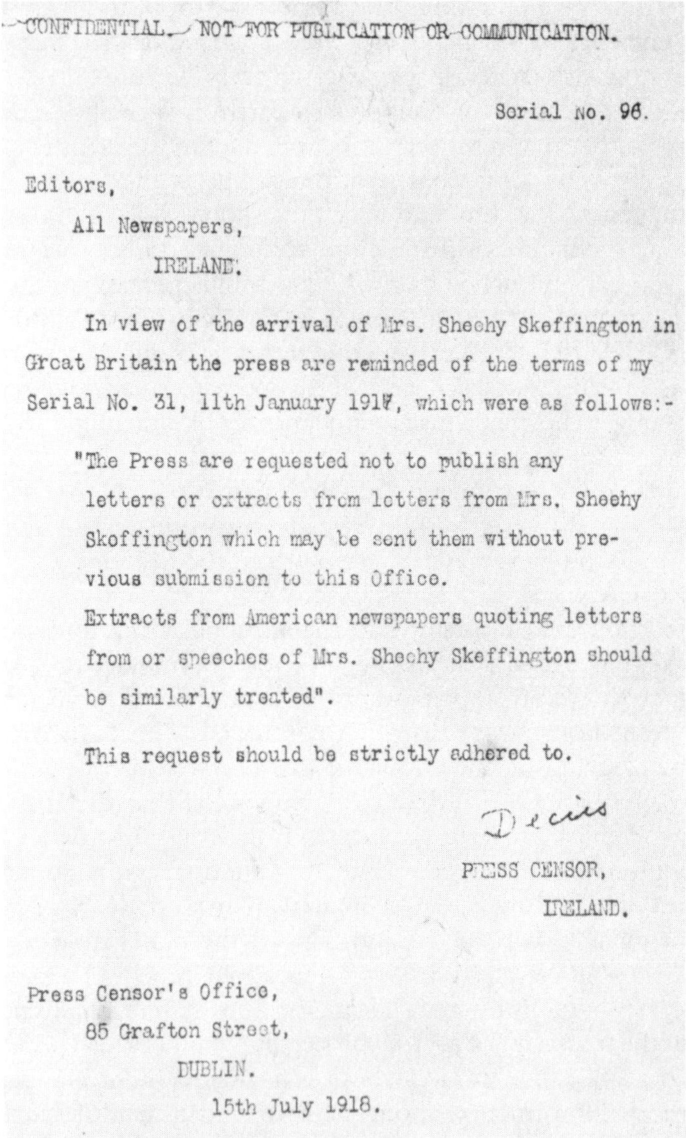

CONFIDENTIAL. NOT FOR PUBLICATION OR COMMUNICATION.

Serial No. 96.

Editors,

All Newspapers,

IRELAND.

In view of the arrival of Mrs. Sheehy Skeffington in Great Britain the press are reminded of the terms of my Serial No. 31, 11th January 1917, which were as follows:-

"The Press are requested not to publish any letters or extracts from letters from Mrs. Sheehy Skeffington which may be sent them without previous submission to this Office.

Extracts from American newspapers quoting letters from or speeches of Mrs. Sheehy Skeffington should be similarly treated".

This request should be strictly adhered to.

Decies

PRESS CENSOR,

IRELAND.

Press Censor's Office,

85 Grafton Street,

DUBLIN.

15th July 1918.

PLATE 3. Although the Irish Press Censor's Office billed itself as both temporary and involved only in matters of British security, Lord Decies, who held the position of Censor during most of World War I, sometimes ventured into the shaping of public opinion through omission. Ironically, his "confidential" reports not only have found a larger audience in students of Irish history but also could escape his control to find a wider circulation in the public streets. It is not surprising that the Censor circulated to

being Done to Death in Silence by the 'Champion of Small Nations.'" And a pamphlet entitled *English Atrocities in Ireland* presented what were alleged to be "Court and Press Records of 31,482 *admitted* British Military Outrages in Ireland, from May 1, 1916 to March 1, 1920," acts including not only murders, raids, and arrests but also reports suppressed by the Censor. Some of the last involved information about cruelty to Irish prisoners held in Belfast.[67]

The most interesting (because the most trivial) instance of censorship that I have discovered involves an article, apparently intended for an Enniscorthy paper, arguing that the Guinness Brewing Company was wrongly importing (and paying *more* for) English barley instead of buying at a fair price the Irish barley that lay at the heart of Guinness's great success. The final sentence in the editorial reads: "Irish hands and Irish brains have gone to build up . . . [Guinness's] present position; and it is unthinkable that now, when the firm is at the zenith of its success, that it should differentiate unfairly against the home producers of its essential product and give preference to the foreigner." The last two words were crossed out by the censor, and the words "imported barley" substituted for "the foreigner." A marginal note by the censor reveals his reasoning: "Surely," he says, "you would not have your readers regard us as foreigners. In England there are more Irish people than in Ireland. These are not, and I can assure you would not like to be, looked upon as foreigners in England."[68]

When, in September of 1919, the Republican press of Ireland was suppressed altogether, that action merely underscored the fact that the British government used D.O.R.A. to maintain, for the last time, dominance over the Irish, in matters ranging from international security to mere personal opinion, but when information about these suppressions circulated by handbill and pamphlet, the

---

various Irish editors the letter above, which instructed newspapers not to print without the consent of the Censor's Office letters written by Hanna Sheehy-Skeffington. Two years before the date on this circular, Francis Sheehy-Skeffington had been brutally killed, along with two other Irish editors, by a British firing squad. As Hanna herself said, "Dead editors tell no tales—though sometimes their wives may" (quoted in *James Joyce Quarterly*, 20 [1982] p. 123, from a lecture given by Hanna Sheehy-Skeffington in 1917 and recorded in *Dublin 1916*, ed. Roger McHugh [London: Arlington Books, 1966]. Photograph courtesy of the National Library of Ireland.)

perennial inefficacy of censorship was again established. Indeed, the necessity for censorship merely signified the already compromised authority of the British army in Ireland. Nonetheless, the military, like other influential institutions in Irish life, structured oppression into the culture, even though consistent resistance to suppression may be traced in the historical records that remain.

In Ireland, then, censure, efforts to control, and outright suppression characterized all aspects of the society. From the formal prohibitions of the church or Castle to the unofficial acts of vigilante groups and publishers to the metaphorical stranglehold of conventions reinforced by press, stage, or popular custom, Irish culture at the turn of the century was constituted by the impulse to censor— that is, to dominate. Of the three institutions addressed here, the church was most often the source of disapproval, while the stage and press were generally the objects of censoring. Yet all three exercised or were channels for power: they transmitted attitudes, perpetuated conventions, and enacted social antagonisms. Modern Irish censorship thus highlights the meeting of competing institutional creeds. More important, it describes nexi in which both members of oppositions remain inextricably interrelated in the struggle for power. These points of concord mark the fact that press, stage, and pulpit conformed to the demands of a market economy: literally or figuratively, they sold their discursive products in order to exist, and their own survival depended on sustaining the contemporary social order.

Joyce introduced his fictions into this field of censorship; each text was part of the repressive network that it responded to. Although it is not possible to argue away past forces of domination and their impact on literary texts, it *is* possible to discern in history areas of unresolved antagonism and hence of cultural alternatives. Throughout this study, I argue that in form and in idea Joyce's narratives draw attention to these contested arenas. In particular, *Ulysses* and *Finnegans Wake* echo the persistent competition of institutional discourses in Irish society. Further, Joyce's major narratives operate like the culture that Joyce experienced in that they may *appear* to force the either/or choices of a censoring society but in fact undermine a simplistic binarism—much as the Irish history I have surveyed here may *appear* to be determined by the enmity of one institutional ideology for another but in fact documents the under-lying unity of design that censorship served to further. That this goal is the maintenance of a commercially favorable social order calls for recurrent attention throughout this study to Joyce's literary deal-ings with economic motivations for action.

NOTES

1. Letter of 17 August 1911, *Letters of James Joyce*, ed. Richard Ellmann, 3 vols. (New York: Viking, 1966), 2: 291, 293.

2. It is of interest that in what appear to be notes for a lecture on Irish publishing, now housed in the National Library of Ireland, Roberts wrote: "The publisher should hesitate to act as censor . . ." (MS. 13274, National Library of Ireland). On some discursive level, Roberts was aware of a "duty" which as a publisher he seems not often to have fulfilled. Richard Burnham suggests that Roberts simply did not know how to deal with people, that Roberts's letters make him "appear inept, capricious, and scheming." Burn-ham maintains, "It was Roberts' ethics and naivete that got him into diffi-culty" ("Poor George Roberts, Dublin publisher [Maunsel & Co.]," *Éire-Ireland* 10 [1975], 146, 145).

3. Cf. Moretti on Freud's *Eros and Civilization*, "The Soul and the Harpy," in *Signs Taken for Wonders*, pp. 36–40.

4. "Metaphor and Social Antagonisms," *Marxism and the Interpretation of Culture: Limits, Frontiers, Boundaries* (conference), University of Illinois at Urbana-Champaign, 9 July 1983.

5. AE, "The Censorship in Ireland," *Nation & Athenaeum*, 22 De-cember 1928, 435–36; rpt. in *The First Freedom: Liberty and Justice in the World of Books and Reading*, ed. Robert B. Downs (Chicago: American Li-brary, 1960), p. 391.

6. See, for example, Francis Hackett, "A Muzzle Made in Ireland," *Dub-lin Magazine*, new ser., 11 (1936), 8–17; rpt. in *First Freedom*, p. 395.

7. W. McDonald, "The Index in Ireland," *Irish Ecclesiastical Record*, 4th ser., 1 (1897), 131, 128.

8. Hurley, "The New Legislation on the Index," *Irish Ecclesiastical Record*, 4th ser., 5 (1899), 448.

9. Ibid., 4 (1898), 432. Below I quote from pp. 429 and 529.

10. George H. Putman, *Censorship of the Church of Rome . . . with Some Consideration of the Effects of Protestant Censorship*, 2 vols. (New York: Put-nam, 1907), 2: 447. Below I refer to pp. 208–10, 267.

11. Hurley, 6 (1899), 243.

12. Ibid., 5 (1899), 336. The following three quotations in the text are from pp. 220–21, 223, and 427.

13. See Frederick Ryan, "The Latest Crusade," *Irish Review* 1 (1912), 522.

14. Rev. R. S. Devane, "Indecent Literature: Some Legal Remedies," *Irish Ecclesiastical Record*, 5th ser., 25 (1925), 197. Elsewhere, Devane mentions that the Canadian Black List (Canadian Customs Memorandum No. 1771 1/2B, 1 March 1914; amended to May 1924) includes not only *Ulysses* but also *Photo Bits* and *Ally Sloper's Half Holiday*, two of Joyce's sources. See Rev. R. S. Devane, S.J., "The Committee on Printed Matter: Some Notes of Evidence," *Irish Ecclesiastical Record*, 5th ser., 28 (1926), 367–70. Bernard Benstock comments on Joyce's "attitude toward the Jesuitical practice of censorship," as evidenced in *Finnegans Wake*. See *Joyce-Again's Wake: An Analysis of* Finnegans Wake (Seattle: University of Washington Press, 1965), p. 94.

15. Cyril C. Martindale, S.J., *Bernard Vaughan, S.J.* (London: Longmans, Green, 1923), p. 112.

16. Conversations with Dr. Cyril Cusack, 3 August and 11 August 1981. He noted, "I have heard my mother—who was English and a convert to Catholicism—when we toured our own Company about the country, declare rather dramatically that one week our company was denounced from the altar, but I doubt if the words were quite so Savonarola-like." And again: "As touring actors we would be open to individual reaction on the part of the clergy who in the main would attend performances. Prior to the play, and as expected from a country audience, there would be a series of variety turns. With our company we had a very lithe young woman, Esme O'Callaghan, who . . . contributed to the variety with a seductive performance of what was billed as a 'Snake Dance'. I did, in fact— about 1919–20—witness two priests stand up and walk out in protest, but the audience (so often spoken of by writers as priest-ridden, tyrannised by the clergy in this country) did not follow suit."

17. Canon P.A. Sheehan, *Sermons*, ed. M. J. Phelan, S.J. (Dublin: Maunsel, 1920), pp. 270–71. In his unfinished novel *Tristram Lloyd*, Sheehan writes with great sympathy of a journalist who tries to improve the conditions of the poor in Dublin through airing them in his column and who is censored by his editor when he goes too far in this mission.

18. Rev. Joseph Guinan, "The Apostolate of the Press," *Irish Monthly* 38 (1910), 321–23.

19. Rev. Denis O'Shea, "Newspaper Controversy," *Irish Ecclesiastical Record*, 4th ser., 27 (1910), 619–20.

20. Rev. Patrick Forde, "Catholic Literature," *Catholic Bulletin* 1 (1911), 4. The quotation below is from p. 5.

21. Rev. Joseph Guinan, "Wanted: Apostles of the Press," *Catholic Bulletin* 1 (1911), 422.

22. See Editorial, *Catholic Bulletin* 1 (1911), 513–15. Stephen J. M. Brown characterizes the *Catholic Bulletin* as often politically vitriolic in *The Press in Ireland: A Survey and a Guide* (1937; rpt. New York: Lemma, 1971), pp. 82–83.

23. Devane, "The Committee on Printed Matter: III— 'Indecency' in Law," *Irish Ecclesiastical Record*, 5th ser., 28 (1926), 460.

24. Devane, "Indecent Literature," p. 185. Cf. his "Committee on Printed Matter," 465, where he calls for a National Vigilance Association to educate and guard public opinion "*not alone* as regards printed matter, but also in relation to the stage, the music halls, the commercialized dance halls that are springing up all over the country, the unmarried mother problem, and, indeed, in regard to prostitution and the diseases which follow in its wake. . . ."

25. "However when I was going to take the next sermon I had to give after this regulation came into force to Fr. Clare for revision he pooh-poohed the matter and would not look at it." *Sermons and Devotional Writings of Gerard Manley Hopkins*, ed. Christopher Devlin (London: Oxford University Press, 1959), pp. 62 and 89. For more information on ecclesiastical censoring, see Graínne O'Flynn's doctoral thesis, *The Dublin Episcopate and the Higher Education of Catholics 1795–1908* (University of Dublin, Trinity College, 1973). O'Flynn points to the attempts by press and clergy in Ireland to cover up the fact of Archbishop Walsh's having been summoned to Rome in 1887 during an investigation of the Irish episcopate. O'Flynn has discovered that the P. J. Walsh biography of Archbishop Walsh silently censored letters and cut information about the Archbishop.

26. F. Ryan, pp. 521–26. Below I quote from p. 525.

27. G. M. G., *The Stage Censor, An Historical Sketch: 1544–1907* (London: Sampson Low, Marston, 1908), pp. 84–85. G. M. G. points out that in 1843 the Licensing Act of 1737 was repealed and in its place was instituted Sir James Graham's Act "for regulating theatres" by which every play to be produced in England had to be submitted for review seven days before performance and by which the Lord Chamberlain could stop an objectionable performance (pp. 114–15). This system was reapproved in 1892 when a Select Committee on Theatres and Places of Entertainment suggested using it also in music halls (pp. 120–21). Below in the text I refer to G. M. G., p. 123.

28. *Theatres and Places of Entertainment: Report from the Select Committee on Theatres and Places of Entertainment* . . . (London: Her Majesty's Stationery Office, 1892), p. 233.

29. Elsewhere Shaw says, "When I add that the lists of forbidden subjects and words include religion, sex, and politics, the strangling effect on

serious drama may be imagined. My early play on the White Slave Traffic was banned for many years, and I myself branded as a blackguardly playwright, because prostitution was a forbidden subject unless it was made voluptuous or funny in the manner of the farcical comedies then in vogue" (G. Bernard Shaw, "Censorship: Comments by Readers. I," *The Bell* 9 [1945], 399).

30. Lady Gregory, *Our Irish Theatre: A Chapter of Autobiography* (New York: Putnam, 1913), p. 115.

31. Gregory, pp. 145–47. Such behind-the-scenes pressure also touched Joyce during his fight to get *Dubliners* published. Ellmann notes that in avoiding publication of the stories, George Roberts "may also have had a private reason: one Dublin rumor of the time said he had promised his fiancée, out of regard for her honor, that he would not publish a questionable book. Joseph Hone suggested later, though Roberts denied it, that the Vigilance Committee, in which one of Maunsel's chief customers, the Lord Lieutenant's wife, Lady Aberdeen, was active, had exerted pressure on the firm" (*James Joyce*, p. 328). For information on the Vigilance Association, see Michael Adams, *Censorship: the Irish Experience* (Dublin: Scepter Books, 1968), pp. 15–17.

32. Séamus de Búrca, "The Queen's Royal Theatre, 1829–1966," *Dublin Historical Record* 27 (1973), 16.

33. Interview with Séamus de Búrca, 14 July 1981, Dublin, and unpublished essay by de Búrca called "*Ireland a Nation*," dated 8 July 1982. This film was the first feature movie to be made in Ireland; it was produced by the MacNamara Feature Film Co., Inc., and reissued in 1920 by the Gaelic Film Co.

34. Micheál Ó hAodha, *Theatre in Ireland* (Oxford: Basil Blackwell, 1974), p. 17.

35. "Notes on the Drama," *Dublin University Magazine* (March 1875), p. 380. Fragments quoted in the following sentence are also from p. 380.

36. The Lord Chamberlain also ran into this problem, especially with pantomime business; see Raymond Mander and Joe Mitchenson, *Pantomime: A Story in Pictures* (New York: Taplinger, 1973), p. 24.

37. *Souvenir of the Twenty-Fifth Anniversary of the Opening of the Gaiety Theatre 27th November, 1871, With Michael Gunn's Compts.*, 27th November 1896, Dublin, p. 37.

38. MS. 4451, National Library of Ireland.

39. "Current Affairs," *Leader*, 6 October 1900, p. 83.

40. "Report on the proceedings of the Jt. Sel. Ctee. on censorship of stage plays, 1909," in P. Ford and G. Ford, *A Breviate of Parliamentary Papers: 1900–16* (Shannon: Irish University Press, 1969), p. 383. Similarly, John Palmer argues that Actor Managers supported the Censor in *The Censor and the Theatres* ([London]: Fisher Unwin, 1913).

41. "A 'Star' Star Stopped," *Evening Telegraph* (Dublin), 27 December 1892.

42. "The Freedom of the Theatre," *Éire*, 4 November 1914, p. 2; also *Scissors and Paste*, 27 January 1915, p. 1.

43. Frederick J. Higginbottom, *The Vivid Life*: *A Journalist's Career* (London: Simpkin Marshall, 1934), pp. x–xi.

44. R. J. Smith, *Ireland's Renaissance* (Dublin: Hodges, Figgis, 1903), p. 8.

45. James Stephen, *The Insurrection in Dublin* (New York: Macmillan, 1916), pp. 3–4.

46. William M. Murphy, *The Story of a Newspaper*, rpt. from the *Irish Independent*, 2 January 1909, p. 21. In "Cyclops" the Citizen calls the *Irish Independent* an un-nationalistic "blasted rag" and Murphy "the Bantry jobber" (U 298).

47. "Index of Irish Newspapers, 1900–1922 (Part I)," *Éire-Ireland* 11 (1976), 84.

48. Moran complains that, as he had predicted, most of the Dublin press did not mention the inauguration of his paper. "Of course had we been published in London, were our pages adorned with the portraits of music hall performers, and had our name . . . been *Snip-Snap* or *Snap-Snip*, our pages would have given work to the scissors of nearly every sub-editor in Dublin" ("Current Affairs," *The Leader*, 8 September 1900, p. 17).

49. "Our Degenerate Press," *Leader*, 10 November 1900, p. 165.

50. "The English Mind in Ireland: At So Much Per Column," *Leader*, 10 November 1900, p. 171.

51. *Leader*, 1 September 1900, p. 2.

52. R. Fullerton, "Social Unrest and Its Remedy," *Catholic Bulletin* 3 (1913), 34–35.

53. Malcolm Brown, *The Politics of Irish Literature*: *From Thomas Davis to W. B. Yeats* (Seattle: University of Washington Press, 1972), pp. 7–8.

54. James Joyce, "Fenianism: The Last Fenian," trans. of "Il Fenianismo: L'Ultimo Feniano," *Il Piccolo della Sera*, 22 March 1907, in *The Critical Writings of James Joyce* (New York: Viking, 1964), p. 188.

55. Marcus Bourke, *John O'Leary*: *A Study in Irish Separatism* (Athens: University of Georgia Press, 1967). Bourke says that the entry and seizing of the *Irish People* office was illegal and that T. Clarke Luby, the paper's proprietor, briefly attempted to lodge a suit against "the Lord Lieutenant, the Under-Secretary and the Chief Magistrate for Dublin" (p. 95—see also pp. 90, 94). Below in this paragraph I refer to pp. 90, 91, 54, 84, 106, 73–74, and 94.

56. F. S. L. Lyons, *Ireland since the Famine* (New York: Scribner's, 1971), p. 235n.

57. Quotations below in this paragraph and the next are from W. P. Ryan's *The Pope's Green Island* (London: Nisbet, 1912), pp. 1, 9, 11, 14.

58. P. S. O'Hegarty, "The Mosquito Press," *The Bell* 12 (1946), 56, 57.

59. Dorothy Macardle, *The Irish Republic: A Documented Chronicle of the Anglo-Irish Conflict and the Partitioning of Ireland, with a Detailed Account of the Period 1916–1923*, 2nd ed. (New York: Farrar, Straus and Giroux, 1951), pp. 125–26.

60. Roland McHugh, *The Sigla of* Finnegans Wake (Austin: University of Texas Press, 1976), p. 25.

61. *Éire*, 28 November 1914, p. 2.

62. *Éire*, 13 November 1914, p. 1.

63. Breandán Mac Giolla Choille prints the British *Intelligence Notes* for 1914–16 about such suppressions in *Chief Secretary's Office, Dublin Castle. Intelligence Notes 1913–16—Preserved in the State Paper Office* (Baile Átha Cliath: Oifig an tSoláthair, 1966), pp. 116–17, 162–65, 223–27. Of interest is the account of the December 1914 suppression of *The Irish Worker*. Replaced less than a month later by *The Worker*, which was printed in Glasgow by the Socialist Labour Press, the paper changed in character, according to the *Intelligence Notes*, from being "anti-English and anti-recruiting" to being "frankly socialistic and anti-capitalistic": "It was subsequently seized by the Police on arrival at the North Wall from Glasgow, and publication then ceased" (pp. 116–17). This suppression on the grounds of anti-capitalism suggests the Censor's reluctance to extricate the demands of military security from political and economic debate. Interestingly, *Scissors and Paste* reported on 2 January 1915 (p. 1) that the *Irish Worker* had been suppressed three weeks earlier but "reappeared" through the auspices of the Socialist Labour Party at Glasgow. For all of their efforts at suppression, the censors could not prevent other organs from publishing the details of such suppressions as well as the circumstances of their own; four days later, *Scissors and Paste* reported the confiscation of its own paper by the Cork police, an act also covered by Dublin's *Daily Independent*.

64. *Éire*, 1 December 1914, p. 2.

65. *Éire*, 21 November 1914, p. 1.

66. Press Censor Circular, Serial no. 96, 15 July 1918, National Library of Ireland.

67. Katherine Hughes, *English Atrocities in Ireland: A Compilation of Facts from Court and Press Records* (New York: Friends of Irish Freedom, n.d.), pp. 26–27.

68. Press Censor Circular, MS. 984, National Library of Ireland.

CHAPTER 2

"Easy all . . . we're in the archdiocese here"

—Christ in our irish times! Christ on the airs independence! Christ hold the freedman's chareman! Christ light the dully expressed! (FW 500.14–16)

What makes power hold good, what makes it accepted, is simply the fact that it doesn't only weigh on us as a force that says no, but that it traverses and produces things, it induces pleasure, forms knowledge, produces discourse.

Michel Foucault, *Power/Knowledge*

History and Form: The Newspaper

A study of the conditions of publication in Ireland during Joyce's lifetime reveals the degree to which the press was both responsible for perpetuating ideological practices of several persuasions and helpless to resist economic and political assimilation. Even though some newspapermen no doubt understood their roles in these processes, the press played out scenarios written by a church- and British-dominated social system. When he revised the "Aeolus" episode to allude to the shape of the newspaper, Joyce brought into his fiction a potent signifying form that speaks of a censorship wrought from economic, political, and religious control as well as of a culture in many ways synonymous with that censorship. The change between the *Little Review* version of "Aeolus" and the headlined version was not merely one of imitative form; in addition to increasing the wit of the chapter, Joyce enriched its large-scale historical references as well as opportunities for cultural critique.

In particular, Joyce interrogates, often comically, the conditions of production of Irish journalism and the replication of those conditions in other professions such as education and law. In "Aeolus" we see barefoot newsboys, a bounder, a disfranchised intellectual, and a

67

failed barrister. We see Bloom go through the motions of trying to place an advertisement in the paper, one that does not blush to pun on the political needs of a nation. We hear "spiritual" patriotic prose which the pressgang can obviously see through but which they print anyway. We encounter an editor with shifting sympathies and censoring tendencies. That is, we see the results of domination and the seemingly innocuous means by which ideological practice is sustained. However, in *Ulysses* as in history, suppression is also speaking; entrapment by institutional mores is also experience of the inevitable undermining of absolutes within cultural discourse. "Aeolus" appears to be organized according to a system of binary oppositions but renounces choice in favor of multiple differentiation. A close reading of the episode suggests, then, that it is an oversimplification to see the issue of censorship in only moral or humanistic terms—it's not enough to advocate free speech and a free press. In "Aeolus" we are suspended in a condition of protean domination and of eternal resistance. The form of the episode signifies the economic and political controls that structured Irish society; it alludes to a cultural reality constituted by dichotomizing institutional restraints upon the imagination; but it also directs attention to the ultimate insuppressibility of even highly censored discourse.

According to the usual view of "Aeolus," the episode is an evaluation of Irish rhetoric.[1] One recent version of this approach occurs in C. H. Peake's *James Joyce: The Citizen and the Artist*. Peake argues that Joyce sets up a contrast in "Aeolus" between noble oratory of the past and the decadence of the modern rhetoric that is best exemplified in corrupt journalistic prose.[2] While this contrast of old and new is present, it serves ends other than the criticism of modern rhetoricians or even of modern consciousness. The several dimensions of dialectic in "Aeolus" suggest the coercive conditions that in Western society shape the production of discourse; they target the institutional competition that composed Irish culture as Joyce knew it.

Certainly the setting of "Aeolus" primes us for this point. The episode opens with an overview of Prince's Street. There the offices of the *Evening Telegraph* and of the *Freeman's Journal*, among the major Dublin newspapers in Joyce's day, stand across the street from the General Post Office, the center of the Easter Rising of 1916. That the episode is set in 1904 does not diminish the association of this spot with the patriotic fervor that prompted the Irish Republican Brotherhood's takeover of the post office two years before Joyce began composing his newspaper chapter.[3] Similarly, the tram stoppage at the end of the chapter, although the result, we are told, of a "short circuit" (U 149), calls up the stasis of the 1913 Tram Lockout.[4] These politically and economically charged scenes enhance the significance of the immediate action as much as the location in the *Freeman's Journal-Evening Telegraph* offices does.

To discuss one of these papers is to include the other. Run by Freeman's Journal, Ltd.,[5] both share in Joyce's work the same attitudes and windy atmosphere. The *Freeman*, circulated throughout the world, was, in Joyce's day, the "Constitutional-Nationalist Organ of the Parliamentary Party,"[6] but, as Father Brown explains, the century and a half during which the paper was published (1763–1924) saw many changes in its policies. From early fluctuation between being pro-independence and anti-Catholic, the *Freeman's Journal* turned in 1783 to being a more or less covert tool of Dublin Castle.[7] In the early nineteenth century, liberal principles again reigned in the *Freeman's Journal* offices, but far from being the chief radical organ of the nation, it "was always moderate and cautious to a fault." The paper supported Parnell before its merger with the *National Press*. Father Brown, however, reported, "Extremists looked upon it with contempt, and the more ardent spirits of the party which it supported were often exasperated by its hesitancy and moderation. It maintained that reputation—not always deserved—to the end."

For example, *Scissors and Paste*, Arthur Griffith's paper, maintained in 1915 that the *Freeman's Journal* was un-Nationalistic, against true Irish freedom and self-determination, and anti-Fenian.[8] So does the Citizen, who calls it a "subsidised organ" (U 298). Similarly, the National Library of Ireland contains an undated throwaway stating that the *Freeman* had "denounced" several causes—"the men of '48," "the men of '98," the Fenians, Parnell, and "the men of 1916"—and now denounced Eamon de Valera. It questioned, "Is *The Freeman's Journal* right today? Do not be misled by a corrupt press."[9] Joyce, of course, believed from his youth that the Dublin press was corrupt.

Another such throwaway entitled "The Freedom of the Press" discussed "the Suppression of the 'Freeman's Journal,' and Seizure of its Machinery by the Military."[10] Closed down on 15 December

1919 by military authorities because of its alleged offenses against
D.O.R.A., particularly in regard to military recruitment, the *Freeman*, it was argued, "was condemned without trial by the Executive, and sentence passed on it and executed by armed military and
police, and the sentence still runs with no limit to it. In fact the suppression has now been so prolonged that it has become obvious that
the aim of the Executive is the destruction of the newspaper. Such is
the Freedom of the Press in Ireland!" Dated 21 January 1920, the
throwaway suggests that at least a part of the population of Dublin
at the time could be moved to regard the paper as a worthy representative of public opinion and that the Castle could view it as a
threat to internal British control.

"Aeolus" refers pointedly to the political inconsistency of the
Freeman: "Myles Crawford began on the *Independent*. Funny the
way those newspaper men veer about when they get wind of a new
opening. Weathercocks. Hot and cold in the same breath. Wouldn't
know which to believe. One story good till you hear the next. Go
for one another baldheaded in the papers and then all blows over.
Hail fellow well met the next moment" (U 125). Crawford's having
been on the *Irish Independent*, a paper excoriated by the Citizen for
its lack of nationalism, has not kept him from becoming associated
with the *Freeman*, the paper against which William Murphy first
set up the *Independent*. *Ulysses* drives home the political inconsistency of pressmen when Professor MacHugh genially calls Crawford
the "sham squire" (U 126)—a reference to Francis Higgins, the
eighteenth-century owner of the *Freeman* who is notorious for
having informed against Irish patriots.

Because of its politically ambiguous status, the *Freeman* often
came under fire in Joyce's lifetime. For example, *Éire-Ireland*, an
aggressively "Nationalist" Dublin daily that began publication in
1914, reported in that year that the wife of the Lord Lieutenant of
Ireland, Lady Aberdeen, "communicated with the 'Freeman' Editor
by letter twice a week, while she communicated with him by tele-
phone practically every day."[11] *Éire* presented the *Freeman* as a paper
that masked its true subservience to British control and that supported the British in World War I because Lady Aberdeen wrote its
policy. By the time Joyce was revising "Aeolus" for final publication,
the setting resonated with a variety of political charges, and the
newspaper form alluded to rifts that cut across both institutions and
persons.

Into this ideologically loaded setting Leopold Bloom comes in search of approval from the typesetter Nannetti and from the editor Myles Crawford for the mildly political ad that he wants to sell to Alexander Keyes. Nannetti, a councilor, was elected, Bloom recalls, on the "workaday worker tack." But despite the "Ireland my country" (U 118) routine of the political election, Bloom still feels the need to explain to Nannetti that his ad is designed to allude to the Manx parliament and to provide an "Innuendo of home rule" (U 120). His explanation does not elicit even a spark of interest or patriotic approval from the foreman, merely a businesslike assessment of how long a renewal will be required from Keyes to assure a profit for the paper. Certainly Nannetti's unresponsiveness suggests both the remoteness of government officials from their constituents (shades of "Ivy Day in the Committee Room") and the sometimes peculiar aloofness of the established press in Ireland from certain political issues.

Further, Bloom's ad-cadging serves to reinforce the point made by the scene in which Myles Crawford praises the journalist Ignatius Gallaher because of his transmittal to the *New York World*, with the help of an ad, of coded information about the Phoenix Park murders. That the censored information was sent via advertisements connects Gallaher's journalistic coup with Bloom's efforts to place the Keyes notice; in both cases, political content is inserted only with difficulty into a press sometimes in complicity with the powers-that-be. Yet the use of ads in the service of a subversive politics does more than ironically highlight the typical collusion of commercial and political power; it warns us against simplistic alignment of these two kinds of strength on the side of an ascendant ideology and allows us to see that the channels established in Ireland for such dominance could be appropriated to communicate opposing positions.

Among the many comings and goings of "Aeolus," of course, Bloom's part in the chapter is relatively small. The chapter's disparate action comes to a focus not on Bloom but on the attempt of J. J. O'Molloy and MacHugh to secure Stephen's approval of their attitudes and of the rhetoric they admire. The editor briefly contributes to this skirmish when, receiving from Stephen Mr. Deasy's letter on foot and mouth disease, Crawford tries to interest Stephen in joining what O'Molloy calls the "pressgang." Lenehan, too, seems to court Stephen's attention by poking fun at MacHugh and by telling riddles and a limerick. Finally, Stephen presents his "vision" about two old women climbing to the top of Nelson's pillar; the artist's work is set against examples of rhetoric from other professional fields to highlight contrasts in intention that are made more urgent by being considered in the midst of confusion, sycophancy, and disagreement.

But when Joyce added the headlines to "Aeolus," he established an even more compelling motion in the chapter by demonstrating the extent to which the press, often a censored means of communication, speaks for the shaky status of the other professions brought into the episode. The occupations of middle-class Dubliners are subsumed under the representative umbrella of the press, a fact to which the editor draws attention under the headline "OMNIUM GATHERUM."

>—All the talents, Myles Crawford said. Law, the classics . . .
>—The turf, Lenehan put in.
>—Literature, the press.
>—If Bloom were here, the professor said. The gentle art of advertisement.
>—And Madam Bloom, Mr O'Madden Burke added. The vocal muse. Dublin's prime favourite. (U 135)

From the "workaday worker" Nannetti to the counselor-at-law, jobholders are controlled by the same lines of economic and political puissance that control the pressgang. On the simplest narrative level, the headlines suggest the subsuming by the press of all the professions dealt with here through their textualization in a newspaper format. The form of the narrative thus communicates the stresses within an oppressed society.

The narrative action plays out the circumstances and results of the domination signified by form. For instance, under the ironic headline, "ITALIA, MAGISTRA ARTIUM," O'Molloy speaks of Seymour Bushe's defense in the notorious Childs murder case, explaining that Bushe "spoke on the law of evidence . . . of Roman justice as contrasted with the earlier Mosaic code, the *lex talionis*. And he cited the Moses of Michelangelo in the vatican" (U 139). After a pause, O'Molloy "resumed, moulding his words":

>—He said of it: *that stony effigy in frozen music, horned and terrible, of the human form divine, that eternal symbol of wisdom and prophecy which, if aught that the imagination or the hand of sculptor has wrought*

in marble of soultransfigured and of soultransfiguring deserves to live, de-serves to live." (U 140)

A barrister, O'Molloy is interested, it would seem, more in effective rhetoric than in matters of law. He appears to respond to the periodic structure of Bushe's phrasing without regard to the adequacy of Bushe's legal stance. Given the evidence provided in this section of "Aeolus," Bushe could have argued that the Old Testament "eye for an eye" conveys a divinely ordained notion of justice which Roman law falls short of, yet the headline reports the opposite conclusion in naming Italy as mistress of the arts. The Roman revision of Mosaic law (hence Moses in the Vatican) seems to have been Bushe's choice after all. O'Molloy is unaware of this narrative tension and of his own irrelevance to the institutional voice which, in the heading, chooses a position for him. Certainly O'Molloy's sensitivity to the similar "moulding" to which both stone and language are subject has not saved him from professional failure. Bloom considers the lawyer in these terms:

> Cleverest fellow at the junior bar he used to be. Decline, poor chap. That hectic flush spells finis for a man. Touch and go with him. What's in the wind, I wonder. Money worry. . . .
> Practice dwindling. A mighthavebeen. Losing heart. Gambling. Debts of honour. Reaping the whirlwind. Used to get good retainers from D. and T. Fitzgerald. . . . Believe he does some literary work for the *Express* with Gabriel Conroy. Wellread fellow. (U 125)

Debts, decline, and journalism appear to be the fate of this well-read Irish practitioner of British law. This national contradiction accounts in part for his being marginalized by a social structure that is all too anxious to entrap with form and deny substance. That O'Molloy is socially superfluous reminds us of Gabriel Conroy's own worries in "The Dead" about the possibility of his being in truth a "West Briton" (D 188) and about his own tendency to indulge in rhetorical posturing.

It is significant that Bloom's assessment of the dreary O'Molloy directly follows the passage in which, to the professor's announcement of Dawson's speech as a Ciceronian fragment entitled *Our lovely land*, Bloom responds, "Whose land?" (U 124). This is not to say that the British control of Ireland is the direct cause of O'Molloy's troubles, but that in a chapter heavy with contention and failure the lawyer's inadequacies speak also for the economic and political problems generated by the pressures of history. Hence, when the conversation turns to Latin and the empires of Rome and Britain, O'Molloy comments "*Imperium romanum. . . .* It sounds nobler than British or Brixton. The word reminds one somehow of fat in the fire." And Crawford responds, "That's it. . . . You and I are the fat in the fire. We haven't got the chance of a snowball in hell" (U 130–31).

To complement the chapter's consideration of the journalistic and legal professions we have MacHugh, the professor of Latin who, as Lenehan jocularly points out to Stephen in his limerick, "*wears goggles of ebony hue*" and "*mostly sees double*" (U 134). Whereas O'Molloy is simply beaten down by failure, MacHugh perversely glories in it. For instance, MacHugh sees his teaching Latin as wrong; he should, he suspects, teach the more "spiritual" Greek. Even worse, though he does nothing to change either situation, he speaks English, which he regards as the most material of languages: "—We were always loyal to lost causes, the professor said. Success for us is the death of the intellect and of the imagination. We were never loyal to the successful. We serve them. I teach the blatant Latin language. I speak the tongue of a race the acme of whose mentality is the maxim: time is money. Material domination. *Domine*! Lord! Where is the spirituality? Lord Jesus? Lord Salisbury? A sofa in a westend club" (U 133). MacHugh speaks for a characteristic that he sees as especially Irish, the inability to combine victory with spiritual wholeness. In fact, he regards failure and spirituality as somehow causally related. To MacHugh, Ireland's ineffectiveness in securing Home Rule is self-justifying.

To an extent MacHugh is right, but only in his gesture toward material domination as intrinsic to Irish culture in his day. Yet it is a measure of how deeply MacHugh has bought into received ideas that he locates the truth of his and Ireland's situation in a "racial" justification. That is, he rests in the characterization of the Irish as being "Loyal to a lost cause" (U 133). Certainly this explanation is not unique to MacHugh; it is a common theme in Irish writing of the time. R. J. Smith, for example, states as much when, in 1903, he speaks of "the undue prevalence of idealism amongst Irishmen."[12] On a similar note, Sir Horace Plunkett wrote in *Ireland in the New Century* (1905) of the need to correct what he saw as flaws in the

Irish character, including a too-ready acceptance of events as destined, a humorousness that masked reluctance to take charge of the future, and a lack of useful education and industry (the Protestant North excluded); clearly, Plunkett's biases informed his vision of an unproductive and spiritually handicapped Ireland, but to an extent the thumbnail characterizations in "Aeolus" seem to support Plunkett's assessment.

Nonetheless, the formal emphasis in "Aeolus" on institutional power[13] suggests that the "truth" is to be found rather in the complexities and complicities of cultural coding—in the social institutions that create "subjects" and explain to them their domination masked as history ("It seems history is to blame" [U 20]) or as genetics ("We are liege subjects," says the professor, "of the catholic chivalry of Europe that foundered at Trafalgar and of the empire of the spirit, not an *imperium*, that went under with the Athenian fleets at Ægospotami" [U 133]). Further, an institution like the press is bound up in and by those cultural concurrences; coding subjects, it is itself subject to domination, a point implicit in the use of capitalized headings.

The Headlines

Like the comic newspaper columns in "Cyclops," these boldface phrases have generally been taken to suggest the oversimplification, sensationalizing, and stereotyping with which the press shapes public opinion. This condition of the establishment press is the reality that Joyce asserts throughout his fiction, often by citing the headlines that no Dubliner could avoid hearing and seeing on every streetcorner. In *Stephen Hero*, Cranly and Stephen discuss the *Evening Telegraph*'s "newsbill which was exposed to public gaze on the roadway," which, as they stand by it, is being read by a handful of other people as well:

Nationalist Meeting at Ballinrobe.
Important Speeches.
Main Drainage Scheme
Breezy Discussion.
Death of a Well-known Solicitor
Mad Cow at Cabra,
Literature &.

Stephen's wry question about whether "it requires great ability to live that life successfully" (SH 221) aligns with the *Wake's* association of boring bourgeois routine[14] with newspaper-reading: "business, reading newspaper, smoking cigar, arranging tumblers on table, eating meals, pleasure, etcetera, etcetera, pleasure, eating meals, arranging tumblers on table, smoking cigar, reading newspaper, business; minerals, wash and brush up, local views, juju toffee, comic and birthdays cards; those were the days and he was their hero . . ." (FW 127.20–25).

Similarly, in the *Wake* the headlines that announce HCE's crime ("The Outrage, at Length") also threaten to bury it in quotidian details:

> the Durban Gazette, firstcoming issue. From a collispendent. Any were. Deemsday. Bosse of Upper and Lower Byggotstrade, Ciwareke, may he live for river! The Games funeral at Valleytemple. Saturnights pomps, exhabiting that corricatore of a harss, revealled by Oscur Camerad. The last of Dutch Schulds, perhumps. Pipe in Dream Cluse. Uncovers Pub History. The Outrage, at Length. Affected Mob Follows in Religious Sullivence. Rinvention of vestiges by which they drugged the buddhy. Moviefigure on in scenic section. By Patathicus. (FW 602.19–27)

Such, too, we take to be the reporting in the "*Weekly Standerd*, our verile organ" (FW 439.36), in which the virile, the vile, and the veridical cannot be extricated. Throughout *Ulysses*, and especially in "Cyclops," where the Citizen rails against the national papers, the press is an agent of stereotyping and distortion; it does not hesitate to "tell a graphic lie" (U 647).

Some readers have questioned the labeling of the capitalized lines in "Aeolus" as headlines,[15] but whether we understand these phrases as headlines, subheads, or captions, the institutional context is evident. Further, all of these verbal phenomena conform to similar syntactic and formal requirements; they are examples of what Heinrich Straumann calls "block language," and they exist not so much to begin chunks of copy or to emphasize as to make obvious the varieties of overstatement that daily feed a dependent and largely uncritical public opinion.[16] By the same logic, the headings signify, among other things, the attempt of the press to hold sway over discourse in Irish society. This effort to control becomes critical when we consider that what the press presents as fact is often a seemingly authoritative version of personal opinion. One writer of the era questioned, "How often does the editorial pretentious 'We' mean an irresponsible, prejudiced, commonplace individual in a dingy office, paid to serve up a highly spiced dish of opinions and criticisms, with a keen eye to his employer's income out of the advertisements in his newspaper? How often does an editorial 'We' mean a clique of nonentities foisting their personal squabbles and jealousies on the unsuspecting reader?"[17] Although Joyce's Aeolian headlines roughly conform, as Stuart Gilbert long ago indicated, to the changes in headline language from the Victorian age to the early twentieth century,[18] they also reflect individual points of view.

In fact, the attitudes of people present in the *Telegraph* office show up in the headlines to create comic and satiric effects.[19] For instance, using "HIS NATIVE DORIC" (U 126) to describe the style of Dan Dawson's overblown laudings of Irish landscape represents professor MacHugh's viewpoint. For a scholar of the classics to describe this style as "native Doric" has a mildly comic effect; it implies a criticism of Dawson's vocabulary at odds with Bloom's thought that "it goes down like hot cake that stuff" (U 126). Similarly, "LENEHAN'S LIMERICK" (U 134) pinpoints what in the scene is important to Lenehan, though the phrase does not touch Stephen's significant thoughts there of Mulligan's mockery. Lenehan's curiously sycophantic self-absorption thus receives a penetrating sidethrust. "FROM THE FATHERS" (U 142) heads up Stephen's recollection of a passage from St. Augustine's *Confessions* but ignores the body of the section that is devoted to MacHugh's recital of the Taylor speech.

Finally, some of the closing headlines bear the imprint of Myles Crawford, that rather irresponsible and certainly prejudiced individual in a disorganized and probably dingy office. So used to diocesan control is he that he automatically reads into Stephen's sketch mildly pornographic possibilities that would require his professional excision. "SOME COLUMN!—THAT'S WHAT WADDLER ONE SAID" (U 147) and "DIMINISHED DIGITS PROVE TOO TITILLATING FOR FRISKY FRUMPS. ANNE WIMBLES, FLO WANGLES—YET CAN YOU BLAME THEM?" (U 150) reflect Crawford's suspicions. And the triumphant editorial headline fragment "PEN IS CHAMP" (U 148) combines the notion of a champion penis[20] (no doubt a "column" in question, along with the newspaper column and Nelson's pillar) with the discursive eminence

of the press (the pen is mightier than the sword). Hence, the headlines make private reality prominent, a conclusion which is supported by the gramophone recording Joyce made in 1923 of the
Taylor speech (H. M. V. Paris). Where the headline "FROM THE
FATHERS" interrupts the speech, Joyce drops his voice so that the
line becomes part of Stephen's thoughts on Augustine. Of course,
some of the headlines appear to show the attitudes only of an imper-
sonal narrator (possibly an embodiment of the press throughout
history),[21] but all of the viewpoint shifts effected in the episode and
emphasized by the newspaper format indicate the process by which
editorial opinion shapes public consciousness, to the extent that the
individual readers making up that public cannot separate a received
opinion from a "personal" one.

But this point is more complicated than it seems to be, for *Ulysses*
repeatedly underscores the synergistic relationship of individual and
institution(s) to indicate how far short of the mark it is to discuss
social communication in the traditional epistemological terms often
used by Joycean critics. Subjective vision and objective experience
are not merely interfused in *Ulysses*; individual viewpoints are not
merely less than adequate to take in reality.[22] Rather, the individual
who shapes public discourse (say, the editor of a newspaper) is gov-
erned by the policies of the institution in question as well as by the
other ideological practices prevalent in the culture, none of which
may be said to represent an objective reality. Joyce's headlines speak
to the "undecidable" relation of the individual, forever exiled from
unmediated experience, and the institution, not to a simple opposition of the two terms. The absorbing of "personal" voices into
Joyce's headlines suggests that there is finally no way fully to separate
Stephen, MacHugh, and company from the public bodies that constitute their reality.

Further qualifying this relationship, Joyce's narrative displays the
tensions among various institutions, specifically the church and
the press. The brief interchange between Red Murray and Bloom
points to this conflict. When the two men watch the editor, William
Brayden, enter the office of the *Freeman's Journal*, Murray sees in
Brayden a resemblance to "Our Saviour," and this piety is reflected
in Murray's comments about John Joyce's self-declared enemy, Dublin Archbishop William Walsh.

> —His grace phoned down twice this morning, Red Murray said
> gravely. . . .

A telegram boy stepped in nimbly, threw an envelope on the counter and stepped off posthaste with a word:

—*Freeman*!

Mr Bloom said slowly:

—Well, he is one of our saviours also. (U 118)

Later, passing through the building, Bloom thinks, "But will he save the circulation?" (U 118). Red Murray's concern over a possible complaint from the Archbishop against the paper,[23] combined with Bloom's critical recognition that the relationship of church and press does not necessarily contribute either to free speech or to economic advantage, alludes to the religious establishment's hostility toward a free press. Bloom's mere pretense of respect for Walsh is interestingly echoed in Stephen's encounter with Crawford as Stephen narrates his "parable of the plums."

The *Freeman's Journal*, the *Suppressed*, and the *Insuppressible*

Beginning his storytelling at the instigation of the editor, Stephen Dedalus is quite careful not to make his tale sensational. When Professor MacHugh asks him where the two women in the story live, Stephen tells him that their street is "Off Blackpitts," and he recalls, "Damp night reeking of hungry dough. Against the wall. Face glistening tallow under her fustian shawl. Frantic hearts. Akasic records. Quicker, darlint!" (U 145). Whether Stephen has witnessed this provocative scene or, more likely, participated in it, he excludes it from his oral narration. Far from presenting the "LIFE ON THE RAW" that the headlines announce, Stephen's story of two old women climbing Nelson's Pillar is a decorous one-dimensional fable. Yet, as noted above, the text begins to record headlines such as "SOME COLUMN!—THAT'S WHAT WADDLER ONE SAID" (U 147) and "DIMINISHED DIGITS PROVE TOO TITILLATING FOR FRISKY FRUMPS" (U 150). The headlines describe as "SLIGHTY RAMBUNCTIOUS FEMALES" (U 148) what Stephen presents as "Two Dublin vestals . . . elderly and pious" (U 145). Rather than censor suggestive material, this journalistic report of the event reverses the usual procedure and heightens in its headlines the sexual implications of Stephen's sketch. No doubt this about-face is Joyce's way of indicating that even a censored press was likely to violate the mores imposed on it as well as those it propounded; it also shows how consistently and immediately suppressed ideas surface in an ideologically charged environment like that of Dublin in 1904. That fact is emphasized by an allusion in "Aeolus" to one of Arthur Griffith's short-lived journals, *Scissors and Paste* (U 117), which pieced together copy from various official newspapers to form ironic commentaries on current events while avoiding censorship.[24]

Another ironic moment occurs when Stephen mentions that the two women "pull up their skirts" to sit down: the editor cautions, "Easy all . . . no poetic licence. We're in the archdiocese here" (U 148). While the text announces in the headlines details that it should suppress, Crawford suppresses what is innocently unoffensive. Or at least Crawford gestures toward such suppression, possibly in order to suggest to his listeners the fact that the Irish clergy often tried, however unsuccessfully, to control the Irish press. It is important in this regard that the 1897 revision of the *Index* regulations included a full chapter on the press because the church regarded the newspaper as "the literary production characteristic of the present age." This new legislation suggested that an evil press "is like a cancer or ulcer that draws to one point everything that is corrupt and fetid in the social body."[25] Father Hurley remarks on the "greater severity" of the *Index* "towards the press than towards books," and he goes on to state that under ecclesiastical law any paper as a whole was conceived of as a "living organism," "a living moral person." A brilliant rhetorical strategy, this metaphor brings the press directly under the domain of the church. (Further, the cultural conception of the press as a person coincides neatly with Joyce's use of headlines in "Aeolus" to display the other side of the coin—the individual as a collection of institutional attitudes and practices.) Given the power and centrality of the press in modern society, the *Index* called for the proscription of all newspapers that "intentionally" wrote against "religion and morals" and requested that bishops warn their "flocks" of dangerous publications in their region. This conscious antagonism of the church and press indicates one reason that Joyce chose to write in "Aeolus" about the *Freeman's Journal–Evening Telegraph* offices as opposed to those of another Dublin paper. The point is that the Freeman's Journal, Ltd. had more than its share of run-ins with the church, especially in the figure of the Archbishop of Dublin, and hence provided a prime historical text for Joyce's homiletic on the relations between clerics and pressmen.

As early as his 1912 broadside "Gas from a Burner," Joyce denounced what he saw as the Archbishop's misguided sense of moral superiority. Yet Joyce must have been aware that Walsh's prohibitions and expressions of dissatisfaction with the moral and political tone of Ireland were mandated by his clerical role as shaped by Pope Leo's constitution on the *Index*. That is, the opposition was not only personal but also institutional. In any event, Joyce's texts present a dim view of Walsh's intrusions into secular journalism.[26] This criticism is made comically in "Eumaeus." When Bloom scans the pink edition of the day's *Telegraph*, the report of his quick run-through of the "captions" includes a concatenation of topics that highlights the presence of the Archbishop's letter as incongruous: "Great battle Tokio. Lovemaking in Irish, £200 damages. Gordon Bennett. Emigration Swindle. Letter from His Grace. William †. Ascot meeting, the Gold Cup. Victory of outsider *Throwaway* recalls Derby of '92 . . . . New York disaster. Thousand lives lost. Foot and Mouth. Funeral of the late Mr Patrick Dignam" (U 647).

At first glance, "Aeolus" thus *seems* to argue somewhat oversimply for a freedom of the press from church control. Myles Crawford, though half-crazed from drink and at best erratic in his judgments, is presented in *Ulysses* as deferring only ironically to Walsh's dictates, and his belligerence reflects the fact that some actual *Freeman* editors accepted ideological encroachment less casually. For example, one conflict between the Archbishop and the *Freeman* involved the *Insuppressible*, which in January of 1891 published an article entitled "Archbishop Walsh and the *Freeman's Journal*." The *Insuppressible*— once Williams O'Brien's *United Ireland*—quoted the British *Pall Mall Gazette* to the effect that the *Freeman* had "recently declined . . . to publish a letter from the Archbishop of Dublin correcting some statements that had appeared in its columns."[27] Not a major instance of censorship, this refusal to publish is nonetheless a retaliatory strategy of containment directed against the church. The article goes on to note that when representatives of the *Freeman's Journal* directors called on Walsh to explain, Walsh would not accept their apologies.

Two weeks later the *Insuppressible* printed a letter from the Archbishop which accused the *Freeman* of writing in "a spirit not unworthy of the traditions of some leading organ of the atheistic Freemasonry of the Continent." This very strong indictment was directed against the *Freeman's* position that Parnell's affairs—in both senses of the word—were to be considered from a strictly political rather than moral perspective. Walsh stated, "[I]t is my duty, the duty of the Bishop of the diocese in which the *Freeman's Journal* is published, to put the Catholics of Dublin upon their guard against its poisonous teaching."[28] At this moment, for the *Freeman*, proscription was apparently imminent. Myles Crawford's sneering reference but cautious deference to Walsh is easy to understand when we realize how directly the Archbishop attacked the "Old Woman of Prince's Street." Using only a few references, Joyce is able to make "Aeolus" reflect the complex tensions that marked the relations of church and press in Ireland and the reluctance of either to limit its claims on the popular consciousness. But to say this is not to say that *Ulysses* argues for freedom of the press—only that such freedom might be impossible to come by.

Of course, journalists had more than one competing institution to struggle against. As reported in chapter 1, in addition to the church, the Irish press had to deal with the formidable force of the British government, especially in 1919 when the *Freeman's Journal* was suppressed along with all of the other Republican newspapers in Ireland. But even in peacetime, Irish publishers could not help finding themselves threatened by English imperialism, just as they had to come to grips with church requirements on matters not only of morality and religion but also of politics. The webs that held together the ideologies forming Irish culture created a network of relationships that severely constrained the autonomy of the press.

Yet, in that Joyce's headlines control much of the reader's reception of the chapter, "Aeolus" argues the *dominance* of the press over public opinion. Rather than fall beneath the burdens imposed on it by church and state, the press actually flourished in Ireland during the early part of this century, and information suppressed by one paper was, as chapter 1 indicated, generally published by another. In addition, journalists proved adaptable to the cultural situation; the political positions of some papers frequently changed and even reversed, depending on editorial policy and constituency—on which way the Aeolian wind was blowing. Overall, the Irish press of the era was an institution marked by contradictory stances, some drawn from other institutions, some self-generated, but all struggling to gain cultural supremacy. Joyce's newspaper, the "Aeolus" episode, deals explicitly with the discursive systems that made up Irish culture; he builds the episode out of motifs that make prominent the similarity of the press, religion, law, education, and politics. Under the schizoid surveillance of Myles Crawford, the church, the British government, the various professions, the creed of art—all compete for ascendancy in the narrative as they did in Irish society. This is not to say that the efforts of church and state to control the Irish were half-hearted or that the social conditions which resulted from such control were liberal and humane. Rather, despite often extreme physical oppression in Ireland, the culture-as-network necessarily accommodated resistance.

The social tensions I have noted mark the presence of the newspaper throughout *Ulysses*. In particular, the enmity of the church and press underlies the passage in "Circe" where newsboys run past Stephen and Bloom crying, "Stop press edition. . . . Safe arrival of Antichrist" (U 506). Their announcement comically alludes to the irreligion that the church endeavored to keep out of the Irish papers. Yet, when we see the "Circe" version of the Antichrist, he turns out to be only Reuben J. Dodd, the moneylender derided by Simon Dedalus and his cohorts. Dodd's being accompanied by a hobgoblin who looks a good deal like the popular cartoon character Ally Sloper points to the fact that Irish mass culture shaped its own class-based notions of impropriety and had already announced those offending ideas. Far from being original in its blasphemies and obscenities, Joyce's fiction played out offenses so common as to be stereotyped.

This point is further stressed when, defending himself against Philip Beaufoy's charges of plagiarism and imposture,[29] Bloom hears "A Voice from the Gallery" chant, "Moses, Moses, king of the jews, / Wiped his arse in the Daily News" (U 459). Notice that Moses, with whom Bloom is consistently identified and who may also be the Ikey Moses of *Ally Sloper's Half-Holiday*, wipes himself not *with* the newspaper but *in* it (appropriately enough, for a cartoon figure).[30] This scatalogical detail represents what would not have been printed in the news in Joyce's Dublin, but Joyce's novel includes all sorts of material generally censored by the public discourses of the time. Certainly, part of Joyce's strategy in *Ulysses* was to evade censoring conventions, yet Joyce's speaking of the supposedly unspeakable does not really open up new ground for the verbal. Despite what was called the "scandal" of *Ulysses*, the fact is that Joyce told his contemporaries nothing that was new. Rather, he said those things that had already been said, but he spoke them in such a way that his readers may still register them as daring revelations of the human condition. The novelty of Joyce's fiction was in the combination of coded elements rather than in the elements themselves, a combination which simultaneously exposed the cultural dynamics of censorship and shifted them according to Joyce's own ideological preoccupations. What Joyce recognized and what his references to the press suggest is that in his era the Irish accepted and lived within the ethos of competition and suppression—even though the horse had usually already left the barn—even though in most cases what was suppressed had always been insuppressible.

Stephen's Story and Cultural Polarities

One of the delights of "Aeolus" is the fact that Stephen's parable bears a relationship to the episode's action similar to that between the episode and the historical context sketched out in chapter 1—that is, a relationship of simultaneous control by and exposure of censoring. Early in the episode Crawford asks Stephen to write some copy for him; Stephen responds with a short narrative about two old women. He describes in some detail the routine life led by Florence MacCabe and Anne Kearns, and their climbing up Nelson's pillar. At the top of the monument, they consume brawn, bread, and plums, and spit the plumstones through the railings. This sketch, often compared with Joyce's stories in *Dubliners*, appears to be a simple and noncommittal rendering of Dublin life in 1904 as it might be experienced by two women who lack youth, husbands, education, and money.

Stephen's portrayal of the women is selective as well as naturalistically descriptive. As noted above, when he mentions that the two live in Fumbally's lane, he is able to move outside of his narrative to tell MacHugh that the lane is "Off Blackpitts," but that concentration on place leads Stephen to thoughts, which he does not voice, of a sexual encounter. This scene of a "Damp night reeking of hungry dough" shows a side of "DEAR DIRTY DUBLIN" (U 145) that would not be explicitly reported in the daily news. Only the "Akasic records" of all thoughts and words, which exist eternally according to Dublin's Theosophists, would include this visceral side of Dublin experience. In separating thought and spoken word, Stephen has internalized an aesthetic censorship that is continuous with the authoritative dictates shaping public consciousness in his city.

The sketch has come in for a lot of critical interpretation. Richard Ellmann, for instance, has seen it as a portrayal of Dublin as the "Promised Land" turned a waste land of "bondage" in which Stephen refuses to serve.[31] More recently, Ellmann states that in the parable Stephen "savagely mocks both British glories and Irish chauvinism."[32] William York Tindall, finding it an "indefinite" but suggestive "epiphany," sees one focus to be the oppression of church and state that results in infertility and "subjection" for the Irish.[33] Stuart Gilbert labels the sketch an "ironic fable,"[34] while Clive Hart describes the story as "a picture of futility and sterility" and links the old women with Moses and their plum-eating with escapism,[35] a position with which Stanley Sultan basically agrees.[36] Finally, M. J. C. Hodgart regards the women as "the two phases of Woman that preside over birth and death," so that the "Mosaic reference suggests that they are the midwives of the New Ireland, and the layers-out of its stillborn corpse."[37] The consensus is that the story denounces the sexual, political, and religious condition of Ireland and obliquely expresses Stephen's disgust or dismay at this condition.

A good deal of textual evidence supports this reading, but I find the interpretation inattentive to the cultural mechanisms being explored and therefore overly selective in considering Joyce's use in the chapter of dichotomous motifs. Just as Joycean culture tends to polarize, so do the critical readings of "Aeolus." A major contrast in the episode is that between mechanism and organism. At the beginning of "Aeolus," trams, mailcars, and printing presses dominate the mechanized "HEART OF THE HIBERNIAN METROPOLIS" (U 116). Doors creak, barrels thud, presses thump. "Machines," thinks Bloom, "Smash a man to atoms if they got him caught. Rule the world today" (U 118). These thoughts coincide with Bloom's idea that Paddy Dignam's death was the result of a mechanical malfunction. In "Hades" Bloom had likened the heart to a pump which "gets bunged up: and there you are" (U 105). Bloom further reflects that the machinery of Dignam's body is "out of hand" but still "Working away," "fermenting" itself to nothingness (U 118). Further, Bloom sees that the printing presses radically affect the lives of the typesetters. Nannetti, the foreman, moves and speaks somewhat mechanically. "Iron nerves," thinks Bloom as he struggles to communicate to the foreman Alexander Keyes's idea for an ad (U 120) while the machines dominate the scene with their incessant noise.

This primacy is countered by Bloom's tendency to humanize the mechanical processes he witnesses. Thus what looks to him like the setting of type backwards reminds him of his father's reading of the hagadah at Passover. And Bloom sees the printing equipment itself as "Almost human. . . . Doing its level best to speak" (U 121), an assertion that is especially comic in the light of the headlines that appear in "Aeolus." The organic or human seems to exist not as a contradiction but as a function of the mechanical, both incidental offshoots of vast processes of generation and decay. The dichotomizing operation by which the cultural paradigm at hand incorporates new data is both highlighted and subverted through Bloom's interchange of terms for the body and the machine.

Sharing the supposed dominance of the machine in the opening pages of the chapter are images of royalty and English power, images that establish at once the historical nexus into which the narrative inserts itself. The central street in the episode's opening is, after all, Prince's street, and Edward VII's mailcars bear the royal insignia (as does Shaun in *Finnegans Wake*), while Nelson presides over Dublin's heart. In 1909, Richard O'Brien reported that "Nelson's pillar standing in the middle of O'Connell Street represents the dominion of England; O'Connell's statue at the end typifies the Irish people"; he added, "When O'Connell's statue was unveiled a coal porter standing by said, as the veil dropped: 'Now Nelson you've got your match. . . .'"[38]

However, the posited relationship between Britain and Ireland is not just that of political sovereignty and servitude, for professor MacHugh extends the opposition to pose the spiritual orientation of Judaism, Greece, and Ireland against the "Material domination" of Roman and English culture. Questioning where spirituality shows up in conquering Britain, MacHugh contrasts "Lord Jesus" with "Lord Salisbury" (U 133), the leader of the English Conservative party and the man whom Joyce, in his essay "The Home Rule Comet" (1910), quoted as saying, "Let the Irish stew in their own juice."[39] Yet existing side by side with the conquering forces of Britain and mechanization is an undercurrent of "LIFE ON THE RAW" (U 145), the ordinary life of the Dublin poor and lower middle class. The king's insignia is on the mailcars, but Irish shoeshiners occupy the high post office porch. Irish laborers transfer barrels of Guinness's from warehouse to wagon. And Davy Stephens, the famous Irish vendor, appears as the first explicit "mockery of victory"[40] in the chapter when he is referred to as a "king's courier" (U 116). The men of or around the press are occupied with quite ordinary and quite local details of day-to-day life, even though they work in the midst of royal emblems and a variously co-opted press. Even Bloom contrasts the official governmental news in the *Dublin Gazette* with "ads and side features" (U 118) that not only account for sales of a newspaper but also are "More Irish than the Irish" (U 119).

"Aeolus" includes a series of these contrasting motifs, including not only institution/individual, censorship/art, royal/common, domination/servitude, and English/Irish but also Latin/Greek, Egyptian/Hebrew, death/life, monument/man, matter/spirit, ephemera/Akasa, frustration/creation, factionalism/humanism, justice/law, and success/failure. Although these oppositions suggest that choices must be made and offensive elements eliminated, it is clear that the episode is less concerned with weeding out than with specifying the conventional formulations defining Irish culture. As Lotman and Uspensky suggest, Western culture as we know it tends to organize information into binary oppositions. The structuralism that underlies their work has sought, especially in its anthropological embodiments, to establish that this operation characterizes the human mind in *any* cultural setting, but the polarizing of data points equally to the economic and political contradictions immanent in modern Western culture. Certainly, the persistent binarism of Joyce's fictions grows out of historical patterns of power and subservience more than out of Joyce's conscious efforts either to build his texts from oppositions or to capture those intellectual operations that might be said to express the intrinsic nature of the human consciousness.

Even the end of "Aeolus" does not dictate the blanket choice of one set of terms over another. It has been observed that after Stephen's recitation of his sketch, the true paralysis of Ireland is symbolized by the short-circuited trams, Ireland's heart being out of touch with its body.[41] This observation fails to take account, though, of the ever-present undercurrent of ordinary activity recorded in "Aeolus." Even though the trams are "becalmed" (U 149), other sources of transportation continue to function as "Hackney cars, cabs, delivery waggons, mailvans, private broughams, aerated mineral water floats with rattling crates of bottles, rattled, rolled, horse-drawn, rapidly" (U 149). The ultimate mockery of England's mechanical and material domination is the steady continuation of life in Dublin suggested by the function of conveyances that do not rely on the electric power source of the trams. The raw side of Dublin, from which Florence MacCabe and Anne Kearns emerge into Stephen's art, is not especially spiritual, nor is it simply mechanical; one could say rather that it is "working class" in the broadest sense of the term, at the point at which differentiations and contradictions coexist, however uneasily. It is the realm of culture, that is, of domination that grows from more than one source and of resistance that is equally multifaceted.

In fact, far from portraying merely sexual frustration or merely political disappointment, Stephen's parable, which indeed bears the traces of sexual innuendo and political commentary, deals principally with cultural domination. The most virginal aspect of Anne and Florence is their intellectual life, for they contentedly accept their place in the shadow of British ascendancy and religious mores. Like the *Dubliners* stories, Stephen's narrative deals with human limitations and with problems of adaptation to inhibiting conditions that refuse to remain external. And the final measure of this refusal, of the internalization of censoring cultural forces, is the reflexive act by which Joyce presents the responses to the parable. Stephen's auditors try to pin down the significance of the work in interpretive maneuvers that speak for the society's need to encapsulate and label the ambiguous. In other words, to see the culture as essentially a network of censoring impulses is to see its fundamental antipathy to Joycean combinations of codings that create ambiguity (the possibility of alternative positions) where ideological clarity had attempted to hold sway. The title that Stephen proposes for his sketch—*A Pisgah Sight of Palestine* or *the Parable of the Plums* (U 149)—is a sop flung ironically to MacHugh and Crawford, for it leads the reader directly into an interpretation of the sketch as a work of doctrinal argumentation, however debatable the point, rather than one of selective description.

MacHugh, for instance, attempts to formulate a reading before he has even heard the whole of Stephen's short recitation. For MacHugh the two women are the "Wise virgins" (U 145) of Christ's parable. Even though the lack of an introductory double dash in Joyce's text makes Stephen appear not to speak aloud the fact that

Florence "takes a crubeen and a bottle of double X for supper every Saturday" while Anne uses "Lourdes water" for her lumbago (U 145), MacHugh mechanically classifies Stephen's narrative as exemplifying "Antithesis" (U 146). He is delighted by Stephen's description of Nelson as a "onehandled adulterer" (U 148), and he follows up the recitation with the statement that Stephen's bitterness is like that of Antisthenes. He then takes credit for giving Stephen the idea for the Mosaic slant to the title. Such unfocused attempts at analysis tell us more about MacHugh than about Stephen or his story; they fit well the character whose eyes are "Witless shellfish" while he recites a speech about right vision. Steeped in classical tradition and cultural patterns, MacHugh demonstrates the efforts of the culture to incorporate works of art and other productions into already existing paradigms, thus stopping the circulation of meaning and confining the counterinstitutional potentiality of such works. That power grows out of Stephen's reliance on Dublin as the source of his material, not because he builds his art on "issues" that will one day be as much "Dead noise" (U 143) as O'Connell's monster-meeting speeches. Rather, the two old women that Stephen saw on the beach, the fruit vendor working at the foot of Nelson's pillar, and the churches of Dublin contribute to Stephen's narrative the specificity of the actual, the ideological content of which binds narrative to history.

One thing that "Aeolus" teaches us, then, is that Joyce's narratives conform to his culture; both fictions and history assent to the demands of press, church, government, and the popular opinion that shapes and is shaped by these institutions. The materials that Stephen uses to compose his parable are similar to those that Joyce used to create his fictions; they are already "censored" by the society. That is, they articulate the accepted, the conventional, and the non-revolutionary. Scorning the censor, Joyce nonetheless had little option, given his encyclopedic program, but to trace cultural power lines in his fictions and to rely for meaning on the conventional discursive frames that comprised life in Dublin. Joyce's works suggest that for most of his characters living *is* the state of conforming to the standardized. On the other hand, to see itself as vital a society requires blind spots; it needs to regard some behavior as spontaneous and to believe that new information is not all automatically digested into prescribed formats that resist radical change. In "Aeolus" we

see the movement between convention recognized as such and what
appears to be unconventional. Myles Crawford, for all of his apparent alcoholic confusion, discerns in Stephen just such a meeting
place between what is obviously censored and what is daring.

Of course, his request that Stephen write something new for the
paper turns to his caveat against offending the religious mores that
the press mostly followed. Even more important, the form of the
episode works to confine the significance of conversation, thought,
and action in "Aeolus" to those ideas that do not violate the proprieties of the press. Anything outside of that framework, readers
have tended to label simple parody of the exaggeration and stereotyping characteristic of journalism in the era of Alfred Harmsworth.
However, "Aeolus" is a good deal more complex than the usual
critical assessment recognizes; the episode follows Irish society in
Joyce's day in generating evidence counter to a vision of that culture
as moribund. Both text and culture forestall in several ways the closure of ideological domination: (1) through the use of establishment channels for antiestablishment messages (as in Bloom's House
of Keyes ad and Joyce's use of the newspaper form), (2) through the
refusal to choose between imposed oppositions (as when the individual and the institution cannot be separated, when Bloom fuses
man and machine, and when free speech and censorship are revealed
as falsely distinguished aspects of the constant circulation of discourse and power), and (3) through the failure of censorship really
to suppress ideas. This final point requires some development because the editor's response to Stephen's parable emphasizes so
strongly the surfacing, during the act of reproof, of offending implications—the whole area of sexuality insofar as it was silenced in
Irish life.

It is, of course, Michel Foucault who discusses the power mechanisms expended on focusing the attention of Western culture on
sexuality. Responding to the widespread theory that in the nineteenth century bourgeois society repressed physical expression,
Foucault states: "All . . . [the] negative elements—defenses, censorships, denials—which the repressive hypothesis groups together
in one great central mechanism destined to say no, are doubtless
only component parts that have a local and tactical role to play in a
transformation into discourse, a technology of power, and a will to
knowledge that are far from being reducible to the former."[42] Al-

though Foucault's argument in *The History of Sexuality* has come under critical fire, the fundamental notion that censorship both represses and stimulates discourse is more than borne out in Irish culture, and Joyce's works echo the deployments of power that Foucault details. As chapter 1 demonstrated, most attempts to censor follow the pronouncements that are to be suppressed, and the suppression itself often serves to incite discursive resistance. In the early twentieth-century Irish press, in particular, suppression resulted in a concrete substitution which cast the cultural spotlight on what the censor had set out to obscure. Joyce's anatomizing narratives document the subversive positions resident within a culture characterized by censorship and confined by tradition. The irony is that many readers of Joyce have paid attention to the stultifying mores that he displays or to his own supposedly aberrant floutings of those conventions rather than to the textual/cultural operations that expose the identity of both Joycean maneuvers.

NOTES

1. A notable exception to the usual emphasis on rhetoric is Stanley Sultan's section on "Aeolus" in *The Argument of* Ulysses (Columbus: Ohio State University Press, 1964), pp. 109–18. Sultan maintains, "The major subject of the chapter is the political character of the Irish nation" (p. 109).

2. C. H. Peake, *James Joyce: The Citizen and the Artist* (Stanford, Calif.: Stanford University Press, 1977), pp. 194–95.

3. For dates concerning the composition of "Aeolus," see Michael Groden, Ulysses *in Progress* (Princeton, N.J.: Princeton University Press, 1977), pp. 68–69. On the G.P.O., see Sultan, p. 110, and Mays, p. 90.

4. Cf. MacCabe's treatment of the Lockout and "Aeolus," p. 140.

5. Glandon, p. 104. This indistinguishability apparently accounts for the fact that Stephen J. Brown's classic study, *The Press In Ireland: A Survey and a Guide* (1937; rpt. New York: Lemma, 1971), does not mention the *Telegraph* even though the *Freeman* is treated at length.

6. Glandon, p. 106.

7. Father Brown calls for "a study of the use made of the Press by Dublin Castle as a political tool" (Brown, pp. 19–20). That was in 1936, and there is still work to be done in this area. Below, I refer to Brown, pp. 21, 35–36 and 39.

8. *Scissors and Paste*, 13 February 1915, p.2; 20 February 1915, p.2.

9. National Library of Ireland, ILB, Item 77.

10. National Library of Ireland, ILB, Item 74.

11. "The Castle & the 'Freeman's Journal,'" *Éire*, 4 November 1914, p. 1. A related article published two days earlier in *Éire* is entitled, "The Castle and the Castle Journal" (p. 1).

12. R. J. Smith, p. [i].

13. In *The Consciousness of Joyce*, Ellmann says that Joyce uses "as his principal emblem of modern capitalism the newspaper, wasting the spirit with its persistent attacks upon the integrity of the word, narcotizing its readers with superficial facts, habituating them to secular and clerical authority" (p. 78).

14. Benstock calls the following quotation a description of "the typical burgher" (*Joyce-Again's Wake*, pp. 186–87).

15. M. J. C. Hodgart finds all but a few to be "unsuitable for headlining: they are rather captions under imaginary illustrations, probably photographs, added by an anonymous sub-editor" ("Aeolus," in *James Joyce's* Ulysses: *Critical Essays*, ed. Clive Hart and David Hayman [Berkeley: University of California Press, 1974], p. 129.

16. Heinrich Straumann, *Newspaper Headlines: A Study in Linguistic Method* (London: Allen & Unwin, 1935), pp. 38–39. When Straumann explains the term "block language," he mentions that the language of Joyce's *Work in Progress* has similarities to it. Straumann argues for "the existence of headlinese as a language, a jargon, a dialect, or whatever it may be called, of its own," and he cites "sociological, psychological, grammatical, and historical evidence to prove this assumption" (p. 25). He discusses the distorting powers of headlines that do more than provide "a simple label" over the story in question (p. 26) and notes, "Supposing there is such a thing as public opinion influenced by the Press, this influence must largely go by way of the headline . . ." (p. 27).

17. Smith, p. 2.

18. Stuart Gilbert, *James Joyce's* Ulysses, 2nd ed. (New York: Vintage-Random, 1955), p. 179n. Hélène Cixous modifies this view, claiming that through changes in headline style, "we watch the devaluation of language" in Joyce's "judgement of the rhetoric practised by his contemporaries." "Not only the language of Dublin or of the newspapers, but the language that claims it can reduce the whole world to words, including the artist's own word, is subjected to destructive criticism . . ." (Cixous, pp. 691, 692). Carol Shloss, "Choice Newseryreels: James Joyce and the Irish *Times*," *James Joyce Quarterly* 15 (1978), points to the parodic nature of the headlines in "Aeolus" and argues that "where a real newspaper supposedly uses headlines as a strategy for claiming attention through clear, summary statements, Joyce's headlines rarely clarify anything" (p. 335). She cites "CLEVER, VERY" (U 137) as primarily a parodic rhetorical device (p. 336), but Joyce's parodies are sometimes closer imitations of

contemporary journalism than she appears to recognize. For example, to head up a 24 November 1914 article about the killing of German and Austro-Hungarian prisoners on the Isle of Man, the Irish newspaper *Éire* printed "REMARKABLE—VERY" (p. 2). It seems likely that along with his chronological presentation of headline styles, Joyce also alludes to the radical press's tendency to critique or even parody the form and content of such establishment papers as the *Freeman's Journal* or the *Irish Times*.

19. Cf. Peake, p. 195.

20. Leslie Fiedler, "Portrait of the Artist: The Academic Perspective," 15 February 1982, State University of New York—College at Purchase.

21. Cf. Karen Lawrence's argument that the "headings" are the novel's often parodying self-commentary; they separate the text from "an originating consciousness" and emphasize the text's "collective" and "public" nature, its voicing of "received ideas" instead of individually authored style (*The Odyssey of Style in* Ulysses [Princeton, N. J.: Princeton University Press, 1981], pp. 62, 64–67). Although I believe that this dichotomy oversimplifies the situation, throughout her book Lawrence usefully focuses on "the voices of culture" (p. 103) such as the press, the epic, and the melodrama.

22. See, for instance, Marilyn French, *The Book as World*: *James Joyce's* Ulysses (Cambridge, Mass.: Harvard University Press, 1976), pp. 98–101.

23. Ellmann notes that in 1909 when Joyce visited the *Evening Telegraph* offices, "The publisher of the *Freeman's Journal* was Thomas Sexton, a Parnellite who was feuding with Archbishop Walsh; consequently his paper minimized whatever the Archbishop did and enlarged upon everything that Cardinal Logue did. Walsh evidently made frequent protests, which Joyce referred to without explanation . . ." (Ellmann, *James Joyce*, p. 288). Hence the irony of the headline "NOTED CHURCHMAN AN OCCASIONAL CONTRIBUTOR" (U 121). For an attempt to locate a specific historical event behind this detail, see John Garvin, *James Joyce's Disunited Kingdom and the Irish Dimension* (Dublin: Gill and Macmillan; New York: Barnes and Noble, 1976), pp. 72–73.

24. Francis Phelan was the first to identify this allusion in "Aeolus" in "A Source for the Headlines of 'Aeolus'?" *James Joyce Quarterly* 9 (1971), 146–51.

25. Hurley, 6 (1899), 56–57. Quotations below in this paragraph are from pp. 61–62 and 67–68. The imagery of disease recurred in discussions of this kind. Cf. Guinan, "Apostolate of the Press," p. 322: "A corrupt Press is the worst of white plagues, exhaling a fatal miasma, carrying deadly microbes on its pestilent breath, and planting them insidiously in the minds of the happy, innocent girl, and the bright, pure-souled boy. . . ."

26. Patrick J. Walsh says that around the end of 1890, during the "early

stages of the Parnell crisis," Archbishop Walsh was less popular than he had been. "Up to that time the *Freeman's Journal* had always been at the Archbishop's service, and its columns were the ordinary medium of his numerous public communications. On the defection of the *Freeman* the Archbishop availed first of the pages of the *Irish Catholic*, but as it was but a weekly publication, he encouraged and aided the issuing of a little daily called the *Insuppressible*, and later of a more substantial paper styled *The National Press*" (*William J. Walsh: Archbishop of Dublin* [Dublin & Cork: Talbot Press, 1928], pp. 426–27).

27. "Archbishop Walsh and the Freeman's Journal," *Insuppressible*, 14 January 1891, p. 1.

28. *Insuppressible*, 29 January 1891, p. 3.

29. When Bloom defends himself to the watch, he says, "I am connected with the British and Irish press" (U 458). This defense accentuates the indistinguishability of Irish journalism from the English columns that made up much of what Irish people read in the establishment papers. It suggests also that what the Irish wrote, the British kept surveillance over.

30. The word "in" occurs here in the Rosenbach Manuscript, the *Little Review* version, the 1922 Paris text, and the "Circe" page proofs and typescripts. An excellent analysis of Ally Sloper and company is Peter Bailey's "Ally Sloper's Half-Holiday: Comic Art in the 1880s," *History Workshop* 16 (1983), 4–31.

31. Richard Ellmann, *Ulysses on the Liffey* (New York: Oxford University Press, 1972), pp. 70–71.

32. Richard Ellmann, *Consciousness of Joyce*, p. 81. See also pp. 38, 53.

33. William York Tindall, *A Reader's Guide to James Joyce* (New York: Noonday-Farrar, 1959), p. 166.

34. Gilbert, p. 181.

35. Clive Hart, *James Joyce's* Ulysses (Sydney: Sydney University Press, 1968), p. 53.

36. Sultan, pp. 114–15. Sultan also emphasizes the political theme of the parable (pp. 115–17). For further discussion of the story, see Bernard Benstock, "What Stephen Says: Joyce's Second Portrait of the Artist," in Ulysses *Cinquante Ans Après*, pp. 140–42; Irene Briskin, "Some New Light on 'The Parable of the Plums,'" *James Joyce Quarterly* 3 (1966), 236–51; James H. Maddox, Jr., *Joyce's* Ulysses *and the Assault upon Character* (New Brunswick, N.J.: Rutgers University Press, 1978), pp. 96–100; J. G. Keogh, "*Ulysses*' 'Parable of the Plums' as Parable and Periplum," *James Joyce Quarterly* 7 (1970), 377–78; French, pp. 97–98; and Harry Blamires, *The Bloomsday Book: A Guide through Joyce's* Ulysses (London: Methuen, 1966), pp. 58, 232.

37. Hodgart, "Aeolus," p. 126. Overall, though, Hodgart gives the

sketch a more hopeful twist: "The midwives have presided over the birth of a miraculous Child, and now a great Modern writer is among us."

38. Richard Barry O'Brien, *Dublin Castle and the Irish People* (Dublin: Gill; London: Kegan Paul, Trench, Trübner, 1909), p. 6.

39. James Joyce, "The Home Rule Comet," trans. of "La Cometa dell' 'Home Rule,'" *Il Piccolo della Sera*, 22 December 1910, in *Critical Writings*, pp. 210, 213.

40. The "sense" or "meaning" of "Aeolus" according to the schema Joyce gave to Carlo Linati.

41. Sultan, p. 117; Hodgart, "Aeolus," p. 119.

42. Michel Foucault, *The History of Sexuality*, trans. Robert Hurley, 2 vols. (New York: Vintage-Random, 1980), 1:12.

CHAPTER 3

Plays and Pantomines
in Joyce's Dublin

Stage Irishman! (U 491)

"Circe" as Script

One question not satisfactorily addressed in discussions of *Ulysses* is what the dramatic form of "Circe" signifies. Like Joyce's other technical experiments and mimeses, "Circe" is not necessarily expected to make clear its formal rationale; we tend to accept that the author moves in mysterious ways and that the explanation for Joyce's stylistic changes rests in the interplay between authorial peculiarities and what he saw as the demands of his Odyssean format. Recently, Hugh Kenner has noted that a play within *Ulysses* was mandatory because Dublin in 1904 was a city marked by theatrical scuffles; he cites the commotion over Yeats's *The Countess Cathleen*, Synge's *In the Shadow of the Glen*, and *The Playboy of the Western World*, and suggests that Joyce was driven to compete with these writers in outraging the Irish public.[1] Certainly, insofar as the theater was a battle zone in the making of cultural mores, insofar as some plays were denounced by the clergy and some by nationalists, and insofar as playwrights like Synge and Yeats frontally attacked the Irish self-concept, Kenner is correct in associating Joyce's interest in the theater and the artist's ability to outrage. But this association is significantly enhanced when we specify the connections among the constraints that society attempted to impose on playwrights, the significance of the theater as an institution, and those stage stereotypes that Joyce's texts encounter, critique, and transform.

Having come to the point in his narrative where his heroes' innermost selves were to be revealed, Joyce used theatrical form to demonstrate the cultural scripting of the "inner." Confronting the traditional concept of selfhood, Joyce dealt in "Circe" with social conventions and economic relations handled routinely on the stages of London and Dublin, especially in the pantomime, music hall, burlesque, and melodrama. To be sure, "Circe" refers to cultural frameworks other than those of the popular stage,[2] but theatrical references mark the episode decisively and indicate that in "Circe" Joyce paid particular heed to the messages, ideological and explicit, that emanated from the highly codified popular theater of his day as well as to the impact of these messages on individual self-concept. In particular, "Circe" deals with those points in which conflict occurred in Joyce's Dublin—class interests, Irish nationalism, the concept of individuality, family relations, and gender definition. In this chapter, I explore the importance of the theater to the characters of *Ulysses*, the conventions of the pantomime in England and Ireland, the ideological positions urged through popular theater, and some features of "Circe" (and, briefly, of *Finnegans Wake* II, i) that allude to or parallel pantomime conventions.

An analysis of the theater as institution is necessary to an understanding of "Circe" because it is obviously this context that the episode responds to—the theater's rituals and codes of expression. As in the presentation of the press in "Aeolus," Joyce refers not to any single play as his chief source; rather, he constructs a composite theatrical text that stands as a "macro-sign"[3] for Irish popular dramatics, especially the pantomime, from the late nineteenth century through the early twentieth century. Hence, "Circe" is as intensely reflexive as it is relentlessly ideological.

Most readings have regarded "Circe" as simply part of the narrative[4] of *Ulysses*, and have analyzed it according to traditional narrative techniques, giving attention to the play of imagery, the handling of irony, and the manipulation of tone and style. Yet in the context of *Ulysses* itself, Joyce did not choose "Circe" to embody the art of literature; "Scylla and Charybdis" has that distinction. In contrast, in "Circe" the focus is not on literary topics or forms; rather, the stage experience is evoked to emphasize that the theater is an institution with different generic determinations and cultural functions from "literature" and with a more immediate, compelling, and widespread influence than narrative form in a city in which *everyone* followed what went on at the Gaiety, at the Queen's, and at Dan Lowrey's. (As poor as she is, Eveline has been to the theater; Frank takes her to an "unaccustomed part of the theatre" for *The Bohemian*

Girl [D 39].) While the literary coterie that Stephen contacts in the National Library is exclusive, the theater provided an experience available in some form to almost all of Dublin's citizens. Even those who could not afford to attend performances saw the melodramatic plot summaries on the playbills that hung in pubs and in shops. Even those who could not read these descriptions could interpret the pictorial posters that covered the hoardings and that often displayed not only music hall stars but also scenes from plays. This is surely one point made by Bloom's occasional thoughts of Marie Kendall, Mrs. Bandman Palmer, and Eugene Stratton—that it would be difficult, considering the extensive presence of the theater in Dublin, not to think of these actors and their roles.

Even though most readings of "Circe" have been what Susan Bassnett-McGuire calls "purely literary," as opposed to semiotic,[5] the multiple significations of cultural context shape the possibilities of meaning in the episode. But our distance from Joyce's Ireland is part of the problem with understanding "Circe" as a dramatic text; many readers, especially Americans, lack experience of the kinds of popular performance to which a Joycean audience was regularly exposed. To supply the specific referents for stylizations or the specific background for comic gags and stereotyped dialogue, the reader must know the contours of popular theater in turn-of-the-century Ireland. Joyce explores the significance of what was merely accepted by the playgoer in his day, but in order to register the nature of Joyce's critique, we do well to attempt recovery of some of the theatrical experience and issues that primed Joyce for the writing of "Circe."

To escape from the "purely literary" reading of "Circe" is to consider what semioticians call the "world-making" function of the drama. Drawing on Lotman's notion that cultures are modeled on the organizational principles of language, Keir Elam says that Lotman would call the drama a "secondary modeling system." He asserts that through the experience of theater, human beings learn to "make sense of . . . [their] lives and their component acts." This sense-making is not, however, absolute; rather, it speaks constantly to the constructedness of the dramatic worlds that shape it.[6] To an extent, then, the culture of any society may be regarded as a version made general of that society's theatrical experience. The world-making of "Circe" is replete with all of the "subworlds" of Stephen and Bloom, the "subworlds" being the possible situations projected, thought about, and hypothesized by characters within a drama or by members of its audience. Elam notes that "each subworld is founded on a particular modality, expressible through verbs such as 'believe', 'wish', 'know', 'hope', 'fear', 'command', indicating the speaker's attitude to the proposition uttered." One might argue that "Circe" is about the playing out of such subworlds. It is much more involved with the subworlds of the wished-for (Bloom) or feared (Stephen) than it is with the "actual."[7] Hence, "Circe" suggests how fully the individual depends for cues on theatrical scripting.

The Theater in *Ulysses*

There is no question that the culture displayed for us in *Ulysses* is heavily coded by the theater, which was viewed both as an intensification of ordinary experience and as a touchstone of excellence by which the everyday could be measured. When Bloom sits with Richie Goulding over lunch in the Ormond, Richie, stimulated by hearing Si Dedalus and his cronies singing in the bar, reminisces: "Never would Richie forget that night. As long as he lived: never. In the gods of the old Royal with little Peake" (U 272). Similarly, even the unnamed principal narrator of the "Cyclops" episode is familiar with the theater and judges life by it. As Bloom, taunting, is pursued by the Citizen out of Barney Kiernan's pub, we are told:

> Gob, the devil wouldn't stop him till he got hold of the bloody tin anyhow and out with him and little Alf hanging on to his elbow and he shouting like a stuck pig, as good as any bloody play in the Queen's royal theatre:
> —Where is he till I murder him? (U 343)

Known at the time principally for its melodramas, the Queen's Theatre stands, however ironically, for a kind of experience far more "dramatic" than the usual course of life. In this case, life is as good as a melodrama, high praise indeed.

As Molly knows, it is rare that experience obliges as the stage does by perfectly matching potential plots to adequate actors. Remembering the occasion on which she took Milly to the Royal to see Martin Harvey in *The Only Way*, Molly thinks,

> she clapped when the curtain came down because he looked so handsome then we had Martin Harvey for breakfast dinner and supper I thought to myself afterwards it must be real love if a man gives

up his life for her that way for nothing I suppose there are few men
like that left its hard to believe in it though unless it really happened
to me the majority of them with not a particle of love in their natures
to find two people like that nowadays full up of each other that would
feel the same way as you do theyre usually a bit foolish in the head.
(U 767)

Stereotypical love scenes obviously condition Molly's thoughts and
dreams even though she is wise enough to recognize that reality
often significantly lags behind art in such matters.

Similarly, Bloom strongly associates Mosenthal's melodramatic
Leah the Forsaken with his father, who saw the play in London and
who consequently shows up in "Circe" in the costume of a stage
biblical Jew:

> How he used to talk about Kate Bateman in that. Outside the Adel-
> phi in London waited all the afternoon to get in. . . . And Ristori in
> Vienna. What is this the right name is? By Mosenthal it is. *Rachel*, is
> it? No. The scene he was always talking about where the old blind
> Abraham recognises the voice and puts his fingers on his face.
>
> Nathan's voice! His son's voice! I hear the voice of Nathan who left
> his father to die of grief and misery in my arms, who left the house of
> his father and left the God of his father.
>
> Every word is so deep, Leopold. (U 76)

Bloom's Circean image of his father is written from Rudolph's passionate attachment to this scene and repetitious reenactment of it.
The scene thus becomes for Bloom a touchstone for filiality as well
as for infidelity. Bloom, fatherless and sonless, is in a pathetic situation, and even though Joyce resisted the temptation to write a melodramatic union between the older man and Stephen, he suggests
Bloom's cultural priming for such an episode. Of course, the words
and situations of melodrama still permeate the modern mind to
shape our expectations and our concepts of the true, just, and satisfying ending, whether to a popular play or to a work like *Ulysses*.

Highlighting the failure of theatrical stereotypes to meet reality
even while they shape expectations of the real, "Circe" burlesques
the encounter of Abraham and Nathan:

RUDOLPH

Second halfcrown waste money today. I told you not go with drunken
goy ever. So you catch no money.

BLOOM

(*hides the crubeen and trotter behind his back and, crestfallen, feels warm and cold feetmeat*) Ja, ich weiss, papachi.

RUDOLPH

What you making down this place? Have you no soul? (*with feeble vulture talons he feels the silent face of Bloom*) Are you not my son Leopold, the grandson of Leopold? Are you not my dear son Leopold who left the house of his father and left the god of his fathers Abraham and Jacob?

BLOOM

(*with precaution*) I suppose so, father. Mosenthal. All that's left of him. (U 437)[8]

Although the setting is theatrical, reality seems to whittle away at the melodramatic stances and values that Bloom's father cherished. During his lifetime, the dramatic burlesque was popular for this very reason, that it staged the unmasking of drama as cultural conditioning.

On the one hand, then, the theater, especially in an era that specialized in the typically clear-cut morality of melodrama, provided a sort of emotional utopian vision. As Michael Booth states in the introduction to *Hiss the Villain*, melodrama "is a simplification and idealization of human experience dramatically presented. For its audiences melodrama was both an escape from real life and a dramatization of it as it ought to be; uncomplicated, easy to understand, sufficiently exciting to sweep away petty cares."[9] On the other hand, the theater impressed itself on the minds of Dubliners not only as an ideal vision but also as a commodity. It neatly mirrored both the class structure of Irish urban life and the commodification of sexuality. For instance, even in alluding to specific performances, Joyce's Dubliners remember where they sat in the theater audience. Richie Goulding could afford to sit only in the gods (cheapest balcony seats), as did Bloom, we are told, when he supposedly saw Mrs. Yelverton Barry's "peerless globes . . . at a command performance of *La Cigale*." When she appears in "Circe" to accuse Bloom, Mrs. Barry wears proper upper-class evening garb ("*lowcorsaged opal balldress and elbowlength ivory gloves . . . a sabletrimmed brickquilted dolman, a comb of brilliants and panache of osprey in her hair*"), and she asserts her connection with the powers-that-be when she mentions that her husband was "in the North Riding of Tipperary on the Munster circuit" (U 465). Though Bloom is seated cheaply, Mrs. Barry occupies a box, a treat that Molly tells us she and Bloom experienced only once, when Michael Gunn gave Bloom tickets for helping him with an insurance transaction. In fact, as much as he enjoys the theater and follows current productions, Bloom has little money to spend on the theater; he thinks, when he sees that *Fun on the Bristol* is scheduled for the Gaiety, that "Martin Cunningham could work a pass" (U 92).

On the occasion of the Blooms' presence in the box, Bloom recalls a "Chap in dresscircle staring down into her with his operaglass for all he was worth" (U 284), the same person that Molly remembers as a "gentleman of fashion staring down at me with his glasses." In both cases, the relative positions of people are important, as is the fact that, according to Molly, some "idiot in the gallery" (U 769) during *The Wife of Scarli* hissed the female protagonist because of her adultery. What is of interest here is not simply the way that class distinctions are maintained in an otherwise intimate theatrical setting but also how much of the business of theatergoing involves another kind of transaction—the costuming of women in an alluring way and the response of men to that sexual showcasing. Bloom recalls that, like Mrs. Barry with her "*lowcorsaged opal balldress,*" in the box Molly wears "Her crocus dress . . . lowcut, belongings on show" (U 284).

Further, Molly thinks about the fact that "a lot of that touching must go on in theaters in the crush in the dark" (U 767) as well as of Milly's antipathy to being touched when she was at the Royal.[10] If the women are ogled and felt, the men are anxious to take advantage of opportunities for such interaction. Bloom recalls that when he was a teenager "A little then sufficed, a jolting car, the mingling odours of the ladies' cloakroom and lavatory, the throng penned tight on the old Royal stairs (for they love crushes, instinct of the herd, and the dark sexsmelling theatre unbridles vice)" (U 548). Bloom, of course, thinks that women like such attentions, even though Molly mentally proclaims that her unpleasant trip to the theater would be "the last time Ill ever go there to be squashed like that for any Trilby or her barebum" (U 767).

Bloom, in a testimony that would have delighted the late nineteenth-century opponents of scanty stage costuming, provides evidence that the exhibition of limbs provokes lustful thoughts. Why, asks the interlocutor of "Ithaca," had Bloom failed to write a topical song for Michael Gunn's 1893 pantomime? One reason provided is "concupiscence caused by Nelly Bouverist's revelations of white articles of . . . underclothing while she (Nelly Bouverist) was in the articles" (U 679). Selling itself, the theater also marketed sex. Indeed, the more popular style of performance emphasized the commodity value of the woman. In pantomime and melodrama, the heroine is often the bone of contention, so to speak, which the villain assumes he can purchase. Strongly coded by censors and by popular opinion alike, the theater house is in *Ulysses* a site for getting the sexual goods, either directly or vicariously.

In addition, the advertisement of stage performances emphasizes their status as merchandise, a fact which explains the presence in *Ulysses* of several such ads. Bloom's reflections on his father's attachment to *Leah* are called forth as he stands looking at "the multicoloured hoardings. Cantrell and Cochrane's Ginger Ale (Aromatic). Clery's Summer Sale. . . . Hello. *Leah* tonight. Mrs Bandmann Palmer" (U 76). Afterward, riding to Paddy Dignam's funeral, Bloom thinks again of *Leah* when he passes the Queen's and the nearby hoardings: ". . . Eugene Stratton. Mrs Bandmann Palmer. Could I go to see *Leah* tonight, I wonder. I said I. Or the *Lily of Killarney*? Elster Grimes Opera company. Big powerful change. Wet bright bills for next week. *Fun on the Bristol*" (U 92). Similarly, passing Dan Lowrey's Empire Music Hall, Lenehan and M'Coy go by a poster of the comedienne Marie Kendall. Like the other ads in *Ulysses*, these posters suggest not only Bloom's professional interests but also the economic system on which his society runs, by which popular culture reinforces and attractively heightens class differences and stereotypes, by which various classes buy their ideological programming according to their ability to pay for it, and by which the ultimate commodity, sex, is put forward more effectively than in any other popular medium.

The Pantomime in Ireland

The signifying form to which Joyce chiefly alludes in "Circe" is the pantomime. By now, much material on the Victorian and Edwardian pantomime in Ireland is beyond recovery. This is not to say that scripts, songbooks, playbills, advertisements, newspaper reviews, theatrical memoirs, diaries, and reminiscences provide us with no useful information about the pantomime. We have, if not a wealth, a sufficiency of such material, but a great deal has either been lost or awaits discovery in the attics of Dublin and Cork.

Here, using published scripts from British performances and information from songbooks, playbills, and reviews of Irish productions in Joyce's time, I sketch out something of what the pantomime was like. Along the way, I indicate the close ties of the panto to the melodrama and music hall, the impact of these essentially British forms on their Irish audience, the class-specific nature of the popular theater's lessons, and the ideological valences of its traditions. My intention in this gathering and interpreting of historical information is to make explicit the social content of the pantomime. This content is *formally* signified in *Ulysses* and mostly overlooked as a heuristic tool.

As writers on the pantomime make clear, the genre has a long and worthy history, but in turn-of-the-century Dublin, the form was quite fixed. The larger parts of these productions were not mime at all but were full of dialogue, music, color, extravagant costume, corny humor, and scenic splendor. At the base of the form was one of perhaps a dozen fairy tales or nursery rhymes; as Michael Booth documents,[11] from approximately 1850 onwards, the most popular titles for pantomimes included *Cinderella, The Babes in the Wood, Dick Whittington, Robinson Crusoe, Jack and the Beanstalk*, and *Aladdin*. In practice, however, most pantomimes told the same story—of lovers who seek, against the odds, to be united, despite the initial and long-sustained disapproval of a father or other authority figure.

Attached to the panto per se was the "harlequinade," the portion descended from the commedia dell'arte. It adhered in dramatis personae to the key figures of that tradition: Harlequin, Columbine, Pantaloon, and Clown.[12] That this tradition held in Dublin is clear from the fact that Stephen tells Emma, who talks to him about pantomimes, that he "liked a good clown" (SH 67). In the eighteenth and early nineteenth centuries, the harlequinade had been the center of the pantomime, and the productions had often had such names as "Harlequin and the Ogress; or the Sleeping Beauty of the Wood" or "Harlequin Don Quixote."[13] Some of the titles were comically long; according to the *Irish Times* for 26 December 1873, the Gaiety production for that year was "King Turko, the Terrible; or, Harlequin Prince Amabel, the Three Magic Roses, and Oberon, King of the Fairies."

Generally, the production began with a short "opening" in which the plot was established, and then the characters were transformed into the stock figures of the commedia dell'arte. As time went on, however, the fairy-tale opening took up more and more of the production, while the harlequinade shrunk to a tail end. R. J. Broadbent, in his 1901 book on the pantomime, documents the resilience of the form when he notes that in the mid nineteenth century, when it appeared "doomed" to demise, it "managed . . . to come again into popular favor," but he then laments the fact that this newfound popularity rested on adoption of the longer opening and shrunken harlequinade.[14] In Dublin, which was among the most important of the "provincial centers for pantomime,"[15] the genre underwent changes similar to those in its sister capital. An article in the *Irish Times* for 24 December 1892 says that the harlequinade had withered in the preceding quarter-century from eight to ten scenes, running one to one and a half hours, down to two or three scenes, running about twenty minutes. In addition, the *Souvenir* that the Gaiety distributed in 1896, which discusses the evolution of the form over the course of twenty-five years, reports: "It is true that in the old days a vast amount of outlay was devoted to elaborately modelled masks,[16] sometimes to colossal spectacular effects, and to the mechanical changes incidental to the Harlequinade. But as time went on, the more grotesque forms of humour were supplanted by scenes and episodes that met more perfectly the changing fashion of the day. . . . And so a different class of work had to be provided."[17]

Another change, which attested similarly to the panto's close relation to the contemporary scene, involved the actors. The month that Joyce was born, W. Davenport Adams published an article in *The Theatre* that found the pantomime's supposedly deteriorated condition to rest in its use of music-hall stars to fill principal roles.

> I object . . . altogether, to the intrusion of such artists into the domain of pantomime, and I do so because they . . . bring with them, so to speak, an atmosphere which it is sad to see imported into the theatre. They bring with them not only their songs, which, when offensive in their wording, are sometimes made doubly dangerous by their tunefulness; not only their dances, which are usually vulgar when they are not inane; but their style and manner and "gags," which are generally the most deplorable of all. The objection to music hall artists on the stage is . . . that they have the effect of familiarising general audiences, and children especially, with a style and kind of

singing, dancing, and "business" which, however it may be relished by a certain class of the population, ought steadily to be confined to its original habitat. . . . Such songs as these would not be tolerated by pater familias in his drawing-room, and yet, when he takes his children to the pantomime, they are the most prominent portion of the entertainment.[18]

Broadbent and Adams were not the only ones who deplored the presence of music hall artistes on the pantomime stage. Booth mentions that although the artistes attracted adults to the theatre, "conservatives complained that they degraded pantomime."[19]

Despite disapproval from some quarters, the artistes were in panto to stay, and the Irish pantomime followed the British practice of using variety turns, whether related logically to the plot or not, to punctuate the action. In describing the Gaiety's 1892 production of *Sindbad the Sailor*, the *Irish Times* reviewer[20] alludes to this propensity: "By one of those curious circumstances only known in stage experience, the song, 'The Man that broke the bank in Monte Carlo,' is interpolated. . . ." Similarly, a programme for the production of *Robinson Crusoe* at Leinster Hall (29 January 1894) cites the presence in one scene of Lilly May and "her famous imitations of leading music hall singers." The programme for the 26 December 1896 Gaiety pantomime includes in the scene in which Cinderella leaves for the ball "The Aerial Ballet of Doves by the Tonerre Troupe." And at Leinster Hall during Easter of 1896, "Babes in the Wood" appeared along with "Gymnastic Comedians," a "Talented Danseuse," and a "Phenomenal Juvenile Double-Voiced Vocalist."[21]

The critics of music hall in the pantomime disregarded the fact that the newer form gave evidence of the genre's most interesting feature—its ability to adapt to its audience's tastes and to survive by absorbing diverse influences. Instead, Davenport Adams and others of his persuasion felt that the presence of music-hall artistes on the pantomime stage brought into the bourgeois world of the popular theater a vulgar working-class element. For the middle class, the theater has always been a fungus on the tree of culture, a place in which the offensive could easily flourish. Middle-class propriety reared its head to protect its domain but in so doing introduced class tensions and the ever-vexing question of economic inequities. Hence, although Booth asserts that the pantomime "entertained all classes, appealing to the patrons of working and lower-middle-class theatres as much as it did to more socially elevated audiences,"[22] the stage during this era remained a site that two classes sought to control.

Of course, because the pantomime was the one theatrical event of the year designed and guaranteed to keep the theater on its feet for the remainder of the season, the pantomime appealed in no uncertain terms to the bourgeois audience which was its principal economic support. The most enduring successes claimed that nobility of spirit could be measured ultimately by a young man's success in getting ahead financially and at winning his place in a higher class by marriage to a pretty and wealthy girl. The culture's dream of success was thus played out on the stages of Dublin and London every Christmas season to enthusiastic approval. In addition, the preparations for the productions themselves carried the mark of the bourgeois work ethic. Even the Gaiety *Souvenir* emphasizes the employment value of the Christmas productions: "For years past Pantomime has engaged the attention of the local scenic artist and his staff . . . and an army of artificers are employed in King-street working out the countless details the preparations involve." The writer goes on to praise the supervision of Mrs. Michael Gunn, the wife of the Gaiety's manager, who personally supervised "the artistic designing and selection of the costumes for the great stage groups and pageants, which have formed a main feature of the Christmas pieces." Approvingly, the writer notes that "she has been the means of giving lucrative employment to hundreds of humble Dublin girls, engaged by her as seamstresses, etc., in the production of the costumes."[23]

The Gaiety was not alone among pantomime employers; the Royal, the Queen's, and smaller halls also put on Christmas season extravaganzas.[24] Yet the pantos also joined the burlesques and extravaganzas in poking fun at the society which held up these expectations of success and offered this painted and sequined pap. In these plays, it is always the rich, especially those who get their money without working for it, who are made fun of. The capitalist is not liked; he is merely domesticated into the authoritarian father whose hostility appears to be directed not at the worker but at the boy (who happens to be poor) who wants his daughter. For the parent-merchant, the child is a commodity to be exchanged for social and economic advantage; only because it's a panto does he relent and let Dick Whittington have his Alice, and only after Dick has made himself wealthy. Enacting such middle-class tastes and

preoccupations while including lower-class performers, the pantomime revealed the entanglement of socioeconomic issues and theatrical practices.

Topicality in the Pantomime

Both burlesque and pantomime thrived on topical allusions which
were generally satiric barbs at the fads and foibles, fashions and politics of the moment. In the absence of many full scripts from the
pantomimes, the programmes and songbooks of the era, which
were often highly topical, are valuable cultural artifacts that can be
read for evidence of the ideological interplay of the economic and
the political.

In particular, Booth tells us, "The topical allusiveness of so much
nineteenth-century light entertainment meant the insertion in many
an extravaganza and burlesque of a principal topical song."[25] As unlikely as it seems, Bloom himself once contracted to write a topical
song for the Gaiety pantomime, and the passage in *Ulysses* in which
this matter is discussed makes clear the extent to which the pantomime was a social event with significance in many cultural areas.

> What had prevented him from completing a topical song (music by
> R. G. Johnston) on the events of the past, or fixtures for the actual
> years, entitled *If Brian Boru could but come back and see old Dublin now*,
> commissioned by Michael Gunn, lessee of the Gaiety Theatre, 46, 47,
> 48, 49 South King street, and to be introduced into the sixth scene,
> the valley of diamonds, of the second edition (30 January 1893) of
> the grand annual Christmas pantomime *Sinbad the Sailor* (produced
> by R Shelton 26 December 1892, written by Greenleaf Whittier, sce-
> nery by George A. Jackson and Cecil Hicks, costumes by Mrs and
> Miss Whelan under the personal supervision of Mrs Michael Gunn,
> ballets by Jessie Noir, harlequinade by Thomas Otto) and sung by
> Nelly Bouverist, principal girl?

> Firstly, oscillation between events of imperial and of local interest,
> the anticipated diamond jubilee of Queen Victoria (born 1820, ac-
> ceded 1837) and the posticipated opening of the new municipal fish
> market: secondly, apprehension of opposition from extreme circles
> on the questions of the respective visits of Their Royal Highnesses,
> the duke and duchess of York (real) and of His Majesty King Brian
> Boru (imaginary); thirdly, a conflict between professional etiquette

and professional emulation concerning the recent erections of the Grand Lyric Hall on Burgh Quay and the Theatre Royal in Hawkins street: fourthly, distraction resultant from compassion for Nelly Bouverist's non-intellectual, non-political, non-topical expression of countenance and concupiscence caused by Nelly Bouverist's revelations of white articles of non-intellectual, non-political, non-topical underclothing while she (Nelly Bouverist) was in the articles: fifthly, the difficulties of the selection of appropriate music and humorous allusions from *Everybody's Book of Jokes* (1,000 pages and a laugh in every one): sixthly, the rhymes, homophonous and cacophonous, associated with the names of the new lord mayor, Daniel Tallon, the new high sheriff, Thomas Pile and the new solicitorgeneral, Dunbar Plunkett Barton. (U 678–79)

The passage comically suggests that composing a topical song would place the writer at the political and economic center of his society and catch up him or her in the whirl of local history, international celebrations, programmed emotional responses (Bloom's reaction to underclothing), the expansion of popular culture in new venues, the desire for personal aggrandizement, and the lust for personal gratification. The difficulty of writing the ideal topical song evoked here makes it not surprising that on occasion the panto producers failed to meet audience expectations on this score. For example, after he had attended the 1908 Gaiety production of *Robinson Crusoe*, Joseph Holloway wrote, "At once be it said that the pantomime is lacking in [fun?], &, taking songs & it is regrettable that there is no attempt at local [hits?] whatsoever. It might as well be played at the North pole as in Dublin for all the reference there is to the latter in it."[26]

In general, however, the pantos succeeded in getting off at least a few satiric thrusts and genial references to current events. A generic example occurs in the text of *Aladdin or Harlequin and the Wonderful Lamp*, performed at Drury Lane in 1874. In Scene VIII, the Harlequinade proper, we are taken into "The Bright Region of Fanta-see, illuminated by the Rays of the Wonderful Lamp." There, this "bright region" looks very like an ordinary railway station, in which two clowns try to purchase tickets: "FIRST CLOWN goes up to window L., knocks. MAN says, 'Too late', slams the window down again. Business. SECOND CLOWN knocks R., says, 'Please, I want a ticket and a half return for the Suez Canal.' Man says, 'Pshaw!', shuts window nearly on CLOWN's nose. Business. CLOWN says, 'We'll give him the Shah—and his diary too.'" Booth explains, "The Shah of Persia arrived in England in June 1868, and left in July; he published a diary of his tour of Europe that included much praise of England, the country he liked best of all those he visited. In England he was something of a social sensation."[27]

Don Gifford and Robert J. Seidman tell us that "Nasr-ed-Din (d. 1896) made two state visits to England, in June 1873 and July 1889. . . . During the 1889 visit the Shah caught the popular fancy and was 'immortalized' in street songs and as the principal figure in innumerable stories of the sort Bloom recalls."[28] In "Sirens" Bloom thinks, "Night Michael Gunn gave us the box. Tuning up. Shah of Persia liked that best. Remind him of home sweet home. Wiped his nose in curtain too. Custom his country perhaps" (U 284). Just as the pantomime turned to local allusions, so Joyce wove into his narratives topical references that could not be understood by future readers except through historical research; in this way, of course, Joyce saved his fiction from being something that might just as well have been produced at the North Pole. Joyce's persistent topicality violated the canons of much traditional fiction but was a version of what all pantomimists were expected to place on stage every Christmas.

So important an aspect of pantomime fun was local color that some end-of-the-century pantomime playbills from Ireland cite, along with costumiers and property specialists, writers and set-designers, "Local topics by . . ." and "Localised by. . . ." Such writers worked in all kinds of current topics. For example, the *Irish Times* review of the 1892 Gaiety production[29] of *Sindbad* states,

In the dialogue between Sindbad's mother and Tindbad the Tailor is a humorous reference to the present craze the "missing word." For instance, to illustrate it, some fun is derived from these lines:—

Tindbad—Where is your son? Behold my little
　　　　　bill; your cheque will much oblige.
Mrs Sindbad—No doubt it will.
Tindbad—To patches, buttons, braid and sundry
　　　　　　　　　　　　　　　　　stitches,
　　　　　Re-seating sundry pairs of sailors'_____
　　　　　　　　　　　　　　　　　boots.

An allusion to a fad could join strictly theatrical references. The reviewer goes on to report that "Captain M'Turco and Mrs Sindbad
join in a duet—'Mrs Enery 'Awkins,' borrowed from Mr Arthur
Roberts' burlesque, 'Too lovely black-eyed Susan.'"[30]

In addition, a satiric slant marked some productions, such as the
Theatre Royal's *Aladdin* for 1876, which included a song with the
lyrics,

> For those who live in cities,
>   Where mad fashion holds her sway
> You'll see the sort of thing I mean
>   Full twenty times a day.
> Girls with dark hair and chignons fair,
>   Which do not match, alas!

Such gentle criticism of the follies of fashion and urban life was enhanced by explicit criticism of the modern era; the Widow sings a
song which begins, "You naughty men have naughty ways / In these
fast-going naughty days." And a specific local reference occurs in a
song called "It Was Told on the Quiet to Me":

Right bang across the College Park a railway is to go,
Its Terminus in Grafton Street, instead of Westland Row,
The College boys when making up their trigonometry,
Will stuff their ears with cotton wool, that was told on the quiet to me.[31]

Unsophisticated lyrics of this kind characterized the songbooks and
dialogue generally presented in Dublin, the words having been
written to fit various popular tunes, as often as not by people other
than professional playwrights.

In fact, in a special sense, the pantomime spoke for its community. Individually authored, the pantos nonetheless went through
major revision in production, generally still undergoing cutting
after the initial performances. The impact of the nominal author
fades further when one considers the internal repetition and conservative nature of the panto, which constantly revised the same stories
and reworked old gags. Given its communal nature, the pantomime,
like the daily newspaper, mirrored the tastes, topics, and tendencies
of an entire era. Directly in touch with ideological forces and stratifi-
cations, the pantomime communicated the preoccupations of demotic culture.

A clear example of this coming together of tradition and topicality occurs in the Queen's Theatre's production of the ever-popular *Mother Goose* (1912), in which Mother Goose is a suffragette. Her daughter Jill asks Colin what a suffragette is, and he replies, "A lady who has never been kissed." Because Mother Goose was played by Mr. Robb Wilton, the humor of his/her being a feminist would be pronounced even without this consensus statement in opposition to votes for women. When Mother Goose gives a speech in favor of suffragism, addressing the "Women of Ireland," she says, "Wait till we get into Parliament, wait. You may get tired of waiting, but wait. Won't there be a revolution. Talk about the debates, fancy me and Mr. Asquith having an all-night sitting. There's young Winston Churchill, too; my word, if I catch him departing from the perpendicular. But the burning question of the hour is, shall women vote?" After some banter passes between Mother Goose and the crowd, the police chase them all away.[32] Later, the pantomime includes gags directed against the police, their presence in the script suggesting the social tensions that the R. I. C. generated in a politically charged Ireland, which in this production were safely displaced onto the highly visible British women's movement.[33]

In another example, the theme of Irish nationalism characterizes a Dublin production of 1888 entitled *Harlequin Bryan O'Lynn or The Sleeping Beauty of Erin*. There, we find five chief Fairy Queens by the name of Hibernia ("The Worker of all Good"), Liberty, Britannia, Caledonia, and Wales.[34] That Hibernia was the chief Fairy Queen points, as does the effort at an Irish motif for the pantomime, to nationalism, however even-handed the writers were in including Britannia among the other Fairies. Further, for a Harlequinade scene in an "Irish and American Meat Market," the action is described on the programme as follows: "Rival Firms—Sad end of the Bobby." No doubt one of the six policemen listed among the dramatis personae met a bad end to create a surely humorous, though clearly political, statement. Significantly, this pantomime was produced not at the Gaiety or Royal but at the National Music Hall, a less commercially successful enterprise than sister theaters in the city.

But even the more commercial theaters allowed their pantos some social content, however inappropriate to their audience. In the songbook to the Theatre Royal's 1902 *Sleeping Beauty* appears "A Pattern to the World," a curious tune that might be taken to signify the utter lack of any popular desire for Home Rule. The song suggests a total identification of the Irish actors, singers, and audience with their English government.[35]

> Brave hearts everywhere, proud of the flag they are under,
>   Ready to face the common foe—
> What though enemies guns volley, and volley and thunder,
>   Fear is the word they do not know.
> Some say the glories of the olden days,
>   Never shall be;
> Well, take it as a joke, and when the ravens croak,
>   Refer them to our brothers o'er the sea—
> Our brave colonial boys across the sea.
>
> REFRAIN.
>
> We can depend on Young Australia,
>   On India, and Canada,
> For they have proved themselves, in Africa,
>   A patriotic pattern to the world.
>
> War clouds darken the earth; rumours of desperate dangers
>   Spring on the startled ears of man;
> Our land, so we are told, soon will be govern'd by strangers—
>   Britons no longer in the van.
> Such foolish notions, born of jealousy,
>   Englishmen despise.
> The other nations fret, and envy us, you bet,
>   Because we know the way to colonise.
>
> REFRAIN—We can depend on Young Australia, etc.
>
> Dear Australian boys, here's to your valour and glory;
>   New Zealand, here's our love to you;
> Shake hands, Canada's sons, long we shall treasure the story,
>   How you have fought, and still would do.
> India, the Englishman is proud of you,
>   Swarthy boys and brave,
> Supported by you all, our colours cannot fall,
>   You've proved you do not fear the soldier's grave—
> For Motherland you'll risk the soldier's grave.
>
> REFRAIN—We can depend on Young Australia, etc.

Certainly there are substantial ironies in an Irish audience's celebrating the British knack at colonizing. A far cry from "The Wearing of the Green," this song comes wholly out of the British viewpoint and yet was the finale to a pantomime in Dublin. It is interesting that the *Irish Times* reviewer, who remarks on the audience's general appreciation of the "time-honoured precedent of introducing Dublin names of streets and localities to give point to dialogues," says of the panto's songs only that they are "not a very remarkable collection."[36]

Like *Sleeping Beauty*, the Royal's 1904 *Dick Whittington* also played the patriotic card in its finale, "The Anglo-Saxon Language":

> As you sail this wide world over, you'll infallibly discover
> There's a language that is known to old and young;
> And wherever you may roam, you'll find yourself at home,
> If you only speak the Anglo-Saxon tongue.
> You'll hear Regent Street at Malta, Bonnie Scotch at old Gibraltar,
> You can hear the "coster" out at Singapore;
> Welsh in India, no finer, and real Irish out in China,
> And the lot combined aboard a man-o'-war—
> You can make yourself at home, by jingo,
> If you only speak the Anglo-Saxon lingo.[37]

Joseph Holloway, who reports on this production in his diary, mentions that it originated in Belfast; perhaps this fact accounts for what Holloway calls the "'jingo' sentiments introduced here & there in the pantomime," which, he says, "were passed over unnoticed by the audience."[38]

Evidently, this onstage treatment of England was not unusual. In 1900 the "Correspondence" column of *The Leader* included a letter from a Kilkenny resident who had attended a recent performance at the Gaiety of *The Messenger Boy*; he or she complains, "Throughout the play it was taken for granted that we were an English audience. . . . at the end about fifty females, attired in English military uniform, marched up and down the stage, to the strains of a song, which voiced England's joyous expectation of the return of her soldiers from South Africa. Some few tried to express their disapproval, but the majority behaved like a crowd of intolerant Cockneys."[39]

Patriotism, of a sort, was joined in the panto by economic concerns. The 1902 *Sleeping Beauty* songbook includes a number that obviously refers to the presence of socialist agitators in the British Isles.

On very clever principles we're working nowadays,
The question how to equalize is getting quite a craze;
Some people vow the wealth of all the dukes and millionaires
Should all be called together and dealt out in equal shares.
Now, why should one man be allowed to roll in so much wealth,
While others have to work and slave, and dislocate their health?
Let's down with ev'rything that's up, no matter what the class—
Let ev'rybody toe the line, and call in all the brass.

CHORUS.

> Share it among the lot—share it among the lot!
>   All the wealth of the millionaires
>   Should be divided in equal shares;
> And when a fellow's "done in" his share,
>   Whether he's careful or not,
> We'll call all the money together again,
>   And share it among the lot!

The next two stanzas cite the case of a harried family man who, unable to afford a medically prescribed trip to the seaside for the whole family, goes by himself and fills up bottles of sea air which he then shares at home; finally, the singer decides that single men should invade the Sultan of Morocco's harem and share that too among the lot.[40] Satiric and sly, the song nonetheless indicates in the midst of its ridicule a popular attention to the unequal distribution of wealth, to the ever-present music hall theme of the poor man who can't make ends meet, and to the barely masked equation of the Sultan's wives with merchandise.[41]

In fact, the nineteenth-century pantomime was preoccupied with the world of goods. Booth fills in the background to this characteristic concern, averring that with the prominence of the Londoner Joseph Grimaldi as the eighteenth-century's great Clown, the focus of the Harlequinade shifted from rural to urban life.

Not surprisingly, therefore, this kind of pantomime dramatized, though confusedly and undiscriminatingly, aspects of contemporary life such as changes in fashion, technological development and new inventions, economic questions, the war against France, and a wide range of topical social matters, a few significant, more trivial and ephemeral. What is immediately striking about the social context of the harlequinade is the extent to which *goods* (from a profusion of *shops*), *things*, and *objects* motivate the characters and determine the nature of the comedy.[42]

Booth speaks here of Regency harlequinade, but the lengthened opening of the later nineteenth century retained and developed many of these tendencies, the pantomime's topical nature making it a magnet for changes in cultural interests and social mores. Thus, Booth remarks of nineteenth-century theater, "Pantomimes and extravaganzas were very aware of the railway age and the industrial scene. Factories, warehouses, docks, and railway stations appear in pantomime scenes." Such events are alluded to in "Eumaeus" when Bloom recalls: " . . . Ludwig, *alias* Ledwidge, when he occupied the boards of the Gaiety when Michael Gunn was identified with the management in the *Flying Dutchman*, a stupendous success, and his host of admirers came in large numbers, everyone simply flocking to hear him though ships of any sort, phantom or the reverse, on the stage usually fell a bit flat as also did trains . . ." (U 636).

Confirming the focus on commerce, Richard Southern prints a drawing of a set, "a typical scene in a shop," from the Drury Lane pantomime of 1851, *Harlequin Hogarth; or, The Two London 'Prentices*: several characters occupy a balconied room, the walls of which are lined with items for sale.[43] As Franco Moretti has rightly observed, "Circe" is "the unsurpassed literary representation of commodity fetishism"; in that episode goods and objects assume animated roles and appear to direct action.[44] That the primary referent of "Circe" is the pantomime accounts for this fact as much or more than the demands of expressionistic form, the usual explanation of the peculiar animations of the Nighttown episode. If anything, expressionism, like *Ulysses* and the pantomime, was informed by the capitalist ethos that, perhaps more than anything else, characterizes the modern era.

One obvious indicator of that concern is the kind of advertisement used on theater playbills (see Plate 5, the programme for the first edition of the Gaiety's December 1892 production of *Sindbad the Sailor*, for the second edition of which Bloom was commissioned to write a topical song). Covering every bit of space not filled with information about the play, these ads lined up on both sides of the Irish political front. On the programme for the Gaiety's 1889 production of *Aladdin or, The Scamp and the Lamp* is an ad that runs

"Parliament House. McNamara, Confectioner, Parliament Street. The only Parliament House in Ireland since 1800." In this witty notice, on the order of Bloom's House of Keyes effort, the plan for Home Rule colors the economic arrangement being solicited. On the other hand, some ads reinforced the Anglophile songs performed in the pantos; examples include "The Dublin Artesian Mineral Water Company, Limited, first-class Mineral Waters, To be had in all the Bars of this Theatre, as supplied to His Excellency the Lord Lieutenant and both Houses of Parliament,"[45] and "J. Thornton, fruit merchant and florist To H. R. H. the Prince of Wales, and Lord Lieutenant, 63, Grafton Street, Dublin. . . . The only Fruit Merchant in Ireland warranted to supply H. R. H. the Prince of Wales."[46] Joining the commercial exploitation of a political situation that was rapidly becoming untenable, comic reference to politics showed up on the same programme as the mineral water ad. Scene 4 of the Gaiety's 1888 production of *Cinderella*, which takes place "In the Baron's Castle," is described using the double meaning of Home Rule that Joyce also capitalizes on in *Ulysses*: "Thisbe composes—Clorinda objects—a fight—peace—prospects of dinner—a financial statement—Home Rule."[47] Appealing to the same middle-class market, advertisers and producers of either persuasion felt free to use politics as a sales device; whatever the school, the cultural consensus, then as now, was that business is business.

A final characteristic of the panto that bears mention is the playfully reflexive use of outrageous puns in the description of characters. For example, a character in the Queen's fifth pantomime (26 December 1888), *The Fair One with the Golden Locks*, who is listed on the programme simply as an "Immortal" called "Adventure," is described in a chiasmus worthy of Lenehan as "a *roving imp*—past *improving*." A Gaiety programme (26 December, n.d.) from the period for *Robinson Crusoe* lists "Parrot" as having "a fine *parrot tone* voice." The Gaiety programme for *Cinderella* for 26 December 1888 speaks of the character Thisbe as "Another *elder* sister far from *yewth*," and of the Fairy Queen says, "Being fond of *change* is naturally a *sovereign*." Finally, two characters from the Gaiety's *Ali Baba and the Forty Thieves* (26 December 1890) are described on the programme as "Two young Gentlemen from across the seas—Who seize everything they sees." Such verbal devices no doubt appealed to Joyce and influenced the verbal comedy of *Ulysses* and *Finnegans Wake*. On the love of wordplay in the music hall and popular theater, Peter Davison comments, "Often the playing with words is embarrassingly puerile . . . but it has helped to keep alive an awareness of language and a delight in words . . . which the legitimate drama had not, on the whole, succeeded in doing."[48] For Joyce and his contemporaries, the pantomime significantly conjoined politics, socioeconomics, and verbal wit. This historical thematic collocation informs my analysis of "Circe" in chapter 4. As a brief appendix to this discussion of the pantomime and its social content, I address below three specific pantomimes that Joyce refers to in *Ulysses* and *Finnegans Wake*—two of them actual productions in the Dublin theater, one a fictional production in the *Wake*.

The Pantomime in Joyce: *Turko*; "Mick, Nick, and the Maggies"; *Dick Whittington*

Although not many Irish actors were as well known as those whose venue was the British stage, Dublin did occasionally draw and hold an especially fine performer like Edward Royce. No less a critic than George Bernard Shaw found him a "brilliant harlequin" as well as a "first-rate burlesque actor and dancer."[49] H. G. Hibbert, in *A Playgoer's Memories*, tells us that Royce was part of "the famous Gaiety quartet" in London and that Royce had been with that company for over forty years, having been on tour for the London Gaiety,[50] and Hibbert includes a picture of the actor in stage Oriental pantaloons, embroidered velvet vest, and curled moustache. Bloom's early morning Oriental reverie includes a reference to a "big man, Turko the terrible, seated crosslegged, smoking a coiled pipe" (U 57); in "Circe" Major Tweedy appears "*moustached like Turko the terrible*" (U 596—see Plate 4). For people of Bloom's station, the panto provided not only pleasant memories but also points of reference for processing the unknown and projecting fantasy.

It is, of course, this same Royce that Stephen thinks of in "Telemachus" when he recalls his mother's few joys: "She heard old Royce sing in the pantomime of Turko the terrible and laughed with others when he sang:

> *I am the boy*
> *That can enjoy*
> *Invisibility.* (U 10)

PLATE 4. Popular images of the Orient surfaced in Joyce's Ireland not only in bazaars like the one portrayed in "Araby," but also in numerous songs, plays, and pantomines. This picture shows Edward Royce (standing) as part of the Gaiety Quartet in London (from H. G. Hibbert, *A Playgoer's Memories* [London: Grant Richards, 1920], p. 57), but it could just as easily describe the "Turco" that Bloom and Stephen think of during their morning cogitations. For them and apparently for much of the mass audience in Joyce's Ireland, the East suggests beneficent magic, melancholy thoughts, and a mystery no less compelling for its two-dimensionality.

In the 1873 *Irish Times* review of this pantomime, we are informed that *Turco the Terrible* (Joyce's "Turko" is a variant spelling) did involve becoming invisible. King Turco, a melancholy monarch who wants everyone else to be unhappy along with him, plots to thwart the love of Prince Amabel and his daughter. Acquiring a white rose that magically causes invisibility, Turco uses it to eavesdrop, unseen, on his courtiers. The reviewer states, "Mr Royce was very amusing as King Turco; his get-up was extremely grotesque, and he infused an amount of spirit into his part that had much to do with the success of the pantomime. His dancing was very fine, his attitudes irresistibly funny, and his singing of the several very comic songs incidental to his monarchical character was most successful, and produced so much laughter that he was repeatedly encored."[51]

There is no mention here of the "Invisibility" song itself, but in the Gaiety's twenty-fifth anniversary *Souvenir* we are told that in a burlesque called *Amy Robsart* (Eldred's Company, 1872, Gaiety) Royce "produced a great impression. His song 'Invisibility' is still remembered. It was to the striking success he achieved in this part that he owed the special engagement to fill the title part in the pantomime of the year following. . . . in Dec., '73, we had what proved to be one of the best pantomimes ever put upon the Dublin stage, namely, 'Turko the Terrible'. . . . Who can forget Ted Royce's inimitable performance, his quaint humour, his unmatched skill as a dancer?"[52] No doubt Royce's "Invisibility" was transferred from its musical-burlesque origin to encore in *Turco*. Like the music hall songs that called into the pantomime performance a theatrical world beyond the dramatic context at hand, Royce's using the same song in two works provides evidence of the exaggerated overt theatrical reflexivity of the period, as does his role in 1892 as Captain M'Turco in the Gaiety's[53] *Sindbad the Sailor* (Plate 5). Like Joyce's works, which forever quote themselves to the consternation of many readers, the theater of Joyce's day was highly and self-consciously intertextual. Melodrama begat burlesque, pantomime begat extravaganza, pantomime quoted burlesque, and music hall interpenetrated the lot. In Dublin, where a common man such as Bloom knew and appreciated the various traditional and local renditions of even more sophisticated material (he is familiar with *Martha, Hamlet, Maritana, La Sonnambula*, and the like), that quality epitomized the theatrical. Joyce exploits this intertextuality of form in composing characters, showing the presence in their thought and behavior of material that emanates from the self-quoting stage.

A similar intertextuality informs *Finnegans Wake*, II, i. As part of the "Mime of Mick, Nick, and the Maggies," Joyce included late in composition a playbill,[54] which is the only part of the "mime" to retain its shape as a formal allusion to the theater. Not until the end of II, i does the narrative complete the theatrical frame which the playbill begins; the applause (FW 257–58) that marks the end of the mime helps us to see the domestic experience of HCE and family as a performance indebted to the conventions of melodrama, pantomime, and burlesque. Of course, that performance roughly follows the dramatic conflict outlined in the playbill, in which Glugg and Chuff compete for the attention of Izod and the Floras, but the playbill also presents a prefabricated form that the story resists when it passes beyond the conventional story of love and competition into exposure of the economics of sexual relations. That is, the girls' choice of Chuff as their man is based on a vision of his rising from "desk jobduty" to "a bank midland mansioner" (FW 235.11–12). During the Mime, the voice of someone very like Gerty McDowell suggests that money is necessary because "exceedingly nice girls can strike exceedingly bad times unless so richtly chosen's by (what though of riches he have none and hope dashes hope on his heart's horizon) to gar their great moments greater" (FW 252.22–25). The German *richt* provides the association of rich and right, so that the drama's morality concurs with the economic bias of Joyce's culture. The discrepancies between playbill and plot thus emphasize that the former is essentially an advertisement, and Joyce's elaboration of it into a parodic commentary on the major popular dramatic modes in Dublin highlights the commodification of the theater in this city of dramophiles.

The playbill reveals the indebtedness of the Mime to both melodrama and pantomime. On the one hand, detective melodrama is represented in the story, which is "adopted from the Ballymooney Bloodriddon Murther by Bluechin Blackdillain" (FW 219.19–20). On the other, although some commentators have assumed the Mime to be of the silent variety, the very different Christmas pantomime has its part too, as is indicated in the "humpteen dumpteen revivals" (FW 219.15) of the play; "Humpty Dumpty" was a popular panto character. The villain Glugg is "the bold bad bleak boy of

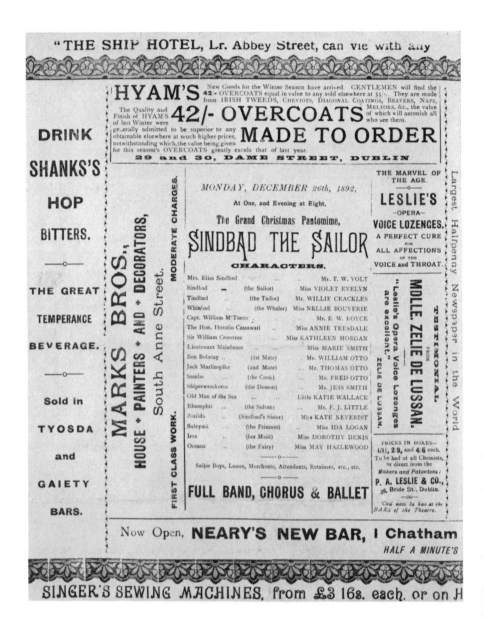

PLATE 5. The manuscript collection of Trinity College, Dublin, includes the original of this pantomime programme. In *Sindbad the Sailor*, Edward Royce played the role of Captain M'Turco, and Sindbad is joined, here as in the "Ithaca" episode, by Tinbad the Tailor and Whinbad the Whaler. Employing the

verbal play and intertextual referentiality characteristic of the Christmas pantomime, Joyce created in his fiction webs of significance that exposed the cultural impact of popular dramatic performances. (Programme reproduced by the kind permission of the Board of Trinity College, Dublin.)

the storybooks" (FW 219.24) and his rival Chuff "the fine frank fairhaired fellow of the fairytales" (FW 220.12–13), both characters having derived from the world typically presented on the Christmas stage.[55] Further, the playbill lists "Dances arranged by Harley Quinn and Coollimbeina," a "Pageant of Past History" (FW 221.25, 18–19), and a "Magnificent Transformation Scene showing the Radium Wedding of Neid and Moorning and the Dawn of Peace, Pure, Perfect and Perpetual, Waking the Weary of the World" (FW 222.17–20).

Again, Joyce's playbill evokes the pantomime in its most degraded or at least most commercial form, that of sheer advertisement. Of course, the playbill announces that to see the play requires payment: "Entrancings: gads, a scrab; the quality, one large shilling. . . . Jampots, rinsed porters, taken in token" (FW 219.3–4,6). As Roland McHugh tells us, in England, children were told they could pay their admission fees with jampots,[56] a tradition taken over in the *Wake*'s Dublin. Similarly, "rinsed porters" can be exchanged for tickets, a detail that alludes not only to porter bottles but also to the film family that in III, iv of the *Wake* substitutes for the Earwickers; one can barter with a version of the self purveyed by the theatrical institution that exacts payment and does so according to class (the "gads"/gods vs. "the quality"). Yet within the playbill we find conflicting evidence on the question of commodification and class difference; the play takes place, after all, in the "Feenichts [fee-nichts] Playhouse" (FW 219.2).

In addition to alluding to the socioeconomic implications of theater commodification, Joyce's playbill refers to the institutional tensions that marked all of Dublin's popular culture. This reference occurs when the playbill claims that the show is "Newly billed for each wickeday perfumance" (FW 219.4–5). Constantly under pressure from various sources to maintain or enhance the moral value of its shows and continually experimenting with the easing of informal but nonetheless effective censorship lines, the theatrical institution was thought by its religious opponents to make each performance day into a "wickeday." But the playbill comically reverses the occasional antipathy of church and stage in its "nightly redistribution of parts and players by the puppetry producer and daily dubbing of ghosters, with the benediction of the Holy Genesius Archimimus and under the distinguished patronage of their Elderships the

Oldens" (FW 219.7–10). No religious censorship in the offing (although the playbill does state, "By arraignment, childream's hours, expercatered" [FW 219.5–6]), the performance has the blessing of God, the Arch-Mime himself, a Punch-and-Judy puppeteer who makes reader and character alike respond to his pulling of strings. The god of the theater, however, is indistinguishable from the playbill's version of HCE, the "Hump" who is played by "Mr Makeall Gone" (FW 220.24). Creator and destroyer in this dramatic universe is the Gaiety's manager, Michael Gunn. That the *Wake*'s theater finds its god in an entrepreneur explicitly states the connection of art and economics that "Circe" suggests.

In fact, because of its rags-to-riches content, the most important pantomime for *Ulysses* is *Dick Whittington*, which more than any other panto stands at the heart of Bloom's experience in "Circe." Coincidentally, that pantomime was produced at the Theatre Royal on 26 January 1904, and the extant songbook provides useful information about the social and economic interests of Dubliners reflected in the production. Based on the life of the late fourteenth-century and early fifteenth-century mayor of London and folklore hero, this simple tale has taken on variations in many countries,[57] yet the general plot lines are clear. In the Theatre Royal version, a poor boy from the country travels to London to seek his fortune, taking with him his best friend, a resourceful cat. On the verge of starving, he is given a chance to prove himself by working for Alderman Fitzwarren, who owns stores stocking every conceivable good. Dick is a fine salesperson, but owing to an error in working the till, he must go to sea, leaving behind his beloved Alice, the Alderman's daughter. Judging from the songbook as well as from other versions of the story, I surmise that Dick arrives at a distant land and accepts the hospitality of a vizier. When Dick and company save the country, through the help of Dick's cat, from an invasion of rats, the vizier is so pleased that he rewards Dick handsomely. Dick returns, an entrepreneurial hero, and reestablishes Fitzwarren as both alderman and wealthy man, in the bargain winning Alice as his wife. As the bells of London had told Dick long before, he will go on to become the Lord Mayor of London three times over.

The fundamental focus of the pantomime as it was produced in Dublin in 1904 is socioeconomic. Early on, Dick and company sing a number together:

Dick—I thought to find Tom Tiddler's ground in this stately London
   town,
   But I found I'd have to work all day to earn a modest "brown."
Fitz.—Quite right, my boy, the way we swells make up our little pile
   Is letting others do the work, and watch it grow the while.

           . . . .

Dick—I will not be afraid, on entering into trade,
Alice—You must;
   The kicks are more than ha'pence when first you go to work;
   But set to with a will, and never rob the till,
   They won't be very cruel if you never shirk.

           . . . .

Fitz.—I won't hurt you for it, I'm a most agreeable man;
   You can please your noble self, while you get me heaps of pelf.
Jack—(mimicking) I won't hurt you, but I'll have a jolly good try,
   You'd best remember, my beaming boy, you're in my eye.[58]

Later, when Dick is thought to have committed the ultimate capitalist crime of robbery, there occurs a number in which Fitzwarren,
the Captain, and the Boatswain talk over the situation, the latter
two averring that "Everybody is on the fake, / Seeing exactly how
much they can make. / When they think your back is turned, they're
at their trickery." Even the Emperor agrees with this assessment of
modern business life:

      To make a living in our days, it's true,
      Lots of funny things one has to do;
      To "Number One" we all have well to look,
      And every business man must know his book.
      In buying aught one must be wide awake,
      For things aren't always what they seem to be:
      For instance, take a grocer, now, who sells
      A splendid brand of coffee at the price of one and three.
      A splendid brand of coffee grand,
      Imported from some foreign land;
      A curious name to make it fiz,
      You think it's Indian coffee, but this is what it is—
      A lot of dust, some roasted peas,
      The scrapings off the rind of cheese,
      The filing from a rusty bar,
      A few dead flies, and there you are.

Of course, the reason that Dick is supposed to have restored wealth to his employer and gained it, along with a wife, for himself, is that he is noble and good—a country boy whose honor wins the day. Indeed, one of his songs argues, with a touch of Gilbert and Sullivan:

> Don't judge a man by the kind of coat he wears,
> No one knows the value of his clothes, and no one cares;
> You'll find that true blue gentlemen are seldom ornamental men—
> And a man's a man in spite of any clothes he wears.
> . . . .
> Hearts are trumps when they're sincere, outside show is but veneer,
> By the poet we are told all that glitters is not gold.

No doubt his audience accepted Dick's truistic assertion that "Noble hearts, we must confess, often beat 'neath ragged dress." Nonetheless, the society that accepted these ideological viewpoints also accepted the fact that Alice could be (if not ought to be) sold to the highest bidder. In Samuel French's Basic Pantomime of *Dick Whittington*, Alice, like many panto heroines, is supposed to marry, on her father's request, a wealthy merchant's son, until Dick comes back and proves himself worthy of her.

Few if any pantomimes left a hero as poor at the end as at the beginning; the culture's values dictated that he gain cash and bride in tandem. In the 1904 *Dick Whittington*, the initial encounters between the successful Fitzwarren and the down-and-out Dick speak for contemporary class tensions, but these realities bow to the triumphant middle-class notion of order when Dick follows in Fitzwarren's footsteps as businessperson and politico. It is obvious that the middle-class ethic of business success won out; in fact, probably the panto sustained its success throughout the industrialization of the modern era precisely because the old fairy tales and nursery rhymes easily adapted to the conveyance of these sentiments. In many ways, *Dick Whittington* is *the* cultural myth, in which the contradictions of poverty and wealth are mediated and class tensions resolved by the elevation of the already deserving hero. Although this pantomime is not a specific structural "source" for "Circe," it embodies the social blueprint for that episode in that Bloom's transformations chart the reconciliation in a single dramatic character of the desires of various classes.

Further, the importance of *Dick Whittington* in Anglo-Irish popular life makes it significant that "Circe" includes occasional specific references to the story, particularly to the social-climbing fantasy which is a cultural topos that Bloom obviously appreciates. Early in Dick's adventures, he decides that there is no hope for him in London, and he begins to return to the place of his birth. On his way out of town, he hears the city bells call out to him, and in "Circe" the same thing happens to Bloom. A workman making a "stump speech," Bloom hears "The Chimes" advise, "Turn again, Leopold! Lord Mayor of Dublin!" (U 478).[59] Immediately, Bloom becomes an alderman, who delivers his program of reform and is acclaimed by his audience. Because Dick traditionally rises to power through his work for Alderman Fitzwarren, Bloom blends the roles of authority figure and son.[60]

Moreover, the theme of commerce links *Dick Whittington* and "Circe." In the Gaiety's 1894 production, written by J. M. Lowry, the final scene before the "Grand Transformation" is called "View of the River Thames" and includes a "Procession of Trades. 1. POPLIN WEAVERS. 2. FAN MAKERS. 3. LACE MAKERS. 4. FRUITERERS. 5. MINERAL WATER MAKERS. 6. WATCH MAKERS. 7. FISHMONGERS. 8. FLORISTS. 9. POULTERERS. 10. POTTERS. 11. DAIRYMAIDS. 12. SADDLERS. 13. BACON CURERS. 14. JEWELLERS. 15. BREWERS. 16. DISTILLERS." No doubt the trades displayed in the pantomime's well-loved device of the procession, one that Joyce also employs more than once in "Circe," are not exactly what Dick Whittington would have encountered in London. These jobs, evidently arranged in order of increasing importance and, judging by the programme, supplying some highly visible advertisement for local tradespeople,[61] represent Dublin businesses more than London's manufacturers.

In "Circe," Joyce gives us processions that reflect as directly as the one in the Royal production the social conditions and interests of the era. For instance, when giving his political speech in the role of alderman and well on his way to becoming emperor, Bloom has his harangue broken off by "Prolonged applause" and the following parade:

The van of the procession appears headed by John Howard Parnell, city marshal, in a chessboard tabard, the Athlone Poursuivant and

Ulster King of Arms. They are followed by the Right Honourable Joseph Hutchinson, lord mayor of Dublin, his lordship the lord mayor of Cork, their worships the mayors of Limerick, Galway, Sligo and Waterford, twentyeight Irish representative peers, sirdars, grandees and maharajahs bearing the cloth of estate, the Dublin Metropolitan Fire Brigade, the chapter of the saints of finance in their plutocratic order of precedence, the bishop of Down and Connor, His Eminence Michael cardinal Logue, archbishop of Armagh, primate of all Ireland, His Grace, the most reverend Dr William Alexander, archbishop of Armagh, primate of all Ireland, the chief rabbi, the presbyterian moderator, the heads of the baptist, anabaptist, methodist and Moravian chapels and the honorary secretary of the society of friends. After them march the guilds and trades and trainbands with flying colours: coopers, bird fanciers, millwrights, newspaper canvassers, law scriveners, masseurs, vintners, trussmakers, chimney sweeps, lard refiners, tabinet and poplin weavers, farriers, Italian warehousemen, church decorators, bootjack manufacturers, undertakers, silk mercers, lapidaries, salesmasters, corkcutters, assessors of fire losses, dyers and cleaners, export bottlers, fellmongers, ticketwriters, heraldic seal engravers, horse repository hands, bullion brokers, cricket and archery outfitters, riddlemakers, egg and potato factors, hosiers and glovers, plumbing contractors. After them march gentlemen of the bed chamber, Black Rod, Deputy Garter, Gold Stick, the master of horse, the lord great chamberlain, the earl marshal, the high constable carrying the sword of state, saint Stephen's iron crown, the chalice and bible. (U 480)

Fritz Senn has pointed out to me that all of the jobs cited in this passage, even that of "riddlemaker," appear in the list of trades in the 1904 *Thom's Directory*—all, that is, except for Bloom's position of newspaper canvasser. Dublin's social spectrum, which is reproduced here and from which Bloom is forever excluded, prominently includes the military, religious, economic, and political hierarchies, and suggests the superstructural competition of church and state.

In addition, the platitudes of much Circean dialogue, especially of Bloom's speech and the responses to it, echo the popular as clearly as does Bloom's Whittingtonian marriage to a woman of high birth. Having "repudiated" his "*former morganatic spouse,*" "Leopold the First" pronounces his horse "Grand Vizier" and takes to wife the "princess Selene, the splendour of night" (U 483, 482). Like Alice Fitzwarren, this panto-styled princess is a political and economic cipher, an emblem of power. Bloom's ambitions, however, are superficial; they pour out of readily available popular scripts, not out of a strictly personal unconscious. Bloom's designs are merely the hopeful financial fantasies embodied in a children's pantomime.

Both the "Mime of Mick, Nick, and the Maggies" and "Circe" almost eliminate, at least as coherent story lines, the fairy-tale narratives on which popular theater in Joyce's day thrived. In their place, Joyce's texts produce scenes that call up dramatic stereotypes in order to make their ideological content the focus of the fiction. The meshing of cultural components normally kept at a greater distance from one another stresses their coagency as well as the reinforcement of socioeconomic conditions by theatrically transmitted roles that speak the ideological conditions of their making.

NOTES

1. Kenner also suggests that the purgations required by Stephen and Bloom need "Aristotle's prescription"—a play. See *Ulysses* (London: Allen & Unwin, 1980), pp. 118–19.

2. Kenner cites Shakespeare, *Faust*, and Flaubert, as well as the panto (*Ulysses*, p. 119).

3. In *The Semiotics of Theatre and Drama* (London: Methuen, 1980), Keir Elam says that the "performance text" as a whole may be seen as a "macro-sign" (p. 7).

4. See Patrick McCarthy's discussion of "Circe" as narrative, "Non-Dramatic Illusion in 'Circe,'" in *Joyce & Paris: 1902 . . . 1920—1940 . . . 1975: Papers from the Fifth International James Joyce Symposium*, II, ed. J. Aubert & M. Jolas (Paris: Editions du C.N.R.S., 1979), 23–26. I disagree with his position that most critics have viewed "Circe" as drama and that the episode "is narration masquerading as drama" (p. 25). To my knowledge, no one has yet recognized the dramatic form of the episode as iconic, signifying, and ideological. Yet "Circe" is less a narrative than a dramatic text differentially related to its narrative context. Given this fact, I would emphasize Ruth Amossy's position, "Contemporary research views the theater not as a literary discourse among many others, but as a global system integrating in its own ways a series of semiotic subsystems." See "Semiotics and Theater: By Way of Introduction," *Poetics Today* 2 (Spring 1981), 5.

5. Susan Bassnett-McGuire, "An Introduction to Theatre Semiotics," *Theatre Quarterly* 10 (1980), 51–52.

6. Elam, pp. 133–4, 108–9.

7. Ibid., pp. 114–15.

8. Throughout, I retain all italics when quoting stage directions from "Circe."

9. Michael Booth, ed., *Hiss the Villain: Six English and American Melodramas* (New York: Benjamin Blom, 1967), p. 9.

10. Cf. U 767: "every two minutes tipping me there and looking away hes a bit daft I think I saw him after trying to get near two stylishdressed ladies outside Switzers window at the same little game I recognised him on the moment the face and everything but he didnt remember me."

11. Michael R. Booth, ed., *English Plays of the Nineteenth Century*, vol. V: *Pantomimes, Extravaganzas, and Burlesques* (Oxford: Clarendon, 1976), p. 57.

12. "Early nineteenth-century pantomime directly descended, not only from the traditions of *commedia dell'arte* as they had evolved for centuries, but also from the distinctively English pantomime of the eighteenth century, an amalgam of serious scenes from classical and modern legend or fable with unrelated harlequinade episodes depicting the love of Harlequin and Columbine, their unsuccessful pursuit by the parent or guardian figure, Pantaloon, and his assistants, and the tricks and transformations wrought along the way by the magic powers of Harlequin's bat" (Booth, *English Plays*, p. 2). In "Circe," Buck Mulligan's costume of "*particoloured jester's dress of puce and yellow and clown's cap with curling bell*" (U 580) alludes to the traditional outfits of both Harlequin and Clown.

13. R. J. Broadbent, *A History of Pantomime* (1901; rpt. New York: Benjamin Blom, 1964), pp. 174, 197.

14. Ibid., p. 221.

15. Booth, *English Plays*, p. 53.

16. Mander and Mitchenson date the phasing out of the "Big Heads" in London from the 1860s on (Mander and Mitchenson, p. 30).

17. *Souvenir*, p. 24. Citing Thomas E. Connolly, James S. Atherton says that Joyce had a copy of this volume and that he "probably" used it in writing *Finnegans Wake*. See *The Books at the Wake: A Study of Literary Allusions in James Joyce's* Finnegans Wake, expanded ed. (Mamaroneck, N.Y.: Appel, 1974), p. 151.

18. Quoted in Mander and Mitchenson, p. 35, from *The Theatre*, February 1882.

19. Booth, *English Plays*, pp. 59–60.

20. *Irish Times*, 27 December 1892, p. 7, col. 5.

21. Advertisement in the Gaiety programme for 9 April 1896.

22. Booth, *English Plays*, p. 2.

23. *Souvenir*, p. 24.

24. Atherton says that Joyce probably went to the Gaiety for pantos. For

those who wanted their fix of popular culture closer to the source, there was (in 1904 at least) a presentation in the Rotunda of the Irish Animated Company's "BIOSCOPE Living PICTURES," including "All the London Successes" such as the then current pantomime "Puss in Boots," while the Empire Palace Theatre had a variety show which included a "Beautifully Arranged Pantomime Absurdity, 'Hilarity'" by Fred Karno's Troupe (National Library of Ireland Manuscript 12073 [Holloway papers], clipping from unidentified newspaper, [15 January 1904?]).

25. Booth, *English Plays*, p. 465.

26. Joseph Holloway, "Impressions of a Dublin Playgoer," July-December 1908, December 26 entry, National Library of Ireland MS. 1806ii.

27. Booth, *English Plays*, pp. 370 and 461n. This version of *Aladdin*, which Booth prints in full, was written by Edward Litt Leman Blanchard.

28. Don Gifford and Robert J. Seidman, *Notes for Joyce: An Annotation of James Joyce's* Ulysses (New York: Dutton, 1974), entry 280:4.

29. "The Gaiety Pantomime," *Irish Times*, 27 December 1892, p. 7, col. 5.

30. This burlesque appears to refer to Charles Coborn's music hall song "Two Lovely Black Eyes" as well as to an original play. Booth states that throughout the nineteenth century, "almost every really successful melodrama, opera, and 'drama' was spiritedly and usually promptly burlesqued." He mentions Frederick Cooper's *Blackeyed Sukey, or All in the Dumps* (1829), "a burlesque of Jerrold's *Black-Eyed Susan*, which had appeared six months earlier . . ." (*English Plays*, p. 34).

31. Theatre Royal, Dublin, *Book of Words of the Songs, Duetts, and Choruses, Sung in the Grand Christmas Pantomime of Aladdin or the Wonderful Lamp* (n.p.), produced Christmas 1876.

32. Vashti Wynne, *Mother Goose* (n.p.), pp. 17, 19. Produced for Queen's Theatre, Dublin, 16 December 1912.

33. For comments on feminism in Ireland, see Bonnie Kime Scott, "Emma Clery in *Stephen Hero*: A Young Woman Walking Proudly Through the Decayed City," in *Women in Joyce*, ed. Suzette Henke and Elaine Unkeless (Urbana: University of Illinois Press, 1982), p. 64.

34. Programme, National Music Hall, 24 December 1888. Irish-theme pantos apparently occurred with some regularity. John McCormick mentions three by the eighteenth-century writer John O'Keefe, with names like *Giant's Causeway; or, a Trip to the Dargle* ("Origins of Melodrama," *Prompts* 6 [September 1983], p. 9). The *Irish Times*, 26 December 1873, reports that the City Music Hall, Capel Street, produced a panto entitled *Slievna Mon, the Demon of the Mountain Crag, Harlequin King O'Connor, or the Fair Princess of the Emerald Isle* (p. 3, col. 2). Such "Irish" productions did not typify the major Dublin theaters, although T. H. Nally's *Finn Varra*

Maa (*The Irish Santa Claus*) was produced at the Theatre Royal in 1917. See Robert Hogan and Richard Burnham, *The Art of the Amateur 1916–1920*, vol. V of *The Modern Irish Drama, a Documentary History* (Atlantic Highlands, N.J.: Humanities Press, 1984), pp. 78–81. Joyce refers to "*Fenn Mac Call and the Serven Feeries of Loch Neach, Galloper Troppler and Hurleyquinn*" (FW 48.14–15), and David Hayman mentions that in the "late notes for *Ulysses* (British Museum Add MS 49975)" there is "a reference under 'Cyclops' to an 'Irish pantomime Brian Boru & Finn Mac-Cool.'" See *A First-Draft Version of* Finnegans Wake (Austin: University of Texas Press, 1963), p. 17.

35. Harry Dacre, "A Pattern to the World," in Theatre Royal, Dublin, *Book of Songs of the "Royal" Pantomime* [Sleeping Beauty] (Dublin: Allen, 1902), p. 16. Produced Tuesday, 21 January 1902.

36. *Irish Times*, 22 January 1902, p. 5, col. 6.

37. Theatre Royal, Dublin, *Book of Songs of the "Royal" Pantomime* [Dick Whittington] (Dublin: Allen, 1904), p. 39. Produced Tuesday, 26 January 1904; song published by B. Feldam & Co., High Street, London.

38. Holloway, "Impressions of a Dublin Playgoer," June-December 1904, January 26 entry, National Library of Ireland MS. 1802i. Holloway panned much of this pantomime.

39. "Correspondence," *The Leader*, 15 September 1900, p. 44.

40. *Sleeping Beauty*, pp. 13–14.

41. Economic issues surfaced repeatedly in the pantos. For instance, the *Irish Times* review of *Sindbad*, 27 December 1892, reported that the character Tindbad "gives us the song 'Once more I sent the usual eighteen stamps'—a satire on the swindling advertiser and his victim." The satire must have been on-target because the reviewer notes tersely, "The song is not as refined as it might be, but the accompanying dance is good" (p. 7, col. 5). (This song was made popular on the music hall circuit by Tom Costello.) Other examples include the repeated problem, drawn from melodrama, of the poor but honest hero or heroine dunned by the villain, and the figure of the Baron in productions of *Cinderella* or *The Babes in the Wood*, whose poverty and/or greed causes much of the mischief.

42. Booth, *English Plays*, p. 6. Below in this paragraph I quote from p. 49.

43. Richard Southern, *The Victorian Theatre: A Pictorial Survey* (Newton Abbot: David & Charles, 1970), p. 36.

44. Moretti, pp. 185, 195.

45. Programme, *Cinderella* (written by T. H. Ebard), Gaiety Theatre, 26 December 1888.

46. Programme, *Dick Whittington*, Gaiety Theatre, 29 December 1894. Cf. an ad on the same programme: "McCLUSKEY, Fruiterers, To the Vice-

regal Court, Trinity College, and Military Officers' Messes in Ireland." As Fritz Senn pointed out to me, Thornton's is where Boylan buys fruit in "Wandering Rocks."

47. Cf. the programme for the Gaiety's 1890 *Ali Baba and the Forty Thieves*: Cogia Baba is described as "Ali's better half—A real Home Ruler—Enquire of Ali."

48. Peter Davison, comp. & ed., *Songs of the British Music Hall* (New York: Oak Publications, 1971), p. 156; cf. pp. 230–31.

49. Mander and Mitchenson, p. 44.

50. H. G. Hibbert, *A Playgoer's Memories* (London: Grant Richards, 1920), p. 56. I am indebted to Ulrich Schneider for pointing out to me Hibbert's treatment of Royce.

51. *Irish Times*, 26 December 1873, p. 3, col. 2. I am grateful to James Hurt of the University of Illinois for a copy of the songbook to *Turco, the Terrible*.

52. *Souvenir*, p. 19. Of *Amy Robsart*, Joseph Holloway records that it was an "operatic extravaganza" performed by "Mr Joseph Eldred's Dramatic & Burlesque Co for 24 nights Mon May 27 to Sat June 22 [1872]" (Holloway, *Gaiety Theatre, Dublin, List of Plays 1871 –85*, National Library of Ireland, MS. 12069).

53. R. M. Adams discusses Royce, *Turco*, and *Sindbad* as well as Bloom's attempts to write a topical song in *Surface and Symbol: The Consistency of James Joyce's* Ulysses (New York: Oxford University Press, 1962), pp. 76–82.

54. Hayman, in *A First-Draft Version*, says that "The list of *dramatis personae* was among the last additions to this chapter. It was written when Joyce was well advanced in his revising of II, ii" (p. 129, n. 1). In *A Reader's Guide to* Finnegans Wake (London: Thames and Hudson, 1969), William York Tindall calls the playbill an "afterthought" (p. 157), but that characterization overlooks the impact of the playbill in focusing the social content of the chapter's action.

55. Other references in the chapter to classic pantomime stories include "Ani Mama and her fiertey bustles" (FW 243.4–5), "Ulo Bubo selling foulty treepes" (FW 243.24), "Rabbinsohn Crucis" (FW 243.31), "bopeep" (FW 227.12), "his fiery goosemother" (FW 242.25), "Cinderynelly" (FW 224.30), and "sin beau" (FW 233.5). J. S. Atherton's early and valuable article, "*Finnegans Wake*: 'The Gist of the Pantomime,'" *Accent* 15 (1955), sets out many references throughout the *Wake* to panto stories and conventions, but Atherton's thesis about the pantomime does not fully connect with the social content of the form and of Joyce's use of it; he claims, "The conclusion to be drawn from Joyce's treatment of the entire theme of pantomime appears to be that in his opinion life is meaningless, repetitive, traditional, and yet entertaining" (p. 26).

56. Roland McHugh, *Annotations to* Finnegans Wake (Baltimore: Johns Hopkins University Press, 1980), p. 219. In my analyses of passages from the *Wake*, I am indebted to McHugh for many confirmations of allusion and for interpretive suggestions.

57. Broadbent, pp. 206–9.

58. *Dick Whittington*, 1904, p. 7. Quotations below are from pp. 17, 29, and 9.

59. FW 248.7: "Turn again, wistfultone, lode mere of Doubtlynn!"

60. Dick's place in Fitzwarren's household is contested by the Cook, who doesn't like the boy; in "Circe," Bloom runs up against the "brothel cook" at Bella Cohen's, who wants to help Bello abuse Bloom (U 533–34).

61. "The Model Saddles supplied by Messrs. W. R. Box & Co., 105, Middle Abbey Street. The Irish Lace supplied by the Irish Industries Association, 76, Grafton Street."

CHAPTER 4

Transvestism and Transformation

You found me in evil company, highkickers, coster picnic-makers,
pugilists, popular generals, immoral panto boys in flesh tights and
the nifty shimmy dancers, La Aurora and Karini, musical act, the
hit of the century. I was hidden in cheap pink paper that smelt of
rock oil. I was surrounded by the stale smut of clubmen, stories to
disturb callow youth, ads for transparencies, truedup dice and bust-
pads, proprietary articles and why wear a truss with testimonial
from ruptured gentleman. Useful hints to the married. (U 545)

We must make no mistake here: with the great series of binary oppositions (body/soul, flesh/spirit, instinct/reason, drives/conscious-
ness) that seemed to refer sex to a pure mechanics devoid of reason,
the West has managed not only, or not so much, to annex sex to
a field of rationality, which would not be all that remarkable an
achievement, seeing how accustomed we are to such "conquests"
since the Greeks, but to bring us almost entirely—our bodies, our
minds, our individuality, our history—under the sway of a logic of
concupiscence and desire. Whenever it is a question of knowing
who we are, it is this logic that henceforth serves as our master key.
                    Michel Foucault, *The History of Sexuality*

"One good turn deserves another" (U 232):
Cross-Dressing in "Circe"

Preparing for his vaudeville act, the famous American female impersonator Julian Eltinge underwent a complex ritual of gender wor-
ship; even when shaved, corseted, rouged, coiffured, and costumed,
Eltinge still had to enact with grace the poses and gestures characteristic of womanhood in his day if he were to establish a convinc-
ing illusion for his audience.[1] The fascinating results of his care may
be seen in those trick photographs in which Eltinge appears both
with and as his mother or bride. Such serious female impersonation
attempts were not, of course, merely endemic to vaudeville or to the
States; the art has been popular in many countries, while the history of extratheatrical cross-dressing could no doubt be traced to
the outskirts of Eden. But it is notable that dramatic transvestism

136

was especially in vogue during the late nineteenth and early twentieth centuries, when sexual impersonation was tolerated poorly, if at all, in routine social settings, and when the theater functioned as a refuge for those phenomena like cross-dressing that Victorian and Edwardian society wanted to see as having no more substance than theatrical illusions. Outside of the stage (or the underground festivities of, say, special clubs), such behavior was viewed as mad and was strongly censured.[2] In a culture that was becoming more and more intent on discovering—with the help of Charcot, Krafft-Ebing, and Freud—the nature of human sexuality and its relationship to identity and consciousness, cross-dressing could be viewed only as an abnormality, a disease, a confusing condition as threatening to the sense of stability deemed necessary to most individuals as was true physical hermaphroditism or an overt behavioral psychosis. But within such arenas as the music hall and the pantomime, sexual impersonation was not only tolerated, it was enjoyed; what is more, it was expected. Onstage, men dressed as women and women dressed as men, mostly to comic effect and often in ways that explicitly performed the culture's unconscious anxieties about the potency and nature of sexual difference.

Given this connection of the theater and costuming, it is a measure of James Joyce's cultural savvy that in *Ulysses* the passages devoted to Leopold Bloom's transvestite experiments occur within the dramatic context of the Nighttown episode. Here we not only learn about Bloom's instances of cross-dressing, but we also discover suggestions of gender melding in the other Dubliners who populate the Circean core of *Ulysses*. For instance, Bloom addresses a "*sinister figure . . . a visage unknown*" who gives him the "*evil eye*" and who, seeming to be designated as masculine by the wearing of a "*wide-leaved sombrero*," is surprisingly addressed by Bloom as "*señorita Blanca*" (U 436). Soon after Molly's trousered apparition, Mrs Breen shows up wearing a "*man's frieze overcoat with loose bellows pockets*" (U 442); similarly, Mrs Dignam later wears pants under her skirt (U 568), and Bella Cohen's female cook not only has a beard but wears "*men's grey and green socks and brogues*" (U 533). Further, when Bloom addresses the jury, he seems to confuse his own gender when he says, "I am the daughter of a most distinguished commander" (U 457), and his "bogus statement" includes his intention "*to reform, to retrieve the memory of the past in a pure sisterly way*" (U 461). In addition, Bloom mentions that he has "moved in the charmed circle of the highest . . . . [Joyce's ellipsis] Queens of Dublin Society" (U 465).

Such ambiguous references to gender, almost always in relationship to Bloom rather than to Stephen, become more puzzling and insistent as the episode proceeds. For example, Virag, Bloom's grandfather, appears on pink stilts in a brown macintosh with a phallic parchment roll underneath it—as though the male signifier itself were merely part of his costume for the Circean festivities. In the midst of a conversation with Bloom about aphrodisiacs and female sexuality, in which he asks Bloom if he likes women dressed as men, Virag "*laughs in a rich feminine key.*" Interestingly, Virag states that "the truffles of Perigord . . . were unsurpassed in cases of nervous debility or viragitis" (U 516); the relation of his name to the latter condition, in which a woman behaves according to the prevailing standards of masculinity, signifies Virag's status not as a womanlike man (as the quality of his laughter suggests) but as a manlike woman. More important, he appears to agree with Krafft-Ebing's *Psychopathia Sexualis*—generally accepted to have been a major source for the "Circe" episode—that viragitis is a sickness on the order of a psychosis, the assumption being that in those who suffer from the condition the masculine has been improperly grafted onto the feminine. But Virag is Bloom's grandfather, and despite his feminine laugh we persist in seeing him as indisputably male until we recognize that the text may be undermining the easy cultural assumption that one is "really" of a certain gender, a recognition which could have profound implications for the paternal quest in *Ulysses* (as Stephen Dedalus suggests when he says, "Paternity may be a legal fiction" [U 207]). Certainly, a grandfather must be anatomically male, but in regard to Virag a definite gender is more than in doubt. When, on top of such curious passages, Henry Flower comes along carrying a "*longstemmed bamboo Jacob's pipe, its clay bowl fashioned as a female head*" (U 517), the union of phallic pipe and womanly bowl epitomizes a textual strategy of mingling sexual traits in beings customarily differentiated.

Critics have long recognized the importance of these passages, and yet most have drastically undervalued their dramatic context. The passage involving Bloom's mother is one of the most revealing of these instances because of the focus there, near the beginning of "Circe," on pantomime transvestism. Ellen Bloom appears dressed in a "*pantomime dame's stringed mobcap, widow Twankey's crinoline and bustle, blouse with muttonleg sleeves buttoned behind, grey mittens and cameo brooch, her plaited hair in a crispine net*" (U 438). The reader not familiar with the British popular theater could easily overlook the significance of this costuming.

Principal Boys and Dames

Regardless of the story to be enacted, the pantomime had a highly codified cast. First, it was mandatory to include not a man but a male impersonator in the role of the fairy-tale hero. This "principal boy" was most often a well-endowed woman in tights, who made little or no attempt to mask her femaleness. The famous male impersonator Hetty King, for example, played her role as Aladdin at the Royal Court Theatre (Liverpool, 1904—see Plate 6) in quite feminine attire, wearing a spangled tricorn and frill-lined velvet cape over her beaded and close-fitting tunic. Most Irish pantomimes of the late nineteenth century also included several other cross-dressing roles for women. For example, in the Gaiety's 1894 *Dick Whittington*, both the "Shop Girls" and the "Apprentices" were played by women, along with Dick him(her)self, while in the 1890 production at the Gaiety of *Ali Baba and the Forty Thieves*, the "Lieutenants of the Forty, but right tenants for the firm of Abdallah, Hassarac & Co." are also four young women.[3]

More important, the panto in Joyce's day always included a man in the role of "dame." Very few men were known solely for their female impersonation as Vesta Tilley was for her male mimicries,[4] but even so, performers like Harry Randall, Dan Leno, George Robey, and Wilkie Bard frequently played panto dames; many such performers regularly used drag acts in their music hall repertoire,[5] always for intensely comic effect. Extended foreheads, sweetly folded hands, saccharine expression—these were among the conventional stylizations that marked the nineteenth-century dame. The widow Twankey—in whose outfit Ellen Bloom appears—fulfilled this role in the pantomime *Aladdin*, which was rewritten from production to production by many hands but which must have included in all versions "Aladdin's mother, 'who,' to quote the 'Arabian Nights,' 'was rather old and who even in her youth had not possessed any beauty.'"[6] In her study of the Victorian dame's transformation in the plays of W. S. Gilbert, Jane W. Stedman describes the character emulated by Ellen Bloom as Aladdin's "knock-down, drag-out, slapstick, widowed mother."[7] She goes on to suggest that "mid-

Victorian dames had always two characteristics in common: they were at least middle-aged and they were at least very plain, if not positively hideous. Their make-up was caricature, their action slapstick. . . . They were, in short, animated comic valentines." Further, the dame might have "a hasty, even a cruel temper; shrewishness; an unrequited passion; an avid love of flattery; and a misplaced dependence on the disguising powers of cosmetics and false hair." A photograph of the beloved Dan Leno, the most famous dame of his era, in his role as the Widow Twankey (Drury Lane, 1896—see Plate 7) does not suggest that the role pictured involved such crusty intolerance and laughable vanity; however, the caricature side of the dame can be read with ease in Leno's mischievous grin, in his exaggerated costume and comical pose.[8] Unfortunately, Leno's costume for this production did not include the mobcap and such that Joyce describes in "Circe"; Leno was fond of wearing a topknot and used it in more than one dame role. More typical of the style in question is Wilkie Bard's Mother Goose (Prince's Theatre, Bristol, 1905—Plate 8).

Whatever the temperament and attire of the dame, his/her function was to make people laugh—not to create an illusion of the sort that Eltinge sought but comically to heighten systematically coded gender differences. Even now, one can read in this picture of Bard the broad comedy that audiences must have enjoyed on seeing a male face peeking out of a bonnet. Similarly, existing pictures of Leno in drag show him in various guises, from the elegant to the ridiculous, but always the collocation of facial expression and dress evokes an incongruity which relies for effect on an audience's knowing the culture's gender codes and styles.

Certainly children who visited the theater for the first time or two were less than attentive to such costume-switching. Mícheál mac Liammóir, for instance, recounts his alter ego Martin's enraptured first visit to a theater to see *Dick Whittington*, focusing on Martin's confusion over the proper sex of the hero, though Martin's sister Tina did comment on first seeing the principal boy in that Cork production, "My God, if I'd legs like that, I'd hush them up."[9] And George Bernard Shaw referred once to the time when he "was a very small child and thought it all real."[10] The point, at least as far as mac Liammóir's testimony goes, is that children did not necessarily know that the humor of the piece depended on gender-switching. For mac Liammóir, the theater was not originally seen as distinct from

PLATE 6. A music hall expert writes of Hetty King that "she topped bills all over the world as a debonair man-about-town, and as the soldiers and sailors of both world wars" (Roy Busby, *British Music Hall: An Illustrated Who's Who from 1850 to the Present Day* [London: Paul Elek, 1976], p. 92). Sharing with Vesta Tilley a popularity based on elegant male impersonation, Hetty King appeared also as the principal boy in pantomimes, in which roles she followed the panto practice of reading male lines while wearing costumes that were regarded by many theatergoers as both feminine and unambiguously suggestive. (Photograph reproduced by the kind permission of the Raymond Mander and Joe Mitchenson Theatre Collection, London.)

life, and his confusion of the sexes was sorted out *through* the
pantomime and after. Yet adults often tend to believe that children
always know the codes by which one sex is differentiated from the
other.

Either way, it would seem that the burlesque tradition that interpenetrated the modern pantomime[11] insured that much of the impact and humor of these productions could be appreciated best by
adults who had gone through the appropriate cultural encoding;
the pantomime itself becomes for uninitiated minors a socializing
arena. But perhaps anyone could pick up the humor of the Widow's
singing the following lyrics in an 1876 Royal production of
Aladdin:

> My husband was an awful cad,
> Thro' drinking he went to the bad,
> And now they've stolen away my lad,
> Nobody knows the trouble I've had.
> Tho' I'm young and lovely as you see,
> And I'm only just turned twenty-three!
>
> Oh! nobody knows the trouble I've seen.[12]

The dame's perennial folly is her vanity and desire for a mate, a folly
which proper hamming up in lines 6 and 7 of the above verse would
surely emphasize. But the implications of such comedy reach far.
Even though many actors might have denied it, cross-dressing on
the stage displayed the ideological practices that made sexual stereotypes operative.

In "Circe," then, Ellen Bloom wears a costume associated by the
text with a role played by male actors only, even though the clothes
seem to signify her femaleness and even motherliness. Peter Ackroyd
quotes the opinion of a contemporary dame, Cyril Fletcher, which
suggests that the gender duality we read in Ellen Bloom forms a
conscious tension in the panto actor: Fletcher notes that the art of
the dame creates "a world of complete fantasy, a world of very subtle
sexual balances, quite as unsettling and provoking as anything in *As
You Like It*." And Ackroyd adds, "The dame is never effeminate; she
is never merely a drag artist, since she always retains her male identity. The performer is clearly a man dressed as an absurd and ugly
woman, and much of the comedy is derived from the fact that he is
burlesquing himself as a male actor."[13] Such vertiginous theatrical
reflexivity characterizes the play in "Circe" with the culture-based

PLATE 7. Some of the sexual comedy that marked cross-dressing in the pantomime and that was designed to be comprehended by adults only is suggested here in Dan Leno's "Widow Twankey" costume. The coy curtsey emphasizes the message embroidered on the satin panel, "No Reasonable Offer Refused." Leno whose music hall and pantomime performances displayed his exceptional comic talent, appeared frequently in Drury Lane Christmas productions. Roy Busby's description of Leno's performance style suggests something of the theatrical presence behind *Finnegans Wake*; he tells us that "Dan's songs were really rambling monologues introducing a legion of brilliant character impersonations, a railway guard, shopwalker, recruiting sergeant, fireman, Beefeater, huntsman, or just telling the audience of a visit to the races, or the latest gossip of the mythical Mrs. Kelly. 'You remember Mrs Kelly!'" (Busby, p. 103). (Photograph reproduced by the kind permission of the Raymond Mander and Joe Mitchenson Theatre Collection, London.)

PLATE 8. Well-known for his work in both pantomime and music hall, Wilkie Bard is here shown dressed for his role as Mother Goose in the 1905 Christmas production at the Prince's Theatre in Bristol. Roy Busby tells us that Bard "developed his own style of comedy, adopting the eccentric but distinctive make-up of the high bald forehead with black spots painted above each eyebrow" (Busby, p. 20). Given the pantomime's exaggeration of gender differences, it is significant that Bard used his "spots" in both male and female roles; the dots are just visible in this photograph. (Photograph reproduced by the kind permission of the Raymond Mander and Joe Mitchenson Theatre Collection, London).

signs of sexual differentiation. Ellen's wearing of a male version of female apparel begins to unsettle—from the outset of the episode— the firm sense of gender distinctions with which most readers in Joyce's time and in our own might be expected to approach "Circe"— or, for that matter, any work. Our notion of Bloom's character has to include a sense that his maternal image shows some gender confusion, albeit in a theatrical and strictly semiotic context, but the point of this confusion is not that we discern in Bloom a significant neurosis. Rather, "Circe" prods us toward some conclusions about how sexual identity was named and known in Bloom's Ireland.

Psychology and "Circe"

To date, most speculation on "Circe" has viewed the chapter as a dark night of the soul, a psychic testing ground for Bloom (and, to a lesser extent, for Stephen). For this reason, Bloom's behavior has usually been read in psychoanalytic terms; some readers have turned for explanations of "madness" such as Bloom's masochistic tendencies and transvestism to Freud or to Krafft-Ebing. Such approaches focus on "Circe" as an expression of the main characters' unconscious minds and see the non-naturalistic parts of the episode as hallucinations. For these critics, the chief points of interest are to what extent the episode reflects Joyce's own repressed sexual dynamics and in what ways the characters may be said to change or grow as a result of their evening's experiences. Thus the dramatics of "Circe" are read as psychodrama, "Circe" itself as the unconscious.[14]

The most thoroughgoing proponent of the psychological approach to *Ulysses* is Mark Shechner, in whose *Joyce and Nighttown* we find extensive application of psychoanalytic principles to further our understanding of the psychic states of Stephen, Bloom, and Joyce himself.[15] Shechner's analysis is careful and in many ways unified, but the casting of "Circe" as a play emphasizes that what may be seen as the surfacing of repressed desires in Bloom—and as a reflection of his creator's own needs—is at least as much dramatization of desire as it is material to be read through Freudian lenses. "Circe" is the enactment of the role of repressed desirer. Where Shechner discovers an identification of Joyce's mind and the predilections of his characters, the Circean drama asks us to find a play of character types—not Bloom and Stephen "in the flesh" but a play about what the text suggests Bloom and Stephen might be like.[16]

The figure of Ellen Bloom is an excellent one to use to display the difference between the Freudian and the dramatic approaches. When Ellen sees Bloom covered with mud, "*She hauls up a reef of skirt and ransacks the pouch of her striped blay petticoat. A phial, an Agnus Dei, a shrivelled potato, and a celluloid doll fall out*" (U 438). Certainly, a Freudian reading in which Bloom's fantasy of his mother signifies the state of his unconscious associations with her could make hay with the material Joyce supplies here—pouch, phial, potato, and doll all having obvious sexual overtones. Such a reading might conclude that although Bloom is not quite able to see his mother as a full-fledged phallic woman of the sort he admires and kowtows to when he meets Bella/o, Bloom's hallucination of his mother nonetheless plants unambiguously in her clothing signs of his neurosis, his psychic need to be at the mercy of such a dual-sexed individual, especially when that person is the mother with whom, so psychologists tell us, such potentially transvestite males typically identify.[17] By some lights, Ellen appears as the phallic mother that Bloom seems to detect in himself, to have married, and to objectify under the stimulation of Bella's masculine presence. She is the mother who, in the mind of the frightened child, has lost the phallus in some mysterious way that threatens the child too—Ellen's pouch containing phallic but detached items.

Such a reading has the drawback of leaving us still in the mode of interrogating the text; we have no way of demonstrating, given the formal properties of "Circe," that the reading is sound, except insofar as it merely restates the dependencies and fetishistic qualities that are abundantly evident in portions of the novel in which Bloom is presented "naturalistically." It seems to me altogether more fruitful to view "Circe" as a script and to consider the stage directions regarding Ellen's costuming and attendant props as the means to our envisioning a bit of stage action—the pantomime dame's playing peek-a-boo with her often very young audience and delighting them by pulling comically from her clothes altogether silly items. This suggestion does not deny that within *Ulysses* those items may carry symbolic import, or that within a true pantomime performance, similar items may not bear similar Freudian implications (Harlequin's magic bat comes to mind), but it is a way of emphasizing the obvious theatrical references in "Circe" as primary interpretive keys.

Hence, Bloom's mind may be chock-full of easily interpreted Freudian images that attest to his infantile experiences, but "Circe" also suggests that such images are themselves cultural constructs[18] and that they are not an expression of a "natural" semiotics, Freud and Krafft-Ebing both having constructed their theories on the basis of people whose notions of life *were* stereotyped by cultural phenomena. It is clear that Joyce was acutely aware of the synergy by which people create their culture and in turn are created by it, so that any text, no matter how seemingly personal and focused on the individual unconscious, is, if not a Lotmanian "text of *the* culture," a text of culture. And any explanation of personal behavior is, like Freud's and like Krafft-Ebing's before him, also cultural creation, subject to influences beyond the control of the individual patient, the individual author, and the interpreter of human behavior. Because the theater and transvestism were associated in the culture, the explanation for that connection is cultural. My approach to "Circe," while centered on Bloom, assumes that he is a creature of his society and that he can experience and think only those thoughts that are somehow—however obliquely—made possible and even codified by the culture. If "Circe" portrays the unconscious, that is only to say that the mind is a text, a drama.

In contrast, although he recognizes that the portrayal of Bloom in "Circe" is "slapstick," an "entertainment," a "vaudeville routine," Shechner finds that, because the various sexual practices that Bloom thinks about in "Circe" are also Joyce's epistolary fantasies, "Circe" is "daringly confessional." Similarly, Shechner discovers Joyce's own fears in the episode, including his apparent fear of going insane. As a result of this apprehension, Joyce's characters also undergo psychic strain:

> The bout with insanity may in fact be the deepest of the conflicts in "Circe," for in that chapter both Bloom and Stephen are provisionally psychotic. They hallucinate their reality. Boundaries evaporate; inner and outer interpenetrate, and identity becomes a flux of interlocking possibilities.[19]

The terms of Shechner's argument unintentionally describe—and even in the same vocabulary—the poststructuralist conception of the literary text: a linguistic space in which characters dissolve into discourse, in which inside and outside interpenetrate to destabilize even the integrity of the aesthetic frame. And it is this description which Hélène Cixous approximates when she analyzes "Circe"; she argues that this theatrical chapter "not only replays all parts of *Ulysses* in one scene but, by de-compartmentalization and by depersonalization, decomposes each and everyone into his several selves, breaks the real into fragments and calls on the multiplicity of entire pieces to speak, without distinction of object, of subject, of interiority or of exteriority, of property."[20] It seems clear that in "Circe" Joyce has used the script format to make inescapable the textuality of the chapter. Like all of *Ulysses*, "Circe" is not so much an intuitive precursor of poststructuralism as it is a model for what many contemporary critics find descriptive of all writing. When Joyce claimed of *Ulysses* that "a transparent leaf separates it from madness,"[21] perhaps he sensed how thoroughly destabilizing his writing had become, especially through the nine revisions of "Circe," which logically played out his metaphysically explosive association of theatrical artifice and the inner self.

"Circe" portrays Bloom not so much psychoanalytically as analytically, as having become part of several different texts or discourses that variously shape his so-called hallucinations, among which discourses those of the popular stage performance are strategically prominent. "Circe" takes the psychic apart into its cultural components and shows their source in popular discourses. Hence, the elaborate play with gender roles does not stop with Ellen Bloom's ambiguous costuming. In fact, the scene in which Bloom meets his mother is followed by a series of manifestations which suggest the theme of theatrical transvestism.

For example, at one point in "Circe," Bloom begins to tell Mrs Breen that he had attended the performance that night of *Leah*. Bloom's earlier thoughts about the star actress in this play are significant: "*Leah* tonight: Mrs Bandmann Palmer. Like to see her again in that. Hamlet she played last night. Male impersonator. Perhaps he was a woman." And Bloom goes on to speculate: "Why Ophelia committed suicide" (U 76).[22] Mrs. Palmer's male impersonation is, of course, part of a legitimate theatrical tradition that stands in contrast to male impersonation in pantos, in which the feminizing of the hero was quite overt, an effect which negated the sexual aspect of the love affair at the heart of so many panto stories. At the same time, the principal boy's leotarded legs also emphasized the sexual element of those presentations in the "normal" or societally conditioned way—in that "panto boys in flesh tights" (U 545) were long associated, as the Nymph in "Circe" makes clear, with the immorality of what Bloom calls the "dark sexsmelling theatre"

(U 548). One conclusion, then, about this topic is that the presentation in "Circe" of gender traits as culturally defined and societally conditioned[23] accurately reflects the theater's varied and tantalizing manipulation of costume codes—the complexity of which Bloom is aware.

Blooming Androgyny?

These contextual references to transvestism and gender ambiguity become more significant to plot and characterization as the episode proceeds to reflect (or perhaps refract?) Bloom's consciousness and culture. The most illuminating references to such matters occur in a two-page interchange between Bloom and Bella Cohen. Bello, whose name changes from feminine to masculine forms to match his or her outfit, is described as wearing not the clothes of the typical whorehouse madam but *"mountaineer's puttees, green silverbuttoned coat, sport skirt and alpine hat with moorcock's feather"* (U 531). Bloom meanwhile is in similarly ambiguous shape. Bello threatens Bloom's unmanning and associates this state with putting Bloom in a "punishment frock" (U 535) and renaming him Ruby Cohen. But Bloom, despite the obvious appeal here to his masochistic tendencies, plays a more complex role in this scene than that of the masochist alone. Under the weight of Bello's oppressive fashion forecast, Bloom is described in the stage directions as a *"charming soubrette with dauby cheeks, mustard hair and large male hands and nose, leering mouth"* (U 536). The phrase "charming soubrette" (U 253) was used in "Wandering Rocks" to describe the music hall comedienne Marie Kendall (though I have never been able to find a picture of her in which she looks nearly as coquettish as Marie Lloyd did—see Plate 9). And the colors of Bloom's hair and cheeks have changed.

It is this point in the novel along with the scene in which Bloom gives birth to several children that most critics of *Ulysses* think about when they argue that in "Circe" Bloom actually *becomes* a woman. In fact, many readers accept without much question that Bloom is in some sense androgynous. As Carolyn Heilbrun notes in her study of androgyny, "Surely no one can deny Bloom's feminine characteristics; he is both man and woman. . . . He is the only androgynous figure in Dublin, one supposes in all of Ireland."[24] Similarly, Richard Ellmann claims that "Bloom changes from man to woman," and critical commentary includes many similar assertions.[25]

A recent widely read article on transvestism and modern literature, written by Sandra Gilbert, provides an interesting variation on this critical theme. Discussing Joyce, Lawrence, T. S. Eliot, Djuna Barnes, Woolf, and H. D., Gilbert argues that "For the male modernist . . . gender is most often an ultimate reality [one that they are anxious to retain while simultaneously affirming a male-dominated social order], while for the female modernist an ultimate reality exists only if one journeys beyond gender."[26] Citing Robert Stoller's study of transvestism in *Sex and Gender* (1975), Gilbert asserts that in Nighttown Bloom's change of clothes is "sexually compensatory" in that it affirms that he is not just a man but a man who has mastered the female and subsumed it in his own body. Thus she finds Bloom's victory to be not over his fantasies and desires but over Molly, so that the end of *Ulysses* is "triumphantly orderly." This assertion would surprise the many readers of Joyce for whom the value of his works resides precisely in their rejection of a conventionally bounded narrative frame. I think that Gilbert underestimates the complexity of Joyce's portrayal of gender. When she argues that women writers "struggled . . . to define a gender-free reality behind or beneath myth, an ontological essence so pure, so free that 'it' can 'inhabit' any self, any costume," Gilbert charts the substitution of a single gender-based identity with a gender-free essence, but she does not register Joyce's frontal attack on that concept—on the notion that any essence, any "pure" selfhood exists beyond and above the scriptings of culture. Joyce's later fiction argues rather vigorously against this idea by insisting on the cultural coding of many characteristics that we ordinarily take to be natural.

To argue that Bloom actually becomes a woman in "Circe" is to ignore Joyce's references to such cultural stereotyping as portrayed through the dramatic form of the chapter. "Circe" is a script, a dramatization of events, based on *Ulysses*. "Bloom" is a character assigned a transvestite role in the drama. Once we are drawn inside the theatrical context, we can no longer tell—based on the roles played—what the "truth" of any character's gender is. Nor can we be sure that it is Bloom who *plays* the dramatic character named Bloom. Cixous's description of "Circe" neatly corresponds to this view: "Fragments of dialogue cut by long stage directions, a system of plays and parentheses comprise the monstrous text. Pieces, tableaux settle for an instant, the time to record a passage, a bit of face; a syntax is produced, by non-logical connection, by heterogeneous

PLATE 9. Had Joyce been less committed to historical accuracy in his references to Dublin's billboard advertisements on June 16, 1904 and had he concerned himself about the future reader's likely knowledge of British music-hall, he might well have chosen to mention, in "Wandering Rocks" and "Circe," Marie Lloyd rather than Marie Kendall. The first performer is universally viewed as the queen of vocal comedy in the halls, but Marie Kendall also had her claims on the public heart. Music hall expert Peter Gammond reports that Kendall's "comedy was as graceful as her presence, her songs . . . sweetly sentimental" (*Your Own, Your Very Own!: A Music Hall Scrapbook*, comp. Peter Gammond [London: Ian Allen, 1971], p. 76). This photograph conveys something of the sweet elegance that charmed her audiences. (Photograph reproduced by the kind permission of the Raymond Mander and Joe Mitchenson Theatre Collection.)

links related through a few references: suspicious subjects who as-
semble their states under the names of Bloom, Stephen, prostitutes,
the madam, names, moreover, which are unstable."[27] Naturally, even
Cixous talks at times of *Bloom's* doing something; part of the madness which *Ulysses* exposes for us is our own inability to discuss the
Circean personae without implicitly reifying them into the supposedly stable characters who populate the rest of *Ulysses*. Ordinary
language fails adequately to meet our needs in describing and talking about Bloom in "Circe"; we still fall back on a single name when
we talk about him and thus seem to be arguing, despite statements
to the contrary, that Bloom is an ontological essence rather than the
character(s) found in "Circe" under the designation "Bloom." With
one hand we show Bloom to be a textual thread; with another we
find him "Good old Bloom! There's nobody like him after all"
(U 491). What takes place in "Circe" is thus a Joycean pantomime
which plays out the confusing implications of how culture not only
determines gender traits but also shapes concepts of selfhood.

Bloom's responses to his feminine costume demonstrate this
power of culture over even the extraordinary Dubliner. Fitted by the
text into the role of a stereotyped music hall soubrette, Bloom goes
on to defend himself and to reminisce over the time that he tried on
Molly's clothes when they lived on Holles Street, an action that he
calls a "small prank" (U 536). Instead of yearning for a true androgyny, Bloom seems always to have gravitated toward only a stereotyped femaleness composed of clothing, makeup, hairstyle, and
mannerism. Whether or not he is to be construed as wearing the
female clothing described by Bello is debatable. Later, the persona
Bloom is assigned certain props—a ruby ring, some bangle brace-
lets, even a vulva—but such items do seem to be little more than
props.[28] They have the same kind of reality that Bello's descriptions
of Bloom's projected female clothing do. That is, they have a semiotic function,[29] and what they signify is the power of clothing over
behavior, the power that one sex wields simply by virtue of a certain
costume and distinctive mannerisms. Although the chapter seems
to look directly at the nature of sexuality, it is always only clothes-
deep into the subject, and it argues that clothes (construed as any
part of the semiotic trappings of one sex: hairstyle, speech patterns,
even physical features such as big noses, vulvas, rosy cheeks) are only
theatrical props which support the role adopted by the actor, who is
not a pure essence but rather a complex of traits and traditions.

But "Circe" does not leave Bloom's transvestite experiences there; instead, Bello accuses Bloom of showing "off coquettishly in your domino at the mirror behind closedrawn blinds your unskirted thighs and hegoat's udders in various poses of surrender" (U 536). Bello goes on to note that Bloom apparently fantasized in this way and acted out his fantasies on more than one occasion—varying with each session the figure of the violator—so that in one case the rapist was not a man at all but the "dowager duchess of Manorhamilton." In defense, Bloom says that, in essence, he is not responsible for this hobby. "It was Gerald," he claims, "converted me to be a true corsetlover when I was female impersonator in the High School play [30] *Vice Versa*. It was dear Gerald. He got that kink, fascinated by sister's stays. Now dearest Gerald uses pinky greasepaint and gilds his eyelids" (U 536–37).[31] As he speaks, Bloom's style changes, the phrases "dear Gerald" and "dearest Gerald" indicating that the text is giving Bloom lines scripted by stereotypes of deviant behavior and subcultural discourse. Significantly, the presentation of Bloom's excuse encapsulates a culture's fear that from playing a role to *being* that role is one very easy step.

As a whole, "Circe" is a performance on paper of the way that the individual—fashioned of cultural threads—in turn fashions experience into a sort of personal drama: in *Ulysses*, culture makes culture, and identity is a by-product of that process. "Circe," of course, bears reference to more forms of experience than just that of the popular theater, but the stage marks the episode in a fundamental way, for when we recognize that Bloom's sexuality is not under investigation here as an exorcism of supposed weakness or abnormality, we find that in *Ulysses* as in life, sexual identity is largely a cultural or even a theatrical phenomenon. Furthermore, "Circe" shows us that we cannot burrow under a character's clothes to any essential nature, to any undiluted and potent identity, sexual or otherwise. Rather, we are always stopped on the level of one semiotic system or another.

On the level of popular culture, we find that the pantomime contained the symptoms of social deviance (the panto dame, the principal boy) which were not viewed as such by their audience. On stage the cross-dressed actor said more than he or she was aware, for impersonation acts both concealed and unveiled the sexual issues they adumbrated. That is, the cross-dressed actor performed two messages at once. First, he or she denied the reality of androgyny by playing off the cultural assumption that each person had to be either male or female; he or she thus acted out the culture's confusion over sexual identity—and its fear of deviations from the norm.[32] Second—and somewhat contradictorily—this acting was a censored announcement that male and female need not be mutually exclusive categories or, indeed, even the principal categories used to identify the sexual dimension of human experience. As "Circe" demonstrates, an individual can readily mix sexual signs and yet be neither androgynous nor psychotic. In *Ulysses*, there is no spontaneous or separate "humanity," no "fully human" androgyny; there is only a perpetual rising to textual consciousness of gender traits that became rigidly entrapping labels, packages, and norms reflecting the culture's characteristic mechanism of binary encoding (male vs. female). *Ulysses* argues that sexuality is sheer theater, at least on the social stage on which we dramatically construct the selves we play.

Impersonation and Selfhood

"Circe" rejects sexuality as a determinant of individual selfhood, authenticity, and autonomy, but the implications of this conclusion extend in *Ulysses* far beyond matters of gender and clothing. From the notion that there's no "natural" or "nonalien" gender, *Ulysses* posits that there is no human nature in the ordinary sense of the term and no inner being that one struggles to understand, develop, or fulfill. Rather, *Ulysses* shows us cultural codes mingling in the minds of each character to the effect that the character—whether known through dialogue, thoughts, or action—is properly construed as a narrative event.[33] In "Circe" we see Bloom, for instance, subjected to a series of situations that call forth from him the distinct roles that in his ordinary social interactions remain merely latent, potential, or partially enacted. The episode exaggerates this "normal" mixture of codings, and it is not alone in doing so. "Oxen" shows us Bloom in a sequence of roles, each of them keyed to a linguistic style and hence an historical period or social setting in which his actions would have been differently constrained by cultural possibilities. Similarly, "Ithaca" gives us, at a substantial remove, a vision of the "scientific" world-view as Bloom would appear in it, just as "Sirens" speaks to the sensuous tropes and turns of the musical world of Dublin insofar as Bloom is scripted by these cultural elements. That Bloom's name shows up throughout *Ulysses* variously distorted ("Old Ollebo, M.P." [U 678], "L. Boom" [U 647]) and mirrored in other cultural phenomena ("*Blumenlied* I bought for her. The name" [U 278], "bloomers . . . I suppose theyre called after him" [U 761]) reinforces these conclusions about the mutual writing of world and individual. Throughout *Ulysses* we are never in touch with a stable character named Bloom but are given access to cultural codings that change, sentence by sentence, thought by thought. The variety that is called "Bloom" is already a fissured discursive entity by the end of "Calypso." Bloom's playing Bloom in "Circe" describes his continuous adoption of one role or another, to the extent that we cannot distinguish character from role. Most readings of that episode want to explain and cure Bloom's condition but to leave his society intact, whereas surely "Circe" provides evidence that to change Bloom we would have to change his culture and to alter the structure of terms in which individuality is positioned.

Such speculation takes us full circle, back to the questions of how culture is composed and whether it is possible to envision a society different in its fundamental mechanisms from the one that surfaces in Joyce's fiction. The fact that sexual impersonation exists at all as *entertainment* is evidence that social institutions thrive on the stable binarisms that transvestism relies on. In this regard, it is worth noting that "Circe" refers at least briefly to another form of impersonation and incorporates a whole range of structuring binarisms.

When Bloom meets Josie Breen in Nighttown, and she threatens to tell Molly of his presence there, he explains that he is in fact on a reconnaissance mission for Molly: "Slumming. The exotic, you see. Negro servants in livery too if she had money. Othello black brute. Eugene Stratton [see Plate 10]. Even the bones and cornerman at the Livermore christies. Bohee brothers. Sweep for that matter" (U 443). Eugene Watters and Matthew Murtagh tell us in their study of Dan Lowrey's Music Hall that "all the blacked-up boys paled before Eugene Stratton." He first performed in Dublin in 1896 and regaled "huge summer evening crowds." In the same year, the Bohee Brothers, George and James, who really were black, entertained the Dublin audience, as they had a decade before: "According to a son of Jack White, the Stage Carpenter [at Lowrey's], the harmony of these men was so moving that they actually cried and the Audience wept with them."[34] Joyce's evocation of the minstrel performers, who, either in minstrel shows or as part of music-hall acts, produced a craze in England from 1843 on,[35] brings forth

PLATE 10. Born in New York, Eugene Stratton arrived on British shores as part of a minstrel troupe. Reports on his performances emphasize the dramatic nature of his singing, the expressiveness with which he danced, and the strong emotions felt by his audiences. His songs included "The Dandy-Coloured Coon" (which became his tag-name), "The Lily of Laguna," and "The Little Octoroon." Bloom seems to use his name in "Circe" as though Stratton were less a famous or representative "black-face" singer than a true black minstrel. (Photograph reproduced by the kind permission of the Raymond Mander and Joe Mitchenson Theatre Collection, London.)

some minstrels in the textual flesh: "*Tom and Sam Bohee, coloured coons in white duck suits, scarlet socks, upstarched Sambo chokers and large scarlet asters in their buttonholes, leap out*" (U 443).

Introducing these figures does not do violence to the decorum of the panto format of "Circe"; Booth[36] tells us that in [Anthony?] Hope's mid-nineteenth-century [?] *Harlequin Alfred the Great*, "Alfred and his supporters enter '*as Ethiopian Serenaders. Their disguise merely consists of a black dress coat, with enormously long tails, white wristbands a good way up their arms, high white collars, black masks down to the mouth, and woolly skull caps.*'" In the National Music Hall's 1888 *Harlequin Bryan O'Lynn*, there is a character called Pompey Washington who is described simply as "A Nigger," and whose name alludes to comic minstrelsy. And the Royal's 1902 *Sleeping Beauty* songbook includes the minstrel tune "Mah Moonlight Lou" ("Out in the moonlight I wait for you, / June bugs and bull frogs am waitin' too; / Night owls am blinkin', I hear dem hoot; / I'se gettin' skeery, I'd like to skoot . . .").[37] Certainly the pantomime audience fully accepted such figures and the impersonation of them.

It *is* impersonation rather than actual Negro minstrelsy that Joyce refers to in "Circe." True, the Bohees were black performers, and here they are said to have "*negroid hands*" and "*smackfatclacking nigger lips*" and to dance the highspirited minstrel "*breakdown*" (U 443), but they are said also to have "*white kaffir eyes*"—a sign of their ambiguous racial status. Popular in Dublin, the famous White-Eyed Kaffir, though he usually made up in black face, was actually Caucasian. The Kaffir, G. H. Chirgwin, distinguished himself from the horde of minstrel entertainers by wearing a large white diamond over one eye—an act that began accidentally and, evoking audience laughter, became a fixed part of the Kaffir's routine.[38] As years passed, the Kaffir sometimes reversed his costuming priorities, so that he wore only white clothing and makeup with a large black triangle over his eye (Plates 11 and 12). That the Bohee brothers here wear Kaffir makeup suggests that, like most pantomime blacks, they could remove their masks to reveal Anglo-Saxon-Celtic skin tones. But after singing their version of "Someone's in the Kitchen with Dinah," the Joycean Bohees "*whisk black masks from raw babby faces*" and "*dance away*" (U 444). Outside of their theatrical roles, they are of indeterminate race—unsocialized, unconventional. The term "babby" is itself a mask. Here, even skin is viewed as a kind of clothing that is no more determining of selfhood than gender distinctions. The "babby" face may be as close as we get in "Circe" to a proto-self or state before cultural coding; if so, that state is simply the condition of being infantile and unsocialized.

It may be relevant that the word *persona* means "mask."[39] Given this meaning, "impersonation," whether sexual or racial or role-based, refers simply to the state of being in a mask; impersonate equals "in-person-ate."[40] Instead of an ontological being, each character in Joyce, as in a panto, can be relied on only to be a coded ideological construct. Impersonation, like individuality, imitates and draws on a repertoire of traits and conventional behaviors; it is an adoption of what seems to be an artificial role as opposed to what is imagined to be an innate one. In the culture that *Ulysses* presents and that "Circe" comically rearranges to collapse distinctions and hierarchies, such characteristics almost always fall into terms that define themselves in relation to opposing labels. Male and female, black and white join Jew and gentile, middle class and aristocratic, married and single, sane and insane, Irish and English, in mourning and not in mourning, audience and performer, human and dehumanized. Such is the diacritical range of terms which serve to define Dublin's citizens. The means of categorization and exclusion, these terms sustained the culture's power relations, but these binarisms must all be recognized as nondefinitive. Although culture relentlessly structures experience, Joyce's fictions play out the interpenetrations of terms and suggest the possibility, however illusory, of freedom from their reign.

Transformation and Utopian Vision

Bloom explains to those near him his schemes for social regeneration. All agree with him. The keeper of the Kildare street museum appears, dragging a lorry on which are the shaking statues of several naked goddesses, Venus Callipyge, Venus Pandemos, Venus Metempsychosis, and plaster figures, also naked, representing the new nine muses, Commerce, Operatic Music, Amor, Publicity, Manufacture, Liberty of Speech, Plural Voting, Gastronomy, Private Hygiene, Seaside Concert Entertainments, Painless Obstetrics and Astronomy for the People. (U 490)

One of the generic features of the pantomime is the easy metamorphosis of one form into another, of the hero into Harlequin and his beloved into Columbine, of a dark forest into a lovely grotto.

PLATES 11 and 12. Pictured here in both of his guises, George H. Chirgwin was a minstrel of whom it has been said that of "all the eccentric music-hall comedians, with their grotesque costumes and strictly individual make-up, George Chirgwin stands supreme. . . . Even after he had been known as 'The White-Eyed Kaffir' for a score of years, when he jerked his head back to reveal the celebrated white lozenge, he was greeted by roars of delight and cries of 'good old George'" (Busby, p. 35). His skilled use of falsetto and playful costume made his act destabilize not only gender categories but also racial distinctions. Furthermore, the fact that one of Chirgwin's standard songs was the sentimental "The Blind Boy" makes him a wonderful analogue to Joyce's Ulyssean "blind stripling," who undermines popular sentimentalizing of physical handicaps. (Photographs reproduced by the kind permission of Roy Busby, London, and the Raymond Mander and Joe Mitchenson Theatre Collection, London.)

Transformations within the play could be positive or negative, helpful or hindering to protagonists. The pantomime writers multiplied the trials of transformation in many ways, and their audiences accepted such outlandish doings as they did the conventional emotional exaggerations of the melodrama. Joyce appears to have taken the pantomime's cues in these matters, in that "Circe" operates by the constant alteration of people, costumes, and scenery, with the dominating logic of the episode being that of mutability itself.

This transformation takes several forms, but generally either the role enacted by Stephen or Bloom will trigger an appropriate response or the change in an environmental factor will create a change in Bloom's costume or in Stephen's mood. The mood and the role are thus extensions of each other; the episode provides a model of cultural enactment. Bloom enters the Nighttown district as "*lovelorn longlost lugubru Booloohoom*," as "*jollypoldy the rixdix doldy*," as "*puffing Poldy*" in search of "*pig's crubeen*" and "*sheep's trotter*" (U 433–34). Almost struck by a "*sandstrewer*," Bloom turns policeman for a moment, holding up a "*whitegloved hand*" (U 435), then speaks Spanish in response to seeing a "*sinister figure*" in sombrero leaning against O'Beirne's. Recalling his letter to the *Irish Cyclist* about the hazards of travel at night, Bloom is a type of the athletic and concerned citizen (U 436); careful of pickpockets, Bloom is a modern Polonius, an advice-giver like his father, and the latter does in fact rise before Bloom so that the son eventually appears garbed in "*youth's smart blue Oxford suit with white vestslips, narrowshouldered, in brown Alpine hat, wearing gent's sterling silver Waterbury keyless watch and double curb Albert with seal attached*" (U 438). Through the clichéd roles of dutiful son, henpecked husband, masochist, "lion of the night" (U 444), secret lover of Josie Breen, king of Ireland, and common workman—to name only some of his roles—Bloom establishes for us a series of possible subworlds for the drama to develop in.

Bloom is, of course, not the only one to change in this episode. His grandfather Virag seems temporarily to adopt elements of a cat (U 516–17); O'Molloy becomes John F. Taylor before transforming into Seymour Bushe (U 464–65); the red-light district itself changes into a scene of Oriental splendor (U 477). Hugh Kenner has viewed such changes as indicating that we all play roles,[41] but because this analysis leaves out of account, except as quasi-hallucinations, attendant changes in setting and among various life forms, I would put it a different way. Certainly Joyce works hard in *Ulysses* and *Finnegans Wake* to undermine the notion that any character is a holistic self rather than a complex of cultural codes or a nexus of societal influences, but in "Circe" we go beyond a concern with the self to find all things in motion and transition. The focus is at least partially kept on the dramatic text and its world-making, and on the way that this process mirrors the culture's continuous generation of roles and scenes for the members of the society in question to run through, to transform at will, and to be transformed by. What "Circe" brings us up against, though, is the hard economic reality that cannot be altered at the touch of imagination but which requires more physical handling. "Circe" shows us the battering of individuals, caught up in their own plights and dreams, by a history that, having the last word, undoes many a hopeful vision.

The "Grand Transformation"

Old style or new style, the pantomime's most attractive feature is the transformation scene. Originally occurring when the opening story turned into the harlequinade, the transformation remained at the end of the much-lengthened opening and served to round off the fairy-tale or nursery-rhyme plot with an assertion of the wonders of fairy power and of magic. A good general description of the classic panto transformation occurs in Percy Fitzgerald's *The World Behind the Scenes* (1881):

> All will recall in some elaborate transformation scene how quietly and gradually it is evolved. First the "gauzes" lift slowly one behind the other—perhaps the most pleasing of all scenic effects—giving glimpses of "the Realms of Bliss," seen beyond in a tantalising fashion. Then is revealed a kind of half-glorified country, clouds and banks, evidently concealing much. Always a sort of pathetic and at the same time exultant strain rises, and is repeated as the changes go on. Now we hear the faint tinkle—signal to those aloft on "bridges" to open more glories. Now some of the banks begin to part slowly, showing realms of light, with a few divine beings—fairies—rising slowly here and there. More breaks beyond and fairies rising, with a pyramid of these ladies beginning to mount slowly in the centre. Thus it goes on, the lights streaming on full, in every colour and from every quarter, in the richest effulgence. In some of the more daring efforts, the *femmes suspendues* seem to float in the air or rest on the frail support of sprays or branches of trees. While, finally, perhaps,

at the back of all, the most glorious paradise of all will open, revealing the pure empyrean itself, and some fair spirit aloft in a cloud among the stars—the apex of all. Then all motion ceases; the work is complete; the fumes of crimson, green, and blue fire begin to rise at the wings; the music bursts into a crash of exultation; and, possibly to the general disenchantment, a burly man in a black frock coat steps out from the side and bows awkwardly. Then to shrill whistle the first scene of the harlequinade closes in, and shuts out the brilliant vision.[42]

Judging from the descriptions of pantomime stage mechanics in Southern's *The Victorian Theatre*, the transformation scene as Broadbent recalls it fits fairly well what Dublin theaters aimed for, although their results must have been less spectacular than most of those on London's stages.[43]

What is significant about these scenes is not only the care, ingenuity, and cash lavished on them but also the social values implied in the transformation. Booth comments that from the mid nineteenth century on,

> moral boundaries in pantomime were much more sharply demarcated [than in Regency productions], probably for the edification of the increasing number of children in the audience, and a fixed moral pattern became apparent in the opening, in both characterization and scenic effect. Many pantomimes of this period began with a gloomy scene in the realm of the evil spirit and his henchmen, followed by a sharply contrasting scene set in the bright dominion of the good fairy, who sets herself against the evil spirit and resolves to frustrate his work. Sometimes it is the other way around. Whatever the order, the good fairy takes the hero and heroine under her protection, and the evil spirit determines to do as much harm to them as he can. . . . A moral confrontation of this kind was obviously and often elaborately expressed.[44]

This change was linked strongly to the pantomime's essentially melodramatic scale of moral values, clear-cut evil being readily recognizable and easily distinguishable from the beautiful good. Similarly, the final "grand" transformation carried ideological messages; always built into a simple framework, these scenes were demonstrably some of the most blatant societal wish-fulfillment ever staged.

A few examples should convey the flavor of the pantomime transformations. In the 1876 *Aladdin* performed at the Theatre Royal, the scene was entitled "The Loves of Hero and Leander!" The songbook's brief description of the classical story summarizes the outcome:

> As upon the occasion of each sweet interview it would be necessary for LEANDER to trust himself to the fostering care of the treacherous waves to bear him to his beloved, APHRODITE, guardian of all true lovers, fearing lest a chance tempest might arise and cause LEANDER to perish in the raging billows, decided upon herself conveying him with HERO nightly to the region of her votaries on the
>
> GOLDEN ISLAND
OF
CEASELESS DELIGHTS!

The producers sacrificed the rationale of the classical myth to provide for their customers a vision of Utopia. Similarly, according to the programme, *Harlequin Bryan O'Lynn* (1888) moves at its close from the "Gloomy Cavern" to the "GRAND TRANSFORMATION: REALMS OF BLISS, or a DREAM OF FAIRYLAND. WITH SPECIAL AND BRILLIANT SCENIC EFFECTS." In the same year the Gaiety followed standard form in ending *Cinderella* with a "Dream of Cloudland and Triumph of Luna." Two years later the Gaiety's *Ali Baba* ended with a transformation scene entitled "NIGHT AND MORNING."

Turning to a seasonal theme, the 1894 *Dick Whittington* at the Gaiety presented a transformation called "THROUGH STORM AND SNOW TO SUNSHINE."[45] This motif informed many panto extravaganzas, including the Queen's 1895 production of *The Forty Thieves*, in which the audience viewed "SPRING'S TRIUMPH OVER WINTER"; the same theater's 1889 *Dick Whittington and His Wonderful Cat!* involved a transformation in four tableaux, one for each season of the year. On the same lines, the Gaiety's 1892 *Sindbad the Sailor*, an important pantomime for Joyce, took ten minutes between scenes to set up a transformation of which the *Irish Times* gives a fine description:

> The transformation scene, entitled "Winter and Summer," is very grand, and thoroughly creditable to the artists . . . who painted all the scenery, which is of the most beautiful description. Winter is suggested by a snow covered scene and a troop of merry-hearted boys romping around Father Christmas. They run off the stage laughing, the Christmas bells begin to peal, and on creeps a poor little lassie in rags, shivering in the snow and moonlight, sobbing out this plaintive ditty, "No one to love me; these Christmas chimes bring no joy to me; no father, no mother, no home; why doesn't Santa Claus bring

me happiness?" and she falls while the pure snow covers her. Then Santa Claus does come in, and she is cared for; and bright summer breaks over the scene and all is loveliness, and speaks volumes for the great trouble that everyone . . . connected with the Gaiety has taken to produce a pantomime so entertaining and full of incident and beauty.[46]

It is, of course, this production that Bloom appears to recall in "Ithaca" as he falls off to sleep.

With?

Sinbad the Sailor and Tinbad the Tailor and Jinbad the Jailer and Whinbad the Whaler and Ninbad the Nailer and Finbad the Failer and Binbad the Bailer and Pinbad the Pailer and Minbad the Mailer and Hinbad the Hailer and Rinbad the Railer and Dinbad the Kailer and Vinbad the Quailer and Linbad the Yailer and Xinbad the Phthailer.

When?

Going to dark bed there was a square round Sinbad the Sailor roc's auk's egg in the night of the bed of all the auks of the rocs of Darkinbad the Brightdayler. (U 737)

Bloom's thoughts, as he falls asleep after a day of both special frustration and routine failures, turn to pantomime and indicate that the presumed center of his consciousness is composed chiefly of elements from the peripheral and enclosing popular culture.

Clearly, ideological content having no overt relationship to *Sindbad*'s story was easily woven into the Gaiety's production. The transformation scene described is a collection of stereotypes—the "little match girl" falling into the snow in her poverty and despair, only to have a vision of happiness that turns out to be true—but the importance of this enactment should not be underestimated. Given the managers' typical efforts to reach the popular mind in as economically beneficial a way as possible, such a scene speaks to basic social issues and voices cultural wish-fulfillment on a mass scale.

Fredric Jameson, in his conclusion to *The Political Unconscious*, argues the intimate and necessary connection between popular cultural phenomena and a culture's Utopian imagination:

. . . if the ideological function of mass culture is understood as a process whereby otherwise dangerous and protopolitical impulses are 'managed' and defused, rechanneled and offered spurious objects, then some preliminary step must also be theorized in which these same impulses—the raw material upon which the process works—are initially awakened within the very text that seeks to still them. If the function of the mass cultural text is meanwhile seen rather as the production of false consciousness and the symbolic reaffirmation of this or that legitimizing strategy, even this process cannot be grasped as one of sheer violence (the theory of hegemony is explicitly distinguished from control by brute force) nor as one inscribing the appropriate attitudes upon a blank slate, but must necessarily involve a complex strategy of rhetorical persuasion in which substantial incentives are offered for ideological adherence. We will say that such incentives, as well as the impulses to be managed by the mass cultural text, are necessarily Utopian in nature.[47]

The pantomime, especially the transformation scene, offers explicit evidence that the popular theater of Joyce's day responded to such idealized impulses. The control of the seasons, the instantaneous and magical conquering of Ireland's long-standing problem of extreme poverty, the consummation of eternal and nonsexual love, the vindication of the deserving poor—these and similar "triumphs" showed up regularly on the Dublin stage during those festal times of year when societies indulge their sense of possibility.

More than indoctrinating children into the moral values of the culture, the pantomime served to school them in the society's visionary goals as well as in the deceptive idea that only through the agency of admittedly unreal conditions (magic, fairy queens, gods and goddesses, folklore heroes) could such dreams be realized. That is, they could never be actualized in society itself; hence, the pantomime lessons served the interests of the middle class, which would not have desired the redistribution of wealth required to alleviate even the most pressing of such conditions.

It is important that precisely the sorts of magical changes that the transformation scene specialized in were eschewed in Joyce's own Circean pantomime. Far from "curing" Stephen and Bloom of their private obsessions and public problems, "Circe" puts them through change after change only to leave them as they were at the outset. Nonetheless, the compensatory longings to which the pantomime spoke have been evinced by the many readers of *Ulysses* who have discovered in Nighttown a magical bonding of the two men or some instant change in Bloom that will put his marriage back on the stereotypical track of marital bliss. Such readers fail to register the subversion of bourgeois ideology in Joyce's uses of popular culture.

Jameson goes on to argue that Marxist criticism must add to its "demystifying vocation" the task of demonstrating how "a given cultural object" fulfills a Utopian function in its "symbolic affirmation of a specific historical and class form of collective unity."[48] One might observe that the Utopian urge asserted by Jameson—this multivalent impulse toward both a pseudotheological plenitude of being and a society in which all share the aims of the dominant class—may also be viewed not as something inevitable and pervasive but as culturally created and transmitted. Whatever the case, given the growing prominence of the transformation scene throughout most of the pantomime's history, and given the amount of money lavished on it annually in West End theaters and provincial halls alike, it is clear that the culture was willing to pay dearly for such visions of amelioration without perspiration.

Significantly, all classes responded to such magical solutions to persistent problems of both culture (poverty, romance) and nature (seasons, elements). That the society went for its answers to the realms of fairyland and folklore suggests the strength of the underlying resistance to significant socioeconomic changes; that Joyce refused to do the same indicates an active critique of this programming for social inactivity.

Class Conflicts and Political Tensions in "Circe"

In "Circe," Joyce deals with wealth and poverty, with unions, and with the economic stalemates of Irish society. The Utopia proposed by Bloom is as wish-fulfilling as those of the pantomime: the Irish theater and Joyce's works provide parallel evidence of the cultural desire for resolution. However, Joyce rejects this impulse in his recourse at the end of "Circe," after concentration on social problems, to the personal level. In fact, this withdrawal from the social panorama characterizes Joyce's aesthetic political stance. Dominic Manganiello documents beyond doubt Joyce's interest in socialist and anarchist politics, but Joyce's artistic activity involves a range of political practices wider than his reading and theorizing might indicate. What is important about Joyce's art is not that at one time he spoke as a socialist and that later his political statements became more evasive, but rather that in his writings he was always driven

back to the personal and that he refused to allow his works fully to
resolve the social conflicts he observed.

In many ways, "Circe" is the most direct treatment in *Ulysses* of
the historical contradictions shaping Irish experience. The atmosphere projected from the beginning of the chapter describes a violent culture in which life is almost insupportable and in which British soldiers act as quasi-lords in a world of victimized women and
"*bandy*" or "*scrofulous*" children (U 430). The fact is that what we
read as expressionistic exaggeration is in some cases more faithful to
the reality of life in an Irish tenement district than one would like to
admit.

"Circe" is as much the world of an imperialized experience as it is
of the unconscious. It is no exaggeration to state that although critics have tended to focus on the significance of the episode for the
purgation of various psychic problems of Stephen and Bloom,
"Circe" insists on being read as a portrait of cultural psychosis. At
one point, Bloom is accosted by a bawd who wants to sell him a
woman ("Ten shillings a maidenhead. Fresh thing was never touched.
Fifteen. There's no-one in it only her old father that's dead drunk"
[U 441]); one reason for such conditions is the capitalist assumption that every item—inanimate or human—can be exchanged on a
market that operates according to a single monetary scale of values.
This cash nexus creates, so "Circe" maintains, much of the violence
of Irish life, especially the conflict of classes and the uneasy relationship of English and Irish. The episode suggests that the economic
situation in Ireland could not be distinguished from the context of
political oppression in which that economy operated.

Although it is often presented in comic ways, the economic dimension of the episode is complex. For example, Philip Beaufoy,
charging Bloom with plagiarism, uses against Bloom the full rhetorical force of a higher class's disgust at a lower's *modus vivendi*.
Beaufoy himself describes his works as "books of love and great pos-
sessions," and he addresses with absolute disdain Bloom's "*hangdog
meekness*" during his attempt to defend himself: "You funny ass,
you! You're too beastly awfully weird for words! . . . My literary
agent Mr J. B. Pinker is in attendance. I presume, my lord, we shall
receive the usual witnesses' fees, shan't we? We are considerably out
of pocket over this bally pressman johnny, this jackdaw of Rheims,
who has not even been to a university" (U 459). True to his type,
Beaufoy wants his payoff immediately and attempts to demolish

Bloom by pulling rank on him in terms of education and connections. Significantly, that confrontation instantly turns to the case of "The King versus Bloom," in which Mary Driscoll charges Bloom with sexual assault. One of the employed members of the working class in *Ulysses*, Driscoll remonstrates when it is suggested that she may be of "the unfortunate class" of streetwalkers. She defends herself by saying that despite Bloom's advances, "I thought more of myself as poor as I am," but Bloom, now adopting Beaufoy's own tactics, says, "I treated you white. I gave you mementos, smart emerald garters far above your station" (U 460–61). Despite his Utopian sentiments, Bloom thinks hierarchically, holding to the class system that defines his moral standards.

It is thus interesting that as part of Bloom's defense, Bloom is reported as wanting to

> lead a homely life in the evening of his days, permeated by the affectionate surroundings of the heaving bosom of the family. An acclimatised Britisher, he had seen that summer eve from the footplate of an engine cab of the Loop line railway company while the rain refrained from falling glimpses, as it were, through the windows of loveful households in Dublin city and urban district of scenes truly rural of happiness of the better land with Dockrell's wallpaper at one and ninepence a dozen, innocent Britishborn bairns lisping prayers to the Sacred Infant, youthful scholars grappling with their pensums or model young ladies playing on the pianoforte or anon all with fervour reciting the family rosary round the crackling Yulelog while in the boreens and green lanes the colleens with their swains strolled what times the strains of the organtoned melodeon Britanniametalbound with four acting stops and twelvefold bellows, a sacrifice, greatest bargain ever . . . . (Joyce's ellipsis, U 462)

This brilliant passage mixes clichés of middle-class Irish life with references to the British sources of many such values and with the advertising language that programs both British and Irish societies to accept a commodified version of Utopia. Not long after this evocation of the ideological complex on which many cultural values depend, "Circe" presents Bloom's defense against the aristocratic women (Mrs. Yelverton Barry, Mrs. Bellingham, and the Honourable Mrs. Mervyn Talboys) who charge him with various indecent advances. It is significant that much of the women's rage centers on Bloom's class more than on the nature of his sexual overtures. Mrs. Talboys thus derides him as a "plebeian Don Juan" (U 467) and bristles, "To dare address me! I'll flog him black and blue in the public streets" (U 469). Even were we to accept this fantasy as simply a reflection of Bloom's neuroses as shaped by Sacher-Masoch and Krafft-Ebing, the class dimension of the narrative suggests also the specific social formation in Ireland into which the text inserts itself, the intersection of Irish and British social hierarchies that not only created tension among rich and poor but also stood as a not very subtle form of international violence.

Throughout "Circe," Stephen and Bloom follow more or less separate tracks, playing out two ideological strands—Bloom these conflicts within politics and economics, Stephen the confrontation with the church. However, Stephen's run-in with the two soldiers dramatizes in its own way the political and economic tensions of his culture. Although he prefers to dissociate himself from the social, Stephen obviously cannot do so. As in a pantomime, in which the police often figured, "Circe" includes agents of British power who pursue Stephen and literally knock him out.

Although he attempts to extend hospitality to the privates, stating that they are his "guests," however "Uninvited," and however much "History [is] to blame" (U 587), he recognizes that to them he is a "Green rag to a bull" (U 592)—at which point Kevin Egan interjects his anti-British sentiments, Patrice skirts the issue by re-announcing his socialism, Biddy the Clap finds Stephen to be "of patrician lineage," the "Virago" plumps for Wolfe Tone, and the "Bawd" sides with the British by cheering, "Up the soldiers! Up King Edward!" (U 592–93). Earlier, the navvy had shouted out against the British (U 451), and here seems to do so again, suggesting the mixed influences in Irish popular ideology reflected when the "Hag" says, "What call had the redcoat to strike the gentleman and he under the influence? Let them go and fight the Boers!" and when the "Bawd" replies, "Listen to who's talking! Hasn't the soldier a right to go with his girl?" (U 602). That the interchange ends in clawing and spitting between hag and bawd epitomizes the displacement of international enmities into interpersonal Irish encounters. As these and other figures take sides in the issue, Rumbold the British executioner, here identified with the Demon Barber of Fleet Street, hangs the Croppy Boy to recall the history of British execution of Irish political enemies. For Stephen it is all "too monotonous." Asserting that Edward VII "wants my money and my life, though want must be his master, for some brutish empire of his"

(U 594), Stephen boils down many cultural discords to the economic motive. Having given away his money, Stephen feels that he has removed himself from that dispute altogether.

With the Citizen and Old Gummy Granny attempting to encourage Stephen to fight and with Bloom pursuing his Circean policy of asserting, based on the participation of the Royal Dublin Fusiliers in the Boer War (U 596; cf. 457), Irish allegiance to the British, Cissy Caffrey pinpoints the reason for the conflict when she notes that they're all going to fight over her. The economic values represented by the prostitute's selling of her body to any political side suggests that the British domination is as much an economic as a political exercise of power, the goal being sustained social control. Bloom charges Cissy to "Speak. . . . You are the link between nations and generations. Speak, woman, sacred lifegiver!" (U 597), but Cissy only insists on her position as commodity by asking Private Carr, "Amn't I your girl?" (U 598). Although the stereotypical connection of woman with lifegiving is one that Bloom tends to buy, here he is educated in the dangers of assuming that the worlds of melodrama and pantomime are accurate portrayals of social reality.

After Apocalypse and Black Mass follow, Carr knocks Stephen to the ground, but within those intervals, which epitomize the culturally catastrophic and perverse, we find another displacement of the British-Irish dissension into Celtic conflict:

> *Armed heroes spring up from furrows. They exchange in amity the pass of knights of the red cross and fight duels with cavalry sabres: Wolfe Tone against Henry Grattan, Smith O'Brien against Daniel O'Connell, Michael Davitt against Isaac Butt, Justin M'Carthy against Parnell, Arthur Griffith against John Redmond, John O'Leary against Lear O'Johnny, Lord Edward Fitzgerald against Lord Gerald Fitzedward, The O'Donoghue of the Glens against The Glens of The O'Donoghue.* (U 598–99)

All of the historical combatants being Irish, *Ulysses* denies the luxury of easy political dichotomies as it does a patriotism that finds the victims free of complicity with their oppressors. Stephen shows his understanding of this complicity when he responds to the inflammatory Old Gummy Granny: "Aha! I know you, gammer! Hamlet, revenge! The old sow that eats her farrow!" (U 595).

"Incidental" documentation of economic concern in the narrative is not difficult to come by. Many of the characters are the poor of

Dublin: a navvy (laborer), a bawd, "Two sluts of the Coombe" (U 552), the "Irish Evicted Tenants," orphans (U 496–97), and the prostitutes themselves. Specifically addressing their situation are two viewpoints—the one capitalistic and exploitative (exemplified by Bella's domineering merchandising of the women), and the other socialistic and Utopian (exemplified by Bloom's social plans and evident concern with abstract justice).[49]

Although Bloom's experience tends to subvert confidence in social equity, he is as deeply scripted by market-economy values as the next character. For instance, Bloom genuinely worries about Stephen's paying too much at Bella's; he finds frustrating Dedalus' laissez-faire attitude about money. In parody of his middle-class outlook, Bloom gives birth to "eight male yellow and white children."

They appear on a redcarpeted staircase adorned with expensive plants. All the octuplets are handsome, with valuable metallic faces, wellmade, respectably dressed and wellconducted, speaking five modern languages fluently and interested in various arts and sciences. Each has his name printed in legible letters on his shirtfront: Nasodoro, Goldfinger, Chrysostomos, Maindorée, Silversmile, Silberselber, Vifargent, Panargyros. They are immediately appointed to positions of high public trust in several different countries as managing directors of banks, traffic managers of railways, chairmen of limited liability companies, vice chairmen of hotel syndicates. (U 494)

From a bourgeois viewpoint, this brood fulfills a parental dream of vicarious upward mobility.[50] The text also brings forth the "eight beatitudes" (a more sinister version of Bloom's children), who state their materialistic credo in which "Bible" has been transformed into "buybull" and in which beer, beef, and business supplant such spiritual values as meekness and peacemaking (U 509).

On the other hand, the union-organized "Chapel of Freeman Typesetters" cheers Bloom after his coronation as "Leopold the First" (U 484, 482), and Bloom's comic platform has elements of Utopian and socialistic thought:

I stand for the reform of municipal morals and the plain ten commandments. New worlds for old. Union of all, jew, moslem, and gentile. Three acres and a cow for all children of nature. Saloon motor hearses. Compulsory manual labour for all. All parks open to the public day and night. Electric dishscrubbers. Tuberculosis, lunacy, war and mendicancy must now cease. General amnesty, weekly carnival with masked licence, bonuses for all, esperanto the universal language with universal brotherhood. No more patriotism of barspongers and dropsical impostors. Free money, free rent, free love and a free lay church in a free lay state. (U 489–90)

But his *"schemes for social regeneration"* lead to Bloom's rejection by Mother Grogan and Mrs. Riordan. They follow the lead of Father Farley, who, accurately reflecting the church's characteristic response to socialism, finds Bloom an "anythingarian" (U 490). Nonetheless, near the end of the episode, as Stephen copes with Privates Compton and Carr, Patrice Egan pops up to shout *"Socialiste!"* (U 592) and to remind us of that politicoeconomic option. In fact, Bloom's alderman speech explicitly voices some of this socialist discourse, although reduced to a handful of clichés:

> These flying Dutchmen or lying Dutchmen as they recline in their upholstered poop, casting dice, what reck they? Machines is their cry, their chimera, their panacea. Laboursaving apparatuses, supplanters, bugbears, manufactured monsters for mutual murder, hideous hobgoblins produced by a horde of capitalistic lusts upon our prostituted labour. The poor man starves while they are grassing their royal mountain stags or shooting peasants and phartridges in their purblind pomp of pelf and power. But their reign is rover for rever and ever and ev . . . (Joyce's ellipsis, U 479)

All of these statements must be accepted in the context of sheer, self-exposing theater. The play provides a site for the intermeshing and reconstituting of cultural codes, not necessarily for the accurate presentation of historical events. Yet "Circe" reflects the problems and possible solutions available in Ireland in Joyce's day as well as the theatrical world and its devices. The popular theater was demonstrably an arena in which cultural problems underwent dramatic transformation to the extent that many plays naively transformed social problems into fairy-tale conventions. Nonetheless, the social content of these plays indicates the depth of the culture's anxieties over apparently irresolvable contradictions. It is a measure of the participation of "Circe" in its social fabric that solutions of any kind are rigorously avoided—are, in fact, ridiculed.

Although the social changes that Bloom posits in "Circe" are the Utopian core of the novel, the popular rejection of Bloom as both a religious and a political leader suggests Irish society's actual turning away from the sort of reform in which he is interested. Hence, Bloom both projects the culture's Utopian fantasies and exhibits its ideological insufficiencies. Bloom "himself" becomes a victim of his cultural fantasies; threatened by wealthy women, he is a perfect image for the lower middle and lower class's belief in its own inadequacy. Acquiescing to the strategy of western culture for at least the past century by which the individual is made to assume responsibility for his or her own psychic condition, most critics have not recognized that in "Circe" masochism is portrayed as a function of the class pressures and ideological practices that have shaped Bloom's personality.[51] Evidence for this position includes the fact that when Bloom confronts Mary Driscoll, a woman of lower social status than his own, the groveling masochism that informs his imagined relations with Mrs. Yelverton Barry is missing.

One might object that the mild sadism that Bloom feels toward Mary Driscoll is matched by his response to the obviously wealthier woman outside the Grosvenor, and that this coalescence undermines the thesis being presented here. However, for Bloom the major consideration is his safety in acting out class aggressions. At a distance, he can easily toy with taking "the starch out" of the woman at the Grosvenor (U 73); near or far, the slavey Mary is no threat to the bourgeois Bloom; but when it appears possible that he may actually be beaten by the women in "Circe," Bloom's class envy turns to fear, his sadism to masochism. The coalescence in Bloom's thoughts of sex and class targets the culture's programming for violence on two important fronts. Nor does Bloom's "real" (as opposed to "imagined") gentleness as a father and husband contradict this viewpoint; it merely evinces the perceived ideological insulation of the familial sphere from the economic and political arenas. In "Circe" the sexual fantasies enacted by Bloom are the space in which he works through the class tensions evident throughout *Ulysses*.

Rudy

Not all of Bloom's "fantasies," though, are sexual. After Bloom explains to Corny Kelleher that he plans to take Stephen home from Nighttown, Kelleher drives off laughing, and "*The jarvey joins in the mute pantomimic merriment . . .*" (U 608). This reference to the nonverbal quality of some pantomime business prepares for the final scene of the episode. Standing over Stephen, Bloom mutters his thoughts about the man as well as fragments of Freemasonic ritual.

(Silent, thoughtful, alert he stands on guard, his fingers at his lips in the attitude of secret master. Against the dark wall a figure appears slowly, a fairy boy of eleven, a changeling, kidnapped, dressed in an Eton suit with glass shoes and a little bronze helmet, holding a book in his hand. He reads from right to left inaudibly, smiling, kissing the page.)

BLOOM

(wonderstruck, calls inaudibly) Rudy!

RUDY

(gazes, unseeing, into Bloom's eyes and goes on reading, kissing, smiling. He has a delicate mauve face. On his suit he has diamond and ruby buttons. In his free left hand he holds a slim ivory cane with a violet bowknot. A white lambkin peeps out of his waistcoat pocket.) (U 609)

In the old-style harlequin pantomime tradition,[52] "silent" Bloom "inaudibly" speaks to an "unseeing," silent, and miming child who has fascinated Joyce's critics from Stanislaus Joyce on. Except for Hayman and Kenner,[53] however, they have tended to skirt the pantomime context of the scene, the transformation format, and the symbolic details—the very theater of the event.

In fact, most commentary on Rudy has been brief and relatively uninformative. For example, Stuart Gilbert tells us that after Bloom's "erotic and perverse" fantasies throughout "Circe," he "redeems himself" with a "wistful vision" of Rudy, and Gilbert adds that in this vision the "trappings of death" are "transmuted into a sparkling panoply of fairyland."[54] William York Tindall says, "That Rudy would be eleven now seems a sign of renewal. Does the white 'lambkin' mean kin of the Lamb or Jesus, the black panther? Is Stephen the lambkin? Rudy's glass shoes suggest Cinderella; his helmet is a warrior's; his reading of Hebrew is scholarly and priest-like; his cane is like Stephen's stick."[55] Underplaying the bizarre trappings of the scene, Richard Kain comments only that Stephen "appears to the paternal Bloom as his beloved Rudy, dressed in an Eton suit, holding a book in his hand, a white lambkin peeping from his pocket."[56] Jackson Cope, in an interesting variation, states that "Little Rudy can merge with Stephen only in the poignant shepherd boy who smiles into the reveries of Bloom as he guards a drunken Stephen."[57]

Quite early, Edmund Wilson claimed that Bloom "beholds an apparition of his own dead son, little Rudy, as Bloom would have had him live to be—learned, cultivated, sensitive, refined: such a youth,

in short, as Stephen Dedalus. Ulysses and Telemachus are united."[58]
Harry Blamires, confusing idealization with stylization, asserts that
as Bloom watches over Stephen, "Paternal longing rises within him
and the figure of his lost son, Rudy, appears before him, eleven years
old as he would have been had he lived, and highly idealized in deli-
cacy of feature, studiousness, cheerfulness, and charm. The 'white
lambkin' establishes him as the paschal victim. The home-rule Son
will yet arise in the north-west."[59]

Hugh Kenner carries on the paschal motif by stating that at the
end of "Circe" Bloom unconsciously plays "the Christly role" of re-
deemer, the vision of his son being "like a resurrection" of Rudy.[60]
More suggestively, Richard Ellmann finds that the "vision of Rudy"
puts the

> seal upon Bloom's Good Samaritan act. . . . Bloom raises Rudy from
> the dead like Lazarus. . . . Bloom harrows hell. The child reading
> Hebrew from right to left creates by his bizarre attitude and detach-
> ment a sense of distance and estrangement from Bloom even as he
> answers his call. . . . Rudy's ivory cane transfigures Stephen's ash-
> plant. He is like a statuette of a child, something to buy it may be in
> Woolworth's, and yet the effect is not maudlin, but genuinely tender.
> At the midpoint of the *Wandering Rocks* Lenehan had said that there
> was 'a touch of the artist about old Bloom', and it is as an artist that
> he now vindicates himself, creating out of love an image which has
> independent life. . . . Here, out of love for his dead child, he does
> more than remember, he reshapes Rudy's misshapen features and raises
> him from the grave. He fathers and mothers this new-old child. . . .
> his vision of Rudy . . . is Bloom's way of damning death . . . and of
> making life easter in us.[61]

But such a description leaves some details as well as Bloom's surprise and awe unexplained. If Bloom truly imagines this figure, then
why are we told that it is conjured—and that Bloom, like Faust in a
similar act of conjuring, is startled at his success?

To account fully for the iconography of Rudy's actions and attire
it is necessary to recognize that first and foremost Rudy is a character in the Circean drama and that his immediate forebear is not
Bloom as much as it is the English pantomime.[62] Rudy is the most
obvious example in *Ulysses* of a character constructed, as all are,
from cultural discourses. Joyce plays off the reader's expectation that
every detail will be significant, by this point in *Ulysses* an automatic
response even without the theatrical promptings, to suggest that the

highly artificial and bizarrely cross-coded Rudy needs to be understood by reference to the several discourses constituting him. Again, the primary frame of reference is the pantomime: Rudy is both silent harlequin and the hero of the twentieth-century panto. In a sense, Rudy, who is "neither one thing nor the other" (U 774), is a classic principal boy. However, purely a role in a drama, Rudy cannot with certainty be assigned any sex or any age.

Attending to the institutional context, Rudy's costume, his miming, and the manner of his materializing bear witness to his dramatic status. As readers have noticed, Rudy owes his mauve face to his coloration at birth, but the oddity of the hue confirms that Rudy wears the spangled costume of a pantomime hero during a transformation scene. Rudy's slow emergence and his fairy status suggest the gradual nature and fairy-world milieu of the transformation. He also has ties with the older Harlequin figure, for his slim cane is a displacement not only of Stephen's stick but also of the magic bat traditionally held by Harlequin; both ivory cane and ashplant may be taken as allusions to the pantomime's transformative baton. Although he would not be out of place on the English stage, Rudy is a specifically Irish concoction, for he is the Yeatsian changeling, kidnapped by the sometimes unpleasant fairies of Celtic folklore; Stephen's muttering of "Who Goes with Fergus" sustains Rudy's indigenous quality.

Rudy's status as dramatic character is important, for, amidst the sentimentality of Bloom's wonder over the "revived" child, we are likely to neglect the fact that the pantomime transformation scene always leads to a world of utter improbability. However allied to the melodrama the panto was, this scene signified the introduction of a world without death, illness, poverty, adultery, and misery. That wish-fulfillment was produced by enterprising theater managers but eschewed by Joyce's narrative. His pantomime—effectively evoking the glittering world of the fairies through the single image of the remote changeling child—reflexively detonates itself by making its audience part of the drama. Because neither Bloom nor Stephen is any more material than the scenes they witness (both character and scene existing only as script), "Circe" tells us that none of what has happened, neither the horror of May Goulding's ghostly apparition nor the wonder of Rudy's appearance, is real.

It is this dramatic view of Rudy that Marilyn French comes close to after she discusses Bloom's characteristic of being loving.

> But lest we permit ourselves the luxury of sentimentalization or idealization of Bloom or the human race, beleaguered as both are, Joyce presents us with one of his great visions. The dénouement, Bloom's vision of Rudy as a cross among Cinderella, Little Lord Fauntleroy, and Bo-Peep, is ironic in Joyce's special way. For noble Leopold Bloom can find a purpose to his life only in a fairy-tale / nursery rhyme symbol—a fact that is at once ludicrous, pathetic, outrageous, comic, and true to human experience.[63]

French has located the exact parameters of Bloom's vision without noting the medium by which such material was transmitted to Bloom and to Joyce's compatriots. Like other vehicles in the popular theater, the pantomime created both Bloom's vision and that of his contemporaries. It has been suggested that the pantomime showed an adult's idea of a child's view of the world and especially of dreamland. The "Rudy" we find in "Circe" is Bloom's idea of childhood generated out of such theatrical experience. Highly artificial, the vision that the drama offers to Bloom places the frontier of his imagination firmly within the settled, not to say exploited, domain of popular culture.

Notably, the quasi-religious nostalgia that Bloom sometimes feels when he thinks of his father has also been absorbed into this vision, as have *Hamlet* and the Scriptures. It is as though Joyce were prompting us to recognize how fully even the most exalted art or highest spiritual mysteries not only coalesce with the popular but also exhibit the same constructedness. Not only a panto figure, Rudy is also an angel of the apocalypse, as iconic as a figure from *Revelations*. In chapter 10 of that biblical text occurs an angel with a little book. Within *Ulysses*, that angel, Hamlet with his tablets, Rudolph Bloom with his Hebrew texts, and Stephen on the strand with his shred of paper all figure one another. By this logic, the cultural traditions alluded to in Joyce's transformation scene make Rudy equal to Rudolph, the son to the father, the angelic to the human, the poet or playwright to the character created. Ultimately, that character is not just a dramatic persona but the culture itself.

Finally, attention must be paid to the Homeric source of Joyce's concern with transformation in "Circe," a source into which Joyce folded the popular theatrical preoccupations of his day. In Homer's version of the Circe story, after Odysseus' sailors are transformed again into men, they are younger, fairer, and taller than they were before their ordeal. This Homeric pattern coincides neatly with the new and, by all accounts, more presentable Rudy who appears at Bloom's summons, as it does with the pantomime's remaking of all things into better and more beautiful versions of themselves in its Grand Transformation. It may be assumed, then, that *Ulysses*, like other cultural artifacts of its time, speaks the utopian drive that Jameson discusses. Stephen, Bloom, and Molly are presented as products of an atomized society; they are as dominated by business and empire as Odysseus' men were by Circe. Yet we are also shown a persistent desire in Bloom, most forcefully aired in the vision of Rudy, for a real family, a real community, and a real nation held together by the love that he tries to describe in "Cyclops." Bloom's recurrent thoughts of happy times with Molly and Milly (the experience on Howth, Milly's bath night) evoke a sense of family as community which stands in contrast to the family life usually encountered in Joyce's fiction. The Breens, the Purefoys, and the Dedaluses exemplify the sad results of domination by church and state—unchecked fertility, impoverishment, anomie, degraded women, hopeless children, maddened men. Bloom's estranged wanderings in Dublin point to conditions in his country that were beyond the power of individuals to correct. It is symptomatic of the need for fundamental social change that even when looking for a flicker of communal warmth from another Jew, Bloom encounters not a spiritual kinsman but Dlugazc the shopkeeper.

The transformed Rudy signifies the family, community, and continuity that Bloom, alone and alienated, seeks, but the transformations Bloom desires cannot take place in the cultural matrix currently shaping his compatriots and himself. The reality is rather Stephen's wariness of Bloom, the offal-toting boy in "Lotus-Eaters" who passes the time with cigarettes, the poverty of Si Dedalus and his cohorts, prostitution, violence, and literature turned from a tool of discovery into a commodity like *Titbits*. As a Jew, Bloom tends to represent to other Dubliners the same kind of usurious connection with an already inequitable economic system that Reuben J. Dodd epitomizes. One of Joyce's less subtle ironies, this situation foregrounds the few things that Bloom argues for against the oppressive culture in which he exists. But like Stephen, Bloom is caught in the nightmare of history, which—whether personal, social, or global—allows no awakening for those who populate Joyce's fictions.

Joyce's use of the pantomime form as part of *Ulysses* accentuates the transformation of convention that the narrative undertakes. Through his aggressive exploration of the theater of gender, Joyce makes inescapable the undecidable relation of individual and institution, by which neither may be said to be separable from the other; [64] the stage transmits sexual ideology, and Joyce uses gender conventions to expose the institutional masking of ideology as nature. Further, in responding to the pantomime's transformation scene, Joyce brings to light the cultural attempt to "masque" violence as community. Joyce relied on biblical iconography, on stage tradition, and on reflexive references to *Ulysses* itself to transform Rudy's death and the social antagonisms seen in Nighttown into a moment of pure "culture" (the utopian child). In this textual moment, many codes converge to reveal their activity in shaping communal desire and expectation. The withdrawal by both Bloom and Stephen from a contradictory social scene to the personal arena is shown to be a centrifugal action which pulls to itself bits of social flotsam and jetsam. These codes and conventions Joyce displays center stage and thereby reverses the retreat to selfhood by setting up an interpretive countermovement toward the social as the source of meaning and, indeed, as the instigation for writing.

NOTES

1. I read a version of section I of the chapter at the Joyce festival held at the State University of New York at Purchase in February of 1982.

2. Peter Ackroyd, *Dressing Up: Transvestism and Drag: The History of an Obsession* (New York: Simon and Schuster, 1979), pp. 61–62, 64, 96, 98.

3. Programme, *Ali Baba and the Forty Thieves*, 26 December 1890.

4. Vesta Tilley appeared seven times at Dan Lowrey's Star of Erin, the final time in 1895. In 1886, Lowrey named her as one of the three performers who had been most successful for him in Dublin. See Eugene Watters and Matthew Murtagh, *Infinite Variety: Dan Lowrey's Music Hall 1879–97* (Dublin: Gill and Macmillan, 1975), pp. 158, 87.

5. Ackroyd, p. 101: "by the 1860s and 1870s, most male and female performers had a 'drag' number in their repertory."

6. Bruce Bradley, S.J., *James Joyce's Schooldays* (New York: St. Martin's Press, 1982), p. 55. At least such is the description of the "Widow Twankay" (variant spelling) which appeared on the programme for the production done at Clongowes Wood College in 1891 and in which Joyce took part. As was traditional and indeed necessary in boys' schools in the British

Isles, such productions always included boys in female roles. In the surviving cast photograph, we find the ten-year-old Joyce dressed for the part of what looks like an imp in drag (Bradley, p. 56). The Widow Twankey "made her first appearance in *Aladdin; or, the Wonderful Scamp* by H. J. Byron, who *invented* her . . . for a burlesque at the Royal Strand in April 1861" (Mander and Mitchenson, p. 22). In *Some Pantomime Pedigrees* (London: Society for Theatre Research, 1963), V. C. Clinton-Baddeley agrees that "The name goes back to 1861—but the part goes back to 1788" (p. 33).

7. Jane W. Stedman, "From Dame to Woman: W. S. Gilbert and Theatrical Transvestism," in *Suffer and Be Still: Women in the Victorian Age*, ed. Martha Vicinus (Bloomington: Indiana University Press, 1972), p. 23. Quotation below in this paragraph is also from p. 23.

8. Joyce was certainly aware of Leno and other music hall artistes who worked during the Christmas season in the pantos. Adaline Glasheen notes several references to Dan Leno in the *Wake*. See *Third Census of Finnegans Wake*, 3rd ed. (Berkeley: University of California Press, 1977), entries "Leno, Dan" and "Drapier."

9. Mícheál mac Liammóir, *Enter a Goldfish: Memoirs of an Irish Actor, Young and Old* (London: Granada, 1977), pp. 19–20.

10. Quoted in Mander & Mitchenson, p. 44, from *The Era*, 30 December 1937.

11. The practice of cross-dressing in the panto grew out of the mid to late nineteenth-century burlesques (Mander and Mitchenson, p. 30), comic dramas that parodied either another contemporary and serious play (especially melodrama) or some well-known story, often based on classical myth. Clinton-Baddeley, however, traces the convention further back, even to the seventeenth century when English actresses began to appear on stage and to adopt male roles: "The beginning of the nineteenth century saw the production of many great musical spectacles and the juvenile lead in these shows was always played by a woman. And since the Regency vogue had exchanged the eighteenth century breeches for tight trousers the male impersonator began to appear in even tighter versions of the fashions. Actresses continued to play the male leads as a matter of course in the extravaganzas and burlesques of the mid-century—those enormously successful entertainments which eventually giggled themselves to death and were firmly replaced in 1892–94 by George Edwardes's new invention of musical comedy. The huge difference between 1892–94 and everything that went before it lay in the rejection of burlesque with its long laughter about serious subjects and its girls dressed as men. Travesty was dead—except in the Christmas entertainment, the fairy tale burlesque with a fragment of harlequinade still clinging to the end; and because travesty survived in the fairy tale the male impersonator survived with it" (pp. 16–17).

This tradition held in England until the 1950s (Mander and Mitchenson, pp. 45–46).

12. Theatre Royal, Dublin, *Aladdin or the Wonderful Lamp*, p. 3. Similarly, the Nurse in the Royal's *Sleeping Beauty* (*Songbook*, 1902, p.5) has some mildly naughty lines: "A maiden with an aching heart, once met her love at night, / He pressed her closely to his breast, and there he held her tight / Said he, 'Give me your answer true, or from your lips I'll force it,' / Said she, 'Don't squeeze me, love, so tight, or you'll break my cor----aching heart.'"

13. Ackroyd, p. 102.

14. In various degrees, many writers on Joyce have taken this stance. For recent examples, see James H. Maddox, Jr., *Joyce's* Ulysses *and the Assault upon Character* (New Brunswick, N.J.: Rutgers University Press, 1978), 114–19, 140; and Suzette A. Henke, *Joyce's Moraculous Sindbook: A Study of* Ulysses (Columbus: Ohio State University Press, 1978), 196–97. Similarly, Hugh Kenner, who emphasizes in his 1974 essay the expressionistic nature of the chapter and denies that it is a "psychological chapter," nonetheless finds Bloom undergoing a "descent through psychic depths," a "course of psychic purgation" (Hart and Hayman, pp. 357, 359, 356). Cf. Kenner's *Ulysses*, pp. 125–27.

15. Mark Shechner, *Joyce and Nighttown* (Berkeley: University of California Press, 1974). Sheldon Brivic's *Joyce Between Freud and Jung* (Port Washington, N.Y.: Kennikat, 1980) also bears mention as a study of the psychoanalytic implications of Joyce's works, but his study is only obliquely related to the issues I am concerned with.

16. For a Lacanian reading of *Ulysses*, see MacCabe. In addition to countering the attempt to read the writer's life through his work (p. 12), MacCabe charts the undermining in "Circe" of the "unitary subject" and of stable bipolar gender definitions. Thus "Circe" becomes the "unconscious" not of Joyce or of Bloom but of the text (pp. 123–24, 128–29). It seems to me that when Maddox suggests that in "Circe" we learn that Bloom has not only a "mysterious" inner core but also "many selves" which play out their roles in the course of the evening (p. 118), he moves toward this position, which contradicts some of his argument about "Circe." Similarly, Kenner walks the line between the theatrical and the psychological, pointing out that Joyce conceived of the self as a "medley" of roles and that this point is abundantly played out in "Circe": "In short, the whole episode is phantasmagoric; the dramatic surface, with its objectivity, its naturalism, is a rhetoric throughout . . ." (Hart and Hayman, pp. 354, 351).

17. Cf. Mark Shechner on the "phallic mother," pp. 69, 112–17, 209–11.

18. Certainly the point must be stressed that Joyce researched much of

his clinical material. Besides having studied Krafft-Ebing, he seems to have known about psychoanalysis by 1912 (Mark Shechner, "Joyce and Psychoanalysis: Two Additional Perspectives," *James Joyce Quarterly* 14 [1976–77], 417). Hence Joyce could have explicitly included images which are now popularly coded as Freudian.

19. Shechner, pp. 101, 150–51, 119–20.

20. Hélène Cixous, "At Circe's, or the Self-Opener," trans. Carol Bové, *Boundary 2*, 3 (Winter 1975), 387. MacCabe comes close to a discussion of conventionality when he argues, "The bisexuality in question does not involve some perfect imaginary union of a disjunct[?]. . . . Rather . . . it implies an infinite and vertiginous regression as Bloom and Bella reflect each other in an endless hall of mirrors. As the text succeeds in giving a voice to the woman in Bloom, it abandons disjunction in favour of a bisexuality which multiplies identity geometrically" (pp. 128–29, cf. pp. 150–51). I find this position slightly erroneous, however, in that there is in *Ulysses* no bisexuality per se except insofar as sexuality is shown to be conventional rather than intrinsic.

21. Quoted in Shechner, p. 120, from Jacques Mercanton, "The Hours of James Joyce," part 1, trans. Lloyd C. Parks, *Kenyon Review* 24 (1962), 700–30.

22. Bloom is not alone in this speculation. In an essay on the producer and director Joe Papp, Marie Brenner notes coincidentally, "Papp has always returned to Hamlets of various kinds. . . . Lately, Papp has talked of producing *Hamlet* with a woman playing the prince. 'What if a young child was brought up from birth and treated like a boy. Think of the relationships . . . Hamlet and Ophelia . . . Hamlet and Horatio! At one point I thought of Hamlet as hermaphroditic, but that's a little weird'" (Marie Brenner, "Joe Papp's Third Act," *New York*, 9 August 1982, pp. 28–32).

23. See Robert Kimbrough, "Androgyny, Old and New," *Western Humanities Review* 35 (Autumn 1981), 197–215. Kimbrough echoes much contemporary thought when he argues persuasively that "the effective determinants of gender differentiation between female and male are social, psychological, and cultural" (p. 199).

24. Carolyn G. Heilbrun, *Toward a Recognition of Androgyny* (New York: Harper Colophon, 1973), p. 95.

25. *Ulysses on the Liffey*, p. 143. Cf. Henke, pp. 7, 93, 194. In her recent dissertation, "James Joyce's *Ulysses*: A Study of the Motifs of Androgyny," *DAI* 38 (1977), 2144A (University of South Florida), Dorothy Hutcherson Roberts argues that the "fundamental theme" of *Ulysses* is "the necessity for a recognition of an alternate mode of consciousness, the feminine, and the concomitant necessity for a re-integration of that second mode

that will result in the ideal androgynous consciousness. . . . The major exemplar and Joyce's ideal is Bloom, the 'new, womanly man.'" Similarly, Gladys Leithauser and Paul Sporn, in "Hypsospadia: Linguistic Guidepost to the Themes of the 'Circe' Episode of *Ulysses*," *Journal of Modern Literature* 4 (1974–75)—their meticulous study of Joyce's use in "Circe" of the term "hypsospadia"—argue that one of the most important themes of "Circe" is "the evolution of biologically divided men and women into a psychologically and even socially advanced state in which each individual, man or woman, incorporates into a single self the polarities of sexual existence." Although they recognize that the idea as applied to Bloom is "farcical," they suggest Joyce's serious advocacy of such an evolutionary possibility (p. 109). And Morris Beja, "The Joyce of Sex: Sexual Relationships in *Ulysses*," *The Seventh of Joyce*, ed. Bernard Benstock (Bloomington: Indiana University Press; Sussex: Harvester Press, 1982), has stated that "the equation between Bloom's so-called weakness and submissiveness and his so-called effeminacy and unmanliness strikes me as abominable. Bloom is 'the new womanly man': there are worse things to be. I recognize that Bloom's androgyny, like every other serious theme in the novel, is undercut and treated ironically: consequently, Bloom also has latent ambidexterity; and he so wants to be a mother; and he sometimes seems less an androgynous being than a hermaphrodite or transvestite. Yet his androgyny is no less real for all that, and no less to his credit" (pp. 262–63).

26. Sandra Gilbert, "Costumes of the Mind: Transvestism as Metaphor in Modern Literature," *Critical Inquiry* 7 (1980), 394. Citations below in this paragraph are from Gilbert, pp. 397–99, 404, and 394.

27. Cixous, "At Circe's," p. 389.

28. Joseph Allen Boone argues that, although Bloom never achieves a full androgyny, he is able to reconcile his male and female traits (pp. 80–82); far from still needing at the end of "Circe" to regain his manhood, Bloom demonstrates the possibility of an individual's moving beyond social stereotypes of masculine and feminine behavior. Hence, when he discusses Bella's change into Bello and Bloom's into a prostitute, Boone comments, "Rather than a complete change of sex, the change is actually one of pronouns and costumes, of sexual *roles*. The fact is significant because it indicates that the perversity of the fantasy lies in social definitions and appearance rather than in Bloom" (p. 76). It seems to me, however, that Boone assumes that there is an authentic self for Bloom to recover or establish and that "Circe" involves Bloom's explorations toward that authenticity. Apparently, Boone sees social stereotypes as things that could be done away with if we were only to develop properly clear vision; this Romantic conception of a self that can operate in an imaginative realm apart from social constraints is at odds with "Circe" and with all of Joyce's work,

in which it is clear that one cannot choose authenticity over stereotype; one can choose only among the conventions offered by the culture. Hence, the term "perversity" to describe either a fantasy of Bloom's or a set of conventions ignores the constructedness of all cultural expression and experience. See Joseph Allen Boone, "A New Approach to Bloom as 'Womanly Man': The Mixed Middling's Progress in *Ulysses*," *James Joyce Quarterly* 20 (1982), 67–85.

29. Beyond the sexual dimension, clothes serve other social functions, most notably the denotation of class status. In "Circe," Mrs. Breen's male attire may be less a reference to transvestism than a sign of poverty (she may be wearing her husband's clothes). In effect, of course, she always wears Dennis's clothes in that her social position depends on her husband's circumstances; in the Dublin that Joyce shows us, a woman is limited to her husband's estate. The function of clothing as a semiotic system, although bound up with the question of sexual definition, is not limited to that role.

30. Bradley indicates that Joyce took part in a Belvedere production during Whitsuntide in 1898 of Edward Rose's adaptation of F. Anstey's novel *Vice Versa*. Again, a picture is extant of Joyce and his schoolmates dressed for their parts in this play, Joyce in the severe garb of the headmaster, Dr. Grimstone. Three or four of the boys are dressed in female costume, looking no doubt much as Bloom might have when he cross-dressed for his role in the same play (Bradley, p. 135–36).

31. Virag, watching a moth, "*cries*," "Who's moth moth? Who's dear Gerald? Dear Ger, that you? O dear, he is Gerald. O, I much fear he shall be most badly burned." The moth, about to be burned by the lamp, is blended in Virag's rhetoric with Gerald, Bloom's transvestite friend. It's a fair guess that Gerald is as susceptible to being burned in his societal setting as any moth or other being that is considered either delicate or deviant. And the Gerald-moth sings that he "was a king" in a former incarnation and then "*rushes against the mauve shade*" saying, "Pretty pretty pretty pretty pretty pretty petticoats" (U 516–17). These comments apparently suggest Gerald's sentiments about his sister's frillies, as well as echo Bloom's about the prostitute's clothing that he will wear.

32. "Such acts are, characteristically, harmless ways of breaking certain sexual taboos. They evoke, for example, fears of feminine aggression and overt sexuality at the same time as they play upon anxieties about male homosexuality; all of these fears are subtly represented, and then detonated" (Ackroyd, pp. 103–4). Similar anxieties marked the early criticism of *Ulysses*.

33. Clive Hart comments (in Epstein, *Starchamber Quiry*, p. 164), "Freed, like his successors the *nouveaux romanciers*, from the old con-

straints of 'character', Joyce nevertheless created highly individual human consciousnesses." Kenner posits that "A character in *Ulysses* (in a city of talk) is an interference phenomenon between 'his' language and language not his, sometimes other characters', sometimes the author's" (*Ulysses*, p. 70). Cf. Kenner on characterization and role-playing in *Ulysses* (in Hart and Hayman, pp. 342–44, 360). Also, cf. MacCabe, who speaks of identity "as a set of social relations" (p. 156).

34. Watters and Murtagh, pp. 164, 167, 83–85.

35. Booth, *English Plays*, p. 25. On a 17 June 1882 programme for the Gaiety now housed in Trinity College Library is an ad for the Leinster Hall's booking of "The World-Renowned Royal BOHEE BROTHERS (Banjoists to H.R.H. the Prince and Princess of Wales and the Princess Louise, by Special Appointment), And Their Company of AMERICAN COLOURED ARTISTS, Thirty in Number." S. Theodore Felstead points out that "the Prince of Wales (King Edward VII), a regular patron of their entertainments, was moved to take a few lessons from them" (*Stars Who Made the Halls* [London: Laurie, 1946], p. 58).

36. Booth, *English Plays*, p. 50. I retain Booth's italics.

37. *Sleeping Beauty*, 1902, p.8.

38. Fritz Senn, "Micro-Cycloptics," manuscript note.

39. Elam, p. 134. Latin *persōna*: a mask worn by an actor or character played by an actor. Cf. Walter W. Skeat, *An Etymological Dictionary of the English Language*, rev. ed. (Oxford: Clarendon Press, [1909]); Skeat derives "person" from "L. *persōna*, a mask used by an actor. . . . As if from L. *persōnare*, to sound through."

40. *The American Heritage Dictionary of the English Language*, 1978, and Skeat.

41. See Kenner's essay in Hart and Hayman. This brilliant article deals extensively with role-playing, as well as with the function of stories in creating individual versions of reality.

42. Quoted in Mander and Mitchenson, p. 28. Broadbent also quotes Fitzgerald and finds the scene "now becoming nearly as obsolete as the Harlequinade" (pp. 185–86), but this assessment must pertain more to the West End theaters than to what was going on in the provinces. Dublin playbills from the 1890s and early 1900s do not indicate a loss of the transformation scene but rather confirm its honored position as the high point of the production.

43. Southern states that in Victorian pantos, "Every plot was so devised that at the crucial moment a complete metamorphosis of the whole scene took place visually—by means of transparencies, rising and falling gauzes, opening pieces, 'rise-and-sinks', etc to provide a crowning miracle of effect" (Southern, p. 39). Southern talks about the machinery used for

raising and lowering scenery and about stages that, from about 1900 on, could be made to rise or sink in sections, but according to Lorcan Bourke, no Dublin stage was this elaborately equipped (Conversation with Bourke at his home in Dublin, 16 July 1981).

44. Booth, *English Plays*, p. 45. This convention was followed in Dublin's productions. For example, *Harlequin Bryan O'Lynn* begins in the "Gloomy Cavern of the Demon Baleful" and moves in scene 2 to the "Fairy Glade," apparently located on the "Island of Perpetual Verdure" (programme, National Music Hall, 24 December 1888).

45. Information in this paragraph about individual transformation scenes is from programmes for the productions cited.

46. *Irish Times*, 27 December 1892, p. 7, col. 5.

47. Jameson, p. 287. For comments on Joyce and "utopianism," see Manganiello, pp. 157, 167.

48. Jameson, p. 291.

49. Bloom's trial (especially U 470–71) is a satire on the possibility of justice in Ireland, a fact emphasized by his being sentenced to death. Later, when Bello denounces him, Bloom cries, "Justice! All Ireland versus one!" (U 543); when he confronts the Nymph, he points to another legal inequity that he suffers under, asserting, "I have sixteen years of black slave labour behind me. And would a jury give me five shillings alimony tomorrow, eh?" (U 554). In response, it would seem, to a lifetime of economic and moral double standards, Bloom, having been tried under a corrupt system, sets up his own tribunal and is acclaimed for his wisdom and fairness. At his "Court of Conscience," Bloom dispenses "open air justice" (U 487) but is attacked and eventually burned at the stake. Whether he is judge or defendant, Bloom ends up with the death sentence. In such a cultural setting, Stephen's skepticism about Bloom is understandable; when at Bella Cohen's Bloom offers to hold onto the younger man's money for him, Stephen says, "Be just before you are generous." Bloom's ambivalence speaks for his mercenary culture: "I will but is it wise?" (U 559).

50. Michael Zimmerman sees these children as "indistinguishable . . . from Bloom's touching petit bourgeois wishes for status, power, and wealth." See "Leopold Paula Bloom: The New Womanly Man," *Literature and Psychology* 29 (1979), 176–77.

51. But Jeremy Hawthorn remarks of Bloom that "as his sadomasochistic sexual fantasies show, the energies that are repressed in public behaviour mould and direct his fantasy life." See "'Ulysses,' Modernism, and Marxist Criticism," in *James Joyce and Modern Literature*, ed. W. J. McCormack and Alistair Stead (London: Routledge and Kegan Paul, 1982), pp. 120–21.

52. The harlequinade was not written in standard script form but in the form of stage directions, much like the scene being discussed.

53. Kenner, in Hart and Hayman, pp. 356, 359–60. Dealing not with social but with personal content, Kenner argues that Stephen and Bloom "are (at least temporarily) changed" during the Rudy scene. See also n. 62 below.

54. Gilbert, pp. 320, 348.

55. *A Reader's Guide to James Joyce* (New York: Noonday-Farrar, 1959), p. 593. Another fairly detailed response to Rudy's attire occurs in John Z. Bennett, "Unposted Letter: Joyce's Leopold Bloom," *Bucknell Review* 14 (1966), 12–13. Commenting on the association of Stephen and Rudy, Bennett notes that "Bloom and Molly both recall seeing Stephen at Dillon's long ago, 'in his lord Fauntleroy suit and curly hair like a prince on the stage'" (U 774), a nice emphasis of the dramatic inspiration for Rudy's attire.

56. Richard Kain, *Fabulous Voyager: James Joyce's* Ulysses, rev. ed. (Chicago: University of Chicago Press, 1959), p. 141.

57. "The Rhythmic Gesture: Image and Aesthetic in Joyce's *Ulysses*," *ELH* 29 (1962), 84.

58. "James Joyce," in *Axel's Castle: A Study in the Imaginative Literature of 1870–1930* (1931; rpt. New York: Scribner, 1959), p. 200.

59. Harry Blamires, *The Bloomsday Book: A Guide through Joyce's* Ulysses (London: Methuen, 1966), p. 207.

60. Hart and Hayman, pp. 360–61. Cf. Ulrich Schneider, "Freemasonic Signs and Passwords in the *Circe* Episode," *James Joyce Quarterly* 5 (1967–68), 310. Referring to the allusive use at the end of "Circe" of the Entered Apprentice's oath of initiation and secrecy from *A Ritual and Illustrations of Freemasonry* (anon., London, 1837), Schneider notes, "In the vision which follows Bloom's recitation of the oath his son Rudy appears, and '*A white lambkin peeps out of his waistcoat pocket*'. . . . The lamb, of course, is a biblical symbol, but it could also allude to the white lamb*skin* which the Entered Apprentice is given as 'an emblem of innocence and purity' (*Ritual*, p. 19)."

61. Ellmann, *Ulysses on the Liffey*, pp. 148–49.

62. Hayman appears to suggest this lineage when he says that "the symbolic link between the two men is confirmed by Bloom's version of Rudy as an eleven-year-old Pre-Raphaelite dream child with a 'mauve' face, a ghastly-sweet emanation hovering over the prostrate poet. The moment is worthy of the Dublin Christmas Pantomime. . . ." See Ulysses: *The Mechanics of Meaning*, rev. ed. (Madison: University of Wisconsin Press, 1982), p. 40. Cf. his "Forms of Folly in Joyce: A Study of Clowning in *Ulysses*," *ELH* 34 (1967), 274, 277–78. Hayman mentions Joyce's use of the pantomime's transvestism and transformation scene in "Circe." Gilbert also mentions, without development, that "Circe" is a pantomime (p. 348).

63. French, p. 206.

64. Karen Lawrence suggests something of my position on theatrical form in "Circe" when she speaks of the "rhetoric of drama" and the conventional content of the unconscious (pp. 146–64), but she tends to keep separate the psyche and the society, while *Ulysses* asks us to discard this inside/outside distinction.

CHAPTER 5

Music Hall—"Circe" and
Finnegans Wake I, iv

We import our amusements and our drama as we import our soap;
no doubt they frequently come over in the same boat.
The Leader (1900)

Matthew Murtagh, an expert on the Irish music hall, tells the story of Oliver St. John Gogarty's being thrown out of Dan Lowrey's—a sort of rite of passage for the college students who flocked to what was by then called the Empire for a cheap evening of jokes, songs, and drink. To Murtagh, that Joyce would have been among them is a foregone conclusion.[1] Whether this assumption is correct or not, Joyce did visit the London halls with his father during a 1900 trip,[2] and his interest in them appears not to have faded away even during his years on the continent; Frank Budgen mentions that he and Joyce would sing tunes from "those vintage years of popular song associated with the names of Dan Leno, Harry Randall, Tom Costello, Gus Elen, Arthur Roberts, and the other music hall giants of that time."[3] But the reader of Joyce's works needs no biographical evidence that he found the halls fascinating. Throughout *Ulysses* and *Finnegans Wake* we find many references to the songs that the halls made popular.[4]

Most of these references have been studied by readers of Joyce as often ironic reinforcements of characterization and theme. Although Joyce did not devote a full chapter of any of his works to music hall mimicry, it has been suggested that the rapid style-changes of *Ulysses* follow the rhythm of the halls with their nightly successions of "turns."[5] Certainly, the scattered references throughout the book to Tom Rochford's automatic turn-marker reinforce this hypothesis, so that the form of *Ulysses* as a whole alludes to the halls. In addition, at times Joyce goes beyond the brief allusion to make more extensive

189

use of specific songs. These "turns" within "Circe" and *Finnegans Wake* I, iv point to the class-specific reason for his attention to these songs and performers.

It is the donnée of music hall material that it expressed lower- and lower middle-class concerns. More precisely, it addressed the cultural contradictions presented by modern industrialization, in particular, the presence in the same society of extreme poverty and conspicuous wealth. Hence, it was both hailed as the communal voice of the people and censured as suggestive, vulgar, and (in Ireland) antinationalistic. A Joycean allusion to a music hall performer or song carries with it an ideological charge derived both from the socioeconomic nature of the material being dealt with in the halls and from the insertion of that material—by way of the importing of English performers—into Irish culture.

Perhaps this charge is what Joyce had in mind when he fashioned the self-conscious mot, "The music hall, not Poetry, a criticism of life."[6] As Martha Vicinus tells us in *The Industrial Muse* and as T. S. Eliot's famous essay on Marie Lloyd confirms, the music hall shaped and projected the working-class identity of England's industrial towns.[7] But music hall acts were not just the communication of the lower class; they were also a revealing intersection of class relations. Through stereotyping, emulation (the kid who attends the halls and dresses like a "toff"), and the general airing of working-class problems, the music hall helped to manage class tensions. (Ironically, this management served ultimately to *contain* lower-class frustration by making expression into a commodity to be purchased by the worker.)[8]

Perhaps most important, the music hall often involved a conscious satire on the part of workers against the upper classes, yet despite this attack, English culture readily manipulated the Irish into enacting roles more beneficial to ruler than ruled, just as, with the help of the halls, it maneuvered its own workers into endurance and even celebration of their lot. If laborers of either nationality could be made to accept, however ironically, the minimal utopia of an urban garden plot (as portrayed in the music hall song, "That Little Back Garden of Mine") and a secure but colorless marriage (as in "My Old Dutch"), so much the better. If the popular culture exported weekly from Liverpool to Dublin strengthened the symbiotic intertwining of British and Irish cultures by conveying the same ideological complex to both audiences, that too enhanced English control of Ireland. I do not maintain that these strategies were plotted and planned; rather they emerged as part of the power relations characteristic of Anglo-Irish culture. In addition, a sea-change occurred between England and the North Wall. The "criticism of life" in England becomes doubly potent when examined in the doubly (that is, economically and politically) contested landscape of Irish culture. As a semiotician might observe, British entertainment acquired a group-specific overcoding in the distinctive environment of Joyce's Dublin,[9] not least because hall owners like Dan Lowrey, deprived in Ireland of the massive working-class audience that England boasted, sought to make their establishments appealing to the Irish urban middle class.[10]

Exposing the matters being mediated in the halls, Joyce's fictions also incorporate them. In this chapter, I discuss the presence of the music hall in Ireland, the social content of this entertainment, and Joyce's satiric uses of both in *Ulysses* and *Finnegans Wake*.

The Halls in Ireland

During the late nineteenth and early twentieth centuries, Dublin and Belfast had to ship in most of their entertainers. In 1892 the Parliamentary Report on "Theatres and Places of Entertainment" mentioned the existence in Ireland of only Dan Lowrey's Star of Erin[11] and the slightly larger Alhambra in Belfast. Nonetheless, a good many music halls managed to survive in Ireland. On and off, from the 1870s on, Dublin also enjoyed the Grafton Theatre of Varieties, the Bijou, the Tivoli, the Lyric Theatre of Varieties, the Harp, and the National or Mechanics'—eventually to become the Abbey. In addition, the Leinster Hall put on minstrel and variety shows, the Theatre Royal had a "Hippodrome" season, and other locations throughout the city were available for the occasional music hall booking. If Dublin were to be reconstructed from *Ulysses*, the complete historical picture of entertainment venues would be distorted; knowledge of that picture suggests the representative function of those establishments that Joyce does mention.

In fact, by 1900, Lady Gregory wrote that "Dublin's normal dramatic diet for some years past" had been "musical farces and other variety entertainments" so that before the success of the Irish National Theatre she had wondered if plays like *The Countess Cathleen* were too "ethereal" for Dubliners.[12] Variety entertainment had a good deal in common with that other major English import, the Christmas pantomime. In both cases, the emphasis was on plurality as the spice of the show. Seriocomics, Lion Comiques, "ballet" dancers, ventriloquists, clog dancers, acrobats and jugglers, tightrope walkers, strongmen, knockabouts, bicyclists, performing dogs, minstrels, sexual impersonators, Jewish and Cockney comics, costers, stage Irishmen, protean and quick-change artists, magicians, and stump speakers—all of these and more formed the pool of performers from which Dan Lowrey and other music hall entrepreneurs formed their bills of eight to ten acts per night.[13]

Despite the various kinds of acts available, the fundamental principle of the hall was repetition. Many an artiste was billed "the one and only," and most performers sought gimmicks that would secure them this accolade, but as early as 1878, a writer in the *Dublin University Magazine* complained that "all . . . classes of music hall songs, seem respectively to have had one original copy, upon the leading idea of which, changes of more or less ingenuity are everlastingly sung. There is in fact a general cookery recipe for each style of song."[14] Vicinus confirms this view in discussing the Lion Comique and the female seriocomic: "Both types sang about such popular subjects as the seaside holiday, beer, patriotism, marriage, hard work, the lodger and mothers-in-law."[15] Everyone knew the naughty-girl songs ("Ta-ra-ra-boom-de-ay," "I'm a Naughty Girl," "Her Golden Hair was Hanging Down Her Back," "A Little of What You Fancy Does You Good"), the antimarriage songs ("Young Men Taken In and Done For," "We All Go to Work But Father," "A Thing He Had Never Done Before," "At Trinity Church I Met My Doom"), the soldier songs ("Jolly Good Luck to the Girl Who Loves a Soldier," "Goodbye Dolly Gray," "The Girl I Left Behind Me"), and the happily-ever-after songs ("Down at the Old Bull and Bush," "Wot Cher!," "My Old Dutch," "Daisy Bell"). The simple themes and easy stylizations of such numbers show us cultural operations of dichotomizing, repeating, socializing, and mediating in almost pure form.

Hence, Clarkson Rose, himself a dame and music hall comedian, reminisces, "The audience in those days never tired of hearing their favourite songs over and over again, and this also applied to favourite acts." Vesta Tilley, Rose recalls, always had to sing "Jolly Good Luck" or "The Army of Today's All Right."[16] And the story is told of the famous Lottie Collins that when in 1896 she played at Dan

Lowrey's, the audience received her coldly because she refused to comply with their desire to hear her great hit, "Ta-ra-ra-boom-de-ay!"[17] What the music hall said, it said often. One impact of this repetition is the scripting of persons according to the announced conventions; that those conventions reproduced the class relations managed in the halls is less often mentioned but equally important.

The most extreme example in *Ulysses* of the power of popular culture is Gerty McDowell,[18] who has bought all of the culture's prescriptions for the care and feeding of the lower- and middle-class female. Gerty follows the advice of Madame Vera Verity and similar sages about everything from her "eyebrowleine" (U 349) to her sexuality; her lameness thus extends into a psychological crippling or entrapment by cultural mores that cause her to yearn for a state— utter conformity to the physical ideal of her society and wedded bliss in a vine-covered cottage—that it is impossible for Gerty to attain. Even if biology had not worked against her, history, given her social setting, would have; as Florence Walzl emphasizes in a fine essay on Joyce's women,[19] many women in Gerty's world never had an opportunity to marry in an Ireland emptied of eligible men by patterns of emigration and late marriage established from the time of the Famine on. What "Nausikaa" reveals is both the power of the conventional and the cruelty, however gratuitous, of a culture straining toward such unattainable ideals.

Similarly, Bloom measures himself against the impossible ideal of the music hall muscleman, Eugene Sandow (Plates 13 and 14). Harold Scott says that when Sandow "appeared at the London Hippodrome in 1902," he was "at the height of his fame," and "the celebrated biceps figured in picture postcards all over the town."[20] Felstead adds, "In the early 1900's there came a perfect spate of mountainous men who wrestled with each other in such ferocious manner that you wondered how they survived the ordeal. The Apollo-like Eugene Sandow was probably the progenitor of this craze. You could not call him a champion at the game, but he was certainly a wonderful showman, marvellously good-looking with classical features, pink skin and curly hair. He became the idol of every boy in England, for he preached and practised the gospel of physical fitness, and demonstrated it, in a way that could do nothing but good."[21] Both Gerty in her longing for marriage and Bloom in his cuckoldry bring to our attention the places in which even the most manipulative conventions break down—when they come face

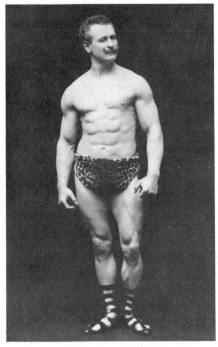

PLATES 13 and 14. Apparently Eugene Sandow saved his fig leaf for photographic sessions and appeared on music hall stages in somewhat more decorous attire. (In a note called "Bloom's Chest" and printed in *The James Joyce Quarterly* in 1979, Hugh Kenner mentions that a fig-leafed Sandow graces the physical improvement manual, *Physical Strength and How to Obtain It*, on Bloom's bookshelf.) That Sandow was a highly successful forefather of the body-building ethic makes rather touching Bloom's choice of this theatrical figure as his physical role model. Molly, too, judges men on the basis of this masculine ideal; more important, during her encounter with Boylan she tests the limits of the type in question. (Photographs reproduced by the kind permission of Roy Busby and the Raymond Mander and Joe Mitchenson Theatre Collection.)

to face with the intractable realities of individual and economic history.

To indict the music hall with the plights of Gerty and Bloom would be absurd, but it is nonetheless demonstrable that the stereotypes offered in the halls of men, women, love, marriage, family relations, and the working life are those that Joyce's characters measure themselves against. Even if Dubliners like Bloom and Gerty were relatively uninterested in music hall fare, its cultural presence was unavoidable. Murtagh and Watters report that Lowrey's posters ("thirty inches long and ten inches wide") "were everywhere—in bars, sweetshops, tobacconists, bunshops, on brick walls and billboards."[22] Not only did the individual theater post playbills, but the well-known stars had personal pictorial posters,[23] and press campaigns followed their comings and goings. As one writer put it, "No one can walk the streets of London, or any other considerable English town, without frequently noticing in the shop-windows of musicsellers certain lithographed frontispieces, representing various persons in grotesque and highly-coloured costumes, each purporting to be the likeness of such-and-such a vocalist, as he or she appeared in singing this, that, or the other 'immense,' or 'favourite,' or 'popular' comic song. . . ."[24] Further, the songs made popular by various artistes were printed in cheap songsheets and gathered into collections, presented on programmes and distributed through the newspapers, in addition to being copied in the annual pantomimes.

The number of people reached inside the halls themselves was substantial. By itself, the Empire-Olympia today seats 1,450 people, and it is reported that by 1897, 3,000 could be handled even though 2,000 of them would have had to stand (Plate 15).[25] Such a figure cannot compare with the estimated 45,000 persons accommodated nightly at the end of the nineteenth century in the London halls,[26] but even if the total nightly attendance in 1904 in Dublin were only 2,000 per night (out of a total urban population of 290,000),[27] that percentage is not inconsequential, given the fact that the patrons would rotate from evening to evening out of a larger pool.

Sociologists often argue that mass culture, as opposed to folk culture, manipulates the lower classes into compliance with hegemonic social goals; if so (and many critics now see this position as simplistic), it is worth questioning what role the music hall played in this or a similar cultural dynamics. The most evident benefit conferred upon the worker who could come up with the money to attend the halls was, of course, escape from the pressures of the working environment and the prospect of a life of unremitting hard labor. Beyond this escapism, the function served by the ritual of attendance was the creation of a communality not experienced either at home or in the workplace. This overcoming of alienation, however temporary, is a phenomenon that Joyce probes in both "Counterparts" and "Sirens." In both narratives, men who are disfranchised, who—like Simon Dedalus—have slipped several rungs on the social ladder, or who—like Farrington—have never had a chance even to catch a glimpse of the second rung up, seek the comfort of drink and talk with others who share their class status.[28] Fritz Senn suggested to me that we might recall here Bloom's thought as he watches the communicants at All Hallows: "There's a big idea behind it, kind of kingdom of God is within you feel. First communicants. Hokypoky penny a lump. Then feel all like one family party, *same in the theatre*, all in the same swim" (U 81—my emphasis).

In the music halls, this soothing unification was especially effective. Normally, the audience responded en masse, with "Ahhhhs" and "Ohhhhs," to the comments of the moderating chairmen and the individual artistes. In the halls an individual became part of an audience that as a body had its favorites and its prejudices, and as a body responded to performers whose lines it often knew by heart. This audience joined in the choruses to songs and expressed communal approval or disapproval of the show. If at their daily tasks these men and women were serfs, in the halls they were lords, often returning to the weak artiste the contempt they suffered on the job. D. J. Giltinan addressed himself to this esprit de corps in 1941 in *The Bell*. There he recalls the old days of the halls when there was "communal singing" and when "Intimacy was the keynote of the whole thing."[29]

Sometimes this solidarity was enhanced by an artiste's satiric attack, from the ordinary person's viewpoint, on the social system. Such a performer was Harry Tate, who had

> his own particular sense of humour—a sense of humour which, today, could be described as "taking the mickey out of the establishment." He will be chiefly remembered, of course, for his famous sketch, "Motoring," and here again, he took the mickey out of motoring with unbridled hilarity. Can anyone who saw him ever forget that wiggling and twitching moustache which he used to convey

PLATE 15. This photograph of the Empire Palace in Dublin as it appeared after its refurbishment in 1897 presents the theatre much as it appears today in its restored state under the name of the Olympia Theatre. During an interval in the Olympia, it is not difficult to imagine the crush of the music hall crowd and their spirited accompaniment to the songs and banter of the many artistes who passed through Dan Lowrey's doors, but the posh interior shown here seems out of keeping with the working-class audience at most music halls. (Photograph reproduced from Eugene Watters and Matthew Murtagh, *Infinite Variety: Dan Lowrey's Music Hall 1879–97* [Dublin: Gill and Macmillan, 1975]; originally printed in the British periodical *Illustrograph*, which ran from 1894 to 1899.)

pomposity, and then to deride pomposity. Harry's work and approach was pure burlesque, and—as true burlesque should be—it was so near the real thing.[30]

Similarly, the chairman, who generally wore formal dress, was the butt of "jokes and a wrath aimed at all who represented authority and order."[31] On the other hand, the working-class resentment of the well-to-do found expression in occasional projection, on the part of the audience and through the person of the artiste, of what it would be like to be of higher birth. Certainly, this imaginative desire explains the popularity in the halls of the Tichborne Claimant, whom Joyce mentions in *Ulysses* (U 650).[32] And those artistes who were not of lower birth drew great interest. A writer in the *Dublin University Magazine* satirized this tendency: "one waiter informed us confidently, and the statement has since appeared in print, that one of the most popular of the music hall singers is son of a peer of the realm. What judgment is there in store for us who shall henceforth call the music hall a low place! It is asserted, moreover, that the long list of comic performers on this stage embraces more than one young man of respectable birth and family. . . ."[33] Although the writer is ironic, these claims were often made, and in the case of George Robey—who "had a middle-class upbringing" but left Cambridge after his family lost their money and finally rose through the halls to be knighted—the claim was true.[34]

The low admission price of the halls facilitated for the worker the attainment of some sort of community,[35] but that togetherness was shot through with contradictions. Generating entertainment out of its resentment of the wealthy, the working-class was further used by the economic system that pandered to its sometimes satiric tastes. Vicinus argues acutely that from the beginnings of the music hall to the end of the nineteenth century,

> The major shift was away from a form of entertainment that spoke directly to the working class out of a shared experience to one that was provided for "the masses" by those familiar with their experience. . . . Some social criticism from a class perspective had been a part of the performances of the earlier halls, but it became muted with the development of the stereotyped comic working man. The broadest humour, the most obvious dupes and the most widely accepted social pleasures came to form much of the subject matter of an artiste seeking fame and popularity.[36]

Although the apparent gradual elimination of social criticism from these performances charts the increased exploitation of the worker, in Dublin the compensatory function of the halls seems to have retained some vitality into the twentieth century. Possible reasons include the local control of these businesses (and the concomitant tailoring, however minimal, of certain performances to meet Irish issues) as well as the cross-class appeal of some of the Irish halls. The communality of Dan Lowrey's exceeded that of the supersized London Palladium just as the smallness of the Irish capital made it possible, as it was not in its British counterpart, for everyone to know everyone else's business.

No Turn Unstoned: Censure of the Halls

The obverse to the music hall community of workers was the antipathy to popular entertainment that surfaced as long as the halls were in operation. This censure occurred on two counts: the suggestiveness of much music hall material and, in Ireland, the English derivation of the halls. The first problem became the brunt of many articles that argued from an upper-class perspective that the halls were demoralizing the lower classes. One writer of the era, seeking to turn "the tide of vulgarity, indecency, and utter imbecility" in the halls, called on both managers and "the more influential and intelligent part of the public" to agitate for more seemly presentations, something on the order of operatic selections, that would elevate the minds and spirits of British hall-goers.[37] Not only song lyrics but also costume and gesture occupy his attention; in the shows he has witnessed, all three are debasing. So extreme is his disapproval that he asks, "where is the power of the Lord Chamberlain? and what is the use of that official, if he cannot interfere with these demoralizing performances?" As the epitome of what he objects to, he describes a generic performer modeled on George Leybourne:[38] "No phase of human nature can be more odious and repulsive than that presented by the typical Music-Hall singer, who, dressed in a bright green coat, a yellow waistcoat, and chessboard-pattern trousers, swaggers on to the stage with his hat on one side, proclaims himself as the 'Howling Swell,' or the 'Rackety Snob,' or the 'Rollicking Cad,' and in that character details the particulars of some low amour, or celebrates the glorious achievement of getting drunk every night, or swindling his landlady out of her rent." Obviously, this outraged writer missed a good deal of the fun that would be had by the ordinary visitor to the halls at the expense of the upper classes, whose interests the writer has at heart. The stereotyping of the wealthy that the Lion Comique engaged in was bound to offend those social sectors, just as the flouting of "taste" (a recurrent, highly ironic criterion in *Finnegans Wake* for judging behavior) and the lauding of such antiestablishment behavior as failing to pay one's rent embodied the lower class's antipathy to its self-proclaimed betters. The tensions aired by this writer, who was published in a Dublin magazine, merely repeat those expressed in the music and milieu of popular entertainment.

The question of censorship for the halls—and of their influence on the young—crops up again and again in the popular press and in magazines in the final quarter of the nineteenth century. Certainly, it is not difficult, when hearing a recording of Marie Lloyd singing "Every Little Movement Has a Meaning of Its Own," to imagine a presentation of the song in which the gestures of hand, eye, and body relayed the message of musical innuendo. No doubt it was this kind of rendition that made Polly Mooney provocative to Bob Doran during the evenings when her mother's music-hall boarders entertained and Polly joined them to sing "I'm a . . . naughty girl. / You needn't sham: / You know I am" (D 62).[39] It is this environment that Bloom fears for Milly: "Twelve and six a week. Not much. Still, she might do worse. Musichall stage" (U 66–67). The fact that Polly indeed lives out the naughty girl role of her song in order to snare a man points to the complicity of popular entertainment, economics, and socially received morality.[40]

Anxious to address the assumed raciness of the halls, Lowrey printed along the top and bottom margins of his programmes a "SPECIAL NOTICE" to the effect that in his desire to keep all acts "ABSOLUTELY FREE FROM ALL OBJECTIONABLE FEATURES, he invites the co-operation of the Public to this end," and asks to be told of any "offensive word or action upon the Stage that may have escaped the notice of the Management" (Plate 16). From the perspective of the music hall habitué or performer, however, the acts were often regarded as tame. Clarkson Rose, in recalling the singers of his early days, avers that "when one reads the comic songs of that era, one finds trite, homely, and sometimes blatant lyrics—but you won't find any sex dirt."[41]

The allegation that popular songs were suggestive is important for an understanding of Joyce's use of music-hall material, but more significant is the fact that the songs grew out of a specifically English socioeconomic context. Developed from inns in which vocalists were employed to increase profits, the halls never lost touch with that financial motivation. Growing to the status of big business, they fed off the burgeoning industrial population in places like London, Lancashire, and Yorkshire. The tensions managed in songs and the situations presented in sketches were often of a "universal" quality (mother-in-law trouble, the unhappy marriage, unrequited love), but these tunes carried evidence of their development in a certain time and place—England in the upsweep of industrialism.

That this background was not totally appropriate to Joyce's Ireland is obvious. For example, in *The New Ireland Review* for June 1903, J. Ryan argues that although an Irish "industrial revival"—particularly for Irish products—was much noised at the time, the 1901 Census Returns in fact indicated significant declines in those employed in areas such as lithography, saddles, textiles, boots, tanning, brush and broom manufacturing, and coopery. Between 1891 and 1901, improvements had been registered in "Coalmining, hemp and jute manufactures, iron working, shipbuilding, [and] the making of machines," but the total "Industrial Class" fell by 17,000 during the same time period.[42]

Despite the fact that Dublin was primarily a commercial rather than an industrial city, the music hall and its principal artistes became popular in Dublin. During 1904 alone, the Tivoli hosted such stars as Vesta Victoria, Charles Coburn ("Two Lovely Black Eyes," "The Man Who Broke the Bank at Monte Carlo"), and Florrie Forde ("Oh, Oh Antonio," "Has Anybody Here Seen Kelly?," "It's a Long Way to Tipperary").[43] Not everyone was happy with this insertion of English mores and morality into the Irish national scene. Like Joyce, *The Leader* maintained that "the drama is nothing if not a criticism of life"; characteristically, it added that the Irish theatrical scene was distinctly disadvantaged by its ties to England. The writer of an article on "Imported Amusements" laments the "low, double-meaning expressions that have been" brought in from England; he decries the photographs of English stars in Irish newspapers; he deplores the estimated £200,000 per year leaving Ireland in exchange for English entertainment of various kinds.[44] The halls in particular—*The Leader* speaks of the Lyric and the Empire—are

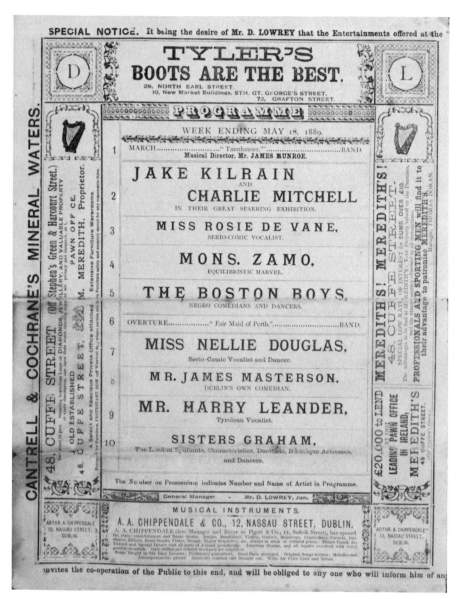

PLATE 16. During the week ending 18 May 1889, Dan Lowrey's Theatre of Varieties presented its usual full complement of artistes and blended the local talents of one James Masterson with the more remote expertise of a "Tyrolean Vocalist" and an "Equilibristic Marvel." Without the benefit of the "ogling" (U 232) machine designed by Tom Rochford in *Ulysses*, Lowrey indicated to his customers the turn currently on simply by posting the number and performer's name on the proscenium. Apart from documenting Lowrey's public concern over keeping the "objectionable features" of music hall at bay, this programme

shows Lowrey's effort, similar to that of William O'Brien and other Gaelophiles, to indicate the Irishness of his enterprise by printing the names of artistes between columns of advertisements headed by harps. Further, *The Irish Cyclist* here advertised its claims to printing the "new," the "startling," and the "amusing"; in "Circe" Bloom claims to have written a letter to the periodical about safety in Stepaside. (Programme reproduced by the kind permission of the Board of Trinity College, Dublin.)

"as a friend of ours very tersely put it, 'regular night-schools for An-
glicisation'" as well as "a powerful propaganda for the lowest and
grossest moral standards."[45] Objecting in particular to the stereotyping of the Irish by performers like "The O'Malleys" and the
"Three Macs" as well as to the glorification of "the harlot" detected
in these shows, The Leader argued for goods of national manufacture.[46] Indeed, part of the problem, according to this journal, was
that not only did Ireland fail to supply her working class with
proper amusement but that other Irish newspapers of all political
persuasions unreservedly praised the music halls.

Of special interest is this journal's claim that the Irish Literary
Theatre had "attempted to swing back the pendulum too far all of a
sudden." Something a bit more commercial appealed to The Leader
as long as it expressed Irish nationality and served to critique "Irish
life and manners."[47] George Moore, as if in response to this position, asserted, "The theatre is the noblest form of art until it becomes a commercial enterprise, then it becomes the ante-room of
the supper club, and is perhaps the lowest."[48]

Three facts stand out here. The English exported music hall stars
to increase profits; Irish entrepreneurs hired them to make money;
the ideological practices implicit in the music hall songs emanated
from the economic situation of an industrialized foreign country.

The Music Hall in Ulysses

In Ulysses, the halls are simply a fact of life, as pervasive in their influence as video games have been in the early 1980s. Only casually
does Bloom think about the halls; seeing Bob Doran "Sloping into
the Empire," he remembers Pat Kinsella's Harp Theatre (U 167).
When we move outside of his "mind," however, into the theatrical
world of "Circe," Joyce includes many references to music-hall turns.
Eugene Stratton, the Bohee Brothers (U 443), and Dolly Gray
(U 589) show up; Bloom *trickleaps* (U 435), juggles (U 486), is
fed straight lines (U 487–91), tells a joke (U 491), and does acro-
batics, magic tricks, and impersonations (U 495). Tom Rochford,
his turn on, "*executes a daredevil salmon leap in the air and is engulfed
in the coalhole*" (U 474). The End of the World walks a tightrope and
sings like the great Scottish artiste Harry Lauder (U 507), and like
a music hall comic, Richie Goulding wears three women's hats
(U 446). Finally, Virag works into his patter phrases from "What

Ho, She Bumps" and "Slap Bang! Here We Are Again" (U 513), and he arrives on the scene on "gawky pink stilts," "sausaged into several overcoats" (U 511). The coats hint of those variety acts in which, to the delight of the audience, several costumes are shed. For instance, a late nineteenth-century description of a music hall act reports:

> Now they are slinging across the stage a slack rope, upon which, when fastened, there mounts a very corpulent man in the dress of a French soldier. Standing on one leg upon the cord, he goes through a pantomime engagement with an invisible German; presents arms, lowers to the charge, fires, receives an invisible wound, falls, springs up again suddenly, flings off his coat, waistcoat, and trousers, revealing underneath the white dress and linen cap of a professional cook. The cook is in like manner transformed into a boy with a red nose; the boy with a red nose into an old woman in petticoats and a coalscuttle bonnet; and, after some half-dozen transformations, a thin, wiry man springs down from the rope, bowing and smiling profusely, and hurries off behind the scenes.[49]

"Wandering Rocks" specifically refers to this pervasive vaudeville-styled presence to emphasize the intertwining of British and Irish cultures. The final section of that episode begins with the journalistic report that "William Humble, early of Dudley, and lady Dudley, accompanied by lieutenantcolonel Heseltine, drove out after luncheon from the viceregal lodge. . . . The viceroy was most cordially greeted on his way through the metropolis" (U 252). Some readers have regarded this section as cumulating many of the chapter's ironies, which center on the fact that the viceregal carriage, that reminder of British imperialism, inspires not rage but courteous respect from many Dubliners. But this definition of ironies should not obscure the fact that the viceroy's presence and Dublin's greeting of him target the mutual dependence of British and Irish hegemonic interests. The music hall references in this section of "Wandering Rocks" make that point beautifully. We're told that "A charming soubrette, great Marie Kendall, with dauby cheeks and lifted skirt smiled daubily from her poster upon William Humble, earl of Dudley" and his party (U 253). A bit later Eugene Stratton is noted as smiling from the hoarding. Within the terms of "Wandering Rocks," these posters are as animated as most of the Dubliners presented; a two-dimensional Kendall and Stratton, both of whom performed in Dublin on Bloomsday, exemplify the plastic poses of the resident populace doing fealty to and enjoying the presence of British nobility. The mockery implied by Kendall's smiling glance at the Lord Lieutenant emerges from the fact that this English performer exaggerates the natives' friendly reception of the viceroy, a reception enhanced by the attitude-shaping entertainment imported into Ireland. Despite political distinctions and well-established animosities, in 1904 the two countries shared much of their popular thought.

Clear evidence of this point is the characterization of Blazes Boylan. As Dublin's resident "lion comique" or "swell," Boylan embodies the class tensions intrinsic to that stock figure. An "aristocrat" and idler, the Lion was, according to Vicinus, "an interesting combination of admiration for and parody of the idle."[50] Stepping along "the provost's wall" to "the refrain of *My girl's a Yorkshire girl*," Blazes receives the nod of the viceregal consort as Humble directs his wife's attention to "the programme of music which was being discoursed in College park. . . .

> *But though she's a factory lass*
> *And wears no fancy clothes.*
> *Baraabum.*
> *Yet I've a sort of a*
> *Yorkshire relish for*
> *My little Yorkshire rose.*
> *Baraabum*" (U 254).

With a flower between his teeth (a carnation, alas, not a rose), Boylan exemplifies the Irish person turned British cliché, shaped by popular culture into a devil-may-care, dandified man-about-town but ready to enact the role of the working-class suitors in the song as he ousts and then is ousted by a Dublin Bloom.

In 1920, Joyce wrote to Frank Budgen requesting that he send a copy of this influential song: "Now I want you to do another favour for me and in a great hurry. The whirligig movement in *Circe* is on the refrain *My Girl's a Yorkshire* etc, but to unify the action the preceding *pas seul* of S.D. which I intended to balance on the gramophone of the opposite kip should be on the air of that same ditty played on Mrs Cohen's pianola with lights. I enclose 10 francs. Will you be so kind as to apply to any vendor (a big one) of musichall airs. It was popular between 1904 and 1908. I want words and music."[51] The complete song runs as follows:[52]

Two young fellows were talking about
Their girls, girls, girls
Sweethearts they left behind
Sweethearts for whom they pined
One said, "My little shy little lass
Has a waist so trim and small
Grey are her eyes so bright,
But best best of all

CHORUS:

My girl's a Yorkshire girl,
Yorkshire through and through
"My girl's a Yorkshire girl,
Eh! by gum, she's a champion!
Though she's a fact'ry lass,
And wears no fancy clothes,
I've a sort of a Yorkshire Relish
for my little Yorkshire Rose."

When the first finished singing in praise
Of Rose Rose, Rose,
Poor Number Two looked vexed,
Saying in tones perplexed
"*My* lass works in a factory too,
And has *also* eyes of grey
Her name is Rose as well,
And strange, strange to say"

CHORUS

To a cottage in Yorkshire they hied
To Rose Rose, Rose
Meaning to make it clear
Which was the boy most dear
Rose, their Rose didnt answer the bell,
But her husband did instead
Loudly he sang to them
As off, off they fled

CHORUS.

Joyce's use of the song introduces into his narrative an English context and stresses the impact in Dublin of this contradictory but powerful social force.

Of course, "Yorkshire Girl" could be viewed as simply reinforcing the favorite Joycean theme of betrayal. A good many music hall songs presented this commonplace—the girl you thought was yours was already somebody else's. More important for my purposes, however, the song projects a social subtext; it displaces the working class's sense of betrayal by the economic system into the narrative of a love affair. That is, in "Yorkshire Girl" two "young fellows" talk in glowing terms about what they discover is the same Yorkshire rose. Both men have "left behind" their sweetheart. Their uprootedness is linked to an industrial society's newfound mobility, one already conventional by the time of the song's composition. We note that the best thing about their girl is not that she is pretty but that she is from Yorkshire; she "wears no fancy clothes" but works in a factory. On the surface, the song is sheer celebration of a stylized working-class experience. Further, the comic ending of the song, in which the husband chases away the two suitors, must have delighted Joyce in its paralleling of Bloom's at least temporary routing of Boylan from Molly's regard.[53] The question lurking in that ending, however, is whether the girl is the sweetheart of at least three men *because* she is a "fact'ry lass." This ambiguity suggests that the song responds in conventional terms to concerns over young men who must leave their homes to seek work in large industrial centers, and over young women who are exposed to temptation because they too must leave their families to work in factories. "Yorkshire Girl" communicates the problems of the class to which the song appealed most, and similar responses to strains in social mores may be traced ion "Ta-ra-ra-boom-de-ay!," "Her Golden Hair was Hanging Down Her Back," "Never Introduce Your Donah to a Pal," and many music hall standards.

The music hall's response to the laborer, therefore, inevitably involved a reaction to the trajectory of power in an industrialized Britain. The problems of power and the plight of the working class are at the heart of Joyce's use of "Yorkshire Girl" in "Circe," especially in the scene in which Stephen dances at Bella Cohen's and swoons into his vertiginous vision of the once-beautiful May Dedalus. While the pianola plays the song, first Stephen and Zoe, then "Bloombella, Kittylynch, Florryzoe, jujuby women" and Stephen dance (U 578). The Yorkshire girl in this case is Zoe, who is quite conscious of herself as such. She is an uprooted, imported part of the British working class—not, like her lyrical namesake, protected from her suitors by a husband but given to them by her tough-minded boss, Bella Cohen.

Further, the "jujuby women" are Bella's girls, who, though not factory lasses in the ordinary sense, are part of a sexual production line. In "Lestrygonians" Bloom pictures Edward VII (as "Circe" does—U 590) as another of the vampires of *Ulysses*, "Sitting on his throne sucking red jujubes white" (U 151), and Bella's employees apparently undergo the same process of being bled white by an economic and political power structure that owns them.[54] The collusion of this structure with the religious hierarchy is suggested when Edward VII appears "with the halo of Joking Jesus, a white jujube in his phosphorescent face" (U 591). References to church, state, and the business of prostitution occur in the "jujuby" passages to underscore the critical fact that there is no difference between Cissy Caffrey and Zoe, between a Dublin girl and a Yorkshire one; both English and Irish workers share the same institutional oppressions. Long subjected to foreign intervention, Ireland is no purer than its rulers, as the substitution of Ireland for England indicates in Stephen's quotation from Blake's "Auguries of Innocence": "The harlot's cry from street to street / Shall weave Old Ireland's windingsheet" (U 597).

The prostitute's status of being property[55] is given specific attention when Bella threatens to put Bloom into a "punishment frock." Speaking of her stable of women, Bella says, "As they are now so will you be, wigged, singed, perfumesprayed, ricepowdered, with smoothshaven armpits. Tape measurements will be taken next your skin. You will be laced with cruel force into vicelike corsets of soft dove coutille with whalebone busk to the diamondtrimmed pelvis, the absolute outside edge, while your figure, plumper than when at large, will be restrained in nettight frocks, pretty two ounce petticoats and fringes and things stamped, of course, with my houseflag . . ." (U 535). Bloom, that is, will wear the mark of the beast Bello and will become the madame's property. It is surely significant that the commercial relations of Bella and her girls are congruent with the husband-wife relationship posited in "Yorkshire Girl"; it is also important that this description of clothing neatly echoes the fashion column lingo that Gerty MacDowell feeds from, a fact that suggests the connection between oppressive cultural institutions and the seemingly innocent code system of fashion. As a woman,

Bloom will join a distinctly dominated part of the Anglo-Irish working class to adopt the status that Zoe, the Yorkshire girl of *Ulysses*, already holds. Again it is significant that Bloom, when he is presented in female costume, is described as a *"charming soubrette with dauby cheeks"* (U 536). That is, he looks like the poster of Marie Kendall described in "Wandering Rocks," and this fact underscores the link between the imported music hall and the kind of business that Bella Cohen does. The halls and the flash houses perpetuate the stereotypes that grow out of the larger commercial network and that reflect both class oppression and sexual oppression. *Ulysses* refuses to see the political opposition of England and Ireland as solely responsible for the quality of Irish life. Rather, the fiction describes a society in which many institutional ideologies create an entrapping system of oppression.

In fact, the implicit comment of "Circe" on the political situation turns Stephen's withdrawal from politics into apocalyptic absurdity. While Dublin burns and the dead arise, *"Factory lasses* with *fancy clothes toss redhot Yorkshire baraabombs"* (U 598—my emphasis). Joining in the general social melee, those working-class women wear decent garb in the inversions and contradictions of an apocalyptic scene. Only then, one supposes, would the social distinctions emphasized in *Ulysses* be erased. Otherwise, Joyce's Dubliners will still be bound by deadening class relations. Joyce's fictions present the political state of affairs in Ireland as both an extension and a displacement of the exploitation of British workers that the music hall chronicled in song and in practice.

Those who bear the burden of this domination are caught up, like Stephen and his companions at Bella Cohen's, in a cultural dance of death that engulfs one of the most pathetic denizens of the city, Dilly Dedalus. When Stephen announces, at the culmination of the pianola's rendition of "Yorkshire Girl," the "Dance of death," the stage directions detail an incongruous caravan in which phrases from the song interlace with references to church and state:

> *Bang fresh barang bang of lacquey's bell, horse, nag, steer, piglings, Conmee on Christass, lame crutch and leg sailor in cockboat armfolded ropepulling hitching stamp hornpipe through and through, Baraabum! On nags, hogs, bellhorses, Gadarene swine Corny in coffin steel shark stone onehandled Nelson two trickies Frauenzimmer plumstained from pram falling bawling. Gum he's a champion. Fuseblue peer from barrel rev. evensong Love on hackney jaunt Blazes blind coddoubled bicyclers Dilly*

with snowcake no fancy clothes. Then in last switchback lumbering up and down bump mashtub sort of viceroy and reine relish for tublumber bumpshire rose. Baraabum! (U 579)

Individual phrases in this social ballet, a sort of "Wandering Rocks" in miniature, bring back to us scenes from the narrative: the not-too-charitable Father Conmee and the one-legged sailor, the supposed midwives with a supposed dead child in their bag, Blazes' jaunting, the viceregal procession, and the like. Yet all of the figures and facts suggested here—the alienation of the blind stripling, the exile of Kevin Egan, the poverty of Dilly—resist being summed up under the platitudes of "My Girl's a Yorkshire Girl." Having defined the social roles of Joyce's characters to the extent that each has become a cultural cliché, the text frees them in this lumbering dance.

In its midst, we find Dilly as Yorkshire girl wearing "no fancy clothes" but presumably only the same tattered outfit that Bloom sees her in earlier, to which has been added the "snowcake" (like "the deathflower of the potato blight" on the breast of Old Gummy Granny? [U 595]). Like many of Joyce's citizens, Dilly is caught in an economic system that generated the music-hall establishment as well as Bella Cohen's style of entrepreneurial activity, a system that was reinforced by religious and political powers and that transmitted the often violent, conventional roles that Dubliners enact. And it is important that the "Yorkshire Girl" dance ends only when Stephen's mother rises before him as if in response to the invocation of the tune, because she is the ultimate example of the conditions it implies. This juxtaposition of song and "vision" emphasizes that the little factory lass in the surrealistic drama of social forces almost inevitably became a deprived, abused, impoverished, or disease-ridden woman. A victim of both sexual oppression and economic exploitation, this grown-up Dilly certainly wore, by the time of her death, no fancy clothes.

The Music Hall in *Finnegans Wake*

Far from ignoring class relations and the financial arrangements that in many social situations substitute for or at least inform personal interaction, *Finnegans Wake* again and again accentuates the extent to which even dreams highlight the economic basis of human relationships in Joyce's Dublin. The use of music hall songs, both in brief allusions and in the slightly more extended parody of "At Trinity Church I Met My Doom"[56] that ends *Finnegans Wake* I, iv, often contributes to this illumination. As is customary in the *Wake*, the text explicitly states the ideological implications of cultural artifacts and institutions that might have gone unnoticed in the experience of Dubliners.

Finnegans Wake I, iv finds the reader caught in the midst of debates and rumors about HCE. As we approach the discussion of the "mamafesta" of "Annah the Allmaziful" (FW 104.1), the narrative-turned-chairman introduces ALP and then steps on stage for a short "turn":

> But there's a little lady waiting and her name is A.L.P. And you'll agree. She must be she. For her holden heirheaps hanging down her back. He spenth his strenth amok haremscarems. Poppy Narancy, Giallia, Chlora, Marinka, Anileen, Parme. And ilk a those dames had her rainbow huemoures yet for whilko her whims but he coined a cure. Tifftiff today, kissykissy tonay and agelong pine tomauranna. Then who but Crippled-with-Children would speak up for Dropping-with-Sweat?
>
> > *Sold him her lease of ninenineninetee,*
> > *Tresses undresses so dyedyedaintee,*
> > *Goo, the groot gudgeon, gulped it all.*
> > *Hoo was the C.O.D.?*
> > > Bum!
> > *At Island Bridge she met her tide.*
> > *Attabom, attabom, attabombomboom!*
> > *The Fin had a flux and his Ebba a ride.*
> > *Attabom, attabom, attabombomboom!*
> > *We're all up to the years in hues and cribies.*
> > *That's what she's done for wee!*
> > > Woe!
>
> Nomad may roam with Nabuch but let naaman laugh at Jordan! For we, we have taken our sheet upon her stones where we have hanged our hearts in her trees; and we list, as she bibs us, by the waters of babalong. (FW 102.22–103.12)

The song on which this parody relies runs as follows:

> > Twelve months ago with decent chances,
> > > Prospects of success in life,
> > Through foolish love of ballroom dances,
> > > Trouble came, I met my wife;
> > Such a noble buxom creature,

> She in my eyes then appeared,
> False she was, though fair of feature,
>   Like to salmon I was speared.

CHORUS:

> She told me her age was five-and-twenty,
> Cash in the bank of course she'd plenty;
> I, like a lamb, believed it all—
>   I was an M U G.
> At Trinity Church I met my doom,
> Now we live in a top-back room,
> Up to my eyes in debt for "renty,"
>   That's what she's done for me!

> In bridal dress with frills and flounces,
>   ('Pon my word, she did look fine),
> Quite sixteen stone and some odd ounces,
>   Weighed then this dear wife of mine.
> People whispered she had money
>   (O! what tales some folk will tell),
> She was simply sixteen stoney—
>   What a swindle—what a sell!

CHORUS

> When she confessed, I'd scarce believe her,
>   Though at last 'twas truth she told;
> She hadn't got a blooming stiver—
>   She was thirty-six years old.
> I can only grin and bear it,
>   Poor indeed is my estate,
> She, poor gal, is forced to share it,
>   Down will drop her mortal weight.

CHORUS[57]

As in "My Girl's a Yorkshire Girl," the duped lover provides the theme, although this time the lover has made a very bad bargain in marrying a woman who is not only older than he but poor to boot. The cultural norm of a good match is upheld by the song's comic woefulness. A similar situation appears to be reflected in Joyce's parody, and even before the song begins we get a hint that the economic arrangement may not be what it had seemed. Referring to another music hall favorite, "Her Golden Hair was Hanging Down Her Back," the text distorts the titular refrain to "For her holden heirheaps hanging down her back." The word "heir" suggests the transfer of wealth, as does the use of "heaps" (of gold?), but the "golden hair" has changed to "holden," and within the parody we find that the woman referred to, here taken to be ALP, has seduced the man by using dyed hair ("Tresses undresses so dyedyedaintee"). The Cockney pronunciation of the final word facilitates Joyce's allusion to the situation of "Her Golden Hair," in which a country girl goes to the city, dyes her auburn hair blonde, appears nude in a music-hall tableau, seduces a "young philanthropist," and returns to the village "With a naughty little twinkle in her eye!"[58] A rousing compilation of several music hall themes, the song connects ALP with those stereotypes and posits her seduction of HCE on not entirely authentic grounds.

Such a lover's ruse is, of course, both comic and serious because of the economic arrangement that marriage represents in Joyce's fiction. More often than not, Dubliners are disadvantaged by their marriages. Her wedding changes Josie Breen from a good dresser to a washed-out drudge wearing her husband's clothing; Farrington and Little Chandler are both caught in a domestic trap that binds them to unsatisfying homes and the debts that go along with them; May Dedalus dies, we are led to believe, partly because of the financial ineptitude of her husband, a situation which, according to "The Mime of Mick, Nick and the Maggies," the Floras hope to avoid by choosing a man with at least as much money as the woeful Bob Doran. Hence, the short passage from *Finnegans Wake* quoted above includes words like "coined," "sold," "lease," and "C.O.D." ALP sold HCE a "lease of nineninenineteee"; this lifetime arrangement would naturally make it easier for her to bear some of the problems that he presents her with—his "haremscarems" with the rainbow girls, for instance. In fact, the passage stresses that "Annah the Allmaziful" fully controls the domestic situation. HCE shows up here as "Goo, the groot gudgeon"; McHugh defines "goo" as Anglo-Irish for "a useless person, or a fool" and "groot" as the Dutch for "great," while "gudgeon" is a "person easily duped."[59] Like the philanthropist who thinks that his country lass really has golden hair and like the duped husband in "At Trinity Church," HCE may not have made the most informed bargain when he bought her lease. As a cod,[60] he has been involved in a strictly cash-on-delivery arrangement that has left him holding the bag. The song maintains, "We're all up to the years in hues and cribies. /

That's what she's done for wee! / Woe!" Woes, cribs, and crybabies seem to be much of what ALP has offered.

On the other hand, HCE has caused her problems beyond mere flirtations. The husband and wife argue and make up on a regular basis and are not especially heartened by this longterm arrangement: "Tifftiff today, kissykissy tonay and agelong pine tomauranna." Yet ALP does "speak up" for him, just as she "bibs" her babes, who seem to include washerwomen by the Liffey spreading their clothing on the stone banks and in the trees as well as ALP's own children (Shem and Shaun, tree and stone). In effect, both parents have gained from the relationship (he benefits from ALP's support; she secures the taking of her lease) and both suffer (they embody the Edenic curse in being "Crippled-with-Children" and "Dropping-with-Sweat").

The transgression of Adam and Eve binds them to this status, but they have apparently enhanced some of the curse's more rigorous elements by making contracts that reproduce a blighted and exiled existence. As the references to Genesis 3 and Babylon ("by the waters of babalong") indicate, they have been cast out of paradise and taken into captivity. They are, in fact, in twentieth-century Dublin, and the balance of power in this song imitates the exchange basis of the marital relationship as Joyce typically portrays it. "At Trinity Church" portrays one man's being duped by an unscrupulous woman, but Joyce's parody addresses more than an individual case. The presence at the chapter's end of tree, stone, and river keeps us connected with the larger-than-individual dimensions of the relationship between HCE and ALP. On the one hand, she is a wife who, though "Shesfaithfultheman" (U 588), is no fool; she made him take out a lifetime contract on her, and it is within and as a result of this arrangement that she is willing to defend him. On the other hand, she is a natural (that is, not personally responsible) force—the Liffey letting down her hair and, even though it's dyed, sustaining washerwomen and children and husband in the cultural stream of life.

In its movement beyond the personal, the passage makes clear the impact of the economic on love and marriage, while suggesting, through the presence of "natural" and elegiac elements, the assumed inevitability of the current constitution of human relationships. The music hall betrayed the same sense of necessity in its endless repetitions of songs on the subject of marriage as well as in the occasional

song that brought the domestic theme into the socioeconomic and
political spheres. At least one example even aired directly the nexus
of politics and marital problems. Richard Kain mentions a song
called "Charlie Parnell" which taunted the Chief, "You want Home
Rule for Ireland / And you can't Home Rule yourself!"[61] The comic
stance of this song masks the anxiety displayed in Joyce's parody
of "At Trinity Church," especially in the dying fall with which the
song ends.

Unfortunately, simple unveiling of anxieties and of their institutional basis does not resolve a society's problems. Although it is
often said that ideology remains effective only as long as it is not
recognized as such, history betrays the oversimplification of that
viewpoint, however congruent it is with the dynamics of popular
Freudianism. The repetitions of *Finnegans Wake* alone should be
enough to convince us that some things refuse to remain demystified.
Like magnetic fields, ideological practices constantly draw to themselves new material along with the old that tangles up with it. The
unmasked cultural process and the openly revealed economic motivation take on ever new forms and are involved in always fresh combinations that insure a large measure of inefficacy in cultural analysis. Despite the penetrations of Joyce's narratives into the conditions
of the interrelated class, sexual, and domestic oppressions voiced by
the music hall, those institutional pressures remained potent within
the part of Irish culture that derived from English commercial enterprises and that masked its purposes in song, its effects in laughter.

NOTES

1. Conversation with Matthew Murtagh, 15 July 1981, at his home in
Dublin. In *Stephen Hero*, Stephen and Cranly "sat sometimes in the pit of a
music hall and one unfolded to the other the tapestry of his poetical aims
while the band bawled to the comedian and the comedian bawled to the
band" (SH 125).

2. Stanislaus Joyce, *My Brother's Keeper*, ed. Richard Ellmann (London:
Faber and Faber, 1958), p. 110.

3. Frank Budgen, *James Joyce and the Making of* Ulysses ([1934]; rpt.
Bloomington: Indiana University Press, 1960), p. 191.

4. For identification and commentary on these songs, see Matthew J. C.
Hodgart and Mabel P. Worthington, *Song in the Works of James Joyce* (New
York: Temple University Publications, 1959); Zack Bowen, *Musical Allu-*

sions in the Works of James Joyce: *Early Poetry through* Ulysses (Albany: State University of New York Press, 1974); and Ruth Bauerle, ed., *The James Joyce Songbook* (New York: Garland Publishing, 1982). Kathleen McGrory and Joseph Phillips are currently continuing research into Joyce and music. Ulrich Schneider's extensive work on the music hall has been helpful to me, especially "Some Comments upon Music Hall in *Ulysses*," manuscript essay; and (with Laurence Senelick and David F. Cheshire) *British Music-Hall, 1840–1923* (Hamden, Conn.: Archon, 1981).

5. For example, Mary Power advanced this position at the Eighth International James Joyce Symposium, University College (Dublin), 16 June 1982. Along these lines, as James Van Dyck Card pointed out to me, Milo O'Shea's performance as Leopold Bloom in Joseph Strick's film version of *Ulysses* is marked by the pacing of music hall turns.

6. The Pola Notebook, in *The Workshop of Daedalus: James Joyce and the Raw Materials for* A Portrait of the Artist as a Young Man, ed. Robert Scholes and Richard M. Kain (Evanston, Ill.: Northwestern University Press, 1965), p. 88.

7. Martha Vicinus, *The Industrial Muse: A Study of Nineteenth Century British Working-Class Literature* (London: Croom Helm, 1974), p. 266.

8. "Until the development of mass entertainment," Vicinus remarks, "working-class literature had expressed a faith in the power of art to change people. But art as a commodity can only be consumed; it acts to prevent change" (*Industrial Muse*, p. 279).

9. For a discussion of overcoding, see Eco, *A Theory of Semiotics*, pp. 133–35.

10. Lowrey actively worked to enhance the good reputation of his establishment. For instance, in 1892 he engaged Kate Santley, who had appeared "in Shakespeare, in Panto, Comic Opera and Opera Bouffe." This artiste drew from the middle-class Gaiety audience. Watters and Murtagh argue that Lowrey's constant attempts to pull in such a class-spanning audience were evident in his calling the Star "A National Theatre of Ireland. Companion piece to a National Parliament. And a National University" (Watters and Murtagh, pp. 68, 138, 132).

11. The Star of Erin became in turn the Star Theatre of Varieties, the Empire (in 1897), and the present-day Olympia Theatre (in 1923). For a thorough history of the Star, see Eugene Watters and Matthew Murtagh, *Infinite Variety*. Even now, the Empire's glass canopy stands in front of the Olympia in Dublin.

12. "Last Year," *Beltaine*, no. 2 (February 1900), pp. 25–28.

13. In contrast, a London hall would put on at least fifteen to twenty acts per night.

14. Tighe Hopkins, "Music Halls," *Dublin University Magazine*, n.s., 2 (1878), 200. Hopkins lists several types of songs customary for the Lion

Comique to sing: "his song bacchanalian, his song amorous, his song sentimental, his song funny, and his song patriotic" (p. 198).

15. Vicinus, *Industrial Muse*, p. 258.

16. Clarkson Rose, *Red Plush and Greasepaint: A Memory of the Music-Hall and Life and Times from the Nineties to the Sixties* (London: Museum Press, 1964), pp. 53–54.

17. Murtagh and Watters, p. 161.

18. For an excellent reading of Gerty's relation to popular culture, see Suzette Henke, "Gerty MacDowell: Joyce's Sentimental Heroine," in *Women in Joyce*, pp. 132–49.

19. Florence Walzl, "*Dubliners*: Women in Irish Society," in *Women in Joyce*, pp. 31–56.

20. Harold Scott, *The Early Doors: Origins of the Music Hall* (London: Nicholson & Watson, 1946), p. 196.

21. Felstead, p. 161.

22. Murtagh and Watters, p. 61.

23. David F. Cheshire, *The Music-Hall in Britain* (Rutherford, N.Y.: Fairleigh Dickinson University Press, 1974), pp. 60–61.

24. "Our Popular Amusements," *Dublin University Magazine* 84 (1874), 233.

25. The source of the current figure is Jay Cruise, recently the manager of the Olympia. When it opened in 1879, Lowrey's hall held 600; this hall was enlarged to hold 1,100 and then in 1892 to hold 1,600. Remodeling in 1897 increased the capacity to 3,000 for the Empire (now the Olympia), "of which 1,000 would be seated" (Murtagh and Watters, pp. 131, 169).

26. "Appendix," "Paper handed in by Mr. J. L. Graydon, 4 May 1892," *Report from the Select Committee on Theatres and Places of Entertainment*, p. 461.

27. Figure from the 1901 Census, O'Brien, *Dear, Dirty Dublin*, p. 39.

28. Walzl discusses the role of male camaraderie in Irish culture (pp. 45–46).

29. D. J. Giltinan, "Variety," *The Bell* 3 (1941), 28–29.

30. Rose, pp. 74–75.

31. Vicinus, *Industrial Muse*, p. 252. It must be noted that the original Dan Lowrey departed from the formal-dress tradition when he sometimes chaired in a "Character Costume"; he often took the comic role of the jarvey "Pat of Mullingar" (Watters and Murtagh, pp. 24–25).

32. The story of the Tichborne Claimant, a pretender to the massive Tichborne family fortune, is told in Watters and Murtagh, pp. 79–81. Working the music hall circuit to tell his story, he appeared at Dan Lowrey's in 1886.

33. Hopkins, p. 203.

34. Davison, p. 155.

35. In fact, the low cost of such varied and extensive an entertainment is what many people still celebrate most about the halls. For instance, in the summer of 1981 I was sitting in Kiely's Bar in Dublin talking about the music hall with Sean White and Thomas Flanagan when a man overheard us and joined us. Our anonymous but enthusiastic friend said that when he was young there were lots of variety shows in Dublin, all of them with "great characters in them" and all of them so cheap that it was a "fuckin' marvel."

36. Vicinus, *Industrial Muse*, p. 239.

37. "Our Popular Amusements," p. 244. Quotations below are from pp. 236 and 241.

38. Typically, Leybourne wore a green jacket; Watters and Murtagh have found him to be the Dubliner's model Lion Comique (Watters and Murtagh, pp. 54–55).

39. Kathleen McGrory and Joseph Phillips have located this song (Workshop: "Eve and the Virgin: Musical Images of Women, Sacred and Secular, in Joyce's Fiction," Eighth International James Joyce Symposium, University College [Dublin], 16 June 1982).

40. As Ulrich Schneider notes in "Some Comments upon Music Hall in *Ulysses*" (p. 2), Polly's "song is modeled upon innumerable music hall songs about 'naughty' young men and girls. From the naughty songs and dances of the music hall stage it was, at least in the eyes of the hostile middle class, only a small step to prostitution. That many of the poorer music-hall singers were not above earning some extra money can be seen in 'Counterparts' where one of the singers from the Tivoli answers Farrington's leering gaze and brushes against him with a provocative 'pardon' on her way out." Patrick A. McCarthy discusses the cycle by which Mrs. Mooney prostitutes Polly and marries her to a man who, in *Ulysses*, is driven to prostitutes because of the complicity of the church and other Irish social forces ("The Jeweleyed Harlots of His Imagination: Prostitution and Artistic Vision in Joyce," *Éire-Ireland* 17 [1982], 91–109).

41. Rose, p. 20.

42. J. Ryan, *New Ireland Review* 19 (1902), pp. 194–98.

43. "Actually, the first singer of 'Tipperary' was Jack Judge, part-author, but Florrie Forde was the singer who mattered," claim Ernest Short and Arthur Compton-Rickett, *Ring Up the Curtain* (1938; rpt. Freeport, N.Y.: Books for Libraries, 1970), p. 193. I am indebted for the list of performers at the Tivoli in 1904 to Matthew Murtagh, who maintains a theater-by-theater and year-by-year catalogue of Dublin entertainment.

44. *The Leader*, 15 September 1900, p. 40. The September 1 issue (p. 2) estimated the loss of money at "half a million sterling a year in exchange for foreign theatrical and music hall amusement."

45. *The Leader*, 1 September 1900, p. 3. Edward Martyn predictably agrees that English theater is dangerous: finding England "little better than a half-civilised country," he sees in its theater audiences "decadence irrevocable and complete," and he claims that their "taste is for nothing but an empty parade, where the stage is degraded to a booth for the foolish exhibition of women, or for the enacting of scenes purposely photographing the manners of society rakes and strumpets of the day" ("A Comparison between Irish and English Theatrical Audiences," *Beltaine*, no. 2 [February 1900], pp. 11–12).

46. *The Leader*, 15 September 1900, p. 39; 1 September 1900, p. 3.

47. 15 September 1900, p. 41.

48. "Is the Theatre a Place of Amusement?" *Beltaine*, no. 2 (February 1900), p. 9.

49. Hopkins, pp. 196–97.

50. Vicinus, *Industrial Muse*, p. 258. Vicinus reports that the "favourite swells" were also parodied in the halls (p. 259).

51. "To Frank Budgen," 10 December 1920, *Letters of James Joyce*, ed. Stuart Gilbert, 3 vols. (New York: Viking, 1966), 1:151.

52. In a letter to me (20 January 1982, Erlangen), Ulrich Schneider said, "The song was one of the hits of Charles Whittle, a Yorkshire blacksmith who became a well-known music hall star. . . . Lancashire and Yorkshire with their industrial centres were important areas for the development of music hall. Yorkshiremen and -girls in shawls and clogs were popular characters on the music hall stage." Bauerle indicates that the song was published in 1908 and was written and composed by C. W. Murphy and Dan Lipton. I use the text of "Yorkshire Girl" that Bauerle prints (pp. 349–51), © 1908 Francis Day and Hunter Ltd. Reproduced by permission of EMI Music Publishing Ltd.

53. Zack Bowen adds another parallel between the song and the story: "Carr, Compton and Caffrey might easily fit the roles of the two British youths in search of their not unwilling Yorkshire girl" ("The Music Hall and Wagnerian Opera: 'My Girl's a Yorkshire Girl' and the Ring Cycle," Eighth International James Joyce Symposium, University College [Dublin], 16 June 1982).

54. McCarthy stresses the "repressive social and moral climate" which engenders the prostitution Joyce portrays in his fiction ("Jeweleyed Harlots," p. 103).

55. Stephen finds the streetwalker to be also a merchant but adds, "In this country people sell much more than she ever had and do a roaring trade" (U 633).

56. "At Trinity Church" was one of Tom Costello's songs. He appeared at Dan Lowrey's in 1887, 1891, and 1892. Costello's persona was working-class "Birmingham Celtic" (Watters and Murtagh, pp. 120, 128–29).

Kathleen McGrory and Joseph Phillips agree with Hodgart and Worthington in finding eleven references to this song in *Finnegans Wake*; they cite Carola Giedion-Welcker's assertion that it was one of Joyce's favorites (panel: "Joyce and the Arts," State University of New York at Purchase, 16 February 1982).

57. The text of the song is quoted from Bauerle, p. 8. "'And Her Golden Hair' was originally sung by Alice Leamar, but it was taken up by Sir Seymour Hicks and sung for some six hundred nights in the musical, *The Shop Girl*, in 1894–95" (Davison, p. 86). Davison states that in the song there is a reference to "Mrs. Ormiston Chant, who, in 1892, began a campaign described even by that violently anti-Ibsen drama critic, Clement Scott, as 'Prudes on the Prowl.'" As Vicinus explains, this campaign was an effort to eliminate prostitutes from the halls (*Industrial Muse*, p. 284n).

58. Song written and composed by Felix McGlennon.

59. McHugh, *Annotations*, p. 102.

60. The initials "C.O.D." show up again in *Finnegans Wake* II, ii, where the marginalia include the following: "CONCOMITANCE OF COURAGE, COUNSEL AND CONSTANCY. ORDINATION OF OMEN, ONUS AND OBIT. DISTRIBUTION OF DANGER, DUTY AND DESTINY. POLAR PRINCIPLES" (FW 270.29–271.11). Glossing the passage, Joseph Campbell and Henry Morton Robinson cite Cash on Delivery as "the fundamental law of history." They claim, "Each of the mystical letters, C.O.D., may be thought of as generating three qualities, and each of the nine resultant qualities is to be found illustrated in history, fact, or legend." They add, "This derivation of nine qualities and of all creation from a Trinity of letters, parodies the cabala." See *A Skeleton Key to* Finnegans Wake (New York: Harcourt, Brace, 1944), p. 171. It is tempting to find Joyce asserting the basic connection of religion, economics, history, and—given the sexual connotation of "cod"—of sexuality, but the passage from *Finnegans Wake* quoted above is not that clearcut.

61. Richard M. Kain, "'The Music Hall, Not Poetry, Is a Criticism of Life'—A Note on Dan Lowrey's Star of Erin," *James Joyce Quarterly* 14 (1976), 97. Watters and Murtagh report that MacDermott popularized this song (p. 110).

CHAPTER 6

The Sermon as "Massproduct" (U 677)

Millions have been already swept down by impurity into hell, there to burn and to scream with agonizing screaming for an unending eternity!

The Rev. Patrick O'Keeffe, C.C., *Sermons at Mass* (1888)

And preach politics from the altar, is it? asked Mr Dedalus. (P 31)

Literary renderings of sermons have varied from the moving beauty of the Easter sermon in *The Sound and the Fury* to the comically pompous rhetoric of Dickens's Reverend Chadband. Idealizations or caricatures, such representations tend to underscore the distance between them and the ordinary reader's experience of religious discourse. In Joyce's writing this critique of homiletics is both compelling and comprehensive. The prominence of sermons in Joyce's works indicates that he deemed the Roman Catholic church's popular presence in Ireland on a par with that of the press and theater. To say this is not merely to reiterate Joyce's amply documented personal antipathy to the political and economic impact of Irish Catholicism. Rather, it is to underscore the participation of that creed in the stereotyping and convention-making of Irish culture; rivalling the newspaper and the stage as entertainment, preaching was a potent force in Joyce's Dublin. Further, it is to recognize that Joyce's texts uniformly portray the church as an organization that walked the path of other institutions in its censoring, competition for power, and ultimate complicity, however unintentional, in shaping an oppressive society. In fact, in Joyce's texts, the church never functions on a transcendental plane in which inspiration and divine dictate hold sway. As Joyce portrays it, the church is a social establishment, involved in the political and economic life of the nation in ways other than purely meliorative ones.

Joyce's narratives are not alone in their critical assessment of religion in Ireland. On the stage and in the press, the popular portrayal of clerics reproduced the often ambiguous or compromised nature of theological discourse in Ireland. In this chapter, I discuss theatrical images of the priest as well as what we would today call "media priests" in order to emphasize the sociopolitical significance of the clergy—and its homilies—in Ireland. I also describe the strict conventionalizing of religious doctrine in the sermon books that flooded the market during Joyce's era. This material reveals the contradictory images of the church and its ministers which resided in the popular mind and in the fiction that emerged from it; in that shared consciousness, the church revolutionary coexisted uneasily with the church repressive. By and large, however, the sermon was a form of popular culture thoroughly accommodated to the pressures and purposes that also marked the press and the stage. The record of both contradiction and accommodation provides a necessary background to Joyce's uses of the sermon form. The latter function informs the ironies of "Grace" and *A Portrait of the Artist as a Young Man*, while the subversion of religious doctrine marks the sermon in *Finnegans Wake*, which I treat in chapter 7.

The Stage Priest

For all of the time he spends with the clergy during his childhood, Stephen Dedalus's notion of the priesthood remains invincibly stagy: "How often he had seen himself as a priest wielding calmly and humbly the awful power of which angels and saints stood in reverence! His soul had loved to muse in secret on this desire. He had seen himself, a young and silentmannered priest, entering a confessional swiftly, ascending the altarsteps, incensing, genuflecting, accomplishing the vague acts of the priesthood which pleased him by reason of their semblance of reality and of their distance from it." The theatrical "semblance of reality" which his clerical performance would be extends in Stephen's imagination even to "the voices and gestures which he had noted with various priests" (P 158). That Joyce recognized the sense in which the church and stage reinforced each other[1] not only in manner but also in message is indicated in *Portrait*, chapter IV, when Stephen amends his life: "He had heard the names of the passions of love and hate pronounced on the stage and in the pulpit, had found them set forth solemnly in books, and had wondered why his soul was unable to harbour them for any time or to force his lips to utter their names with conviction" (P 149). Even though he does not yet understand what they signify, Stephen registers the emotional codes propounded in both popular theater and homily.

Reaching beyond censorship, the church-theater connection found a locus in the portrayal of priests on the Irish popular stage. From the mid nineteenth century on, this stock character indexed the culture's responses to clerical authority. In particular, the exigencies of Irish history merged with melodramatic convention to create the politicized p. p. who was encountered regularly in the Queen's Theatre and in various halls throughout rural Ireland; Irish melodramas like Hubert O'Grady's *The Eviction* and Thomas Finigan's *The Bride of Garryowen* regularly included him in the cast. Perhaps the prototype—and certainly the exemplar—of many such clerics was the famous rebel priest martyred by the British, Father John Murphy. Throughout the early years of the current century, the priest's story was told in Ira Allen's play *Father Murphy Or, The Hero of Tullow*. Although no copy of this play is thought to exist, the story is well known and easily pieced together from information presented on the detailed playbills of the era. For instance, the Queen's playbill for 3 June 1912 indicates the conflict between the infamous John McNabb, "a Creature of Dublin Castle," and the Wexford patriots of 1798. In Act I, Father Murphy "Denounces the Rising," but his subsequent radicalization leads to his choosing "Death before Dishonour" even under torture. The keynote scene, which is the final one of Act 4, portrays the "Death of Father Murphy—'Love them that hate you, bless them that curse you.'"

Similarly, in P. J. Bourke's *When Wexford Rose* (1910), the manuscript of which is extant, Act II, scene 2 finds Father Murphy encouraging the Wexford rebels: ". . . let us go forward with our hearts light to meet the foe. Too long have I preached peace to one and all of you, but peace shall never again be restored until an Irish Republic is declared." He goes on, "Now, men, the time for action has come & we must realise our responsibilities as soldiers of Ireland and a greater or holier cause no nation ever had than the cause that calls on you Wexfordmen to-day. Each one of you has a duty to perform, and I hope each of you shall acquit himself as a man and as a soldier." In this rousing speech, the duties of the Christian are subsumed into those of manhood and patriotism if not altogether subordinated to the struggle at hand. Later, Father John's arrest is reported, and although the play ends with the encouraging arrival of French support for the rebels, the untimely end of the priest was common knowledge. By melodramatic convention, Father Murphy's conversion to patriotism over peace had to be decisive and unequivocal; by historical tradition, he had to be sacrificed, whether on stage or off. The unavoidable message of such plays was thus deeply contradictory.

The conflict between the religious doctrine of nonviolence and the pressing need for revolutionary action in Ireland divided the clergy not only in '98 but up to Joyce's own time and beyond. Some argued the sacredness of peaceful acquiescence to divine will; others argued the sacred cause of freedom. One thing seems certain; the radicalized cleric of the melodramas, like that of history, differed from the parish priest of Irish fiction whom Antony Coleman has characterized as the "professional leader of the community, autocratic and severe, exacting a complete and reverential deference from his parishioners, a rigorist in theology whose obedience to the law, moral and divine, was total and unquestioning."[2] Although the Father Murphys of the stage shared some stern qualities with the Dr. Grays of fiction, the most engaging popular portrait of the priest imaged him as not only spiritual taskmaster but also political revolutionary.

The synergy by which historical events molded stage figures who then molded cultural perceptions worked in favor of those clerics whose political dispositions were somewhere to the left of center. In an article tracing the responses of the Roman Catholic church in Ireland to political movements between 1898 and 1918, David W. Miller charts the wide range of attitudes among the clergy at all levels, the loss of ecclesiastical power which followed the defeat of Parnell, and the eventual acceptance by many clergymen of political activism. To accept this role, priests had to "persuade themselves that Sinn Fein was not the kind of revolutionary movement upon which the theology textbooks had taught them to pronounce anathema." Many were able to do so, particularly younger priests.[3] Certainly, one older priest able to walk the line between church doctrine and patriotic imperative was Father Thomas Burke, who, during an 1872 lecture tour, spoke in New York to this effect:

What future is before Ireland? Oh, my friends, what can I say? Before
me lies the past of my native land: I can weep over her wrongs. Before
me lies the Ireland of to-day, and I can sympathize with her sorrows. I
believe I can see the dawning of her hopes. Of the future it becomes
me not specifically to speak. I am a man of peace, not of war. It only
remains for me to say that, next to the duty that I owe to God and
His holy altar, is the duty that I owe to thee, oh! land of Ireland; to
pray for thee; to sigh for thy coming glory; and to be ready—whenever the necessary conditions shall convince me that the fit hour has
come—to take a man's part in the vindication of thy name.[4]

Clergy holding these sentiments lived out in their preaching the role
provided for them by the patriotic hero of Tullow.

The Chief Secretary's *Intelligence Notes* from 1913 to 1916 document the Castle's keeping of tabs on the clergy, some of whom are
reported as sharing *Sinn Féin* interests or as uttering antirecruiting
opinions from the pulpit. Breandán Choille's edition of these notes
includes a nine-page chart titled "Clergymen who have come under
notice owing to their disloyal language or conduct during the year
1915," which covers all four provinces and lists name, date, place,
and "Nature of Language" reported. For example, in Belfast on November 25, the Rev. M. O'Flanagan, C.C. is said to have stated that
"The work of the Irish people was to break the connection with England." Further, "He prayed that victory would alight on the banner
of any enemy that would deprive England of her power." Another
instance, this time in Wexford, involved the Rev. Albert Lennon,
C.C., who on January 17, "In the course of his sermon told the
people not to leave their places if the Germans came, that the Germans were not as bad as they were painted, and that the information
the people were getting about the success of the Allies was not
true." Several of the noticed clergy had spoken to their congregations in favor of a letter written by the Bishop of Limerick and "reproduced in circular form by the thousand, in which he states that
this war is England's war and that Irishmen have no interest in it";
these same priests advised people to join the Irish Volunteers and
arm themselves rather than accept conscription. One priest told his
flock to do so "even if the only arms they could get was a two-
pronged fork."[5]

The priest of action and revolutionary fervor thus existed both in
fact and in popular culture, but he does not appear in any vivid way

in Joyce's works. In *Stephen Hero*, Stephen witnesses a political debate between Mr. Fulham and his neighbor, Mr. Heffernan. Stephen's conservative host, referring to the Gaelic language movement and the efforts to revive Irish traditions, argues that Ireland's "lot is thrown in with England," but Mr. Heffernan says, "The young generation is not of your opinion. My son, Pat, is studying at Clonliffe at present and he tells me all the young students there, those who are to be our priests afterwards, have these ideas." Mr. Fulham responds, "The Catholic Church, my dear sir, will never incite to rebellion" (SH 247). Between such conservatism and the stage example of Father Murphy, the actual Irish Catholic church of Joyce's day positioned itself. The Father Michael of *Finnegans Wake* comically stands for the "old regime" (FW 116.8), and Joyce's priests, often construed as charlatans or showmen, are broadly anti-revolutionary. Like Father Keon of "Ivy Day in the Committee Room," who is described as "resembling a poor clergyman or a poor actor" (D 125), they represent the political status quo that Joyce associated with Archbishop Walsh.

The church run by Joyce's clerics provides Joyce's Dubliners not with inspiration but only with self-justification. Some Dubliners, like Maria in "Clay" and the offstage Mrs. Farrington in "Counterparts," are pious out of need; they have no other place to turn for support in their brutal sector of society. Others, like Tom Kernan and his friends in "Grace," have less need and more information, except that what they know tends to be a mixture of error, superstition, and popular folklore about religion. For both of these groups, the church is an institution that legitimates the individual who connects herself or himself with it. The reader is led to believe that there are in Dublin relatively few Blooms who see the church as a business organization that "Stupefies" (U 80) its followers in return for their support.

Media Priests

"Fr. B.V. is the most diverting public figure in England at present. I never see his name but I expect some enormity."[6] So wrote Joyce to Stanislaus in 1906 from a small flat on the Via Frattina in Rome. It was not surprising that the name of the Jesuit preacher Bernard Vaughan (1847–1922) was equally familiar in Ireland and in Rome;

from 1900, when he was involved in the first of his public controversies,[7] Vaughan was the best-known preacher of his day, a "public figure" as well as a priest. Joyce refers to Vaughan in *Dubliners*, *Ulysses*, and *Finnegans Wake*, always with a critical eye on his mass impact and appeal. If, in Joyce's estimation, the church were often at fault for the very fact of being not a Body but an Institution, Father Vaughan appeared to epitomize that flaw. For many people, the church of the modern era was to a large extent the one that Father Vaughan represented—an organization led by what Father Denis O'Shea critically labeled the "actor-preacher."[8]

According to his biographer, Vaughan enjoyed meeting his audiences' tastes; he "is best remembered by the world at large as an eloquent preacher in the pulpit and as an impassioned speaker on the platform, who . . . could always and everywhere attract and hold a large and attentive audience."[9] Perhaps the best example of his efforts at popularizing theology was the mission of April and May, 1911, when he and another priest presented from the pulpit a series of "Dialogues" in "dramatic" style between a pastor and a layperson, Vaughan taking the second part. Because this mission took place in a poor parish in London, Vaughan adapted his voice, though reportedly not very well, to a Cockney accent.[10] It is this notorious dramatizing in the pulpit that Father Conmee thinks about in "Wandering Rocks":

> Father Conmee walked and, walking, smiled for he thought on Father Bernard Vaughan's droll eyes and cockney voice.
> —Pilate! Wy don't you old back that owlin mob?
> A zealous man, however. Really he was. And really did great good in his way. Beyond a doubt. He loved Ireland, he said, and he loved the Irish. Of good family too would one think it? (U 219–220)

Martindale observes that outsiders thought that Vaughan was using not dialect but slang and therefore disapproved of his approach; in America, Vaughan's preachings were regarded as "vaudeville performances," and Conmee's condescending, qualified approval of Vaughan characterizes many popular responses to him. Yet Martindale quotes a "distinguished prelate" to the effect that Vaughan was not so much an actor as a dedicated priest who had discovered the efficacy of wearing "motley before the public" to draw them to God.

It appears to be precisely this quality that offended both Joyce and his brother. Stanislaus reports in *My Brother's Keeper* that

Vaughan was "a very popular evangelist . . . whose name was frequently in the newspapers and who had appeared to crowded congregations also in Dublin. He was a Jesuit, a member of an old English family, and a vulgarian priest in search of publicity. Besides
preaching from his legitimate stage, the pulpit, he used to deliver
short breezy talks from inappropriate places, such as the boxing
ring before a championship match." As is well known, Stanislaus
claims that Vaughan is the model for the Father Purdon of "Grace,"
the name change indicating his brother's "contempt for him" in that
"The old name for the street of the brothels in Dublin was Purdon
Street."[11] That the Pola Notebook (1904) records the phrase "The
vulgarian priest"[12] would appear to support Stanislaus's contention
that his brother was seriously troubled by Vaughan's mixing of entertainment with homiletics. Scholes and Kain suggest that Joyce
drew the phrase from Stanislaus's *Dublin Diary* and note its appearance in *Stephen Hero*. There, the patriotic, playful, handsome, singing Father Moran appears to be a priest of Vaughan's type; Joyce
says that he looks like "a pleasant tender-hearted vulgarian" (SH 65).
This connection seems not to have diminished in force over time.
Even in *Finnegans Wake*, Joyce gets in a dig at the late Vaughan.
Under the heading "Vaughan," Glasheen notes that the Buffalo
Workbook #10 includes the phrase "Fr Bern. Vaughan granted
privilege of portable altar" and that *Finnegans Wake* picks up this
idea when, in two pages that sum up much church tradition, the
increasingly "holy" Kevin is said to have "been graunted the prav-
iloge of a priest's postcreated portable *altare cum balneo*" (FW
605.7-8)—an altar with bath.

Despite his likely intolerance for Vaughan's religious showmanship, Joyce was to remember him for over a quarter of a century and
to mention him in three works of fiction. In another letter to
Stanislaus from the same apartment in Rome, Joyce indicated the
basis of this attention: speaking of the *Sinn Féin* campaign against
"venereal excess," Joyce observes:

> Anyway my opinion is that if I put down a bucket into my own
> soul's well, sexual department, I draw up Griffith's and Ibsen's and
> Skeffington's and Bernard Vaughan's and St. Aloysius' and Shelley's
> and Renan's water along with my own. And I am going to do that in
> my novel (inter alia) and plank the bucket down before the shades
> and substances above mentioned to see how they like it: and if they

don't like it I can't help them. I am nauseated by their lying drivel
about pure men and pure women and spiritual love and love for ever:
blatant lying in the face of the truth.[13]

It would seem that Joyce attributed to Arthur Griffith, Shelley,
Vaughan, and anyone else who advocated physical purity the same
desires and energies that characterized his own sexual life. Con-
comitantly, of course, Joyce's responses were marked by his knowledge of the very attitudes he despised; Vaughan and Company had
contributed their share of substance to Joyce's "soul's well," and not
to acknowledge his relationship to their ideological practices would
be to falsify his own position and to undermine the cultural validity
of his writing. The stage priest, the revolutionary cleric, and Father
Vaughan were equally important variants in the culture that Joyce
attended to.

Another well-known "actor-preacher," whose social impact Joyce
addresses in "Grace," is the Father Thomas Burke mentioned above.
Born in Galway in 1830, he traveled around the world, appealing
especially for Irish self-determination. For instance, in November
and December of 1872, Burke delivered six lectures in the U.S. on
this topic. In a book on eighteenth-century Ireland, James A. Froude
had attempted to justify English oppression (past, present, and future) of Ireland, which he saw as a nation unfit to govern itself.
Burke discussed incident after incident in Irish history to discredit
Froude as an historian and to refute his argument. Often humorous, always passionate, Burke captivated his packed audiences. In
the National Library of Ireland is a collection of press clippings,
most of them dealing with Burke's American tours.[14] Many of his
sermons and lectures were published in versions that in the main he
had quickly revised from newspaper transcriptions. But the clippings themselves are of greater interest because, typical of the day's
journalism, they recorded not only details about the size of the congregation but also its "applause," "laughter," "cheers," and the occasional "sensation." These reports make clear the secular appeal of
Burke, his substantial rhetorical talents, and the extent to which his
appearances, whether in churches or academies or hired halls, constituted an evening of popular entertainment.

Hence, at the Boston "Coloseum," 40,000 people paid to hear
Burke speak on "The Genius and Character of the Irish People," before which a band played "selections of National music." In refer-

ence to his lecture on "The Immaculate Conception" at St. Andrew's Church in New York, the newspaper remarks that "Father Burke . . . wore over his Dominican habit a white lace surplice instead of the black cloak in which he usually preaches. . . ." On another instance, the topic "The Exiles of Erin" brought forth the following report:

> Fully one half the audience was composed of ladies, whose brilliant costumes added not a little to the magnificent *coup d'oeil* presented by the house, which was literally crammed 'from pit to dome,' even the space railed off for the musicians, and which, at lectures, is usually allotted to the reporters, being invaded and taken possession of by the crowd. On the stage were over a hundred of the clergy.
>
> Precisely at eight o'clock Father Burke, attired in his Dominican habit, came forward on the stage, and was received with a genuine Irish *cead mille failthe*. The immense audience rose impulsively, and for some minutes the cheering was deafening, while the ladies waved their handkerchiefs with an enthusiasm equaling that of the male portion of the audience.

Such reports, of which this selection is typical, with their attention to fashionable behavior and dress, call to mind the parodic press reports of "Cyclops." Indeed, the similar style of the real press clippings is often comical, as this example demonstrates:

> From the very outset of his discourse, he was completely *en rapport* with his audience; and at many of the striking points of his lecture, particularly where he referred so feelingly to his old father and mother, in the old and beloved land of his birth; and, also, when he pathetically invoked the Saint of whom he spoke [Saint Laurence O'Toole], in his reference to the Irish famine of '46 and '47—in these instances, his hearers seemed scarcely to be able sufficiently to testify the full extent of their sympathy and appreciation.

The conventional language used by the press was one of the means by which the church theatrical reached the popular mind. Throughout Joyce's era, on the stage, in the papers, and from the pulpit, the priest increasingly spoke to more and more contested issues and thus made evident the pressures that threatened to unsettle the status quo.

Sermon Books: Theology as Convention

The maintenance of that state of affairs depended on the church's proselytizing not only against socialism and revolution but also for the idea that the current class-based capitalistic social order was divinely ordained. To sustain these positions, the clergy were bound to the theological defense of many matters that Joyce's fiction presents as strictly conventional. Such stylizations of behavior and vision show up constantly as early as *Dubliners* and run through *Finnegans Wake* in more and more aggressive narrative form. When we find Mangan's sister described in "Araby" in terms appropriate to the iconography of the Virgin Mary, we see the impact on the adolescent consciousness of the church's conventional and ultimately deceptive portrayal of women. When we find Issy openly rejecting Jaun's views about premarital sex, we locate both a critique of religious doctrine as outmoded (to the point of repressiveness) and also a realism that marks all of Joyce's presentations of the individual's responses to institutional pressures. Those pressures were especially evident during the final years of the nineteenth century and the beginning of the twentieth in that, as Joyce lets us see, the whole mechanism of preaching was thoroughly refined and conventionalized. In the next chapter I indicate the extent to which Jaun's sermon in *Finnegans Wake* III, ii comically addresses the homiletic topics characteristic of the era. Here I first discuss the phenomenon of the handbook and the parodic sermons of the music hall, and then turn to Joyce's use of the sermon form in "Grace" and *Portrait*.

Joyce's day saw a boom in the publication of sermon books. The homilies of especially eloquent and well-known preachers—the Donnes, the Newmans, the Bossuets—had always been published for the perusal of the faithful as well as the literary, but to this kind of publication were increasingly added manuals on the preparation of sermons and ready-made messages so simple and orthodox that they could be appropriated by the busy and the uninventive. Such books, constantly reviewed in the press as well as in religious periodicals, and evidently much employed by the preaching orders, directly influenced the popular culture of Catholics and non-Catholics alike. The sheer quantity of this literature makes either a survey of them or an enumeration of them beyond the scope of my inquiry, but that fact alone indicates that the handbooks were part of a concerted effort by the church to hold, maintain, educate, and indoctrinate the popular audience. Even those who did not attend religious meetings would have difficulty avoiding these works, staples as they were of "all the book-stalls which offered old directories and volumes of sermons and unheard-of treatises" (SH 145).

A representative guide to sermon material was published in the 1920s by the famous Jesuit scholar, Father Stephen J. Brown. In *The Preacher's Library*, Father Brown categorizes the publications available to help the Catholic preacher prepare his addresses; he cites "The Teachers," "The Scripture Book-Shelf" (Bible dictionaries, concordances, and the like), "Models" (such as Newman), "Preachers' Aids" (outlines, notes, illustrations), "Published Sermons" (some divided into categories, such as sermons for Lent, sermons for children, sermons for "Special Occasions"), and an "Alphabetical List of Preachers and Their Works." Although not comprehensive, Brown's list targets some of the most popular preachers of the era and gives a good sense of the extent of literature surveyed. In particular, he names thirty-one Irish priests, including Thomas Burke, whom Brown says is "generally acknowledged to be the greatest of Irish preachers."[15] Among the works he lists are many collections of anecdotes, such as W. Gwynne's *Five Hundred Stories and Illustrations, Adapted to the Christian Year for the Use of Catechists, Preachers, and Teachers* (1897), and Henry Ward Beecher's *Five Hundred and Ninety-Five Pulpit Pungencies* (1866). In addition, the busy preacher could find volumes of instructional materials such as quotations from religious volumes, and ideas for sermon development, topically arranged.[16]

As for published volumes of sermons, Brown states, "I take it that such works are mainly intended not for the laity, but for the clergy, and again, not so much for the spiritual improvement of the latter as for utilization by other preachers." One such volume was published in 1886 by Dublin's Gill & Son: Rev. Joseph Farrell's *Sermons. With an Appendix Containing Some of His Speeches on Quasi-Religious Subjects*. Like most if not all of these works, the book bears the censor's imprimatur to guarantee the soundness of the theological doctrine presented. Farrell, a priest of the diocese of Kildare and Leighlin, wrote for the *Irish Ecclesiastical Record* and the *Irish Monthly*. Straightforward in doctrine, his pieces are also unexceptional in character, although on occasion he mentions specifically Irish matters such as the Catholic University Education Question. Another such work is *Sermons at Mass* by the Rev. Patrick O'Keeffe, C.C., from Borrisoleigh, Archdiocese of Cashel. Having "aimed at simplicity not less than at comprehensiveness,"[17] this slim volume includes twenty short sermons from "On Detraction and Backbiting" to "Extreme Unction."

Other books took it upon themselves to instruct the preacher in the writing and presenting of the sermon; in doing so, they followed up on the training provided by college sermon clubs for those preparing for the priesthood.[18] For example, the Rev. John B. Murphy's *The What-Why-How? Plan for Preaching a Sermon with One Hundred and Four Specimen Sketch Sermons* (Dublin: Browne & Nolan, [1925]) provides one page of ideas for each of the many topics covered. Similarly, the Rev. George Edward Howe published *Sermon Plans: Being Four Outlines of Sermons, Chiefly on the Epistles and Gospels, for Each Sunday and Holiday of the Year* (London: St. Anselm's Society, 1904). Mostly dealing with basic biblical and theological doctrine, the book provides two-page outlines for each topic, a plan that would enable the sermon writer to string together a short, orthodox sermon with very little work. The kind of aid evidently desired by the target market for these books is made clear in the Rev. Thomas Flynn's *Preaching Made Easy*, which provides in the appendices relevant scriptural references to Christ's "discourses," "miracles," and "parables."[19] The Rev. W. O'Dowd's *Preaching* not only deals with several types of sermons (including "controversial" ones, five-minute sermons for Low Mass, and sermons for children) but also provides "A Course of Sermons for Three Years" with references to source material in the Scriptures, Aquinas' *Summa Theologica*, the Catechism of the Council of Trent, the *Catholic Encyclopaedia*, and Newman, among other sources.[20] Father O'Dowd's intentions in composing this instructional volume are made clear when he stresses that Christ's own preaching was "popular, that is, it was adapted to the intelligence of the fishermen and peasants who listened to it." He adds, "Seminarists are often exhorted by their professors to get themselves ready to 'popularize theology'"—a task which is accomplished by emphasizing basic doctrine and by simplifying difficult theological points for laypersons.[21]

I have dealt at some length with sermon books to indicate the extreme codification of Catholic theology during Joyce's lifetime. A popularizing activity, preaching stylized form and content, and it was the exceptional preacher who violated convention. Again, one recalls Gerard Manley Hopkins's homiletic troubles; conforming to the prescriptions of many preaching books to be concrete, he followed his examples and images into the realm of the theologically objectionable. The sermon books of Joyce's era not only offered recommendations but also defined the acceptable.

Another point that must be made is that it would be possible for a priest to speak to his congregation year after year without deviating from the conventional run of topics. Although many of the manuals include attacks on socialism, freemasonry, and divorce, such pressing matters as class division, labor disputation, poverty, and nationalism might never be addressed by the individual clergyman in contact with his parishioners. In fact, a restlessness among both Catholic and Protestant clergy with the kinds of sermons that emerged from use of these handbooks is easily documented. For instance, the anonymous author of a review of one such volume—the Rev. Stopford A. Brooke's *The Fight of Faith: Sermons Preached on Various Occasions* (1877)—wrote, "The fact is that the vendors of cheap and musty theology do a large trade, and the preacher who is without the literary gift grinds out what should be living food from a mixture of these dead old bones. Or he buys manuscript sermons written by nameless persons whose style is so colourless as not to endanger the preacher of suspicion of being a borrower."[22] The writer suggests that preachers simply own up to their being overworked and tell their congregations that they plan to *preach* a sermon *written* by a well-known orator. A similar point was made in 1915 by the Rev. Denis O'Shea in the *Irish Ecclesiastical Record*. Father O'Shea notes that "those who do their preaching entirely from sermon books will find it very hard to escape the accusation" of plagiarism. He adds that this grievous error was in fact easy to commit "when sermon books are in such abundance" and lauded by the press, yet these same books he finds to cause dull sermon delivery. Too many preachers memorized their material from someone else's writings; too few priests took on themselves fully the "sacred duty" for which they were ordained—"to preach."[23]

Hence, while the excitement of modernism pushed people out of the churches to other forms of popular entertainment, preaching itself often became more and more standardized and hence less interesting; although in the melodrama, for instance, the reliance on conventions enhanced audience satisfaction—at least to a point—in the pulpit this procedure could undermine the appeal of what everyone already recognized as prescriptive material. My review of ser-

mon manuals argues that much of the theology to which Dubliners
were exposed must have been every bit as boring as Bloom suggests.
A means of offsetting such standardizations, the cult of personality
which actor-preachers encouraged can be seen as of strategic importance to a church actively vying for a share of people's leisure time.
In the figure of the media priest various cultural tensions come together. He adumbrates both the tradition by which the priest resides at the heart of the Irish community and the modern popularizing efforts of the church. He spells out the conventionality of
its messages both religious and nationalistic as well as (possibly) the
revolutionary sympathies of many clerics. And, most important, he
articulates the church's role in the cultural drama that tended to
transform all ideas into ideological practices and socioeconomic
strategies.

The Sermon in Song, the Sermon as Stump Speech

Nothing revealed the conventionality of the church in the popular
mind more clearly than parodies of religious doctrine and of the sermon form itself. Joyce's sermons in fact mirror the popular use of
the form for subversive purposes. Principally, parodic sermonizing
showed up or was referred to in the London music halls, as an article in the August 1874 *Dublin University Magazine* mentions:

> There is now a character popular at the Music Halls, personated by
> more than one vocalist, announced in countless advertisements, and
> celebrated on street hoardings, by the title of the "D----d Scamp!"
> . . . This personage, who is dressed in a manner denoting apparent or
> superficial respectability, is furnished with a string of verses set to a
> "catching" air, wherein he proceeds to accuse himself of a series of the
> most despicable rogueries (of which preaching a street sermon against
> intemperance, and getting drunk on the proceeds, may serve as an
> example . . .).

The author laments the evil influence of such a song on "all the
street boys in London," who currently sang it.[24] The vocalist in
question was, of course, the Irish performer G. H. Macdermott,
who appeared at Dan Lowrey's in 1882, 1884, 1885, and 1889,[25]
thus insuring that the Dublin audience, too, was more than familiar
with "The Scamp" and his outrageous lyrics.

But songs were not the only vehicles for allusion to sermons,

street variety or more formal. *The Leader* for 1 September 1900 deplores the fact that at the Lyric Music Hall in Dublin such songs,
although overshadowed by even more disturbing references to religion, were allowed. The writer mentions a comedian whose song
described "how he collected in church and went off with the proceeds." Another turn involved "living statuary," of which the writer
comments that "better taste would have been displayed if they kept
them on such subjects as 'Mars and Venus,' for dragging in 'The
Rock of Ages,' a young girl clinging to the Cross, and 'The Angelus'
into such a moral atmosphere was a disgusting example of British
hypocrisy, if not indeed flat blasphemy." A further act during the
same evening at the Lyric—indeed, the star performer's turn—included a song which the writer found marked by "vulgar grossness"
even though the vocalist had described it as "the prettiest little
hymn you ever heard in your life."[26] But the act that most offended
was the appearance of an artiste who, "dressed up as a sort of lay
preacher, and no doubt intended to personify Religion, managed to
get a large amount of indecent suggestion into his mock sermonis-
ing about the danger of mixed bathing and like matters."[27] Given
that these references to religion allegedly occurred within a single
evening's entertainment in a Dublin hall, it seems clear that the music hall as a whole took on the ecclesiastical institutions of its day as
fully as it did the swell, the boss, and the mother-in-law—those perennial comic representatives of oppression. The music-hall sermon
spoke for social discomfort over the church's position of power, and
provides historical evidence of the conflicts which religious institutions generated in the popular mind.

Such satire was not sophisticated; it operated mainly by inversion
in that it celebrated behavior deplored by the churches. The message of the halls was that one could have more fun when stealing
tithes than when contributing them. In addition, only the "unique"
lion comiques and seriocomics could get away with such behavior.
They seemed to be freer and more authentic individuals for their
picaresque undermining of conventions and bohemian disregard for
middle-class mores. Of course, performers such as Macdermott and
Marie Lloyd were not so much unique as they were epitomes of a
style. As has been indicated, the halls immediately standardized any
successful act and generated from it endless spin-offs. But that conventionalizing seems to have remained secondary in the popular
mind to the primary impact of enhanced freedom and singularity

which antiestablishment turns celebrated. *The Leader*, for all of its efforts to free Ireland from British control, remained insensitive to the halls' lauding of the individual at the expense of the institution and to the proletarian's need to attack the social forces that confined him or her. On some level, the worker recognized what for the middle classes was masked—the power links among church, economy, and all other organs of cultural control to which the lower orders were abandoned.

To this point, I have argued that the theology of Joyce's era was conventionalized on a mass scale, especially in sermon books, and that the doctrinal rigidity suggested by this fact found responses on the stage and in the pulpit in several ways. The stage priest of the melodrama sometimes lived the doctrine of acceptance, peace, and love without questioning it; other priestly dramatis personae were revolutionaries. The often theatrical preachers of Joyce's day were similarly divided. Clearly, the institutional acts of the church did not satisfy all of the clergy's or the society's desires for social change. In addition, music hall parodies of sermons signify the questioning which took place throughout the culture (but perhaps especially in the disfranchised classes) of religious authority over social relations. The rest of this chapter examines the social impact of the sermon in "Grace" and *Portrait;* it demonstrates that in Joyce's work, the sermon signifies the economic matrix in which Irish culture operated, a matrix responsible for the divided images of the church that popular culture presented.

"Grace"

"Grace" stands as one of Joyce's most direct indictments of the financial enterprise of the church and of its accommodation of theology to secular demands, specifically to the attitudes represented by the backsliding businessmen pictured in the sketch. When Martin Cunningham silences the men in Tom Kernan's bedroom with stories of the church, it is power that he evokes, a power which plays over those gathered and persuades even the comically reprehensible tea taster to affiliate himself, quite apart from belief, with an institution that wields clout. Their awe over the doctrine of papal infallibility provides evidence of their cultural conditioning in that they respond to the image of a potent church more or less independently of their knowledge, inadequate as it is, of theology. The story as a whole attacks this automatic response to the sacred, especially when the briefly presented sermon speaks its content more directly than was often true in conventional published sermons. Openly asserting his modestly matter-of-fact aim for the retreat, the priest actually defuses the men's expectation of conversion. Far from being too challenging, the church reflects the society's everyday behavior while it benefits from the shared desire for personal change. Joyce's cultural anatomy operates here as always to undermine our sense of individual value and development as something other than a complex by-product of social forms and cultural operations. Really to change Tom Kernan would require alteration of the institutions that shape him.

As Joyce's story presents it, the church is not distinct from any secular institution: it defines behavior according to binary codes that appear to be fixed; it seeks to enlarge its membership and to preempt other institutions in the struggle for social control. The conversion of the individual has become a function of hegemonic maneuvers in that the church teaches its members to become better businesspeople and to help themselves to a bigger piece of the financial pie. Joyce's using as a model for Father Purdon the Jesuit Bernard Vaughan enhances our recognition of the church's intimate ties to the economic system from which it often attempted to distance itself in the public mind.

Like Purdon, Vaughan followed and even exaggerated the contemporary popularizing of theology for the masses. Part of this effort centered on offering specialized retreats for people in different walks of life. Vaughan conducted many such retreats; he also published an address given to a group of businessmen and entitled "The Uses of Advertisement." The preacher argues that he is "a member of the oldest advertising firm in religion on this planet." Asserting that "expediency" is more important than "taste" where religion is concerned, Vaughan defends himself against those "superior-minded people" who "object to modern methods of advertisement" and who believe that the preacher should not "turn the House of God into a sort of theatre." He responds that such a stance makes religion "the only . . . tabooed" subject "in the modern world." About advertising itself, Vaughan speaks with great regard. He calls it both an art and a science that requires a knowledge of human psychology and the means of "arresting attention." He adds, "I do not say that advertising is free from abuse. Cheap and nasty things which nobody needs are forced upon our attention un-blushingly and boldly. But what good thing is there in the world which is not equally misused? The honest advertiser of an honest article has my approbation all the time, and the attitude of those who condemn him is little short of hypocritical."[28]

It seems unlikely that Joyce was aware of this speech—one which suggests that Bernard Vaughan and Leopold Bloom could easily have talked shop—but Joyce did know of similar clerical presenta-tions. As is well known, Stanislaus reports that a "retreat for busi-ness men" was held by a Jesuit in Gardiner Street Church and that John Joyce had been persuaded to attend. "Out of sarcastic curi-osity," Stanislaus continues, "I followed them to the church on the last evening of the retreat to listen to the sermon and watch my fa-ther fumbling shamefacedly with his lighted candle. The sermon was a man-to-man talk in a chatty tone. I came out into the fresh air before the end." Stanislaus also mentions that his brother had at-tended a sermon on the subject of grace "and had come away angry and disgusted at the inadequacy of the exposition. He said the preacher had not even tried to know what he was talking about, but assumed that anything was good enough for his listeners. It an-gered him that such shoddy stuff should pass for spiritual guid-ance."[29] Drawn from both experiences and from the media image of Vaughan, Father Purdon in part represents the oversimplification, inaccuracy, and reliance on showmanship that characterized many popular sermons. In contrast, consider Stephen's attendance at the Capuchin church, where he finds that "the sermons of the priests were grateful to him inasmuch as the speakers did not seem inclined to make much use of their rhetorical and elocutionary training nor anxious to reveal themselves, in theory, at least, men of the world" (SH 177).

One other acclaimed preacher drew Joyce's attention in "Grace." Kernan and his friends all agree that Father Tom Burke was one of the greatest preachers of their day. Drawing "crowds of Protestants" along with Catholics, Burke was known for his "style" and "voice" (D 165), and yet he is questioned, even by the likes of Kernan and his cohorts, for theological imprecision:

—And yet they say he wasn't much of a theologian, said Mr Cunningham.
—Is that so? said Mr M'Coy.

—O, of course, nothing wrong, you know. Only sometimes, they say, he didn't preach what was quite orthodox. (D 165)

Given this comment, it is of interest that Burke's 1872 volume of lectures does have the imprimatur, yet in his preface, Burke (who was perhaps aware of such criticisms) remarks, "If . . . there be anything in them contrary to the teachings of the Catholic Church, that, I am the first to condemn and repudiate."[30]

In that both the style and the content of popularized sermons seem to have irritated Joyce, both informal delivery and uninformed preacher receive attention in "Grace." Skepticism over the doctrine aside, he appears to have objected to any job poorly done and especially to sermons that reflected only the lowest state of the art. This ineffectuality is linked explicitly in the story with sermons that do not differentiate theological doctrine from sound financial methods, for "Grace" shows us the harmony of the business world with the religious teachings available for popular consumption.

From the outset of the story we are led to see that religious conversion is not the answer to the Kernans' problems. Proud of being a tea taster and commercial traveler, the once-successful protagonist has been destroyed not so much by drink as by changes in the economic environment: "Modern business methods had spared him only so far as to allow him a little office in Crowe Street on the window blind of which was written the name of his firm with the address—London, E.C." (D 154). Like an out-of-date Jehovah, Mr. Kernan passes judgment, spitting teas into the grate. Directly following the description of Kernan's background and job, the narrative introduces the aptly named Mr. Power, the "much younger man" who rescued Tom when he drunkenly fell down the stairs and who is employed, like Martin Cunningham, in Dublin Castle. That the "arc of his social rise intersected the arc of his friend's decline" (D 154) is significant because those two trajectories describe both the access to power provided by political employment and the inevitable failure of those who have not made the economic choices necessary for survival in the modern business world, even in the seemingly casual way in which that world established itself in early twentieth-century Dublin. Not religion but economics has defined Mr. Kernan's obsolescence and his family's rude poverty.

The relationship of the church to social change is playfully suggested at the story's opening by several uses of the word "curate."

This slang term for bartender appears to have amused Joyce (compare the playbill in *Finnegans Wake* in which Saunderson is described as a "spoilcurate" [FW 221.10]) and implies the church's role in a modernizing world, for the curates first set up Tom Kernan for his fall by serving him liquor and then cover up the evidence of the fall ("a curate set about removing the traces of blood from the floor"—D 153). Like Father Purdon, whose discourse on grace ignores the doctrine of original sin, these secular curates efface the signs of Kernan's decline. What they have to offer addresses the causes and cures of Kernan's woes as poorly as Father Purdon does.

The economic relationships that define the state of affairs in the story surface in many details. For instance, we are led to believe that Mrs. Kernan is kept from thinking the emblematic Mr. Power responsible for her husband's dismal state by "remembering Mr Power's good offices during domestic quarrels as well as many small, but opportune loans" (D 155). Mr. Fogarty, the grocer whom Kernan owes money, has already "failed in business in a licensed house in the city because his financial condition had constrained him to tie himself to second-class distillers and brewers" (D 166). Mr. M'Coy is mildly ostracized because he mooches off his friends, and Mr. Harford the financier is quietly censured because he charges usurious rates to lend money to the workers and failing businesspeople of Dublin. Similarly, the very Jesuits who offer the retreat are presented as not just "an educated order" but also as "the boyos [that] have influence"; as Mr. M'Coy crassly notes, "The Jesuits cater for the upper classes," and Power agrees, "Of course" (D 163–64). Such references to the dominating socioeconomic relations are too insistent to be ignored. In this Dublin, money talks, while poverty is both powerless and quietly resentful.

The retreat itself turns out to be a microcosm of the culture. Mr. Harford attends along with politicians, a pawnbroker, a pressman, and, no doubt, more than one "commercial figure" on the way down (D 173). Father Purdon, who is "powerful-looking" but too bulky to get into the pulpit with grace, is the perfect speaker for them. Mimicking the theatrical media priest of his day, he pauses before speaking to roll "back each wide sleeve of his surplice with an elaborate large gesture" (D 173). The priest, far from being there for a "terrifying" or "extravagant" purpose, came "as a man of the world," a "spiritual accountant" (D 174). The priest is not the only one who does not expect much from religious experience. Of

Mrs. Kernan we are told that "Her beliefs were not extravagant. She believed steadily in the Sacred Heart as the most generally useful of all Catholic devotions and approved of the sacraments. Her faith was bounded by her kitchen but, if she was put to it, she could believe also in the banshee and in the Holy Ghost" (D 158). Like her husband and even the wise Martin Cunningham, Mrs. Kernan owns to beliefs that are liberally mixed with superstition or misinformation, but she does not attribute any extraordinary power to religion itself.

The preacher's focus is the parable of the unjust steward, which most critics of "Grace" have discussed.[31] The text quoted by Father Purdon is, of course, taken out of context. He intones: "*For the children of this world are wiser in their generation than the children of light. Wherefore make unto yourselves friends out of the mammon of iniquity so that when you die they may receive you into everlasting dwellings*" (D 173). From this unsettling and perhaps permanently murky quotation, Purdon arrives at the unlikely point that Christ would have businessmen set the pattern of behavior for the world, that their living "to a certain extent, for the world" is perfectly all right as long as they have balanced the books of their "spiritual life" (D 174).[32] On several counts, Father Purdon deviates from even the most generously conceived Christian doctrine.[33] For one thing, he validates a worldly orientation toward economic gain even though those who are involved with "the mammon of iniquity" are not merely friends of the rich but are also allies of those who have gained wealth through wickedness. (The OED entry on "mammon" emphasizes the diabolic connotations of the word.) The cloak of religiosity seemingly typical of the comrades of mammon appears to be asserted when the *Wake* sums up the writers of the gospels as "Mammon Lujius" (FW 13.20). For another thing, Purdon portrays a Christ who almost condones failings as long as one is "straight and manly with God" (D 174): to be courteous and "never to peach on a fellow" (P 9) turn out to be, as Simon Dedalus counseled his son, a sufficent moral code after all. Further, the priest misleadingly allots the burden and indeed the power of achieving grace to the individual rather than to God. By this logic, the businessman can say either "I find all well" or "I find this wrong and this wrong. But, with God's grace, I will rectify this and this. I will set right my accounts" (D 174). Divine grace enters this audit in the form of a casual expression rather than a theological concept, in a qualifying phrase set off between commas, while the repeated "I" controls the spiritual inquiry. At the very least, the priest's portrayal of the mechanisms of contrition and absolution would leave his auditors not only unredeemed but also egotistical. The myth of selfhood which "Circe" attacks subsumes Purdon's theology.

Further, the thrust of the sermon is that newness of spirit ("We'll make a new man of him," says Mr. Power) may be achieved by following Purdon's advice. Such distortion of doctrine emerges from Purdon's twisting of the biblical text itself. Although the parable is extremely ambiguous, it is perhaps most readily interpreted as a displacement of spiritual terms by mundane ones. Hence, the steward's fixing of his master's books, which would ordinarily be seen as a corrupt action, may be compared to the laying up of treasure in heaven.[34] This substitution is ignored by Purdon, whose businesslike outlook reinforces the implications of his name. Not just a gibe at the church because of the connection of prostitution to Purdon Street, "Purdon" also signals the brand of simony that prostitution represents. The trading of sex for money makes the body a site of economic exchange. The priest would have his auditors enact his bogus and socially damaging system of "spiritual" accountancy.

Robert Jackson suggests the prevailing critical opinion of Purdon's brand of religion when he says that Joyce "condemns . . . the church which supports the set of values by which Kernan is obliged to repent."[35] Similarly, Howard Lachtman finds the story implicitly deploring the fact that in "his betrayal of spiritual values, Father Purdon is another perverse paradigm of what is wrong in Joyce's Dublin. Religion has gone mad, departed, or become, as here, the bastard of business." He adds that the story "has a dark undercurrent of complaint about a faith which has become a social league and a business proposition."[36] Both of these commentators seem to have accepted as definitive Stanislaus's lead in interpreting the story. That his brother found Joyce angry at the befuddled theology he heard from the pulpit does not guarantee, however, that "Grace" became the vehicle for that anger in its initial form. Joyce's personal values might have included many traditional humanistic and Christian qualities, but there is nothing in his writings to suggest that any church can or should be the means by which the modern man or woman achieves any kind of grace. Readers who find here primarily a critique of the church rather than an anatomy of its cultural function attribute to Joyce an underlying belief in religion as the vessel of truth; they ignore his identification of the church as an economic institution. In effect, much of what "Grace" does is to provide evidence of this status.

Certainly, the commercial forces in Joyce's society could do nothing with traditional religious values except use them to further hegemonic ends in a society utterly lacking the possibility for sustained application of such ideals. In addition, the efforts of Dubliners to live by a religious code perpetuate their willed blindness to the economic and political conditions which guarantee the poor quality of their lives. Even Martin Cunningham, who suffers long and is kind to his drunken wife and his comical friends, spends most of his days serving mammon at Dublin Castle. That Bernard Vaughan, the best-known preacher of his day, stands as a likely model for Purdon and provides a definite analogue for his brand of preaching indicates Joyce's assessment of the popular sermon as the means by which not only bogus theology but also economic ideology was transmitted to the mass mind. What looks like Purdon's intentionally deceptive equation of spiritual values with shrewd financial dealing turns out to be merely a clue to the economic underpinnings of religious doctrine in the prevailing capitalistic recoding of scriptural ideas. As "Grace" presents it, the church is undeniably among the powers responsible for the "paralysis" of Dubliners. That state is not just a result of personal ineptitude: Tom Kernan has fallen from social grace not simply because he is not up on the latest business methods but also because he is controlled by institutions that respond to an oppressive economic system. Kernan goes to church to remedy the ills wrought in him by the business world and discovers in the chapel more of the same. Purdon does not so much deviate from doctrine as he reveals its practical impact.

The Sermon in *Portrait*

In extension of this revelation, the sermon presented in *Finnegans Wake* III, ii both adumbrates and actively preaches economic motivations. In this light, the fragment of Alexander J. Dowie's preaching that shows up in "Oxen of the Sun" documents the continuity of Catholic and Protestant theology in accommodating social exigencies. Dowie parodies the theatrical salespitch of a Vaughan and

targets the ease with which the language of popular religion co-
alesces with an economic vocabulary:[37] "The Deity aint no nickel
dime bumshow. I put it to you that He's on the square and a corking
fine business proposition. . . . He's got a coughmixture with a
punch in it for you, my friend, in his back pocket. Just you try it on"
(U 428). When this evangelistic huckster performs in "Circe" as
Elijah, he continues his merchandising: "Rush your order and you
play a slick ace. . . . Bumboosers, save your stamps" (U 507–08).
But in *Portrait*, not the sermon's language but the impact of the sermon on the individual is the mechanism for revealing the church's
power interests.

Part of the mechanism for the religious conditioning of Dubliners
was the sermon to children (in *Portrait* and in *Finnegans Wake* the
sermons are delivered to schoolchildren). Many readers of Joyce
have regarded the *Portrait* sermons as his anguished recreation of his
own pious childhood. Whether or not the motive for composition
was therapeutic, the conventionality of Father Arnall's retreat addresses is perhaps their most important characteristic. More than
the church itself, it is the power of institutionalized cultural convention that Stephen learns to recognize and resist through his spiritual
bout with the church. By the end of chapter iv of *Portrait*, Stephen
has turned not just from the religious life but toward what he sees as
the wild, the free, the uninhibited—all the things symbolized for
him by the bird-girl on the strand. She defies convention by the
twisted height of her skirts and bareness of her thighs as well as by
her direct gaze, which Stephen interprets as neither seductive nor
shrinkingly virginal. Many critics have argued that the girl combines for Stephen the sacred and the secular, but she also represents
a cultural quantity not immediately categorized into one stereotyped realm or the other. In fact, the representation of Stephen's vision of her as birdlike signifies a willing fusion of the two categories—the animal or bestial and the human—that Father Arnall's
sermons set in opposition.[38] The priest's assertion that the "lower
nature" (P 123) tends always toward the "gross and beastlike"
(P 127) takes on a personal shape in Stephen's dream of "Goatish
creatures with human faces" (P 137); yet that visionary concretion
of Father Arnall's metaphoric language may be viewed, too, as the
dark side of an imaginative desire to transform cultural dichotomies
into continuities. The bright side of this creative impulse determines

Stephen's complex vision of the avian girl. Certainly, the girl signifies the mortal danger of conventional ideas and the power of the
ambiguous to remake an outlook founded on religious absolutism.

Power is indeed one of the most important terms in chapters iii
and iv of *Portrait*, for it is power that Stephen craves and the church's
cultural ascendancy that excites him to repentance and to temporary
religious amendment of his life. When the rector recalls to the boys'
attention the story of St. Francis Xavier, he labels him "A saint who
has great power in heaven, remember: power to intercede for us in
our grief, power to obtain whatever we pray for if it be for the good
of our souls, power above all to obtain for us the grace to repent if
we be in sin" (P 108). Similarly, the sermon on death and judgment
calls forth more than any other image that of "God Omnipotent"
(P 113), no longer meekly forgiving but judging and punishing. In
the face of such power, "the jeweleyed harlots" that Stephen has
sinned with both imaginatively and actually are replaced by fear,
and the evoked potency of God wins the place in Stephen's soul previously held by "his presumptuous peace" and arrogant independence (P 115).

Once the physical and spiritual torments of hell have been graph-
ically presented by Father Arnall, Stephen's personal hell begins in
earnest. The effect of the sermons is such that he has trouble entering his room for fear of devils and is able to go into the shadows
only after praying "that the fiends that inhabit darkness might not
be given power over him" (P 136). Stephen's intellect directly as-
saults itself when his curiously auditory hallucinations speak to
him: "We knew perfectly well of course that although it was bound
to come to the light he would find considerable difficulty in endeav-
ouring to try to induce himself to try to endeavour to ascertain
the spiritual plenipotentiary and so we knew of course perfectly
well—." At the moment, Stephen needs to locate a priest to hear his
confession because only a priest is empowered by the church to help
him, but Stephen lacks the strength that confession will require of
him. So forceful is the sermon's rhetoric that he is weakened by it
before he is strengthened in the faith. Fearfully, he tells himself
"that those words had absolutely no sense which had seemed to rise
murmurously from the dark" (P 136), but at least one word—"plenipotentiary"—resonates with the issue at the heart of Stephen's
trial and the church's institutional efforts. In its mythic role as all-

powerful, the church offers its potency only to those who follow its directives, who surrender individual control to institutional ends. Hence, to continue the process of redemption, in his postnausea prayer Stephen identifies himself with Christ: "*So He came Himself in weakness not in power . . .*" (P 138).

Although Stephen eventually humbles himself to enter Church Street chapel and make his confession in the company of laborers, chapter iv finds him characteristically trying to obtain and wield the might of the institution that has educated him. He works to accrue for souls in purgatory "fabulous ages of canonical penances" (P 147). He monitors his every sensation and thought so that all seemed to "revibrate radiantly in heaven: and at times his sense of such immediate repercussion was so lively that he seemed to feel his soul in devotion pressing like fingers the keyboard of a great cash register and to see the amount of his purchase start forth immediately in heaven" (P 148). The economic metaphor attributed to Stephen underscores Joyce's usual connection of religion and the commercial enterprises that ruled his Dublin. Further, Stephen assumes various attitudes of devotion so that the "world for all its solid substance and complexity no longer existed for his soul save as a theorem of divine power and love and universality" (P 150).

It is finally the sense of his own strength that pushes Stephen into doubt: "It gave him an intense sense of power to know that he could by a single act of consent, in a moment of thought, undo all that he had done." Each time he resists temptation, he feels "a new thrill of power and satisfaction" (P 152). This theme of individual and institutional power comes to a head when the director, who has summoned Stephen to discuss a vocation for the priesthood, pridefully enlarges on the benefits of being a priest:

> —To receive that call, Stephen, said the priest, is the greatest honour that the Almighty God can bestow upon a man. No king or emperor on this earth has the power of the priest of God. No angel or archangel in heaven, no saint, not even the Blessed Virgin herself has the power of a priest of God: the power of the keys, the power to bind and to loose from sin, the power of exorcism, the power to cast out from the creatures of God the evil spirits that have power over them, the power, the authority, to make the great God of Heaven come down upon the altar and take the form of bread and wine. What an awful power, Stephen! (P 158)

The concentrated repetition of "power" makes inescapable the fact that in this final bid for his allegiance, the church plays on Stephen's most vulnerable spot—his intense desire for a mastery and for a social validation that will enable his personal talents to find an outlet.

What follows in the narrative provides for us one reason that Joyce included in the novel the transcript or narrative record of Father Arnall's introductory address and three long sermons. Stephen responds to an "instinct" that is "stronger than education or piety," to the "pride of his spirit which had always made him conceive himself as a being apart in every order." The sovereignty of the church that had educated him falls away, its "hold" over him "frail" despite "years of order and obedience" (P 161). Although the conditioning is in place (he recalls the "voice of the director urging upon him the proud claims of the church and the mystery and power of the priestly office"), Stephen elects "to be elusive of social or religious orders" (P 162); he chooses the "freedom and power of his soul" (P 170) over the omnipotence of the Deity as presented in the accumulated traditions of hundreds of years. The retreat sermons thus mark for Stephen not the beginning or renewal of piety but the inception of his awareness of the church as a cultural institution. Even though the very terms used to define his individual goals have been appropriated from the institution he wants to elude, Stephen begins to anatomize the church which Joyce presents as a creature of convention and social function.

The material that Joyce used as an immediate source for Father Arnall's lectures helps the reader to that same realization. In separate articles, James R. Thrane, Elizabeth F. Boyd, and James Doherty have together argued that the sermons on hell derived from an 1889 edition of an English translation of the seventeenth-century Jesuit Giovanni Pietro Pinamonti's devotional volume *L'Inferno aperto (Hell Opened to Christians)*. They also explain that Joyce and Pinamonti alike drew on a long tradition of writing about hell which had its own conventions about the landscape and conditions of the Christian Hades. Doherty comments, "Almost any nineteenth-century Catholic sermon book has a sermon for the Fifth Sunday after Epiphany that sounds quite a bit like Pinamonti."[39] Although I believe that assessment to be exaggerated, a perusal of the Rev. Charles J. Callan's section on hell in his *Illustrations for Sermons and Instructions* quickly reveals that the *Portrait* sermons represent virtually a compendium of folklore about such topics as the remorse and self-accusation of the damned, the fire of hell, and eternal punishment.[40] Such matters as the stench of hell, and eternity expressed through the image of a bird's carrying away grains from a mountain of sand were ready topoi in nineteenth-century Catholic preaching.[41] In defense of Joyce's "plagiarism," Boyd observes, "He probably wanted his borrowing to be recognized, for it is a kind of silent comment on the unyielding traditions of the type of Catholicism he grew up with, toward which he maintained all his life the ambivalent attitude of admiration and rejection."[42]

Partly by being more fiery than most sermons typical of the era, Joyce's text announces its desire to be compared with this tradition of conventions that so often substituted in the popular mind for the established doctrine of the church. That tradition had the power not just to move the heart but also, owing to constant repetition, to hold the mind. For Stephen, these conventions constitute much of the church's power and define a relationship that his will alone cannot sever. The issue of plagiarism becomes ludicrous in the light of this recognition, for quotation and allusion are for Joyce always the way toward dissection of culture and exposure of institutional control of the individual.

Joyce's attention to the church's place in the social network in fact eludes the formulations of much criticism of *Portrait*. For instance, one writer states: "Through the sermons of Father Arnall during the Belvedere school retreat, Joyce bodies forth the Irish church in all its narrowness and perversion. In these sermons Stephen comes face to face with that virulent form of Irish Catholicism he must escape if he is to be free."[43] Scholars have also noted the presence in the sermons of errors in biblical reference and have charted the rhetorical role of those errors. However, the "deception" practiced on Stephen involves not only misquotation and distortion but also, and more important, a censoring of context that Stephen chooses not to sustain. A retreat is, after all, an isolation from all cultural influences but one ("A retreat, my dear boys, signifies a withdrawal for a while from the cares of our life . . ." [P 109]). The terms in which the church presents its power force a choice between adherence to a single code of conduct in isolation from all others and what Stephen sees as "freedom"—a recognition of the many aspects (though, to be sure, most are institutional) of experience. Predisposed to act first and discriminate later, Stephen prefers to test institutional practices and reject that which would cut him off from all others.

A major irony of *Portrait* is that what Stephen chooses and finds cannot be the freedom he seeks. The cultural operations that Joyce's texts adumbrate more than document the illusoriness of that state. To be truly free, the artist would have to exist absolutely apart from society, but if it were possible for him to move beyond the nets of culture, Stephen would cease to be even an incipient artist; he would have no conceptual codes with which to accomplish the artist's work of transformation. Instead, *Portrait* places the church at the heart of the culture's predilection for binarisms such as good/evil, human/animal, saved/damned, and liberated/entrapped. In doing so, Joyce's narrative portrays the community's belief that the moral and spiritual dichotomies of religious doctrine provide intellectual power over existential ambiguities. Just as the church offers Tom Kernan and his friends what appears to be a measure of personal control over the ravages of socioeconomic conditions, so the church entices Stephen with a vision of his future command over the incertitudes of life, sexual identity, and death. But Stephen rejects this offer and the isolation of the priesthood to plunge into the contradictions of cultural experience. His decision to "forge . . . the uncreated conscience of . . . [his] race" (P 253) suggests that in some sense Stephen has learned that personal salvation cannot occur apart from communal change.

But Stephen does not choose only a bogus freedom; he chooses also the three tools of "silence, exile, and cunning." Announcing as much, Stephen elicits Cranly's amusement: "Cunning indeed!" (P 247). To be sure, the third term poses the biggest obstacle to Stephen's success; whereas silence and exile suggest a movement out of the linguistically communicated ideology that Stephen finds constraining, cunning brings Stephen back into language. The Middle English "conning," from which "cunning" derives, means both knowing and reading. Further, through what *The American Heritage Dictionary of the English Language* asserts to be the term's Indo-European root (*-gno*), cunning shares its linguistic soil with the word "narrate." For Stephen—as for anyone in his society—reading, knowing, and narrating depend on access to the cultural matrix from which Stephen would exile himself; the unreachable outside of culture may be construed as silence, but it is the constraining interior which provides the artist's words.

Irish culture as Joyce knew it revealed not only the power of traditional Catholic theology but also the tensions within the church that grew from its role in history. The popularity of stage priests and of media priests demonstrated the centrality of the church as a social presence and of the sermon as a significant cultural voice. But despite the modern publications of the church's received conventions and the standardized preaching that resulted, the Catholic establishment was riven by political and other differences. The theatrical presence of the priest and of parodic sermons in the music halls argues for the culture's awareness of what Joyce explicitly defines—the status of the church not as spiritual guide but as socioeconomic institution—a fact that Stephen Dedalus recognizes even though Tom Kernan remains trapped by powers in which he does not even believe.

NOTES

1. Perhaps for this reason the drama of "Circe" includes many religious figures among the dramatis personae. In addition to "Simon Stephen cardinal Dedalus, primate of all Ireland" (U 523), there are such figures as Father Farley, Brother Buzz, Father Coffey, Don John Conmee, Father Dolan, Alexander J. Dowie, and two Archbishops of Armagh. And, of course, both Buck Mulligan at the beginning of *Ulysses* and Shaun in *Finnegans Wake* enact priestly roles. For a discussion of the significance of the priest in Joyce, see Bernard Benstock, "A Covey of Clerics in Joyce and O'Casey," *James Joyce Quarterly* 2 (1964), 18–32.

2. Anthony Coleman, "Priest as Artist: The Dilemma of Canon Sheehan," *Studies* 58 (1969), 38. Coleman is discussing Sheehan's *The Blindness of Dr. Gray.*

3. David W. Miller, "The Roman Catholic Church in Ireland, 1898–1918," *Éire-Ireland* 3 (1968), 89.

4. Final lecture: "Reply to Mr. Froude's Last Words," Academy of Music, Brooklyn, 19 December 1872, *English Misrule in Ireland* (New York: Lynch, Cole & Meehan, 1873), p. 223.

5. Choille, pp. 166, 170, 227, 173. The chart covers pp. 166–74.

6. "To Stanislaus Joyce," 18 October 1906, *Letters*, 2: 182.

7. Martindale, p. 57.

8. Rev. Denis O'Shea, "Preaching from Sermon Books," *Irish Ecclesiastical Record*, 5th ser., 6 (1915), 498.

9. Martindale, p. 72. The quotation is from the foreword to Martindale by Francis, Cardinal Bourne, Archbishop of Westminster, p. vii.

10. Martindale, pp. 140–42. The passages from Martindale referred to below in this paragraph are from pp. 140–43 and 231–32. Father Robert Boyle, S.J., mentions Vaughan's "cockney imitation" and discusses Conmee's reaction to Vaughan in *James Joyce's Pauline Vision: A Catholic Exposition* (Carbondale: Southern Illinois University Press; London: Feffer & Simons, 1978), pp. 70–71, 117. Cf. Fritz Senn, "A Rhetorical Account of James Joyce's 'Grace,'" *Moderna Språk*, 74 (1980), 123n; Senn cites Father William T. Noon on Vaughan's accent.

11. S. Joyce, p. 225. Martindale confirms that Vaughan visited Ireland many times, including the slums of Dublin (pp. 147–48). Bradley notes that Vaughan directed the Clongowes retreat in 1896 (Bradley, pp. 165–66n); by that time, Joyce had moved on to Belvedere.

12. Scholes and Kain, p. 88.

13. "To Stanislaus Joyce," 13 November 1906, *Letters*, 2: 191–92.

14. The quotations below are from unidentified clippings in the National Library of Ireland, IR 92 b 140.

15. Stephen J. Brown, S.J., *The Preacher's Library* (London: Sheed & Ward, [1928?]), p. 102.

16. Brown, pp. 51, 52, 55–56. The quotation from Brown below is from p. 66.

17. Rev. Patrick O'Keeffe, *Sermons at Mass* (Dublin: Gill & Son, 1888), p. 9.

18. O'Shea, "Newspaper Controversy," p. 622.

19. Thomas Flynn, *Preaching Made Easy* (London: Burns, Oates & Washbourne, 1923), pp. 195–200.

20. Rev. W. O'Dowd, *Preaching* (New York: Longmans, Green, 1919), pp. 225–33.

21. O'Dowd, pp. 150, 154.

22. "Current Literature," *University Magazine* 1 (1878), 118.

23. O'Shea, "Preaching from Sermon Books," pp. 493–94.

24. "Our Popular Amusements," p. 234.

25. Watters and Murtagh, pp. 58–59, 71–72, 75–76, 110–11.

26. The star in whom *The Leader* found such fault was Madge Ellis. According to the *Irish Times* for 1 September, 1900, she appeared on a bill at the Lyric which included the famous Percy Honri; the August 20 advertisement in the *Times* (p. 4, col. 2) for her engagement in Dublin called her "Dublin's Favourite," "America's Star," and "London's Sensation."

27. *The Leader*, 1 September 1900, pp. 2–3.

28. Rev. Bernard Vaughan, *What of To-Day?* (London: Cassell, 1914), pp. 350, 349, 348. This collection of addresses was first published in 1914, but it includes no information about the original delivery date of the sermon on advertising. Martindale says that it is "the transcript, I think, of an address given to those whose business advertising was." Martindale also

states of Vaughan that "in Manchester, he willingly used trade expressions—he liked to say that he belonged 'to the firm that defied all competition,' and was for ever talking about 'delivering the goods' . . ." (Martindale, pp. 230, 56–57).

29. S. Joyce, pp. 223, 224–25. See also pp. 104–6 in *The Complete Dublin Diary*, ed. George H. Healey (Ithaca, N.Y: Cornell University Press, 1962), where Stanislaus dates the retreat attended by his father around 1902. He says that the presiding priest was Father Vernon, which the editor emends to Father John T. Verdon—a name close to Purdon.

30. Rev. Thomas Burke, *Lectures and Sermons* (New York: Haverty, 1872), p. [5].

31. See especially Robert Sumner Jackson's elaborate reading of Joyce's use of this parable, "A Parabolic Reading of James Joyce's 'Grace,'" *Modern Language Notes* 76 (1961), 719–24.

32. Eugene R. August comments that "part of his [Joyce's] point about the Irish Jesuits is precisely that they have sold their religious heritage in order to make friends with the mammon of iniquity. '—And they're a very rich order, aren't they, Simon?' asks Mrs. Dedalus in *A Portrait*. To which her husband replies, '—Rather. They live well, I tell you. You saw their table at Clongowes. Fed up, by God, like gamecocks' . . . . In 'Grace' Joyce lets the passage from Luke 16: 8–9 comment ironically upon the worldly Jesuit and his well fed order." See "Father Arnall's Use of Scripture in *A Portrait*," *James Joyce Quarterly* 4 (1967), 275.

33. Cf. Senn, "Rhetorical Account," pp. 126–27. Similarly, much has been made of the errors in the *Portrait* sermons. Bernard Duyfhuizen, "'Words [Mis]taken': The Opening Sentence of the Retreat Sermons," *James Joyce Quarterly* 16 (1979), discusses a "mistaken reference to Ecclesiastes" (p. 489), and August deals with both this reference and ones in Isaiah and Psalms which reveal Father Arnall's willful distortion of the scriptures to suit his own rhetorical ends (pp. 275–78). (Father Boyle's discussion of Arnall is also of interest; see "Joyce and Faith," in *Work in Progress: Joyce Centenary Essays*, ed. Richard F. Peterson, et al. [Carbondale: Southern Illinois University Press, 1983], pp. 135–37.) But compare J. Mitchell Morse, *The Sympathetic Alien: James Joyce and Catholicism* (Washington Square: New York University Press, 1959), who discusses the relationship of Purdon's accommodating doctrine and St. Ignatius' *Spiritual Exercises*: "The whole burden of his friendly talk is that Jesus Christ is not a hard taskmaster but only wants them to correct any errors there may be in their accounts. This is straight out of the *Spiritual Exercises*" (pp. 74–76).

34. Of course, as Jackson argues, the steward never does achieve worthiness of salvation; he is rather granted grace by God. Hence, the lord in the parable commends the steward despite the latter's persistent unworthiness (Jackson, p. 721).

35. Jackson, p. 723.

36. Howard Lachtman, "The Magic-Lantern Business: James Joyce's Ecclesiastical Satire in *Dubliners*," *James Joyce Quarterly* 7 (1970), 89.

37. Duyfhuizen calls Father Arnall in *Portrait* "nothing more than an old huckster trying to sell genuine rattlesnake oil in a wild west medicine show" (p. 490).

38. I am indebted to Tim Ireland, a student of mine at Swarthmore College in the fall of 1984, for his valuable discussion of the destabilized distinction in Chapter 3 of *Portrait* of body and soul, beast and human being.

39. James Doherty, "Joyce and *Hell Opened to Christians*: The Edition He Used for His Sermons," *Modern Philology* 61 (1963), 119. Boyd, "James Joyce's Hell-Fire Sermons," *Modern Language Notes* 75 (1960), 563, Doherty (pp. 111–18), and Thrane, "Joyce's Sermon on Hell: Its Sources and Backgrounds," *Modern Philology* 57 (1960), 189, discuss Joyce's condensation and intensification of Pinamonti's meditations.

40. Rev. Charles J. Callan, O.P., ed., *Illustrations for Sermons and Instructions* (New York: Wagner, 1916), pp. 93–99. On conventions of doctrine about hell, see also Bradley, pp. 125–28. Sullivan points to the parallels between Father Arnall's statements and *The Sodality Manual or a Collection of Prayers and Spiritual Exercises for Members of the Sodality of the Blessed Virgin Mary*, compiled by Fr. James A. Cullen, S.J. But Sullivan asserts the presence of the sermon's dominant ideas in devotional materials written over "hundreds of years" (pp. 138–41).

41. Thrane, pp. 184–87. Once Bernard Vaughan stayed the night with a man who felt himself pursued by the devil; afterwards, Vaughan "insisted that the stench of evil made itself perceptible to the very nostrils, and he would explain what he meant by that, leaving little enough to the imagination" (Martindale, pp. 53–54).

42. Boyd, p. 571.

43. August, p. 175.

CHAPTER 7

"Politicoecomedy" (FW 540.26–27) in *Finnegans Wake* III, ii

> All authority comes from God, and from Him descends to the
> Church, the family, and the state. . . .
>> Rev. T. Hurley, *Irish Ecclesiastical Record* (1899)

> We must at the same time conceive of sex without the law and
> power without the king.
>> Michel Foucault, *The History of Sexuality* (1978)

Demystifying Form

In the dream of culture which is, among other things, fiction, a man
named, among other things, Jaun, delivers, among other things, a
sermon. It is generally agreed that this section (III, ii) is one of the
most linguistically accessible in the *Wake*, and—possibly because of
its apparent relative simplicity—this chapter has received little critical attention.[1] Yet Jaun's homily (gotten out in bits), the most consistently satiric of Joyce's sermons, prominently includes in its many
arenas of signification a complex statement of the intersection of
Roman Catholic doctrine and socioeconomics. Wakean parody,
reflexivity, and dream distortion do not mask the fact that Jaun's
sermon goes beyond mere reflection of twentieth-century Irish
popular theology (although it does allude to that theology quite
specifically); rather, III, ii offers a critique of the usually concealed
messages to which popular theology kept itself more or less blind.
The economic message in the sermons of Joyce's era has been made
explicit in the *Wake*, the homily being allowed to speak its own content in Joyce's subversive appropriation of that form. In the sermon,
that is, we find a contradiction between the church's ideology of absolute morality and the economic strategies played out by popular
religious dictates. More wittily than in "Grace" or *Portrait*, the *Wake*
enunciates this contradiction.

I might add here that, as there is always more going on in *Finnegans Wake* than meets even the collective eye of Joyce's readers, my focus on the homiletic side of III, ii does not pretend to "explain" the chapter or to contain it within the province described by the mass theology of Joyce's day. Further, although the sermon defines the framework of much of this chapter, the sermon-as-form is destabilized in that other parts of the mass also find parallels in Jaun's oration.[2] While the mass seems to encompass the sermon, Jaun's impromptu but thoroughly conventional sermon may also be seen as enclosing the larger service. Similarly, although I shall speak here primarily of Jaun's attitudes, I do not mean to imply that the Shaun figure is a coherent, unchanging character. Roland McHugh has theorized that the siglum that includes Shem provides the view of Shaun rendered in Book III and that the narrative voice in III, ii is implicated by the siglum that indicates the four old men.[3] This sense of the layering or overlapping of visions enhances our understanding that Shem and Shaun are not separate but interrelated figures. One brother's censure of another is also self-censorship of the sort that Stephen exercises in "Aeolus," and both brothers are products of social discourses. Even when Shaun-Jaun speaks, in some sense, out of religious doctrine, his discourse reminds us that the church was a relational entity and that in history it was interpenetrated by rival institutions. The sibling tensions that shape III, ii are themselves predicted by social forces.

The means by which Joyce conveys his analysis of popular theology is the sermon which is woven into Jaun's dealings with the schoolgirls in III, ii. Just as Father Arnall lectured to Stephen and his schoolmates, so Jaun preaches to "twentynine hedge daughters out of Benent Saint Berched's national nightschool" (FW 430.1–2). Both preachers repeat the church's efforts to capture young minds and hearts in order to preserve in them a state of innocent receptivity to spiritual doctrine. The meditations of the Rev. Charles Gobinet[4] are not alone in suggesting that the longer one waits to repent, the harder the heart, the more difficult the conversion, the more likely one is to backslide. However, although in *Portrait* the impact of preaching on an individual child occupies much of the narrative, in *Finnegans Wake* the larger audience of sermons is evident.

Similarly, in *Portrait* Joyce relied on the specific model of Pinamonti's meditations on hell as well as on the hellfire sermons he heard at Belvedere, and in "Grace" he patterned his priest on the well-known figure of Father Vaughan, but in *Finnegans Wake* Joyce is after bigger game: he takes in a representative sample of the contemporary preaching scene. The target becomes more clearly than ever the generic sermon, the parody a summary of the church's social impact treated with comic accuracy. Here, satire emerges from the anatomy of the sermon form as it appears in popular culture. The fact that we cannot go back to a specific source for Jaun's sermon is important, for throughout the *Wake* Joyce emphasizes the circulation of cultural ideas and ideals that lack definite origin. Truth thus emerges, even in its absolute state of Religion, as conventional wisdom that serves various ends, some hegemonic and phallocentric, some counterinstitutional. The *Wake*, then, probes the connections among religious doctrine, cultural convention, and economics. Further, Jaun's homily attacks as mythic the Edenic origin of the moral system and the sanctity of the priesthood as well as the reality of miracles and divine inspiration.

Contributing to this demystifying challenge of the church's transcendence of the everyday is the fact that Issy, Jaun's primary auditor, quite easily sees through his injunctions. Far from reenacting Stephen's terrorized conversion, Issy remains unmoved by the sermon she hears. She is like Molly Bloom, who thinks of "that old Bishop that spoke off the altar his long preach about womans higher functions about girls now riding the bicycle and wearing peak caps and the new woman bloomers God send him sense and me more money" (U 761); in fact, the twenty-nine girls with "their eight and fifty pedalettes" (FW 430.9) appear to be familiar with bicycles.

Having established in earlier works that the sermon format implies a coercive exercise of power and often connotes spiritual or economic deception (or both), Joyce let the popular sermon display the tensions it generally masked. As both sadist and dispenser of moral wisdom, the two-faced Jaun typifies the priest as Joyce presents him in Fathers Arnall and Purdon, duplicitous to the extent that they distort the scriptures. But in *Finnegans Wake* the exaggeration of this condition also creates comedy. Here no priest fashions a noose for Stephen's neck; there is only the silliness and ideological transparency of Jaun's demented commentary, which the Floras ignore as they wish. Issy's response makes the church not only innocuous but also incredible. In the oddly ideal world of the *Wake*, the sermon is harmless entertainment, and the church is effectively defused as a social force. Jaun's sermon becomes as much a revolt against religion's assumption of authority as a music-hall sermon was. Both concentrate ultimately on worldly wisdom. Both level the church to the order of other cultural institutions.

It is true that in "Grace" this leveling is suggested, but not enough totally to efface for many readers a hovering nostalgia for an incorruptible, fully ethical church that could provide spiritual enlightenment and become a true vehicle of grace. Similarly, *Stephen Hero* and *Portrait* seem at times riven by adolescent disappointment over the unsanctified condition of the church, but *Finnegans Wake* takes a much more genial approach to the ecclesiastical establishment's economic orientation and oppression of joie de vivre. Comedy comes to the fore when out of the church's scriptings emerges their opposite—the ideology that they camouflaged and that the early Stephen conveyed to himself only humorlessly.

Not blind to its own mode of production, *Finnegans Wake* constantly attests to the institutional tensions and cultural operations that provided its materials and account for its complexity. At the very least, Jaun's sermon demonstrates on the level of metaphor the compatibility of his brand of moral absolutism and a system of economic exchange which seeks to encompass all phenomena in its own value system. To support these assertions, I first look at three topics in the *Wake* sermon that were regularly discussed by popular preachers: sex and marriage, bad books, and the general corruption of the modern era.[5]

Love and Marriage

The chapter opens, of course, with Jaun's encountering twenty-nine convent girls, one of whom, on the family level, is his sister Issy. To her Jaun directs an oration—at times a philippic—on sexual virtue. He advises the girls to obey as many precepts of the church "as probable" (FW 432.26), and he specifies a few of these rules: "First thou shalt not smile. Twice thou shalt not love. Lust, thou shalt not commix idolatry" (FW 433.22–23). A partly clear, partly suppressed message, like all ideological statements, the sermon maintains that to commix and commingle in adultery is equivalent to committing idolatry. (Of course, "commix" also suggests the *comic* side of any institution's attempt to control human sexuality.) In fact, Jaun avers that to enjoy oneself in only idle courtship without the goal of marriage or simply to answer spontaneously to any of the various calls of nature and pleasure is to violate a religious—a universal—law. In more personal terms, the implied emphasis of Jaun's sermon is two-fold: as Issy's brother, he wants no one in bed with her but himself; as priestly father, he wants the girls to avoid sex until they trade hymens for husbands. If Stephen Dedalus is a sexually adept young man in whom the "cursed jesuit strain" is "injected the wrong way" (U 8), then Jaun is a priest in whom the sexuality is injected the wrong way—at least given the norms of the vocational role he plays in III, ii.

Jaun's clerical viewpoint was shared by preachers contemporary with Joyce, for whom not only did sex have its dangers, but marriage itself was in danger. The late nineteenth and early twentieth centuries saw the church, threatened by the advance of civil divorce in England and America, mounting a propaganda offensive to bolster belief in the sanctity of the Christian marriage bond; it was said that in the quarter-century preceding 1908, divorces rose 50 percent in the United Kingdom.[6] Bernard Vaughan, an advocate of marriage so pious in his declamations that, his country of origin aside, he was more than once referred to or claimed as an Irish priest,[7] preached on the subject in his famous Mayfair sermons of 1906, published as *The Sins of Society*. Later, Vaughan's collection *What of To-Day?* (1914) discussed divorce and a projected decline in the birthrate in terms of "race suicide." Given the fact that without happy families, children would not be able to mature into good citizens of the state, Vaughan found that "Those . . . who seek to weaken the bonds of matrimony . . . are working to undermine the very foundation upon which the social order rests." Hence, Vaughan argued against what even Jaun might have found innocent enough: "Such aids to marriage as moonlight strolls [or] . . . dreamy music . . . ought to play no part in a man's final choice [of a wife]."[8] Vaughan's denunciation of modern laxity in these matters echoes Father Thomas Burke's rather untheological argument that "the most important of all the sacraments" is marriage.[9] Such works as Father Callan's *Illustration for Sermons and Instructions* (1916) and *The Preacher's Vademecum* ("by Two Missionaries"—1921), typical of the sermon handbooks of the era, treat the topic of marriage in such a standardized fashion as to indicate that in the pulpit deviation from such doctrine was unthinkable.

In fact, the section of the *Vademecum* that summarizes ideas to be presented in an "Address at a Marriage" deserves quoting in full because of its representative coverage of the topic in terms familiar at the turn of the century:

> Marriage was instituted and established by God Himself in the Paradise, when he created a helpmate for Adam. There is another reason why the marriage bond is sacred. Matrimony is a sacrament. It is one of those sacred channels through which the grace of Jesus Christ flows into the hearts of the faithful. Duties of the husband. True, sincere and enduring love of the wife, require nothing that is unworthy, and bear the little imperfections of which the best of us are not entirely free.
>
> Duties of the wife. Do not neglect your home but make it a place of domestic happiness. Make your beloved husband happy. Stand by his side as a faithful helpmate. Share his joys with sincere sympathy, and when troubles come, as they are bound to come, comfort the husband and place in him courage and confidence. Make the home the safe refuge for the busy husband when the world's affairs are stormy.[10]

Similar advice occurs in the papers that make up Vaughan's *What of To-Day?*, which echoes and develops these stereotypical but very useful roles. Vaughan advises husbands to accept their wives' "little feminine ways." In addition, he says, "Never attempt to check the flowing tide of her talk" (given ALP's flowing finale to *Finnegans Wake*, surely HCE excels in this connubial duty), and he suggests humoring the wife. As far as the husband is able, he should give her not criticism but the clothes and "finery" that women love (here Bloom appears to shine, at least as far as good intentions go). In return for praise and pampering, the wife should be a good housekeeper, a good cook, "neat and smart" in her attire, and patient in the face of the reasonable "whims and fancies" of the spouse. In no case should she resort to nagging or tears to get her own way.[11]

One further citation from a sermon handbook of the era, Callan's *Illustrations for Sermons and Instructions*, will suffice to portray the church's profamily propaganda; he quotes Thomas J. Gerrard:

> A large family is a means of developing character, both in the parents and in the children. In the case of the father, it is a question as to whether he will face the task of working and saving for the means of bringing up a large family. He certainly needs courage. He certainly

needs self-denial and self-restraint. . . . Who has not looked with dismay on the spoilt child, the only one of the family? Who has not observed the ugly self-consciousness, pride and vanity of two children, the miserable two who have had no other companions but each other during the years when the foundation of their character was laid? And who has not seen the beautiful unselfishness and generosity of the children of a family of seven, or better still of a family of fourteen? Why even their faults and their sins are due to excess of generosity rather than to defect in it.[12]

The fact that nowhere in Joyce's works do we find the ideal family suggested in these religious prescriptions is not surprising, but it does emphasize the fact that the existing social order, far from resting on the firm foundation of the Christian family, in fact contributed to the connubial and filial sorrows visited on Joyce's Dubliners. Yet the church's interests were vested in perpetuating the unattainable stereotypes of an often vicious social system. The coalescence in the home of Stephen Dedalus of many children, Catholic conviction, poverty, and connubial tensions is neither unusual in that system nor coincidental.

Censorship

Having mapped out for Issy and her friends their ideal futures as wives, Jaun turns to denounce "Secret satieties and onanymous letters" (FW 435.31). We recall Stephen Dedalus's anguish over his own "secret satieties," including the scandalous letters that he left about for girls to discover, but we think also of the church's denunciation of groups like the Freemasons. Clearly, to the church that Joyce portrays secret social organizations were as dangerous as sexuality. For example, the charges leveled against Freemasonry were many: the Freemasons opposed the Pope; they were atheists; they sought to overthrow the authority of both church and state; they participated in blasphemous rituals; they supported cremation, a quasi-socialist civilization without classes or property, and "civil marriages and funerals"; they opposed both infant baptism and the Catholic press.[13] In particular, Pope Leo XIII adopted a hard line against secret societies such as the Freemasons and Fenians. The popular theology of the era inevitably reflected Leo's dictates, especially once they were codified in his 1897 revision of the *Index prohibitorum librorum*.

That work, of course, concentrated primarily on bad books and harmful periodicals, which the popular mind conceived of as sweeping in waves from France up to England and over to Ireland to contaminate the minds and hearts of schoolboys and convent girls. For instance, the editor of the *Catholic Bulletin* for 1914, in talking about a new monthly magazine published by the Christian Brothers and entitled *Our Boys*, mentions "the torrent of impure cross-channel literature daily pouring in upon" Irish youth.[14] Jaun's sermon contains several pointed references to this major propaganda issue. Mentioning "Autist Algy" (Swinburne/Shem), Jaun says that the figure had been "stated by the vice crusaders to be well known to all the dallytaunties in and near the ciudad of Buellas Arias" (FW 434.35–435.2). As in most of the sermon, the language appears to differ from ordinary English by only minor distortions, one result being to emphasize the transparency of the church's ideological messages. Just as for Issy there is no masking of the principal message of the address (which is to control not her morality but her sexuality), so too for the reader there is no question that the transformation of Swinburne into both a lower form of life ("Algy" / algae) and a victim of exaggerated subjectivity (the artist as "Autist") parodies the church's popular mistrust of art and artists. If the girls were to accept Jaun's jaundiced view of art as autism, as a production of discourse characterized by an almost masturbatory self-engrossment and disconnection from the world, they would quite logically reject the alternate views of reality which art has always provided. Perhaps the Pre-Raphaelite vision of Swinburne and associates such as D. G. Rossetti and William Morris would be particularly disquieting to a church intent on holding onto its monopoly on the route to right conduct and paradise.

Jaun's charge against "Autist Algy" is characteristically evasive: the artist was known to the "dallytaunties" (dilettantes, certainly, but also dalliers—no doubt in sexual activities—and those who would deride and mock Jaun's lessons ["taunt" him]). That "Algy" is known to such folks is bad enough, but that they live in "Buellas Arias" suggests a double condemnation. It has been argued that Eveline might have faced substantial danger had she gone with Frank to Buenos Aires; there she might easily have been sold into the white slave trade. This "ciudad" (see you dad?) speaks its own farewell to the religious fathers who would control human sexuality in ways as effective as those of the traders in prostitution. Further, "bellas arias," though presumably more acceptable to an early twentieth-century middle-class Irish audience than, say, music-hall songs, are nonetheless part of the world of art from which Jaun wants to distract his audience.[15] In sum, dalliance, mockery, and a life of sin are some of the possibly soul-damaging results of reading bad books which the "vice crusaders" of Joyce's day fought against. And Jaun specifically asserts in a typically illiberal moment, "I'd burn the books that grieve you . . ." (FW 439.34).

He then proceeds to cite those works of "pious fiction" which, having been "licensed and censered by our most picturesque prelates" (FW 440.8,11), are acceptable reading, all of them written by what seem to be members of the Wakean church establishment: Carnival Cullen, S. J. Finn, and the Curer of Wars. Here the text implies that to censor and to cense (offer incense, possibly with the suggestion of consecrating or blessing) are equivalent and related functions. The comic names of the priests are enhanced by calling them "picturesque." Probably Joyce alludes to media priests like Vaughan or Burke, whose every activity and every word were reported by the press, even down to the type of clerical costume they wore to deliver important sermons and lectures.

Jaun goes on to advise: "Strike up a nodding acquaintance for our doctrine with the works of old Mrs Trot, senior, and Manoel Canter, junior, and Loper de Figas, nates maximum. . . . *Egg Laid by Former Cock* and *With Flageolettes in Send Fanciesland.* Chiefly Girls." And he notes that he "used to follow Mary Liddlelambe's flitsy tales, espicially with the scentaminted sauce" (FW 440.15–21). That these works demand only a "nodding acquaintance" is perhaps indictment enough of their spiritual or intellectual worth, but Jaun's lack of interest even in this material is easily betrayed ("I used to follow . . ."). Typically, he is more interested in food than in doctrine or art; it is the "scentaminted sauce" and lamb that occupy his language, as well as the "sacramental tea" (though possibly the same sort of tea that Mother Grogan is so handy with) that the "saucerdotes" serve up (FW 440.21,22). Finally, this censoring postman-preacher recommends "the long lives of our saints and saucerdotes, with vignettes, cut short into instructual primers by those in authority for the bittermint of your soughts" (FW 440.21–24).

What we cannot help noticing, of course, is the comic irony of some of Jaun's choices of supposedly worthwhile books. Mrs. Trot's name alone gives us pause, betraying as it does her status as old crone and suggesting the slang meaning of "trot"—diarrhea. No doubt a good friend of Mrs. Grundy, Mrs. Trot seems to have a verbal disease which places her in the ranks of Hawthorne's sentimental "scribbling women," which Mary Liddlelambe also occupies. This latter name is puzzling because it suggests not only the fable world of Mother Goose and the looking-glass world of Alice Liddell but also the linguistic expertise of Henry George Liddell, the nineteenth-century Greek lexicographer.[16] That these worlds of fancy and fantasy use language in sophisticated ways is perhaps enough to yoke them together here and to explain why they failed to keep Jaun's attention; indeed, he regards them as "flitsy tales," and "flit" seems here to imply his own changeableness (the OED offers one definition of "flit" as "To change from one state, condition, or direction to another") as well as the flightiness of fairy tales. In addition, a sexual undercurrent runs through this passage. Lope de Vega's name has become "de Figas" and obviously suggests the obscene gesture of making a fig, an appropriate transformation of name considering his appended title of "nates maximum" or "biggest buttocks."[17]

Similarly, *"Egg Laid by Former Cock"* sounds like a fairy tale version of a yellow press headline, the story of a transsexual who performs badly (lays an egg)[18] or who discovers in himself procreative powers beyond the normal. *"With Flageolettes in Send Fanciesland,"* the title of a story supposedly designed for schoolgirls, implies that every work of literature—even a fairy tale—carries sexual content. "Send Fanciesland" is, no doubt, Assisi (St. Francis's land), but it is also the place of fancy. In the word "flageolettes," self-scourgers (flagellaters) blend uneasily with the French *flageolet* (wind instrument, species of bean) and the French *flageoler* (to tremble, shake). The world of Catholic charity associated with St. Francis is here mingled with the darker side of Catholic sainthood—its trembling mortification of the flesh—as well as with the fanciful nature of some of its dictates. Given the "Sirens" episode, where Bloom's "little wee . . . piped eeee" (U 288), a reader may be tempted to see the wind instrument allusion as scatological, while the bean reference reinforces the several allusions in this passage to legumes. *"Lentil Lore"* (FW 440.9) and *"Pease in Plenty"* (FW 440.10) are two books recommended by Jaun on the basis of their being authored by religious figures and authorized by "Their Graces of Linzen and Petitbois" (FW 440.11, 12), the "picturesque prelates" in question.

One suspects that Jaun is more interested in eating beans than in reading books, and as many readers have noticed, in *Finnegans Wake* we can often assume a surrogate relationship between sexuality and eating.[19] Both food and sex are, like sermons, destined for consumption. On the most innocent level, beans, tea, lamb, mint sauce, and figs all provide more evidence that Jaun's mind is not totally occupied with religious "instructual primers." To cap off the general absurdity of Jaun's recommendations, we can note that "Trot," "Canter," and "Loper" show Joyce's fondness for grouping associated words. Obviously, an important part of the rhythm and delight of his prose comes from the trot, canter, and lope of such sequences, but these devices also contribute significantly to the comedy of the sermon, to undermining any pretense to logical soundness in Jaun's counsel. Hence, just as he recommends questionable books, so the sermon's language distorts the title of at least one story that was unquestionably sound, the Reverend Francis J. Finn's "The Best Foot Forward."[20] Warning the girls of the dangers of sexual encounters, Jaun contradictorily says, "Put your swell foot foremost on foulardy pneumonia shertwaists, *irriconcilíb*le with true *fimínín risirvítí*on and ribbons of lace, limenick's disgrace" (FW 434.19–21—my emphasis). That is, he tutors them in seductive dressing (like a "swell" and with the *ego* to the fore, as the italicized letters indicate) in advice which is in every way opposed to that of Finn's Father Noland. In "The Best Foot Forward," Noland teaches Eddie Miller and the boys of the Second Academic Class to help a new teacher realize their unselfish desire to be truly good.

To return to the Dublin of Joyce's day, we might note that during that period the indictment of bad books—often almost as badly argued as Jaun's—turned up constantly in sermons and Catholic periodicals. For instance, the Right Rev. George Conroy, in his essay "Dangerous Reading" (publ. 1884, Dublin), wrote not a defense of the *Index* as such but an explanation to Catholics of the hazards of undisciplined reading. Novels he finds especially frivolous and irrational: "The constant perusal of works of fiction unduly develops the imagination at the expense of the reasoning powers, thus disturbing that order of the faculties which nature has established. Besides, it extinguishes all taste for serious studies, especially for the study of history, and where laborious habits of patient and steady work are thus neglected, the mind loses its vigour, and the whole character, dwarfed by the want of healthy exercise, becomes puerile and feeble."[21] Canon P. A. Sheehan, himself a famous and much-translated novelist, preached early in his priesthood a sermon in which he claimed that "corrupt literature" "is the most powerful enemy of God, and the most powerful ally of His enemy." He adds, "You may pass from end to end of France, and you will not find a single book in a single bookstall that you can touch without fear of committing mortal sin."[22] Such denunciations—intended especially to suppress sexual material—are parodied in III, ii by Jaun's lascivious dwelling on the details of seduction. His general enhancement of titillating discourse recalls the argument of Michel Foucault in *The History of Sexuality* that after the Council of Trent the Roman Catholic church extended its power through the ritual of confession into all private spheres of behavior and literally encouraged the penitent's discourse on his or her sexual desires and actions.[23]

It should not be assumed, however, that none of the clergy chafed under the aegis of Mother Church as Mrs. Grundy. Canon Sheehan, by the time he had become an honored Irish Catholic novelist, felt the constraints placed upon art by dogma, and he played out this conflict in his fictions about the priestly life. In *The Blindness of Dr. Gray*, a young priest is told to burn any of his books that do not pertain to theology; instead, he disposes of the keys to his bookcase by throwing them into the sea.[24] But it was customary for the priest to adopt the role of book censor and to specify for his congregation those works that were forbidden and those that could be read without danger to spiritual health. Not all priests knew which books to recommend, however. Hence, the Rev. Arthur Barry O'Neill, C.S.S., advises in his book *Priestly Practice* that such clerics "consult the book reviews of our Catholic magazines and of well-edited Catholic papers,"[25] a suggestion which effectively kept the lines of authority on such matters firmly within church discourse. Such automatic acceptance of authority is what Jaun's comic and inappropriate list of books questions.

The Modern Age

The denunciation of bad books, of flirting and courtship and the like, coalesced in popular theology into the pulpit's oft-repeated denunciation of the Modern Age. In this period, it was argued, yielding to one of the era's typical pleasures inevitably led to indulgence in others. Hence, again in his sermon on bad books, Canon Sheehan observes that "novel-reading" can be compared to opium-eating, since readers become unfit "for the real practical business of life" and inclined to sin: "They fancy, feed upon their fancies, live by fancy and the consequences [sic] is they become dissatisfied with their condition in life, they preform [sic] their duties mechanically, they acquire a love of dress and finery."²⁶

An implicit wholesale denunciation of the age is a topos so common at the end of the nineteenth century that Father Thomas Burke began a lecture in Cork by the title of "The Catholic Church and the Age We Live In" with these words:

> There may, perhaps, be some amongst you who imagine from the title of this lecture that I am come here to praise the Catholic Church and to denounce the age we live in. I am going to do one and not to do the other. One of the common errors of our day is that a Catholic priest, as such, must make it his especial business to denounce this age of ours. I myself received a curious illustration of this when I asked a poor man in the west of Ireland some time ago what he thought was the proper business of a Catholic priest. He scratched his head, thought for a few moments, and then: "I suppose, your reverence," said he, "the proper business of a Catholic priest is to tell us all we are going to the devil."²⁷

While Burke went on to praise the late nineteenth century as an era of accomplishment, he found the "moral spirit of the age" in disarray.²⁸ Jaun's sermon makes clear his reflection of this assessment: "O," he says, "the frecklessness of the giddies nouveautays!" (FW 435.11–12). "Frecklessness" incorporates "recklessness," "fecklessness," and perhaps "fickleness" (with the Middle English meaning of false or treacherous?)—all of which Jaun denounces along with the giddiness of the kiddies in a "nowadays" that is composed of novelty and change, dictionary descriptions of the French word *nouveauté*.

To this indictment, Jaun adds a comment on modern sex and society: "All blah! Viper's vapid vilest!" (FW 435.16). At the center of satanic viper and moral vileness we have not absolute *evil* but only vapidity; as always, such flatness characterized much of the popular culture, including the popular religion, of the era. Hence it is important that, despite the associations of this chapter with Lent,²⁹ Jaun seems to locate his sermon in the liturgical calendar as occurring "Several sindays after whatsintime" (FW 432.33). Apparently taking place not long after Whitsuntide (or Pentecost) and therefore outside of any festal period in the church,³⁰ Jaun's oration refers only to a lethargic "lithurgy" (FW 432.32) befitting his sense of an age both *in* time and in *sin*time ("whatsintime"). Later mentioning the "slack march of civilisation" (FW 438.25), Jaun worries over the effect, especially on Issy, of what the frame narrator for III, ii calls, using an obvious political pun, the oncoming "devil era" (FW 473.08)—with its bad books, empty flirtations, too-willing seductions, and general carryings-on.

The Authority of Convention: Economics, Taste, and Folklore

No one would argue, despite the correlation of Jaun's sermon topics and those typical of the time, that *Finnegans Wake* in any way supports the church's assessment of modern society and its mores. Nor, as is often assumed by readers, is Joyce simply criticizing church doctrine as out of touch with the needs of contemporary Dubliners. Rather, the satire, punning, irony, and wordplay of this sermon-parody insist on a dispersion of authority from the church into the social conventions and economic exigencies that made up the modern age in Ireland. In fact, part of the project of the *Wake* as a whole is to disseminate key tenets of Catholic doctrine into these determining cultural forces. Jaun presents his ideas as theological dictates, but his sermon suggests that what we tend to see as moral absolutes are economically conditioned. Hence, it is not enough for us to note that Jaun's ideas derive from popular theology. We need also to recognize that the *Wake*, like Joyce's earlier fiction, posits a compatibility of religious doctrine and the capitalist frame of mind.

Certainly, there is no mystery about the congruence of religious and economic designs. The church's attempt to repress premarital, nonprocreative sex (an attempt that is one theme of Joyce's parody in the *Wake* sermon) by upholding the institution of marriage did more than censor the messages of instinct and hormone. As Foucault has repeatedly argued, the repressive measures taken by an institution must be regarded not merely as "negative" but also as forwarding "positive effects" of power.[31] The clerical repression that Jaun's sermon parodies did more than shut down a portion (undoubtedly a small one) of the sexual energy in Ireland; it also involved the society in discussion of sexuality and directed a certain amount of explicit cultural attention to how and why libidinous urges should be controlled. Further, the focus on marriage as the only acceptable arena for sexual expression sought to instigate the kind of procreative sexuality which would lead more or less inevitably—and within, ideally, a stable and productive home environment—to the birth of more children than would be true in casual, nonmarital relationships.

The effect of this population growth would be of strategic benefit to the church, maintaining and extending as it would that institution's social hegemony. But to accomplish this growth in power, the church had to support the cultural status quo. The sermons in Joyce's day which denounced the modern era did so largely because the changes they saw threatened the church's place in it as well as the foundations of its society. Striking evidence for this position is the fact that during the 1911 summer of strikes and lockouts on the Dublin docks, the "general public . . . received solemn warnings from the press and pulpit" about the dangers of labor organization.[32] While trying to be separate from the world, the church actually fought for active control of the culture. This competition for mastery is targeted in Jaun's sermon, which is far from otherworldly in its local and large-scale intentions. In fact, the *Wake* sermon tends to demystify the church's assumption of authority and possession of absolute truth by emphasizing the presence of economic strategy within religious dictates.

Of course, the Catholic church of the era actively forestalled criticism to this effect by announcing the social order and the family unit to be direct reflections of divine law. Popular sermons of that time as of our own reinforced the class structure by speaking to the Christian's task of, as Father Arnall puts it in *Portrait*, "fulfilling the duties of his station in life" (P 114).[33] Father Burke, although an ardent nationalist, in his address "The Church and Civil Government" states unequivocally, "Civil government is the ordinance of Almighty God, coming as the reflection of His glorious and greatest authority."[34] More specifically, Stanley B. James, writing in the 1930 *Irish Ecclesiastical Record*, argues that the Catholic church "stands above all classes."[35] In this aggressive article, which deals with the question of a class-structured society, James argues that the church works actively against the "essentially bourgeois" and thoroughly standardized civilization present in the United States, a culture termed "tyrannical" in its assumption that its value system is as authoritative and "universal as that of Christian morality." James cites the popular argument that the various Protestant sects grew during the Reformation in response to and as a support for middle and upper-class aims. Yet he maintains the freedom of the Catholic church from such ties, citing Pope Leo XIII's "Encyclical on the Condition of the Working Class" to the effect that class division is natural. Hence the Catholic church, says James, resists threats to this natural order as to the family itself, and popular preaching of the time agreed that preserving both aspects of society conforms to divine law. It is not difficult to see either the defensive posture of the church in such assertions or the way that the *Wake* undermines any notion that modern European family life and social organization are anything but mundane, conventional, and pragmatic. That the church encouraged marriage and a higher birthrate—especially in Ireland, where late marriages and a declining birthrate were the norm [36]—may be attributed without disrespect as much to its assessment of societal needs as to its spiritual mission.

The compatibility of theological doctrine and a received economic orientation is suggested repeatedly throughout Jaun's discourse. In fact, the sermon presents all relationships in terms of economic exchange. When Jaun cautions the girls, "Collide with man, collude with money" (FW 433.32–33), we could accept his statement as ironic or even bitter, yet such a tonal imposition is out of place in his sermon, which straightforwardly argues that Issy and her friends should have the ring in hand before they hand over their own precious jewels: Jaun says, "Never lose your heart away till you win his diamond back" (FW 433.14–15). Further, Jaun echoes Parnell in advising, "Ere you sail foreget my prize" (FW 433.33).[37] The emphasis is on *fore*-getting (getting beforehand) as well as on simply not remembering that at the basis of the marital agreement is an essentially financial arrangement.

Such cynical "look before you leak" (FW 433.34) attitudes are enjoined by Jaun as a supplement to the moral system which, according to church doctrine and public opinion, normally determines religious counsel. For Jaun, even the trinity of essential virtues is associated with an economic matrix: "Keep cool faith in the firm, have warm hoep [38] in the house and begin frem athome to be chary of charity" (FW 434.2–3). No longer does faith have anything to do with man's relationship to the deity; faith is placed in the corporate "firm," economic as well as sexual. Displacing God, Jaun loses authority for his statements except insofar as he relies on the system of economic exchange to ground and guarantee the soundness of his advice. And the notion that charity begins at home undergoes significant revision: "begin frem athome to be chary of charity." The suggestion of the German *fremd* (foreign, unknown) counters the conventional association of home and divinely ordained familial bliss; being "athome" thus seems to be a less congenial state than being "at home." Joyce's argument cuts doubly—against the church's principle of the family's spiritual sanctity, a doctrine tending to conceal its economic utility, and against the likelihood of any family's conforming to the roles prescribed by religious theory (at least any family in Joyce's fictional world).

Jaun's "brokerly advice" (FW 439.27) continues unabated throughout the sermon. If the girls forget themselves, he says, they will "pay for each bally sorraday night every billing sumday morning" (FW 436.26–27),[39] a statement which connects their sorrow not to spiritual contrition for sexual acts but to the pain of having to pay a debt. This replacement of divine retribution with a kind of one-to-one accounting system is not unique in Joyce's works. When in "Grace" Father Purdon relies on an accounting metaphor to "explain" and thereby substitute for the concept of theological grace, when in *Portrait* Stephen Dedalus sees his acts of virtue as going directly into a divine cash register to keep his account well in the black,[40] both situations reflect Joyce's larger assessment of the church as an economic institution.

Joyce's presentation of the church's function in the social power structure obviously works to undermine that institution's spiritual authority as codifier of modern behavior. In its place, the social order itself becomes important as a determinant of meaning and morality. This fact is made clear when Jaun discusses exercise and food. It is characteristic of his discourse that his thoughts tend to slide from religious doctrines to economic notions to thoughts of the body. As a result, he mixes up categories which we normally regard as distinct. Hence, not only does he underscore the church's reliance on the socioeconomic system, but he also treats what he eats as a moral issue. First, Jaun lectures the girls about exercise and manages to place menstruating on an economic scale of meaning. Nature, he says, is "the great greengrocer" and as such must be paid ("pay regularly the monthlies"—FW 437.16–17). He goes on, "Stamp out bad eggs. Why so many puddings prove disappointing, as Dietician says, in Creature Comforts Causeries, and why so much soup is so muck slop" (FW 437.21–23). One point of this aside is that the church's making ladylike behavior and female sexuality a matter of morality is as silly as is Jaun's clerical concern with palatable food.

In fact, taste (in both senses) becomes a criterion for right action. Telling the girls to avoid dalliance with "furnished lodgers," Jaun derides "basking in his loverslowlap, inordinately clad, moustache-teasing, when closehended together behind locked doors, kissing steadily" as "malbongusta, it's not the thing you know!" (FW 437.27, 36–438.2). Right conduct is revealed here as a matter of good taste, and the tonal shift from Jaun's mildly lecherous portrait-painting to his upper-class British "it's not the thing you know" emphasizes that his morality is always conventional. For Jaun, virtue is a matter of correct upper-class behavior. Underlining this class connection is the fact that Jaun proceeds at this point to evoke a picture of Issy's possible affairs being exposed in the press and causing her to become a part of the demimonde. Substituting gold for God, Jaun says, "Anything but that, for the love and fear of gold" (FW 438.31). If you're bad, he says, you will fall in social status. And with this thought, Jaun says, "Amene" (FW 439.14) to end the first arc of his preaching to the twenty-nine girls.

Because Jaun delivers his opinions as moral dictates, they are subject to the *Wake*'s general subversion of an absolutist and essentially bourgeois system of conduct, especially in the novel's recasting of the Garden of Eden myth.[41] For example, Joyce has his girls begin III, ii "learning their antemeridian lesson of life, under its tree, against its warning" (FW 430.3–5). Their ignoring the warning brings evil directly into the "antemeridian" world of presexuality which the girls may be supposed to represent (although they are already sexually knowledgeable).[42] Thus the allusion to Eden constituted by the tree with its warning refers only to a world in which evil is present within the good; it is the possibility of doing evil that constitutes the Edenic for Joyce. The distinction between good and evil becomes as meaningless as the Fall in a text which resists the priority of the good and finds it always to have been tainted by its ever-present opposite. Speaking of the sacredness of virginity, Jaun comments: "A coil of cord, a colleen coy, a blush on a bush turned first man's laughter into wailful moither. O foolish cuppled! Ah, dice's error!" (FW 433.28–30). Joyce's handling of the Adam and Eve exemplum suggests that our moral system is not a result of disobedience (error is not "willful" but only "wailful") so much as it is a result of misfortune or sheer chance; Dies Irae—or day of judgment—becomes "dice's error."[43] The coil (presumably a stand-in for the snake), the colleen, and the blushing fruit simply coincide. Certainly sex is at fault here: "felix culpa" is now "foolish cuppled." But egotism is equally to blame: we have not murder but *moi*ther. Finally, the pressure of a kind of conventional inevitability also shares responsibility for man's sin: in the *Wake*, Satan is not only tempter but also a theatrical "prompter" (FW 435.20)[44] for what we must take as an already scripted fall. In fact, we could say that there is no tempter at all, no evil power to generate the moral system, only a coil of rope read according to cultural convention. Instead of an immortal tragedy, Adam and Eve can be said to have enacted a melodrama in which an absolute system of good and evil is not so much proven as assumed.

And such a comparison is appropriate in this case, for Jaun tells Issy as he begins his sermon that he is only retelling to her the "gross proceeds" (FW 431.28) of her own teachings, which seem to have been heavily informed by melodramatic literature. That is, Jaun describes the way that Issy, when they were children, used to tell the two brothers, Shem and Shaun, bedtime stories, which he calls her "oldworld tales of homespinning and derringdo and dieobscure and daddyho" (FW 431.31–32). The provisional truths which Issy has shared with her brothers are no more than the moral imperatives of popular culture. She speaks to them of the family ("homespinning"), of the father ("daddyho"), of good and brave deeds ("derringdo"), and of the proletariat's fate ("dieobscure"). As sistermother, Issy narrates the tales that propagate the Western world's version of right conduct. And Jaun decides to recapitulate these tales in his own form, telling Issy, in his authoritative role of priest, what she already knows. The priestly Jaun's taking possession of these folk stories suggests a patriarchal appropriation of cultural topoi as Truth, topoi which developed as much in response to economic conditions as to putatively higher matters.

Support is lent to the *Wake*'s demystification of religious doctrine by the fact that Jaun himself has no more elevated source of information than Issy for the moral message he delivers. His only other authority is the disgruntled parish priest, Father Mike, who, as a "poorish priced" (FW 432.12), is himself preoccupied with money and whose advice Jaun claims to pass on to the twenty-nine girls. Armed with Issy's stories and "mikeadvice" (FW 432.18), Jaun nonetheless asserts that his ideas are "From above" (FW 432.19). Yet he slips to let us know that his particular "inspiration" has grown out of what he calls the "lessions of experience" (FW 436.20–21).

Religion and Incest

Finnegans Wake does not let the matter rest when it locates some of the determinants of religious doctrine in the economic matrix of society and in social convention, whether middle-class, aristocratic, or folkloric. Rather, these factors are themselves kept from assuming the authority of final causes through narrative attention to the metaphor of the family that ties together discussion of the social order and discussion of religion. On the one hand, the narrative presents the family circle as the arena in which social—and especially sexual—relations are learned. On the other hand, the *Wake* undermines the notion that those learned relations are in any way "right," or conversely that incestuous desires, for instance, are "wrong." Describing the world through the dream culture of a desirous father, the narrative sets up the priest as false parent and the church's dictates as merely the opinions of such. In particular, the repeated connection in *Finnegans Wake* of family relations with incest casts a comically lurid light on the society's ideals of parent-child and sibling behavior[45] and on the sanctity of the priesthood itself.

Jaun, of course, is one of the false fathers in question. Shortly after Jaun meets the twenty-nine schoolgirls by the riverbank, the girls rush for the post, in this case both their letters and Jaun himself, and express their desire to "read his kisshands" (FW 430.20–21). We know that the girls respond to him in typically adolescent fashion—they're attracted to his smell, his sexy look, and, in particular, his "full fat pouch" (FW 430.30). Interestingly, Jaun responds to their anticipated enthusiasm for him by dropping the guise of a postman (or even of a wanderer) and adopting an episcopal (or higher) role. That is, as they come toward him, he takes on a priestly role to suit his audience of supposedly virginal convent girls. As they crowd around him, Jaun in greeting "doffed a hat with a reinforced crown" (FW 430.17–18). What Roland McHugh finds to be a "crown of thorns"[46] is just as much part of the costume of a bishop or other ecclesiastic, the peaked hat worn for ritual functions. Hence Jaun's being kissed by the girls is significant; like the pope, he has "kisshands" or hands more appropriate for kissing than for delivering mail.

To reinforce the implications developed by the term "kisshands" and by the wearing of a mitre, Jaun is called not only Issy's brother but also her "benedict godfather" (FW 431.18). The term is curious and suggests both that Jaun is well-disposed toward Issy to the point of wanting to father her and to deliver to her not a letter but a blessing (Latin *benedictus*: blessing),[47] and that he is also a pope, perhaps a false one. Although the eighteenth century saw Benedict XIV installed as a legitimate pope, in the eleventh century the antipope Benedict X had a brief reign. Beyond its Latin meaning and its Elizabethan sense, "Benedict" thus suggests also the political tensions which led to the election and forced investiture of the pretender popes. Not only is Jaun associated with this ambiguous papal name but his priestly role is as assumed as is his role of "godfather." Within this conflation of paternalisms, he plays out the desire of HCE for Issy and his own sibling lust. Although as a priest Jaun would be barred from sexual activity, he does begin his discourse with the assertion, "I rise" (FW 432.4), and the sermon is punctuated throughout by his obvious verbal advances to his sister/fantasy-lover/ mother Issy. Jaun maintains that love is good when it is "cistern-brothelly" and that the right man is a husband or another "respectable relative of an apposite sex" (FW 436.14,17). As with Father Mike, who speaks in "soandso many nuncupiscent [nun-desiring?] words" (FW 432.10), for Jaun sex is verbal, and preaching is a means to physical excitement.[48] Ironically, a clerical economy is posed against the economy of desire. The church attempts to fill, via good books, magazines, sermons, and retreats, the mind of the populace, but Jaun's experience suggests that in practice, desire not only fills every gap in religious discourse but also usurps that discourse.

For all of its efforts to maintain the sanctity of the Catholic home, the church that *Finnegans Wake* presents sets up surrogate parental relations with its spiritual children only to taint those relations with the persistent demands of the flesh. Jaun's deceitful use of the priestly-paternal role comically critiques the authority of the church in that he associates religion with sexual desire. The discourses that are antithetical in Western tradition (the church repudiating sexuality in its pastors, creating from the very absence of sexuality a kind of religious presence) are in the *Wake* identified—to the discomfiture of both sides. Ultimately, in *Finnegans Wake*, most if not all events, artifacts, and relations are surrogates for sexual activity; sex both describes the vibrating center of Wakean culture and circumscribes all functions.[49]

Hence, Jaun echoes the concerns of the church in Joyce's Ireland, but all propriety is undermined by the heated call of consanguinity. Not only is the church's authority thus questioned in the narrative, but so is the familial and social order which it regards as divinely ordained. To see incest as a sin does, after all, presuppose a norm: the "right" relations of a family and of sexual beings in a society. Yet the *Wake* persistently undoes our confidence in labeling anything "right." Hence the opposition of normative and deviant sexuality, of natural and unnatural family relations, falls away in the dreamworld of the *Wake* in which all desires are in some sense spoken and all scenarios played out. In fact, the *Wake* provides a good deal of evidence that family sexuality is indeed the "norm" from which intercourse with the Other developed.[50] Ultimately, Joyce rewrites the moral system of Western culture to account for incest as a sexual model, the results in *Finnegans Wake* being to sever the sexual from the moral. While the historical religious morality alluded to in Jaun's sermon and throughout the *Wake* reinforced the hegemonic interests of the church by extending its influence into every corner of Irish family life, *Finnegans Wake* destabilizes that system of conduct by highlighting economic imperatives, the dictates of conventionality, and the indiscriminate demands of the flesh.

In sum, the *Wake* targets the sources—not revelation but economic utility and cultural conventions—of popular religious doctrine. Of course, the preachers of Joyce's day *were* disconcerted by those phenomena Jaun denounces—loose behavior, bad books, the change in tenor of the age—but Jaun's send-up of a sermon would have us agree that the denunciatory posture of the institution had a lot more to do with maintaining its social hegemony than with anything approximating divine afflatus. The "lessions of experience" on which Jaun bases his message to the girls are thus not only lessons but also lesions—spots in the cultural surface which reveal the perhaps not diseased but certainly dis-eased intertwining of dogma and economics, of spirituality and the social order. The countercurrents to authority established in III, ii epitomize Joyce's anatomy of his culture, for his narratives persistently expose conditions of censorship, institutional competition, and a deceptive binary structuring of ideas in order to challenge domination in all of its protean forms.

NOTES

1. One useful essay that deals with III, ii–iii is Hugh B. Staples's "Growing Up Absurd in Dublin," in *A Conceptual Guide to* Finnegans Wake, ed. Michael H. Begnal and Fritz Senn (University Park: Pennsylvania State University Press, 1974), pp. 173–200.

2. At the meeting of the James Joyce Society held on March 24, 1985 in the Gotham Bookmart (New York), the actor Patrick Corgan demonstrated the parallels between III, ii and the service of the mass specific to the third Sunday in Lent; he followed Nathan Halper's "The Date of Earwicker's Dream," in *Twelve and a Tilly: Essays on the Occasion of the 25th Anniversary of* Finnegans Wake, ed. Jack P. Dalton and Clive Hart (Evanston, Ill.: Northwestern University Press, 1965), pp. 72–90, in arguing that the night of *Finnegans Wake* is March 18–19, 1922. Mr. Corgan's reading from both III, ii and the service in question made apparent the fact that Joyce's text aggressively undermines one typical response to the inert metaphors and well known rhythms of institutional language—boredom. The parallels with the mass enhance the ironic destabilizing and comic power of Jaun's oration by selectively recasting traditional locutions into Jaun's "personal" commentary. The *Wake* sermon is thus both conventional and counterinstitutional, both prescribed form and individual transformation.

3. Roland McHugh, *The Sigla of* Finnegans Wake, p. 31.

4. Rev. Charles Gobinet, *The Instruction of Youth in Christian Piety; Taken Out of the Sacred Scriptures and Holy Fathers* (Boston: Patrick Donohoe, n.d.). For a discussion of Gobinet and the *Portrait* sermons, see Bradley, pp. 125–28.

5. For example, published in London in 1921, *The Preacher's Vademecum* cites ten topics suitable for a men's retreat which were "chosen with a view to combating the moral disorders at the present day." Among these top ten problems are "Immoral publications," "Divorce and its victims," and "Limitation of the family." The other problems are "Irreligion," "Godless education," "Love of money," "Class hatred," "Vice," "The tyranny of alcohol," and "Murder" (p. 379).

6. Father Bernard Vaughan, S.J., *Society, Sin and the Saviour: Addresses on the Passion of Our Lord* (London: Kegan Paul, Trench, Trübner, 1908), p. xxvii.

7. Although Vaughan was born in Courtfield, England, Martindale found "that the room of his birth was being shown, at a shilling a head, in

an Irish village." He states, "By dint of hearing so much about him, no one knew what he was like. The editor of *John Bull* himself proved his intuitive knowledge of men by sitting next to him at lunch and then declaring him to be 'the typical Irish priest'" (Martindale, pp. 1–2, 119).

8. Vaughan, *What of To-Day?*, pp. 255–61, 238.

9. Burke admits that baptism and holy orders are technically greater sacraments but avers that without marriage there would be no children to baptize, no priests to ordain. See Very Rev. J. A. Rochford, O.P., comp. and ed., *Lectures and Sermons Delivered by the Very Rev. Thomas N. Burke, O.P., Since His Departure from America* (New York: P. J. Kenedy, 1878), pp. 229–30.

10. *The Preacher's Vademecum*, by Two Missionaries, trans. from the French (New York: Wagner; London: Herder, 1921), pp. 338–39.

11. Vaughan, *What of To-Day?*, pp. 246–48. To help the women involved in this endeavor, the *Catholic Bulletin* (Dublin) regularly included a column entitled "For Mothers and Daughters," which included recipes along with helpful and pious information of interest to homemakers.

12. Callan, pp. 236–37.

13. C. M. O'Brien, "Catholics and Freemasonry," *Irish Ecclesiastical Record*, 4th ser., 6 (1899), pp. 311, 313–17, 322–23; Right Rev. George Conroy, D.D., *Occasional Sermons, Addresses, and Essays* (Dublin: Gill, 1884), pp. 264, 374. O'Brien reproduces a chart from *The Masonic Token* (n.d.) which claims that in Ireland there existed 396 Masonic lodges with a total of 20,000 members.

14. *Catholic Bulletin* 4 (1914), 663.

15. It might also be argued that the phrase "bellas arias" refers to the beauty of the so-called higher and purer arts which Jaun is simply too dense to appreciate. Along this line, note also that "dilettante" means not just a dabbler but also, though rarely, a connoisseur, which one might argue Swinburne might have been but Jaun is not.

16. Brendan O Hehir and John M. Dillon, *A Classical Lexicon for* Finnegans Wake (Berkeley: University of California Press, 1977), pp. 384, 610–11.

17. McHugh, *Annotations*, p. 440.

18. Harold Wentworth and Stuart Berg Flexner, eds., *The Dictionary of American Slang*, 2nd ed. (New York: Crowell, 1975), cite this term as in popular use in the 1920s, especially in reference to failure in a stage performance.

19. For example, see Fritz Senn, "Every Klitty of a scolderymeid: Sexual-Political Analogies," *A Wake Digest*, ed. Clive Hart and Fritz Senn (Sydney: Sydney University Press, 1968), p. 30. Senn discusses the "replacement of sex by food" in FW 239:16–22 and in relation to Freud's *The Interpretation of Dreams*.

20. McHugh, *Annotations*, p. 434. Francis J. Finn, S.J., *The Best Foot Forward And Other Stories* (New York: Benziger, 1890).

21. Conroy, p. 345.

22. Canon P. A. Sheehan, "Bad Books," *Sermons*, pp. 267, 268. "It is specially painful to a priest to go into the house of the poor, and to find the *Young Lady's Journal*, *The Family Herald*, the *Halfpenny Journal*, the *London Reader* on the same shelf, but much better cared for, than the *Garden of the Soul*, and the *Imitation of Christ*" (p. 274).

23. Foucault, *History of Sexuality*, pp. 18–20.

24. Coleman, pp. 35, 30, 40.

25. "Some New Books," *Irish Monthly* 42 (1914), 592.

26. Sheehan, p. 273.

27. Rochford, p. 234.

28. Ibid., p. 246.

29. See Adaline Glasheen, *Third Census of* Finnegans Wake: *An Index of the Characters and Their Roles* (Berkeley: University of California Press, 1977), lx. The Pentecost association of the arrival of Dave the Dancekerl complicates the time-layering in this chapter. See also Halper, pp. 72–90.

30. *The New Catholic Encyclopedia* 11 (1967) states, "The two great liturgical cycles of Easter, from Septuagesima to Pentecost, and of Christmas, from Advent to Epiphany, have developed into a continuity of from 6 to 7 months, leaving from 5 to 6 months with no special festal character" (p. 110).

31. Alan Sheridan, *Michel Foucault*: *The Will to Truth* (London: Tavistock, 1980), p. 138.

32. O'Brien, *Dear, Dirty Dublin*, p. 220.

33. In *Stephen Hero* Mr. Fulham mentions "the duties of our station in life," and he is described as "leaning comfortably on the . . . phrase" (SH 249).

34. Rochford, p. 224.

35. Stanley B. James, "The Church and the Class War," *Irish Ecclesiastical Record*, 5th ser., 36 (1930), 170. Quotations to follow in this paragraph are from p. 167.

36. "The Catholic population [in Ireland] enjoys on the average a lower standard of well-being. . . . they constitute very largely an underpaid proletariat unable to marry in youth and unwilling to marry when youth is past." See Rev. P. J. Gannon, S.J., "A Study of Religious Statistics in Ireland," *Irish Ecclesiastical Record*, 5th ser., 17 (1921), 154; Gannon finds the Catholic marriage rate lower than the non-Catholic rate in Ireland. FW 438.21–23 mentions the "marriage slump" and the fact that wives are "at six and seven."

37. McHugh, *Annotations*, p. 433.

38. Not only is "hope" scrambled here into "hoep," suggesting at the very least a distortion or confusion of that virtue in Jaun's world, but the Dutch *hoep* (barrel hoop or petticoat hoop) calls to mind the replacement of hope with liquor (often kept in barrels) or with sex (to be found inside petticoats).

39. Compare FW 5.10–12: "Comeday morm and, O, you're vine! Sendday's eve and, ah, you're vinegar! Hahahaha, Mister Funn, you're going to be fined again!" Fun always leads to fines on the church's day of reckoning—"sumday" / "Sendday."

40. Cf. P 145: "As long as you commit that sin, my poor child, you will never be worth one farthing to God."

41. Cf. Bernard Benstock, who observes that "Joyce is utilizing the Adam-Eve incident as myth, a myth that embodies man's feelings of sexual guilt" (*Joyce-Again's Wake*, p. 82). Benstock's fine extensive commentary on religion in *Finnegans Wake* and on Joyce's rejection of Christianity is very useful. See esp. pp. 101–7.

42. "Since the Floras attend 'St. Bride's Finishing Establishment' (220.03) they are, in fact, schooled. The knowledge tends to be carnal and they betray their knowingness in multiple ways" (Senn, "Every Klitty," p. 27).

43. McHugh, *Annotations*, p. 433.

44. FW 435.19–20—"Stick wicks in your earshells when you hear the prompter's voice."

45. On incest and the social order, see Margot Norris, *The Decentered Universe of* Finnegans Wake: *A Structuralist Analysis* (Baltimore: Johns Hopkins University Press, 1976), pp. 54–61.

46. McHugh, *Annotations*, p. 430.

47. Ibid., p. 431. McHugh points to Benedict X as antipope (see below).

48. On Jaun's achieving a "sadistically induced erection," see E. L. Epstein, "James Joyce and the Body," in *A Starchamber Quiry*, p. 101.

49. Cf. Margaret C. Solomon, *Eternal Geomater: The Sexual Universe of* Finnegans Wake (Carbondale: Southern Illinois University Press; London: Feffer & Simons, 1969): "The sexual symbolism of the novel is pertinent to all historical, religious, cultural and psychological human processes . . ." (p. viii).

50. Cf. Foucault, *History of Sexuality*, I, 108–14.

Afterword

As Joyce knew and as his insistent alluding testifies, it is not possible to separate art and life. Try as we may to isolate the literary text for strict "scientific" interpretation, narrative inexorably resists that isolation and pulls us for explanation toward the contradictory field of history. Recent critical thought, though in many ways different from the New Criticism of the 1930s, sometimes reinforces in practice the New Critical effort to cut off the literary work from the social forces which are in some sense responsible for its production. Writers like Edward Said have pursued a countereffort to reinstate the work in its cultural surroundings. In part, my decision to pursue the research involved in this study grew out of my effort to rethink Joyce's relationship to history in some of the ways suggested by literary critics like Said and Jameson as well as by cultural semioticians. In their work, I have discovered many illuminating theoretical positions, but I have recognized too that a gap exists between the theoretical assertion of our need to "historicize"[1] and the practice of much contemporary criticism.

My initial effort here has been to delve as specifically as existing documents allow into the historical conditions under which popular journalism, drama, and homily were produced during Joyce's lifetime in Ireland. Second, but not secondarily, I have tried to bring into relation the cultural subtexts of that material and my understanding of Joyce's uses of it. What has impressed me most as a result of these efforts is that the gap between "theory" and "practice" may be narrowed but not entirely eliminated. Always, the interpretive activity intervenes to make merely provisional our readings of history and of the art that cannot be severed from history. It may not be possible for Joyce's readers, especially those who are members of the world's premier capitalist society, to encounter *Ulysses*, *Finnegans Wake*, or any other text free from a preoccupation with the self, sexual identity, and the existing social order, yet I would maintain that the effort to work beyond that limiting vision has become necessary if we are to move away from the terms that have held in deadlock much criticism of modern writers. Many of the best readings of Joyce to date have continued to play out the binarisms that his works expose as artifices and have persisted in seeing only "style" where the ideological practices in language "censor" the cultural field at every trope. When Yeats recovered from his initial puzzlement over *Ulysses*, he wrote, "It is an entirely new thing—neither what the eye sees nor the ear hears. . . ."[2] Yeats recognized the fundamental commitment of Joyce's work to ideological exposure—to demonstrating that what Yeats thought he saw and heard was only part of the story.

In his valuable and urbane study *Surface and Symbol*, R. M. Adams explores the relationship between the possibly meaningless details that are part of Joyce's *Ulysses* ("the things which were put into the novel because they are social history, local color, or literal municipal detail")[3] and those that bear obvious and important symbolic significance. The Wildean dichotomy on which he based his work has always seemed to me eminently sound and perfectly suited to Joyce's works. However, in my exploration of those social issues that cling to the surface and the symbol, I have become convinced that this dichotomy, like so many of the cultural binarisms that Joyce evokes, must be questioned. When the most inert detail of Irish life can be—indeed, must be—recognized as bearing a relation to one or another social institution, and when all such institutions are demonstrably the means by which fundamental social relations are reproduced, who is to say where surface ends and symbol begins? Even more important, who is to say that "symbol" is the correct term for the meaning-bearing components of Joyce's fictions? If we take at all seriously the continuity of history and narrative, we must view each word and phrase as, among other things, the possible signifier of a socioeconomic condition. Yet, the conviction that some details are present in Joyce's fictions for the sake of verisimilitude, conceived of in terms that are largely nondynamic, reigns not only in the study of Joyce but in most areas of literary exploration. My concentration in this book on institutional forms and on their function in a narrative anatomy of culture directs attention to an alternative vision of the surface of Joyce's fiction.

The possibility of alternative vision is, I think, what Joyce's anatomy of culture is all about. Although his fictions bear witness to a writer's being bound by cultural binarisms, conventions, codes, and ideological practices, works such as *Ulysses* and *Finnegans Wake* clearly expose those restrictions, and in doing so force us to recognize the oppositional or even subversive content that characterized both the institutional forms studied in this volume and Joyce's own writings. I have indicated those places where these "sub-versions" seem to me most pronounced—for instance, when "Aeolus" reveals that censorship is also speaking, when "Circe" displays the culture's covert dramatic recognition that gender is not nature and, sadly, that the utopian vision of the middle class could not efface the violence of a competitive and colonized society, when Jaun's sermon suggests the sexual energy existing within and around even the most repressive efforts to maintain the economic and political status quo of Irish culture. Indeed, as early as "Grace," Joyce's work tutors us to look at institutional power relations and to see personal conversion as partly contingent on social change. It is fair to say that if we were to stress too heavily the roles played by institutions in Joyce, we would tend to see him as the proponent of individual freedom and his works as operating solely in opposition to the institutions that would curtail that freedom.[4] However, this reading is short of the mark. Repeatedly, Joyce's texts emphasize that the individual and the institution cannot be dichotomized, that the two terms form a dialectic.

To be sure, Joyce the writer always felt himself circumscribed by cultural institutions: his "exile" directly responded to that encirclement. In fact, his writings document the pressures of culture on his thinking; formally and otherwise, the ideological practices of his society left their mark on his works. Nonetheless, many readers of Joyce have found his writings to be among the least constrained of the major modernist fictions. The world has tended to see him as openly flouting convention and openly courting social ostracism. In reaction to this view of Joyce, I have attempted here to argue that Joyce did not speak beyond the terms laid out for him by his culture; there was a firm limit to the novelty of what he could say. But this limitation was not so much because of censorship but because even with conditions of suppression being pervasive in Anglo-Irish life, what was suppressed was always insuppressible. What Joyce courted exile to announce had already been said.

On the other hand, Joyce's steady and various undermining of the absolute opposition of those binarisms (male/female, saved/damned, upper class/lower class, and good/evil) on which Western cultural mores are built engineers in his text what we might call a liberating vision of culture. The anatomizing undoes oppositions as absolutes and enables us to see that the institution, however formidable, is also man-made. Joyce's narrative transformations of institutional ideologies document the presence of cultural sub-versions within the dominant social formations of Irish life. Hence, it is no surprise that attention to the conditions under which institutional discourses were produced in early modern Ireland reveals the presence of op-posing voices within them. Joyce's formal explorations of those dis-courses encourage the reader to participate in the prying apart of the institution as monolith. About the institution, Stephen asserts, "Subtract its human members from it and its solidity becomes less evident" (SH 233). If the reader is interested in this sort of thing, Joyce's narratives can participate in the mental repositioning that Stephen implies, yet the fictions resist the conclusion that they as-sert a political position or that they provide access to intellectual freedom. Rather, the works refuse to allow the exposed sociopoliti-cal fact of experience-as-ideology to be recontained by a single so-cial stance. Similarly, they suggest that freedom is a term that has been made meaningful only in relation to its opposite. Like being, gender, nationalism, and sanctity, even liberation is an idea that re-quires our careful scrutiny. Given the intimate relationship of indi-vidual and institution, it is useless to argue either for Joyce's vic-timization by his culture or for his extrication from it. Just as his society constantly created and constantly undermined its networks of conventionality, so Joyce's works both resolve and renew the nur-turing conflicts of history.

NOTES

1. Jameson, p. 9—"Always historicize!"
2. Letter to John Quinn, 23 July 1918, Quoted in Ellmann, *James Joyce*, p. 530.
3. Adams, p. xvii.
4. Cf. Norris, pp. 71–72.

Selected Bibliography

I. JOYCE SCHOLARSHIP AND CRITICISM

Adams, Robert Martin. *Surface and Symbol: The Consistency of James Joyce's* Ulysses. New York: Oxford University Press, 1962.

Atherton, James S. *The Books at the Wake: A Study of Literary Allusions in James Joyce's* Finnegans Wake. Mamaroneck, N.Y.: Appel, 1974.

―――. "*Finnegans Wake*: 'The Gist of the Pantomime.'" *Accent* 15 (1955), 14–26.

Attridge, Derek, and Daniel Ferrer, eds. *Post-structuralist Joyce: Essays from the French*. Cambridge: Cambridge University Press, 1984.

Aubert, J., and M. Jolas, eds. *Joyce and Paris 1902 . . . 1920–1940 . . . 1975: Papers from the Fifth International James Joyce Symposium: Paris, 16–20 June 1975*. Vol. 2. Paris: C.N.R.S., 1979.

August, Eugene R. "Father Arnall's Use of Scripture in *A Portrait*." *James Joyce Quarterly* 4 (Summer 1967), 275–79.

Bauerle, Ruth, ed. *The James Joyce Songbook*. New York: Garland, 1982.

Beck, Warren. *Joyce's* Dubliners: *Substance, Vision, and Art*. Durham, N.C.: Duke University Press, 1969.

Beckett, Samuel, et al. *Our Exagmination Round His Factification For Incamination of Work in Progress*. New York: New Directions, 1929.

Begnal, Michael H., and Fritz Senn, eds. *A Conceptual Guide to* Finnegans Wake. University Park: Pennsylvania State University Press, 1974.

Beja, Morris. "Dividual Chaoses: Case Histories of Multiple Personality and *Finnegans Wake*." *James Joyce Quarterly* 14 (1976–77), 241–50.

Bennett, John Z. "Unposted Letter: Joyce's Leopold Bloom." *Bucknell Review* 14 (1966), 1–13.

Benstock, Bernard. "A Covey of Clerics in Joyce and O'Casey." *James Joyce Quarterly* 2 (1964–65), 18–32.

―――. *James Joyce: The Undiscovered Country*. New York: Barnes and Noble; Dublin: Gill and Macmillan, 1977.

―――. "James Joyce: The World of Monomedia." *Revue des Langues Vivantes* 42 (1976), 56–63.

―――. *Joyce-Again's Wake: An Analysis of* Finnegans Wake. Seattle: University of Washington Press, 1965.

————. "Leopold Bloom and the Mason Connection." *James Joyce Quarterly* 15 (1977–78), 259–62.

————. "Redhoising JJ: USSR/II." *James Joyce Quarterly* 6 (1968–69), 177–80.

————, ed. *The Seventh of Joyce.* Bloomington: Indiana University Press; Sussex: Harvester, 1982.

Blamires, Harry. *The Bloomsday Book: A Guide through Joyce's* Ulysses. London: Methuen, 1966.

Bonheim, Helmut. *Joyce's Benefictions.* Berkeley: University of California Press, 1964.

Bonnerot, Louis, with J. Aubert and Cl. Jacquet, eds. Ulysses *Cinquante Ans Après: Témoignages Franco-Anglais sur le Chef-d'Œuvre de James Joyce.* Paris: Didier, 1974.

Boone, Joseph Allen. "A New Approach to Bloom as 'Womanly Man': The Mixed Middling's Progress in *Ulysses*." *James Joyce Quarterly* 20 (1982), 67–85.

Bowen, Zack. *Musical Allusions in the Works of James Joyce: Early Poetry through* Ulysses. Albany: State University of New York Press, 1974.

————. "The Music Hall and Wagnerian Opera: 'My Girl's a Yorkshire Girl' and the Ring Cycle." Eighth International James Joyce Symposium, Dublin, 16 June 1982.

Boyd, Elizabeth F. "James Joyce's Hell-Fire Sermons." *Modern Language Notes* 75 (1960), 561–71.

Boyle, Robert, S.J. *James Joyce's Pauline Vision: A Catholic Exposition.* Carbondale: Southern Illinois University Press; London: Feffer and Simons, 1978.

Bradley, Bruce, S.J. *James Joyce's Schooldays.* New York: St. Martin's Press, 1982.

Briskin, Irene Orgel. "Some New Light on 'The Parable of the Plums.'" *James Joyce Quarterly* 3 (1965–66), 236–51.

Brivic, Sheldon R. *Joyce Between Freud and Jung.* Port Washington, N. Y.: Kennikat, 1980.

Brown, Norman O. *Closing Time.* New York: Random, 1973.

Budgen, Frank. *James Joyce and the Making of* Ulysses. Intro. Hugh Kenner. [1934]; rpt. Bloomington: Indiana University Press, 1960.

Bushrui, Suheil Badi, and Bernard Benstock, eds. *James Joyce: An International Perspective.* Gerrards Cross, Buckinghamshire: Colin Smythe; Totowa, N.J.: Barnes and Noble, 1982.

Campbell, Joseph, and Henry Morton Robinson. *A Skeleton Key to* Finnegans Wake. New York: Harcourt, Brace, 1944.

Card, James Van Dyck. "'Contradicting': The Word for Joyce's Penelope." *James Joyce Quarterly* 11 (1973–74), 17–26.

Cheng, Vincent John. *Shakespeare and Joyce: A Study of* Finnegans Wake. University Park: Pennsylvania State University Press, 1984.

Chesnutt, Margaret. "Joyce's *Dubliners:* History, Ideology, and Social Reality." *Éire-Ireland* 14 (1979), 93–105.

Cixous, Hélène. "At Circe's, or the Self-Opener." Trans. Carol Bové. *Boundary 2*, 3 (1975), 387–97.

———. *The Exile of James Joyce*. Trans. Sally A. J. Purcell. New York: David Lewis, 1972.

Cope, Jackson. "The Rhythmic Gesture: Image and Aesthetic in Joyce's *Ulysses*." *ELH* 29 (1962), 67–89.

Davies, Stan Gébler. *James Joyce: A Portrait of the Artist*. London: Davis-Poynter, 1975.

Deming, Robert H., ed. *James Joyce: The Critical Heritage*. 2 vols. New York: Barnes and Noble, 1970.

Doherty, James. "Joyce and *Hell Opened to Christians:* The Edition He Used For His Sermons." *Modern Philology* 61 (1963), 110–19.

Driver, Clive, annot. *James Joyce:* Ulysses: *The Manuscript and First Printings Compared*. New York: Octagon-Farrar; Philadelphia: Philip H. and A. S. W. Rosenbach Foundation, 1975.

Duyfhuizen, Bernard. "'Words [Mis]taken': The Opening Sentence of the Retreat Sermons." *James Joyce Quarterly* 16 (1978–79), 488–90.

Ellmann, Richard. *The Consciousness of Joyce*. New York: Oxford University Press, 1977.

———. *James Joyce*. Rev. ed. New York: Oxford University Press, 1982.

———, ed. *Letters of James Joyce*. Vols. 2, 3. New York: Viking, 1966.

———. *Ulysses on the Liffey*. New York: Oxford University Press, 1972.

Epstein, E. L. *A Starchamber Quiry: A James Joyce Centennial Volume 1882–1982*. London: Methuen, 1982.

Feshbach, Sidney. Review of *Joyce's Politics* by Dominic Manganiello. *James Joyce Quarterly* 19 (1981–82), 208–13.

Fiedler, Leslie. "Portrait of the Artist: The Academic Perspective." State University of New York—College at Purchase, 15 February 1982.

French, Marilyn. *The Book as World: James Joyce's* Ulysses. Cambridge, Mass.: Harvard University Press, 1976.

Garvin, John. *James Joyce's Disunited Kingdom and the Irish Dimension*. Dublin: Gill and Macmillan; New York: Barnes and Noble, 1976.

Gifford, Don, and Robert J. Seidman. *Notes for Joyce: An Annotation of James Joyce's* Ulysses. New York: Dutton, 1974.

Gilbert, Stuart, ed. *Letters of James Joyce*. Vol. 1. New York: Viking, 1957.

———. *James Joyce's* Ulysses. 2nd ed. New York: Vintage-Random, 1955.

Givens, Seon, ed. *James Joyce: Two Decades of Criticism*. New York: Vanguard, 1948.

Glasheen, Adaline. *Third Census of* Finnegans Wake. 3rd ed. Berkeley: University of California Press, 1977.

Golding, Louis. *James Joyce*. 1933; rpt. Port Washington, N.Y.: Kennikat Press, 1972.

Groden, Michael, ed. *The James Joyce Archive*. New York: Garland, 1978.

———. Ulysses *in Progress*. Princeton, N.J.: Princeton University Press, 1977.

Halper, Nathan. "The Date of Earwicker's Dream." In *Twelve and a Tilly: Essays on the Occasion of the 25th Anniversary of* Finnegans Wake. Ed. Jack P. Dalton and Clive Hart. Evanston, Ill.: Northwestern University Press, 1965. Pp. 72–90.

Harmon, Maurice, ed. *The Celtic Master: Contributions to the First James Joyce Symposium held in Dublin, 1967*. Dublin: Dolmen Press, 1969.

Hart, Clive. *Structure and Motif in* Finnegans Wake. Evanston, Ill.: Northwestern University Press, 1962.

———, and Fritz Senn, eds. *A Wake Digest*. Sydney: Sydney University Press, 1968.

———, and David Hayman, eds. *James Joyce's* Ulysses: *Critical Essays*. Berkeley: University of California Press, 1974.

Hayman, David. "The Empirical Molly." In *Approaches to* Ulysses: *Ten Essays*. Ed. Thomas F. Staley and Bernard Benstock. Pittsburgh: University of Pittsburgh Press, 1970. Pp. 103–35.

———, ed. *A First-Draft Version of* Finnegans Wake. Austin: University of Texas Press, 1963.

———. "Forms of Folly in Joyce: A Study of Clowning in *Ulysses*." *ELH* 34 (1967), 260–83.

———. Ulysses: *The Mechanics of Meaning*. Rev. ed. Madison: University of Wisconsin Press, 1982.

Henke, Suzette. "James Joyce and Joris-Karl Huysmans: What Was Leopold Bloom Doing with that Circus-Lady?" *Modern British Literature* 5 (1980), 68–72.

———. "Joyce and Krafft-Ebing." *James Joyce Quarterly* 17 (1979–80), 84–86.

———. *Joyce's Moraculous Sindbook: A Study of* Ulysses. Columbus: Ohio State University Press, 1978.

———, and Elaine Unkeless, eds. *Women in Joyce*. Urbana: University of Illinois Press, 1982.

Herring, Phillip F. "The Bedsteadfastness of Molly Bloom." *Modern Fiction Studies* 15 (1969), 49–61.

———, ed. *Joyce's* Ulysses *Notesheets in the British Museum*. Charlottesville: University Press of Virginia, 1972.

Hodgart, Matthew J. C., and Mabel P. Worthington. *Song in the Works of James Joyce*. New York: Temple University Press, 1959.

Jackson, Robert Sumner. "A Parabolic Reading of James Joyce's 'Grace.'" *Modern Language Notes* 76 (1961), 719–24.

James Joyce Centenary 1882–1982. riverrun. Ireland: Bord Fáilte—Irish Tourist Board, [1982].

Joly, Ralph Robert. "Chauvinist Brew and Leopold Bloom: The Weininger Legacy." *James Joyce Quarterly* 19 (1981–82), 194–98.

Joyce, Stanislaus. *My Brother's Keeper*. Ed. and intro. Richard Ellmann. London: Faber, 1958.

———. *The Complete Dublin Diary of Stanislaus Joyce*. Ed. George H. Healy. Ithaca: Cornell University Press, 1971.

Kain, Richard M. *Dublin in the Age of William Butler Yeats and James Joyce*. Norman: University of Oklahoma Press, 1962.

———. *Fabulous Voyager: James Joyce's* Ulysses. Rev. ed. Chicago: University of Chicago Press, 1959.

———. "'The Music Hall, Not Poetry, Is a Criticism Of Life'—A Note on Dan Lowrey's Star of Erin." *James Joyce Quarterly* 14 (1976–77), 96–99.

Kenner, Hugh. *Dublin's Joyce*. 1956; rpt. Gloucester, Mass.: Peter Smith, 1969.

———. *Joyce's Voices*. Berkeley: University of California Press, 1978.

———. *Ulysses*. London: Allen and Unwin, 1980.

Keogh, J. G. "*Ulysses'* 'Parable of the Plums' as Parable and Periplum." *James Joyce Quarterly* 7 (1969–70), 377–78.

Lachtman, Howard. "The Magic-Lantern Business: James Joyce's Ecclesiastical Satire in *Dubliners*." *James Joyce Quarterly* 7 (1969–70), 82–92.

Lawrence, Karen. *The Odyssey of Style in* Ulysses. Princeton, N.J.: Princeton University Press, 1981.

Leithauser, Gladys Garner and Paul Sporn. "Hypsospadia: Linguistic Guidepost to the Themes of the "Circe" Episode of *Ulysses*." *Journal of Modern Literature* 4 (1974–75), 109–14.

Levine, Jennifer. "Rejoycings in *Tel Quel*." *James Joyce Quarterly* 16 (1978–79), 17–26.

MacCabe, Colin. *James Joyce and the Revolution of the Word*. London: Macmillan, 1978.

McCarthy, Patrick A. "The Jeweleyed Harlots of his Imagination: Prostitution and Artistic Vision in Joyce." *Éire-Ireland* 17 (1982), 91–109.

———. *The Riddles of* Finnegans Wake. Cranbury, N.J.: Associated University Press, 1980.

McCormack, W. J., and Alistair Stead. *James Joyce and Modern Literature*. London: Routledge & Kegan Paul, 1982.

McGrory, Kathleen. "The Music Hall in *Ulysses*: Class, Convention, Popular Culture." Eighth International James Joyce Symposium, 16 June 1982.

McHugh, Roland. *Annotations to* Finnegans Wake. Baltimore: Johns Hopkins University Press, 1980.

———. *The* Finnegans Wake *Experience*. Dublin: Irish Academic Press, 1981.

———. *The Sigla of* Finnegans Wake. Austin: University of Texas Press, 1976.

Maddox, James H., Jr. *Joyce's* Ulysses *and the Assault upon Character*. New Brunswick, N.J.: Rutgers University Press, 1978.

Manganiello, Dominic. *Joyce's Politics*. London: Routledge & Kegan Paul, 1980.

Mason, Ellsworth, and Richard Ellmann, eds. *The Critical Writings of James Joyce*. New York: Viking, 1964.

Miller-Budnitskaya, R. "James Joyce's *Ulysses*." Trans. N. J. Nelson. *Dialectics* 5 (1938), 6–26.

Morse, J. Mitchell. *The Sympathetic Alien: James Joyce and Catholicism*. New York: New York University Press, 1959.

Noon, William T., S.J. *Joyce and Aquinas*. New Haven, Conn.: Yale University Press, 1957.

Norris, Margot. *The Decentered Universe of* Finnegans Wake: *A Structuralist Analysis*. Baltimore: Johns Hopkins University Press, 1976.

O'Brien, Darcy. "A Critique of Psychoanalytic Criticism, Or What Joyce Did and Did Not Do." *James Joyce Quarterly* 13 (1975–76), 275–92.

O Hehir, Brendan, and John Dillon. *A Classical Lexicon for* Finnegans Wake: *A Glossary of the Greek and Latin in the Major Works of Joyce*. Berkeley: University of California Press, 1977.

O'Neill, Michael J. "The Joyces in the Holloway Diaries." In *A James Joyce Miscellany*. 2nd series. Ed. Marvin Magalaner. Carbondale: Southern Illinois University Press, 1959. Pp. 103–10.

Peake, C. H. *James Joyce: The Citizen and the Artist*. Stanford, Calif.: Stanford University Press, 1977.

Perlmutter, Ruth. "Joyce on Cinema." *Boundary 2*, 6 (1978), 481–502.

Peterson, Richard F., Alan M. Cohn, and Edmund L. Epstein, eds. *Work in Progress: Joyce Centenary Essays*. Carbondale: Southern Illinois University Press, 1983.

Phelan, Francis. "A Source for the Headlines of 'Aeolus'?" *James Joyce Quarterly* 9 (1971), 146–51.

Power, Arthur. *Conversations with James Joyce*. Ed. Clive Hart. New York: Barnes-Harper, 1974.

Riquelme, John Paul. *Teller and Tale in Joyce's Fiction: Oscillating Perspectives*. Baltimore: Johns Hopkins University Press, 1983.

Roberts, Dorothy Hutcherson. "James Joyce's *Ulysses:* A Study of the Motifs of Androgyny." Ph.D. diss., University of South Florida, 1977.

Schneider, Ulrich. "Freemasonic Signs and Passwords in the *Circe* Episode." *James Joyce Quarterly* 5 (1967–68), 303–11.

———. "Some Comments upon Music Hall in *Ulysses*." Manuscript essay.

Scholes, Robert. "*Ulysses:* A Structuralist Perspective." *James Joyce Quarterly* 10 (1972–73), 161–71.

Scholes, Robert, and Richard M. Kain, eds. *The Workshop of Daedalus: James Joyce and the Raw Materials for* A Portrait of the Artist as a Young Man. Evanston, Ill.: Northwestern University Press, 1965.

Scott, Bonnie Kime. *Joyce and Feminism*. Bloomington: Indiana University Press; Sussex: Harvester, 1984.

Senn, Fritz. *Joyce's Dislocutions: Essays on Reading as Translation*. Ed. John Paul Riquelme. Baltimore: Johns Hopkins University Press, 1984.

———. "Micro-Cycloptics." Manuscript note.

———. "A Rhetorical Account of James Joyce's 'Grace.'" *Moderna Språk* 74 (1980), 121–28.

Shechner, Mark. "Exposing Joyce." *James Joyce Quarterly* 13 (1975–76), 266–74.

———. "Joyce and Psychoanalysis: Two Additional Perspectives." *James Joyce Quarterly* 14 (1976–77), 416–19.

———. *Joyce in Nighttown: A Psychoanalytic Inquiry into* Ulysses. Berkeley: University of California Press, 1974.

Solomon, Margaret C. *Eternal Geomater: The Sexual Universe of* Finnegans Wake. Carbondale: Southern Illinois University Press; London: Feffer & Simons, 1969.

Sullivan, Kevin. *Joyce among the Jesuits*. New York: Columbia University Press, 1958.

Thomas, Brook. *James Joyce's* Ulysses: *A Book of Many Happy Returns*. Baton Rouge: Louisiana State University Press, 1982.

Thornton, Weldon. *Allusions in* Ulysses: *An Annotated List*. 1968; rpt. New York: Touchstone-Simon and Schuster, 1973.

Thrane, James R. "Joyce's Sermon on Hell: Its Sources and Backgrounds." *Modern Philology* 57 (1960), 177–98.

Tindall, William York. *A Reader's Guide to* Finnegans Wake. London: Thames and Hudson, 1969.

———. *A Reader's Guide to James Joyce*. New York: Noonday-Farrar, 1959.

Tompkins, Phillip. "James Joyce and the Enthymeme: The Seventh Episode of *Ulysses*." *James Joyce Quarterly* 5 (1967–68), 199–205.

Vickery, John B. "*Finnegans Wake* and Sexual Metamorphosis." *Contemporary Literature* 13 (1972), 213–42.

Voelker, Joseph C. "'Nature it is': The Influence of Giordano Bruno on James Joyce's Molly Bloom." *James Joyce Quarterly* 14 (1976–77), 39–48.

Weir, Lorraine. "The Choreography of Gesture: Marcel Jousse and *Finnegans Wake*." *James Joyce Quarterly* 14 (1976–77), 313–25.

Wicht, Wolfgang. "The Politics of Impersonality: an East German Perspective." *James Joyce Broadsheet*, No. 8 (June 1982), 1.

Wilson, Edmund. *Axel's Castle: A Study in the Imaginative Literature of 1870–1930*. 1931; rpt. New York: Scribner, 1959.

Zhantieva, B. G. "Joyce's *Ulysses*." In *Preserve and Create: Essays in Marxist Literary Criticism*. Ed. Gaylord C. LeRoy and Ursula Beitz. New York: Humanities Press, 1973. Pp. 138–72.

Zimmerman, Michael. "Leopold Paula Bloom: The New Womanly Man." *Literature and Psychology* 29 (1979), 176–84.

II. HISTORY, THEORY, AND METHODOLOGY

Alter, Robert. *Partial Magic: The Novel as a Self-Conscious Genre*. Berkeley: University of California Press, 1975.

Bailey, Peter. "Ally Sloper's Half-Holiday: Comic Art in the 1880s." *History Workshop* 16 (1983), 4–31.

Barthes, Roland. *The Pleasure of the Text*. Trans. Richard Miller. Note on the Text by Richard Howard. New York: Hill and Wang, 1975.

Bassnett-McGuire, Susan. "An Introduction to Theatre Semiotics." *Theatre Quarterly* 10 (1980), 47–53.

Bennett, Tony. *Formalism and Marxism*. New York: Methuen, 1979.

Blavatsky, H. P. *Isis Unveiled: A Master-Key to the Mysteries of Ancient and Modern Science and Theology*. Vol. 2. New York: Bouton, 1882.

Bouissac, Paul. "Semiotics and Spectacles: The Circus Institution and Representations." In *A Perfusion of Signs*. Ed. Thomas A. Sebeok. Bloomington: Indiana University Press, 1977. Pp. 143–52.

Brown, Frederick. "The Heroic Hermaphrodite." [Review of *Herculine Barbin: Being the Recently Discovered Memoirs of a Nineteenth-Century French Hermaphrodite*, intro. Michel Foucault.] *New York Review of Books*, 9 October 1980, pp. 8, 10.

Conference. "Marxism and the Interpretation of Culture: Limits, Frontiers, Boundaries." University of Illinois at Urbana-Champaign, 8–12 July 1983.

Coward, Rosalind and John Ellis. *Language and Materialism: Developments in Semiology and the Theory of the Subject*. London: Routledge and Kegan Paul, 1977.

Craib, Ian. "*Criticism and Ideology*: Theory and Experience." *Contemporary Literature* 22 (1981), 489–509.

Culler, Jonathan. *Structuralist Poetics: Structuralism, Linguistics, and the Study of Literature*. Ithaca, N.Y.: Cornell University Press, 1975.

Davis, J. L. "Criticism and Parody." *Thought* 26 (1951), 180–204.

Derrida, Jacques. *Of Grammatology*. Trans. Gayatri Chakravorty Spivak. Baltimore: Johns Hopkins University Press, 1976.

Diacritics 12 (1982). Special issue: "Fredric Jameson: *The Political Unconscious*."

Donato, Eugenio. "'Here, Now'/'Always Already': Incidental Remarks on Some Recent Characterizations of the Text." *Diacritics* 6 (1976), 24–29.

Douglas, Mary T. *Purity and Danger: An Analysis of Concepts of Pollution and Taboo*. New York: Praeger, 1966.

Eagleton, Terry. *Criticism and Ideology*. London: Verso Editions, 1978.

———. "Marxism and Deconstruction." *Contemporary Literature* 22 (1981), 477–88.

———. *Marxism and Literary Criticism*. Berkeley: University of California Press, 1976.

———. "Text, Ideology, Realism." In *Literature and Society: Selected Papers from the English Institute, 1978*. New series, No. 3. Ed. Edward W. Said. Baltimore: Johns Hopkins University Press, 1980.

Eco, Umberto. "Rhetoric and Ideology in Sue's *Les Mystères de Paris*." *International Social Science Journal* 19 (1967), 551–69.

———. "Semiotics of Theatrical Performance." *Drama Review* 21 (1977), 107–17.

———. *A Theory of Semiotics*. Bloomington: Indiana University Press, 1976.

Elam, Keir. *The Semiotics of Theatre and Drama*. London: Methuen, 1980.

Finegan, John. *The Story of Monto: An Account of Dublin's Notorious Red Light District*. Dublin: Mercier, 1978.

Ford, P., and G. Ford. *A Breviate of Parliamentary Papers: 1900–16*. Shannon: Irish University Press, 1969.

Foucault, Michel. *The History of Sexuality*. Trans. Robert Hurley. Vol. I, *An Introduction*. New York: Vintage-Random, 1980.

———. *Power/Knowledge: Selected Interviews and Other Writings 1972–1977*. Trans. Colin Gordon, Leo Marshall, John Mepham, Kate Soper. Ed. Colin Gordon. New York: Pantheon Books, 1980.

Goldmann, Lucien. "The Sociology of Literature: Status and Problems of Method." In *The Sociology of Art and Literature: A Reader*. Ed. Milton C. Albrecht, James H. Barnett, and Mason Griff. New York: Praeger, 1970. Pp. 582–609.

Goodlad, J. S. R. *A Sociology of Popular Drama*. London: Heinemann, 1971.

Gwynn, Stephen Lucius. *The Famous Cities of Ireland*. Dublin: Maunsel; New York: Macmillan, 1915.

Harari, Josue V., ed. *Textual Strategies: Perspectives in Post-Structuralist Criticism*. Ithaca, N.Y.: Cornell University Press, 1979.

Hawkes, Terence. *Structuralism and Semiotics*. Berkeley: University of California Press, 1977.

Heath, Stephen. *The Nouveau Roman: a Study in the Practice of Writing*. London: Elek, 1972.

Iser, Wolfgang. *The Act of Reading: A Theory of Aesthetic Reading*. Baltimore: Johns Hopkins University Press, 1978.

————. *The Implied Reader: Patterns of Communication in Prose Fiction from Bunyan to Beckett*. Baltimore: Johns Hopkins University Press, 1974.

Jameson, Fredric. *Marxism and Form: Twentieth-Century Dialectical Theories of Literature*. Princeton, N.J.: Princeton University Press, 1971.

————. *The Political Unconscious: Narrative as a Socially Symbolic Act*. Ithaca, N.Y.: Cornell University Press, 1981.

Kavanagh, James H. "Marxism's Althusser: Toward a Politics of Literary Theory." *Diacritics* 12 (1982), 25–45.

————, and Thomas E. Lewis. "Interview: Etienne Balibar and Pierre Macherey." *Diacritics* 12 (1982), 46–51.

Kristeva, Julia. *Desire in Language: A Semiotic Approach to Literature and Art*. Trans. Thomas Gora, Alice Jardine, and Leon S. Roudiez. Ed. Leon S. Roudiez. New York: Columbia University Press, 1980.

Larrain, Jorge. *Marxism and Ideology*. London: Macmillan, 1983.

Lotman, Ju. M. "Primary and Secondary Communication-Modelling Systems." In *Soviet Semiotics: An Anthology*. Trans. and ed. Daniel P. Lucid. Baltimore: Johns Hopkins University Press, 1977. Pp. 95–98.

————, and B. A. Uspensky. "On the Semiotic Mechanism of Culture." Trans. George Mihaychuk. *New Literary History* 9 (1978), 211–32.

————, B. A. Uspenskij, V. V. Ivanov, V. N. Toporov, A. M. Pjatigorskij. "Theses on the Semiotic Study of Cultures (As Applied to Slavic Texts)." In *Structure of Texts and Semiotics of Culture*. Ed. Jan Van Der Eng and Mojmír Grygar. The Hague: Mouton, 1973. Pp. 1–28.

Lyons, F. S. L. *Ireland since the Famine*. New York: Scribner, 1971.

Macardle, Dorothy. *The Irish Republic: A Documented Chronicle of the Anglo-Irish Conflict and the Partitioning of Ireland, with a Detailed Account of the Period 1916–1923*. 2nd ed. New York: Farrar, Straus and Giroux, 1951.

McCaffrey, Lawrence J. *The Irish Question: 1800–1922*. Lexington: University of Kentucky Press, 1968.

McCall, Patrick Joseph. *Irish Nóiníns (Daisies), Being a Collection of 1. Historical Poems and Ballads. 2. Translations from the Gaelic. 3. Humorous and Characteristic Sketches. 4. Miscellaneous Songs.* Dublin: Sealy, Bryers and Walker, 1894.

Macherey, Pierre. *A Theory of Literary Production.* Trans. Geoffrey Wall. London: Routledge & Kegan Paul, 1978.

Miller, J. Hillis. "Narrative and History," *ELH* 41 (1974), 455–73.

———. "The Problematic of Ending in Narrative." *Nineteenth-Century Fiction* 33 (1978), 3–7.

Moretti, Franco. *Signs Taken for Wonders: Essays in the Sociology of Literary Forms.* Trans. Susan Fischer, David Forgacs, David Miller. London: Verso Editions, 1983.

Mykyta, Larysa. "Jameson's Utopias." *Critical Exchange* 14 (1983), 90–102.

Nakhimovksy, Alexander D., and Alice Stone Nakhimovsky, eds. *The Semiotics of Russian Cultural History: Essays by Iurii M. Lotman, Lidiia Ia. Ginsburg, and Boris A. Uspenskii.* Ithaca, N. Y.: Cornell University Press, 1985.

O'Brien, Joseph V. *"Dear, Dirty Dublin": A City in Distress, 1899–1916.* Berkeley: University of California Press, 1982.

O'Connell, John Robert. *The Problem of the Dublin Slums: Three Papers on the Present Condition of the Housing of the Poor in the City of Dublin.* Dublin: Hodges, Figgis, [1913].

Plunkett, Horace. *Ireland in the New Century: With an Epilogue in Answer to Some Critics.* 3rd ed. London: Murray, 1905.

Poetics Today 2 (1981). Special issue: "Drama, Theater, Performance: A Semiotic Perspective."

Ryan, J. "The Census and the Industrial Movement." *New Ireland Review* 19 (1903), 193–202.

Ryan, Michael. *Marxism and Deconstruction: A Critical Articulation.* Baltimore: Johns Hopkins University Press, 1982.

Said, Edward W. *Beginnings: Intention and Method.* Baltimore: Johns Hopkins University Press, 1975.

———. "Interview." *Diacritics* 6 (1976), 30–47.

———. "The Problem of Textuality: Two Exemplary Positions." *Critical Inquiry* 4 (1978), 673–714.

Segre, Cesare. "Culture and Modeling Systems." Trans. John Meddemmen. *Critical Inquiry* 4 (1978), 525–37.

Sheridan, Alan. *Michel Foucault: The Will to Truth.* London: Tavistock, 1980.

Slaughter, Cliff. *Marxism, Ideology and Literature.* London: Macmillan, 1980.

Smith, R. J. *Ireland's Renaissance*. Dublin: Hodges, Figgis, 1903.

Spivak, Gayatri. "Feminism and Critical Theory." *Women's Studies International Quarterly* 1 (1978), 241–46.

Stambolian, George, and Elaine Marks, eds. *Homosexualities and French Literature: Cultural Contexts/Critical Texts*. Ithaca, N. Y.: Cornell University Press, 1979.

Stephens, James. *The Insurrection in Dublin*. New York: Macmillan, 1916.

Williams, Raymond. *The Sociology of Culture*. New York: Schocken Books, 1982.

Winner, Irene Portis, and Jean Umiker-Sebeok, eds. *Semiotics of Culture*. The Hague: Mouton, 1979.

———, and Thomas G. Winner. "The Semiotics of Cultural Texts." *Semiotica* 18 (1976), 101–56.

III. CENSORSHIP

Adams, Michael. *Censorship: The Irish Experience*. Dublin: Scepter Books, 1968.

———. "State Censorship in Ireland 1967–1973." *Position Paper: Applications of Catholic Church Teaching* [Dublin], No. 38 (February 1977), pp. 508–10.

Benstock, Bernard. "The Assassin and the Censor: Political and Literary Tensions." *Clio* 11 (1982), 219–38.

Bourke, Marcus. *John O'Leary: A Study in Irish Separatism*. Athens: University of Georgia Press, 1967.

Brown, Malcolm. *The Politics of Irish Literature: From Thomas Davis to W. B. Yeats*. Seattle: University of Washington Press, 1972.

Burnham, Richard. "Poor George Roberts, Dublin Publisher." *Éire-Ireland* 10 (1975), 141–46.

Choille, Breandán Mac Giolla, ed. *Chief Secretary's Office, Dublin Castle. Intelligence Notes 1913–16—Preserved in the State Paper Office*. Baile Átha Cliath: Oifig an tSoláthair, 1966.

Davies, Sidney. *Dublin Types*. Dublin: Talbot Press, 1918.

Devane, Rev. R. S., S.J. "The Committee on Printed Matter—Some Notes of Evidence." *Irish Ecclesiastical Record*, 5th ser., 28 (1926), 357–77, 449–66.

———. "The Committee on Printed Matter: III—'Indecency' in Law." *Irish Ecclesiastical Record*, 5th ser., 28 (1926), 583–95.

———. "Indecent Literature: Some Legal Remedies." *Irish Ecclesiastical Record*, 5th ser., 25 (1925), 182–204.

Dougherty, Kerry. "But Dubliners Remain Vexed." *Washington Post*, 3 February 1982, Sec. B, p. l, col. 1; p. 4, cols. 1–4.

Downs, Robert B., ed. *The First Freedom: Liberty and Justice in the World of*

Books and Reading. Chicago: American Library Association, 1960.

Ernst, Morris L. "Reflections on the *Ulysses* Trial and Censorship." *James Joyce Quarterly* 3 (1965–66), 3–11.

Gregg, Frederick J. "The National Library of Ireland *versus* Walt Whitman" [letter to the editor on the suspension by the National Library of Ireland of Whitman's *Leaves of Grass*]. *Dublin University Review* 1 (1885), 97–98.

Hughes, Katherine. *English Atrocities in Ireland: A Compilation of Facts from Court and Press Records*. New York: Friends of Irish Freedom, n.d.

Hurley, Rev. T. "The New Legislation on the Index." *Irish Ecclesiastical Record*, 4th ser., 4 (1898), 423–37, 525–40; 5 (1899), 61–76, 110–23, 212–29, 328–41, 427–50, 531–46; 6 (1899), 49–69, 242–66.

Kelly, J. M. *The Irish Constitution*. Dublin: Jurist, 1980.

Lennon, Peter. "The Pattern of Systems of Oppression in Ireland." *New Ireland* [Belfast], 1967, 41–47.

Leonard, John. "Film censorship in Ireland." *Position Paper* 38 (1977), 511.

McDonald, W. "The Index in Ireland." *Irish Ecclesiastical Record*, 4th ser., 1 (1897), 110–32.

O'Brien, Richard Barry. *Dublin Castle and the Irish People*. Dublin: Gill; London: Kegan Paul, Trench, Trübner, 1909.

Palmer, John. *The Censor and the Theatres*. London: Fisher Unwin, 1913.

Press Censor's Circulars, 1916–21. National Library of Ireland MS. 984.

Putman, George H. *The Censorship of the Church of Rome . . . with Some Consideration of the Effects of Protestant Censorship*. 2 vols. New York: Putnam, 1906–7.

Roberts, George. Papers. (Maunsel and National Theatre Society.) National Library of Ireland MSS. 13272–79.

Ryan, Frederick. "The Latest Crusade." *Irish Review* 1 (1912), 521–26.

Semar, John. "The New Censor." *Mask* 4 (1911–12), 183–84.

Shaw, Bernard. "Censorship: Comments by Readers. I." *The Bell* 9 (1945), 395–401.

———. *The Shewing-Up of Blanco Posnet: with Preface on the Censorship*. New York: Brentano's, 1911.

Venclova, Tomas. "The Game of the Soviet Censor." *New York Review of Books*, 31 March 1983, pp. 34–35.

IV. THE PRESS

Barry, Rev. David. "The Ethics of Journalism." *Irish Ecclesiastical Record*, 5th ser., 19 (1922), 514–26.

Brown, Stephen J. M. *The Press in Ireland: A Survey and a Guide*. 1937; rpt. New York: Lemma, 1971.

Chief Secretary's Office, Dublin Castle. Irish news cuttings, with some annotations, 1880–1920. National Library of Ireland ILB 0822.

Cork Celt, October—November 1914.

Cudlipp, Hugh. *The Prerogative of the Harlot: Press Barons and Power*. London: Bodley Head, 1980.

Dunlop, Andrew. *Fifty Years of Irish Journalism*. Dublin: Hanna and Neale; London: Simpkin, Marshall, 1911.

Éire Ireland, 26 October—3 December 1914.

Fianna Fáil: A Journal for Militant Ireland, 19 September—5 December 1914.

Freeman's Journal. The Freedom of the Press. [Memorandum on the suppression of the *Freeman's Journal* and seizure of its machinery by the military. n.p.: 1919?]. National Library of Ireland ILB 300, Item 74.

Glandon, Virginia E. "Index of Irish Newspapers, 1900–1922 (Part I)." *Éire-Ireland* 11 (1976), 84–121.

Higginbottom, Frederick J. *The Vivid Life: A Journalist's Career*. London: Simpkin Marshall, 1934.

"An Irish Treasure in a London Laneway: The Fugitive Irish Bulletin." *Irish Press*, 19 January 1934, p. 8, cols. 3–6.

The Leader, 1900, 1915.

Madden, Lionel, and Diana Dixon. *The Nineteenth-Century Periodical Press in Britain: A Bibliography of Modern Studies 1901–1971*. New York: Garland, 1976.

Murphy, William M. *The Story of a Newspaper* [*Irish Independent*]. Rpt. from *Irish Independent*, 2 January 1909.

O'Hegarty, P. S. "The Mosquito Press." *The Bell* 12 (1946), 56–65.

The Police Gazette, or Hue-and-Cry (Dublin), 1882–85.

Ryan, W. P. *The Pope's Green Ireland*. London: Nisbet, 1912.

Scissors and Paste, 12 December 1914—27 February 1915.

Sinn Fein Bulletin, 1919.

Straumann, Heinrich. *Newspaper Headlines: A Study in Linguistic Method*. London: Allen and Unwin, 1935.

United Ireland: Suppressed, 6—16 December 1890; *Insuppressible*, 17 December 1890—24 January 1891.

V. THE STAGE

Ackroyd, Peter. *Dressing Up: Transvestism and Drag: The History of an Obsession*. New York: Simon and Schuster, 1979.

Anstey, F. (Thomas Anstey Guthrie). *Vice Versa; or, A Lesson to Fathers*. New York: Appleton, 1913.

Black, Hester M. "The Theatre in Ireland before 1900." *Threshold* 1 (1957), 20–23.

Booth, Michael R., ed. *English Plays of the Nineteenth Century.* Vol. 5, *Pantomimes, Extravaganzas and Burlesques.* Oxford: Clarendon, 1976.

———. *Hiss the Villain: Six English and American Melodramas.* New York: Benjamin Blom, 1967.

Bouissac, Paul. "From Joseph Grimaldi to Charlie Cairoli: A Semiotic Approach to Humour." In *It's a Funny Thing, Humour.* Ed. Anthony J. Chapman and Hugh C. Foot. New York: Pergamon Press, 1977. Pp. 115–17.

The Bourke Collection of Theatre Programmes. Library of Trinity College, Dublin. Presented by Dr. F. S. Bourke.

Bradby, David, Louis James, and Bernard Sharratt, eds. *Performance and Politics in Popular Drama: Aspects of Popular Entertainment in Theatre, Film and Television 1800–1976.* Cambridge: Cambridge University Press, 1980.

Brenner, Marie. "Joe Papp's Third Act." *New York,* 9 August 1982, pp. 28–32.

Brierly, Harry. *Transvestism: A Handbook with Case Studies for Psychologists, Psychiatrists and Counsellors.* New York: Pergamon Press, 1979.

Broadbent, R. J. *A History of Pantomime.* 1901; rpt. New York: Benjamin Blom, 1964.

The Joan Burke Collection. Concert and Theatre Programmes. Dublin Public Library, Pearse Street Branch.

Busby, Roy. *British Music Hall: An Illustrated Who's Who from 1850 to the Present Day.* London: Elek, 1976.

Cheshire, David F. *The Music-Hall in Britain.* Rutherford, N.J.: Fairleigh Dickinson University Press, 1974.

Clinton-Baddeley, V. C. *Some Pantomime Pedigrees.* London: Society for Theatre Research, 1963.

Collection of Playbills from the Queen's Theatre (Dublin), the Theatre Royal (Dublin), and the Gaiety Theatre (Dublin). Dublin Public Library, Pearse Street Branch.

Cusack, Cyril. "The Irish Actor." *Prompts: Bulletin of the Irish Theatre Archive* 2 (1981), 3–14.

Davison, Peter, comp. and ed. *Songs of the British Music Hall.* New York: Oak Publications, 1971.

de Búrca, Séamus. "Growing-Up in Dublin." *Dublin Historical Record* 29 (1976), 82–99.

———. "The Olympia Theatre 1879–1979: A Hundred Years of Glorious Music Hall and Theatre in Dublin." Unpublished MS. dated 25 July 1980.

————. "The Queen's Royal Theatre, 1829–1966." *Dublin Historical Record* 27 (1973), 10–26.

————. *The Queen's Royal Theatre, Dublin: 1829–1969*. Dublin, 1983.

Disher, M. Willson. *Clowns and Pantomimes*. 1925; rpt. New York: Benjamin Blom, 1968.

————. *Music Hall Parade*. New York: Scribner; London: B. T. Batsford, 1938.

Duggan, G. C. *The Stage Irishman: A History of the Irish Play and Stage Characters from the Earliest Times*. 1937; rpt. New York: Benjamin Blom, 1969.

Eliot, T. S. "Marie Lloyd." In *Selected Essays: 1917–1932*. New York: Harcourt, Brace, 1932. Pp. 369–72.

Feinbloom, Deborah Heller. *Transvestites and Transsexuals: Mixed Views*. New York: Delacorte Press, Seymour Lawrence, 1976.

Felstead, S. Theodore. *Stars Who Made the Halls: A Hundred Years of English Humour, Harmony and Hilarity*. London: T. Werner Laurie, 1946.

Foster, Sally E. "Irish Wrong: Samuel Lover and the Stage-Irishman." *Éire-Ireland* 13 (1978), 34–44.

G. M. G. *The Stage Censor, an Historical Sketch: 1544–1907*. London: Sampson Low, Marston, 1908.

Gaiser, Gottlieb. "A Note on the Principle of Dramatization in 'Circe.'" *James Joyce Quarterly* 16 (1978–79), 501–5.

Gammond, Peter, comp. and ed. *Best Music Hall and Variety Songs*. London: Wolfe, 1972.

Gammond, Peter, ed. *Music Hall Song Book: A Collection of 45 of the Best Songs from 1890–1920*. Devon: David and Charles; London: EMI Music Publishing, 1975.

Gilbert, Sandra M. "Costumes of the Mind: Transvestism as Metaphor in Modern Literature." *Critical Inquiry* 7 (Winter 1980), 391–417.

Giltinan, D. J. "Variety." *The Bell* 3 (1941), 28–39.

Glassie, Henry. *All Silver and No Brass: an Irish Christmas Mumming*. Dublin: Dolmen, 1976.

Gregory, Augusta. "Last Year." *Beltaine*, No. 2 (1900), 25–28.

————. *Our Irish Theatre: A Chapter of Autobiography*. New York: Putnam, 1913.

Heilbrun, Carolyn G. *Toward a Recognition of Androgyny*. New York: Harper-Colophon, 1973.

Hibbert, H. G. *Fifty Years of a Londoner's Life*. New York: Dodd, Mead, 1916.

————. *A Playgoer's Memories*. London: Grant Richards, 1920.

Hickey, Des, and Gus Smith. *A Paler Shade of Green*. London: Leslie Frewin, 1972.

Hogan, Robert, and Richard Burnham. *The Art of the Amateur 1916–1920*. Vol. 5, *The Modern Irish Drama, A Documentary History*. Atlantic Highlands, N.J.: Humanities Press, 1984.

Holloway, Joseph, comp. Articles [newscuttings] by A. B. Walkley in *The Star, The Times, The Morning Leader*, etc. National Library of Ireland MS. 14989.

———. A Dublin Playgoer's Impressions. National Library of Ireland MSS. 1794, 1802, 1806, 4451.

———. Gaiety Theatre, Dublin. List of Plays, 1871–85. National Library of Ireland MS. 12069.

———. Gaiety Theatre, Dublin. Complete List of Plays, 1893–1905. National Library of Ireland MS. 12071.

———. Queen's Royal Theatre. List of Pieces Performed, 1898–1905. National Library of Ireland MS. 12074.

———. Theatre Royal, Dublin. List of Plays, 1897–1923. National Library of Ireland MS. 12073.

Honri, Peter. *Working the Halls: The Honris in One Hundred Years of British Music Hall*. Hampshire: Saxon House, 1973.

Hopkins, Tighe. "Music Halls." *Dublin University Magazine*, n.s., 2 (1878), 192–206.

Howard, Diana. *London Theatres and Music Halls: 1850–1950*. London: Library Association, 1970.

Hunt, Hugh. *The Abbey: Ireland's National Theatre: 1904–1978*. Dublin: Gill and Macmillan, 1979.

Irish Times, 1872–73, 1892.

Johnston, Denis. "Dublin Theatre." *The Bell* 3 (1941), 157–61.

Kavanagh, Peter. *The Irish Theatre*. Tralee: Kerryman, 1946.

Kiell, Norman. *Varieties of Sexual Experience: Psychosexuality in Literature*. New York: International Universities Press, 1979.

Kilroy, James. *The 'Playboy' Riots*. Dublin: Dolmen, 1971.

Krafft-Ebing, R. V. *Psychopathia Sexualis with Especial Reference to the Antipathic Sexual Instinct: A Medico-Forensic Study*. English adaptation by F. J. Rebman of the 12th German ed. Brooklyn, N.Y.: Physicians and Surgeons Book Co., 1931.

Krause, David, ed. *The Dolmen Boucicault*. Dublin: Dolmen, 1964.

Laurie, Joe., Jr. *Vaudeville: From the Honky-Tonks to the Palace*. New York: Holt, 1953.

Lawrence, W. J. "Music-Hall Elements: Their Origin and Antiquity." *Dublin Magazine* 2 (1924–25), 420–22.

———. Personal Newspaper Cuttings. Vol. 3 (1904). National Library of Ireland MS. 4294.

———, comp. Twenty-two volumes of programmes and miscellaneous information about the history of theatre in Ireland, 1883–1940.

Leno, Dan. *Dan Leno Hys Book*. Ed. John Duncan. 1901; rpt. London: Hugh Evelyn, 1968.

London Hermit. "The Conventionalities of the Stage." *Dublin University Magazine* 85 (1875), 503–12.

mac Liammóir, Micheál. *Enter a Goldfish: Memoirs of an Irish Actor, Young and Old*. London: Granada Publishing, 1977.

Mander, Raymond, and Joe Mitchenson. *Pantomime: a Story in Pictures*. New York: Taplinger, 1973.

Marbham. "The Stage Englishman." *Catholic Bulletin* 3 (1913), 617–19.

Martyn, Edward. "A Comparison between Irish and English Theatrical Audiences." *Beltaine*, No. 2 (February 1900), 11–13.

Moore, George. "Is the Theatre a Place of Amusement?" *Beltaine*, No. 2 (February 1900), 7–10.

Nally, T. H. *Finn Varra Maa (The Irish Santa Claus): an Irish Fairy Pantomime in Four Acts*. Dublin: Talbot, 1917.

Nelson, James Malcolm. "From Rory and Paddy to Boucicault's Myles, Shaun and Conn: The Irishman on the London Stage, 1830–1860." *Éire-Ireland* 13 (1978), 79–105.

"Notes on the Drama." *Dublin University Magazine* 85 (1875), 204–09, 379–84.

Ó hAodha, Micheál. *Theatre in Ireland*. Oxford: Basil Blackwell, 1974.

"Our Popular Amusements." *Dublin University Magazine* 84 (1874), 233–44.

Paskman, Dailey. *"Gentlemen, Be Seated!" A Parade of the American Minstrels*. 1928; rpt. New York: Potter, 1976.

Prompts: Bulletin of the Irish Theatre Archive 6 (1983). Special issue: "Dion Boucicault and the Irish Melodrama Tradition."

Rose, Clarkson. *Red Plush and Greasepaint: A Memory of the Music-Hall and Life and Times from the Nineties to the Sixties*. London: Museum Press, 1964.

Scott, Harold. *The Early Doors: Origins of the Music Hall*. London: Nicholson and Watson, 1946.

Senelick, Laurence, David F. Cheshire, and Ulrich Schneider. *British Music-Hall 1840–1923: A Bibliography and Guide to Sources, with a Supplement on European Music-Hall*. Hamden, Conn.: Archon, 1981.

Short, Ernest Henry, and Arthur Compton-Rickett. *Ring Up the Curtain*. 1938; rpt. Freeport, N.Y.: Books for Libraries Press, 1970.

Southern, Richard. *The Victorian Theatre: A Pictorial Survey*. Newton Abbot: David and Charles, 1970.

Souvenir of the Twenty-Fifth Anniversary of the Opening of the Gaiety Theatre 27th November, 1871. With Michael Gunn's Compts. Dublin: 27 November 1896.

Theatre Royal, Dublin. *Book of Songs of the "Royal" Pantomime [Dick Whittington]*. Produced Tuesday, 16 January 1904. Dublin: Allen, 1904.

————. *Books of Songs of the "Royal" Pantomime [Sleeping Beauty]*. Produced Tuesday, 21 January 1902. Dublin: Allen, 1902.

————. *Book of Words of the Songs, Duetts and Choruses, Sung in the Grand Christmas Pantomime of Aladdin or the Wonderful Lamp*. [n.p.]: Produced Christmas 1876.

Theatres and Places of Entertainment: Report from the Select Committee on Theatres and Places of Entertainment; Together with the Proceedings of the Committee, Minutes of Evidence, Appendix, and Index. London: Her Majesty's Stationery Office, 1892.

Toll, Robert C. *On with the Show: The First Century of Show Business in America*. New York: Oxford University Press, 1976.

Turco, the Terrible; or, Harlequin Prince Amabel, the Magic Roses, and Oberon, King of the Fairies. Christmas Pantomime, Gaiety Theatre, Dublin, December, 1873. Words of the Songs. By Edwin Hamilton. 3rd ed. Dublin: [n.p.], 1874.

Van Holt, J. "Eternity and Soap Bubbles." *Mask* 4 (1911–12), 43–45.

Vicinus, Martha. *The Industrial Muse: A Study of Nineteenth Century British Working-Class Literature*. London: Croom Helm, 1974.

————. *Suffer and Be Still: Women in the Victorian Age*. Bloomington: Indiana University Press, 1972.

Watt, Stephen M. "Boucicault and Whitbread: The Dublin Stage at the End of the Nineteenth Century." *Éire-Ireland* 3 (1983), 23–53.

Watters, Eugene, and Matthew Murtagh. *Infinite Variety: Don Lowrey's Music Hall 1879–97*. Dublin: Gill and Macmillan, 1975.

Wynne, Vashti. *Mother Goose*. Queen's Theatre, Dublin. Produced Monday, 16 December 1912.

Yeats, W. B. "The Irish Literary Theatre, 1900." *Beltaine*, No. 2 (February 1900), 22–24.

VI. THE PULPIT

Addresses Delivered on Various Occasions by the Most Rev. Dr. Walsh, Archbishop of Dublin. . . . Dublin: Gill, 1886.

Ayscough, John. "A Novelist's Sermons—XI: Of Preaching and Practice." *Irish Ecclesiastical Record*, 5th ser., 2 (1913), 246–59.

Brown, Stephen J., S.J. *The Preacher's Library*. London: Sheed and Ward, [1928?].

Burke, Rev. Thomas Nicholas, O.P. *English Misrule in Ireland*. New York: Lynch, Cole and Meehan, 1873.

————. *Lectures and Sermons*. New York: Haverty, 1872.

————. A Miscellaneous Collection of Newspaper Cuttings on His Life and Work. National Library of Ireland IR 92 b 140.

Callan, Rev. Charles J., O.P., ed. *Illustrations for Sermons and Instructions.* New York: J. F. Wagner, 1916.

Catholic Bulletin (Dublin), Vols. 1 (1911), 3 (1913), 4 (1914), 5 (1915), 10 (1920).

"The Catholic Truth Society of Ireland." *Irish Monthly* 28 (1900), 443–45.

The Church Times: An Ecclesiastical and General Newspaper (London), Vol. 51 (1904).

Clery, Arthur E. "The Religious Angle in Ireland." *Studies* 4 (1915), 432–40.

"Clongowes and Father Conmee: Two Filial Tributes." *Irish Monthly* 38 (1910), 421–27.

Coffey, Rev. P. "James Connolly's Campaign Against Capitalism, in the Light of Catholic Teaching." *Catholic Bulletin* 10 (1920), 212–24, 275–79, 346–54, 407–12, 489–92.

Coleman, Antony. "Priest as Artist: The Dilemma of Canon Sheehan." *Studies* 58 (1969), 30–41.

Conroy, Right Rev. George, D.D. *Occasional Sermons, Addresses, and Essays.* Dublin: Gill and Son, 1884.

Curran, M. J. "Dublin Diocesan Archives." *Reportorium Novum* 2 (1957–58), 1–5.

"Current literature." Rev. of *The Fight of Faith: Sermons Preached on Various Occasions*, by Rev. Stopford A. Brooke. *Dublin University Magazine* 1 (1878), 118–21.

D'Arcy, Charles Frederick. *The Adventures of a Bishop. A Phase of Irish Life: A Personal and Historical Narrative.* London: Hodder and Stoughton, 1934.

E. M. Rev. of *Addresses by the Most Rev. Dr. Walsh, Archbishop of Dublin*, by Patrick Walsh. *Irish Ecclesiastical Record*, 3rd ser., 7 (1886), 1133–36.

Farrell, Rev. Joseph. *Sermons: With an Appendix Containing Some of His Speeches on Quasi-Religious Subjects.* Dublin: Gill, 1886.

Finlay, Rev. Peter, S.J. "Divorce in the Irish Free State." *Studies* 13 (1924), 353–62.

Flynn, Rev. Thomas. *Preaching Made Easy.* London: Burns, Oates and Washbourne, 1923.

Foy, Fehcian A., O.F.M., ed. *1982 Catholic Almanac.* Huntington, Indiana: Our Sunday Visitor, 1981.

Gannon, Rev. P. J., S.J. "A Study of Religious Statistics in Ireland." *Irish Ecclesiastical Record*, 5th ser., 17 (1921), 141–57.

Gobinet, Rev. Charles. *The Instruction of Youth in Christian Piety; Taken*

Out of the Sacred Scriptures and Holy Fathers. Trans. from the French. Boston: Patrick Donahoe, n.d.

Guinan, Rev. Joseph. "The Apostolate of the Press." *Irish Monthly* 38 (1910), 320–27.

———. "Priest and People in Ireland." *Catholic Bulletin* 1 (1911), 62–65.

———. "Wanted: Apostles of the Press." *Catholic Bulletin* 1 (1911), 420–23.

Hitchcock, Rev. George S., S.J. *Sermon Composition: A Method for Students.* London: Burns and Oates, 1908.

Hogan, J. F., D.D. "The Jubilee of His Grace the Archbishop of Dublin." *Irish Ecclesiastical Record*, 4th ser., 28 (1910), 225–27.

———. "Sir Horace Plunkett's Lecture." *Irish Ecclesiastical Record*, 4th ser., 15 (1904), 289–314.

Howe, Rev. George Edward. *Sermon Plans: Being Four Outlines of Sermons, Chiefly in the Epistles and Gospels, for Each Sunday and Holiday of the Year.* London: St. Anselm's Society, 1904.

The Irish Monthly: A Magazine of General Literature. Vols. 28 (1900), 38 (1910), 42 (1914).

James, Stanley B. "The Church and the Class War." *Irish Ecclesiastical Record*, 5th ser., 36 (1930), 165–72.

Johnson, E. J. "Pentecost Cycle." *New Catholic Encyclopedia* 11 (1967), 109–11.

Kelleher, Rev. J. "Priests and Social Action in Ireland." *Studies* 4 (1915), 169–83.

Kevin, Rev. Neil. "Fiction Priests." *Irish Ecclesiastical Record*, 5th ser., 60 (1942), 253–57.

MacCaffrey, Rev. James. "The Papal Encyclical on Modernism." *Irish Ecclesiastical Record*, 4th ser., 22 (1907), 561–75.

McCarthy, Michael J. F. *Priests and People in Ireland.* Dublin: Hodges, Figgis, 1902.

MacDonagh, Frank. "The Viceroyalty and Catholic Disabilities." *Irish Ecclesiastical Record*, 5th ser., 5 (1915), 373–83.

MacHale, Thomas, D.D. *Sermons and Discoveries.* Dublin: Gill, 1883.

Martindale, Cyril C., S.J. *Bernard Vaughan, S.J.* London: Longmans, Green, 1923.

Miller, David W. "The Roman Catholic Church in Ireland, 1898–1918." *Éire-Ireland* 3 (1968), 75–91.

Mitchel, John. *1641: Reply to the Falsification of History by James Anthony Froude, Entitled "The English in Ireland."* Glasgow: Cameron and Ferguson, n.d.

Murphy, Rev. John B. *The What-Why-How? Plan for Preaching a Sermon with One Hundred and Four Specimen Sketch Sermons . . .* Dublin: Browne and Nolan, [1925].

O'Brien, C. M. "Catholics and Freemasonry." *Irish Ecclesiastical Record*, 4th ser., 6 (1899), 309–26.

O'Callaghan, Edward P., O.F.M. "Correspondence between Bishop O'Dwyer and Bishop Foley on the Dublin Rising, 1916–17." *Collectanea Hibernia: Sources for Irish History*. Nos. 18 and 19, (1976–77), 184–212.

O'Connor, Gerald. *James Connolly: A Study of His Work and Worth*. Dublin: Curtis, n.d.

O'Dowd, Rev. W. *Preaching*. London: Longmans, Green, 1919.

O'Faolain, Sean. *The Irish*. Rev. ed. Harmondsworth, Middlesex, England: Penguin, 1980.

O'Keeffe, Rev. Patrick, C.C. *Sermons at Mass*. 3rd ed. Dublin: Gill, 1888.

O'Riordan, Rev. M. *Catholicity and Progress in Ireland*. 3rd ed. London: Kegan Paul, Trench, Trübner; St. Louis: B. Herder, 1906.

———. "The Martyrdom of a Nation (From a Sermon Preached at St. Patrick's Church in Rome on March 17th, 1916, by Rt. Rev. Mgr. O'Riordan)." [Partly censored]. *Catholic Bulletin* 6 (1916), 266–68.

O'Shea, Rev. Denis. "Newspaper Controversy." *Irish Ecclesiastical Record*, 4th ser., 17 (1910), 619–27.

———. "Preaching from Sermon Books." *Irish Ecclesiastical Record*, 5th ser., 6 (1915), 493–502.

———. "The Preparation of Sermons." *Irish Ecclesiastical Record*, 5th ser., 6 (1915), 362–70.

P. J. W. "Archbishop Walsh and the Irish Ecclesiastical Record." *Irish Ecclesiastical Record*, 5th ser., 18 (1921), 561–76.

Phelan, Michael J., S.J. "A Gaelicized or a Socialized Ireland—Which?: Socialism and Social Reform." *Catholic Bulletin* 3 (1913), 768–74.

Plater, Charles, S.J. "Retreats for Working-Men." *Studies* 10 (1921), 97–108.

The Preacher's Vademecum: Sermon Plans for Sundays, Feasts of our Lord, the Blessed Virgin and the Saints, Advent and Lenten Courses, Forty Hours', Sacred Heart Devotions, Retreats, Conferences, May and October Devotions, Special Occasions, etc. By Two Missionaries. Trans. from French. New York: Joseph F. Wagner; London: B. Herder, 1921.

R. J. R. Rev. of *Sermon Matter*, by Rev. F. Girardey, C.S.S.R. *Irish Ecclesiastical Record*, 5th ser., 6 (1915), 666.

Redmond Papers: Correspondence with John Redmond, chiefly from Patrick O'Donnell, Bishop of Raphoe, concerning the censoring of correspondence between the Irish bishops and the Irish College in Rome, 1915. National Library of Ireland MS. 18292.

Roche, Katharine. "Priests in Fiction." *Irish Monthly* 36 (1908), 421–28, 501–9.

Rochford, Very Rev. J. A., O.P., comp. and ed. *Lectures and Sermons Delivered by the Very Rev. Thomas N. Burke, O.P., Since His Departure from America*. New York: P. J. Kennedy, Excelsior Catholic Publishing House, 1878.

Russell, Matthew. "A Relic of Father Conmee, S.J." *Irish Monthly* 38 (1910), 389–92.

Sheehan, Canon P. A. Sermons. National Library of Ireland MSS. 4675–80.

———. *Sermons*. Ed. M. J. Phelan, S.J. Dublin: Maunsel, 1920.

———. *Tristram Lloyd; the Romance of a Journalist. An Unfinished Story*. Completed by Rev. Henry Gaffney, O.P. Dublin: Talbot Press, n.d.

Silke, John J. "The Roman Catholic Church in Ireland 1800–1922: A Survey of Recent Historiography." *Studia Hibernica* 15 (1975), 61–104.

"Some New Books." *Irish Monthly* 42 (1914), 53–58, 351–56, 591–96.

Tozer, Basil. "Roman Catholics and Journalism." *Monthly Review* 23 (1906), 57–65.

Vaughan, Father Bernard, S.J. *Notes of Retreats Given by Father Bernard Vaughan, S.J.* London: Burns, Oates & Washbourne, 1928.

———. *Society, Sin and the Saviour: Addresses on the Passion of Our Lord*. London: Kegan Paul, Trench, Trübner, 1908.

———. *What of To-Day?* London: Cassell, 1914.

Walsh, Patrick J. *William J. Walsh: Archbishop of Dublin*. Dublin: Talbot Press, 1928.

Woods, C. J. "The Politics of Cardinal McCabe, Archbishop of Dublin, 1879–85." *Dublin Historical Record* 26 (1973), 101–10.

Index